W9-AED-436

FRUITFUL
AND
MULTIPLYING

JEWISH LIFE ON THE MODERN AMERICAN STAGE

ESTHER: A VAUDEVILLE MEGILLAH
by Elizabeth Swados

Alive with music and song, this postmodern version of the prototypical Jewish play reflects the madcap humor of Purim, as well as the historic menace of anti-Semitism. The result is a magical, timeless work.

ANNULLA, AN AUTOBIOGRAPHY *by Emily Mann*

Two actors—the Holocaust survivor Annulla and a young American woman—weave together monologues that enmesh past and present as two women's stories become point and counterpoint in this riveting, true drama.

FALSETTOLAND *by William Finn and James Lapine*

The middle play of the trilogy *Falsettos,* this high-energy musical uses a bar mitzvah as a focus on such issues of contemporary Jewish life as becoming a man, alternative lifestyles, and even baseball.

SIGHT UNSEEN *by Donald Margulies*

When a wife's old lover—who calls her his first *shiksa*—comes to call on her and her artist husband in a rural English cottage, the stage is set for conflict and commentary on creativity, lost values, and the price of success.

And five more masterful plays from the 1980s and 1990s.

Ellen Schiff, Ph.D., is a former professor of French and world literature. She edited *Awake and Singing: 7 Classic Plays from the American Jewish Repertoire,* the first book in this two-volume set on American Jewish theatre, also available in a Mentor edition. The author of *From Stereotype to Metaphor: The Jew in Contemporary Drama*, Schiff has contributed essays to numerous books. Her articles about theatre of Jewish interest have appeared in many periodicals, including *The New York Times, Modern Drama,* and *American Jewish History.* A consultant on theatre to the National Foundation for Jewish culture, she lives in the Berkshires.

FRUITFUL AND MULTIPLYING

9 Contemporary Plays from the American Jewish Repertoire

EDITED AND WITH AN INTRODUCTION BY

Ellen Schiff

A MENTOR BOOK

MENTOR
Published by the Penguin Group
Penguin Books USA Inc., 375 Hudson Street,
New York, New York 10014, U.S.A.
Penguin Books Ltd, 27 Wrights Lane, London W8 5TZ, England
Penguin Books Australia Ltd, Ringwood, Victoria, Australia
Penguin Books Canada Ltd, 10 Alcorn Avenue,
Toronto, Ontario, Canada M4V 3B2
Penguin Books (N.Z.) Ltd, 182–190 Wairau Road, Auckland 10, New Zealand

Penguin Books Ltd, Registered Offices:
Harmondsworth, Middlesex, England

First published by Mentor, an imprint of Dutton Signet,
a division of Penguin Books USA Inc.

ISBN 0-451-62870-5

Grateful acknowledgment is made to the following for permission to quote lyrics in *Conversations with My Father:*
Excerpts from "Santa Claus Is Coming to Town," by Fred J. Coots and Ha-

(The following two pages constitute an extension of this copyright page.)

 REGISTERED TRADEMARK—MARCA REGISTRADA

Printed in the United States of America.

For tonight's audiences and tomorrow's—
and among the latter,
Sarah, Max, Hannah, and Millie

Contents

Acknowledgments xiii

Introduction
by Ellen Schiff xv

Esther, A Vaudeville Megillah
by Elizabeth Swados 1

Conversations with My Father
by Herb Gardner 81

Goldberg Street
by David Mamet 179

Annulla, An Autobiography
by Emily Mann 187

The Value of Names
by Jeffrey Sweet 211

Falsettoland
by William Finn and James Lapine 259

The Substance of Fire
by Jon Robin Baitz 333

Sight Unseen
by Donald Margulies 381

A Vow of Silence
by Allan Havis 453

Acknowledgments

With warm thanks for their generous help to Dennis Aspland, Dorothy Chansky, Carole Kessner, Sanford Marovitz, Seymour Press, and Laurie Wessely-Baldwin. And with gratitude to the playwrights who graciously contributed their personal comments on the focus of this book.

Introduction

I

As an index to what late twentieth-century American audiences will buy tickets to see, the yearly *New York Times* schedule of summer theatre festivals is hard to beat. These program listings for nearly three hundred producing companies coast to coast offer a comprehensive guide to plays that have attracted national favor. That there will be multiple productions of *Fiddler on the Roof,* for example, is altogether predictable. But *Fiddler* is far from the only work of explicit Jewish content whose appeal to end-of-the-century audiences is evident in the *Times* lineup. Nor is it just musicals that fill auditoriums. Even a brief sample from a recent schedule reveals the widespread popularity of straight Jewish plays. Among the dozens billed for summer 1995 were *Beau Jest* in western Massachusetts and rural Wisconsin, *Lost in Yonkers* in Idaho and Vermont, and *The Sisters Rosensweig* in Alabama and New Hampshire.

So extensive a reception of plays about Jews would have been close to unthinkable some sixty years ago. In 1931, two of Elmer Rice's plays opened within a month of one another on Broadway, where they enjoyed extended runs. Assessing the 1931–32 season for the influential *Year Book of the Drama in America,* editor and drama critic Burns Mantle explained why he had chosen for his annual list of the Ten Best Plays Rice's *The Left Bank,* a long-since forgotten work about American expatriates in Europe, over *Counsellor-at-Law,* Rice's now-classic play about a Jewish lawyer in New York. Though Mantle conceded that *Counsellor* had a "stronger dramatic theme," he deemed the play "fairly local to New York in situation and written with a racial consciousness that minimizes its appeal."[1]

Whatever Burns Mantle's personal biases may have been,

it would be a mistake to attribute his judgment to anti-Semitism. (Mantle's esteem for Rice as playwright, producer, and director is unmistakable.) As I have demonstrated in *Awake and Singing*, the companion volume to this collection, Jews have been writing plays about Jews in America for receptive general audiences since at least the 1920s. It is exoticism rather than racism that once distinguished drama about Jewish life. Well into the second half of the century, Jewishness on stage continued to be regarded as foreign.

In 1959, for instance, Paddy Chayefsky reworked the Yiddish classic, *The Dybbuk* as *The Tenth Man*. He set his play in a present-day Long Island synagogue and strove to ensure broad comprehensibility, for example in dialogue that refers to "praying shawls" rather than *tallitot* and a "quorum" rather than a *minyan*. Still, in his review of Chayefsky's play, eminent critic Kenneth Tynan was quick to focus on Chayefsky's "Jewish dialogue," calling it "as meaty as any I have heard since the heyday of Clifford Odets." Then, in a sentence that may well have captured the prevailing attitude, Tynan good-naturedly admitted, "I failed to understand all the Jewish expressions . . . but like most Gentiles, I laughed anyway."[2]

Obviously sea changes have since taken place, both on stage and off. If it is true, as one perceptive observer noted in retrospect, that by the early 1950s, "the Jew was well on his way to becoming the American Everyman,"[3] it is no surprise that explicitly American Jewish plays would ultimately earn a familiarity and universal acceptance rivaled only by bagels'. For a society grown accustomed (if not invariably sympathetic) to pluralism, seeing Jews on stage—as well as on the large and small screens—is as routine as meeting them in supermarket aisles. Correlatively, in the multicultural climate that marks the end of the century, Jews have come to feel utterly at ease writing out of and about their American Jewish lives.

It is impossible to determine which has altered more drastically in the last half of this century: the image of Jews in America or the America in which Jews live. Both transformations—they are, of course, interconnected—are everywhere apparent in post–World War II arts and letters. The widening opportunity for and increasing eminence of Jewish intellectual and artistic activities have fortified the position of Jews in society. "The American Jew has entered the cultural life in all its aspects, has made important contributions and exerts signal influence," noted historian Abraham J. Karp in 1969. "A good deal of American culture today has taken on a kind of Jewish coloration. . . . Being Jewish is no handicap today in American cultural life or in American life in general."[4]

Indeed, Jewish contribution to shaping postwar America has engendered a new concern. "The very Jewish enlargement and invigoration of American culture that has enabled Jews to identify so fully with it has made Jewish identity under such conditions problematic," comments historian Stephen J. Whitfield of Brandeis University's American Studies Department. "That national culture is not so much a distant threat as a distorted mirror, but the Jewish faces that it reveals are coming to resemble everyone else's."[5] That observation is not uniformly valid throughout American society, for Jewishness continues to carry implications of geography and social class. However, one emphatically positive way to respond to fears about homogenization and diminished continuity is to recognize the vitality of art that draws on explicitly Jewish subjects, traditional as well as contemporary.

While this introduction is hardly the context for a cultural history of Jewish creativity, it does provide the opportunity to make and substantiate a long overdue statement: In no sphere have Jewish artists contributed more to the Jewish image in American culture than the theatre. The present-day prominence of Jewish plays in English and their popularity with the general public evolve from a well-established tradition. Jewish plays and playwrights have been part of the indigenous American theatre since its emergence after World War I. Ironically, perhaps for that very reason they often pass as an unremarked and unremarkable component of the national repertoire.

The first volume of this collection, *Awake and Singing: Seven Classic Plays from the American Jewish Repertoire,* documents their presence between 1920 and the beginning of the cultural revolution of the 1960s. This book represents the blossoming of American Jewish drama since the 1960s, during which, as Robert Lowell put it, Jewishness became "the theme of our literary culture."[6] Throughout, the term "American Jewish drama" denotes plays, typically by Jewish authors, that explore specifically and emphatically some aspect of the American Jewish experience and that are written in English for general audiences.

The primary purpose of both volumes is to draw merited attention to the *fact* of the American Jewish repertoire. My intent is to illustrate its extent, diversity, and its worth, as art and as mirror of the changing profile and position of Jews in America. In the introduction to the earlier book, I distinguished between the American Jewish and the Yiddish stages. While the latter is still frequently understood to mean "Jewish theatre," the former speaks in English for the dual citizenship stated in its name. It is important to judge the Jewish content of American Jewish drama on its fidelity to the goals it sets for itself. Those objectives regularly include representing Jews or Jewish life intelligibly to the theatergoing public. Particularly in the last four decades, the drama that results departs significantly in characterization, tone, style, and point of view from the Yiddish repertoire, as it increasingly does from earlier American Jewish plays. As the plays in these books demonstrate, American Jewish drama frequently relies on fundamental and ingenious connections with the Jewish past, while asserting a lively interest in the American Jewish present.

Curiously, drama rarely figures in the discourse of literary critics and cultural historians assessing American Jewish writing. Discussions of what is commonly designated the Jewish literary renaissance of the fifties and sixties regularly refer to inarguably brilliant prose writing in fiction (Bellow, Malamud, and Roth) and criticism (Trilling, Kazin, and Howe). Two examples illustrate the prevalent unawareness of the dramatic repertoire. Scholar and critic Robert Alter, not altogether ready to accept the fact of a Jewish literary renaissance, grants that the "illusion" of such a renaissance would have Bellovian borders. Alter assigns to this theoretical period the twelve years from the publication of *The Adventures of Augie March* in 1953 to that of *Herzog* in 1964.[7] By contrast, writers and editors Ted Solotaroff and Nessa Rapoport subscribe to "belief in the ongoing flowering of Jewish letters in America."[8] However, seeking to illustrate that phenomenon from 1967 through the 1990s, Solotaroff and Rapoport also turned to what the former called the "sense of confidence, openness, and diversity [that is] particularly evident in American-Jewish fiction."[9]

But surely fiction is not the only showcase where these

qualities are on display. Self-assured, candid, and versatile American Jewish voices also speak thrillingly across the footlights, as the artistry in this collection attests. Still, an anthology can provide only a sample of a worthy abundance. Since this one intends to represent four decades of Jewish accomplishment in drama, the last two of which have been phenomenally fertile, it seems reasonable to return for a closer examination to the modest boundaries Robert Alter concedes to the Jewish literary renaissance.

The postwar efflorescence of American Jewish drama did not occur in the same time frame or manner as the explosion of American Jewish fiction. While the novels of Bellow, Malamud, and Roth transformed their genre, no comparable iconoclastic plays changed the course of the American theatre either during the epoch Alter circumscribes or afterward. Rather, the late fifties and the sixties saw the production of an increasing number of plays that aimed at more than entertainment. These were the years in which an era emerged (it is described in the next section of this essay) that fostered innovation and ever more ethnic-specific theatre. The period between 1953 and 1964 is thus most appropriately viewed as prologue to the expansion of sophisticated drama that begins in the seventies. It is not until the eighties and nineties that American Jewish plays and playwrights achieve the dominance and authority that the fiction had earned three decades earlier. That is the primary reason that the plays in this book were selected from the riches of these two decades. Nonetheless, especially since this two-volume collection aims to show that American Jewish plays have historically been part of the national repertoire, it is well worth answering the question suggested by the notion of "Alter's era." What American Jewish plays *were* on stage between 1953 and 1964?

For starters, there were works that drew on a variety of Jewish texts. By pure coincidence, Alter's alpha and omega dates correspond to Arnold Perl's *The World of Sholem Aleichem* (1953) and Joseph Stein's *Fiddler on the Roof* (1964), whose resounding successes signify renewed appreciation of the celebrated Yiddish storyteller made available in English. In *The Tenth Man* (1959), as previously noted, Paddy Chayefsky drew on another Yiddish classic, Ansky's *The Dybbuk,* which, having entered the English-speaking psyche, would subsequently appear in a number of ingenious adaptations.

The Bible remained a wellspring of inspiration. Paddy Chayefsky's *Gideon* (1961) dramatizes the conflict between self-determination and complete trust in God's will. A similar theme animates Clifford Odets's *The Flowering Peach.* A recasting of the story of Noah as a Jewish tale, *Peach* was selected by the *Year Book of the Drama in America* as a Best Play of 1954.

There were Jewish treatments of a gamut of concerns that were on many minds during these twelve years: life in the military, making a living—and escaping it all. The implications of being a Jew in American uniform during World War II were probed in the courtroom drama Herman Wouk adapted from his novel *The Caine Mutiny Court-Martial* (1954), and by Arthur Laurents in *Home of the Brave* (1960). Various aspects of the needle trade, long a locus of Jewish commercial life, provided the setting of Sylvia Regan's *The Fifth Season,* launched on an extended Broadway run in 1953, Paddy Chayefsky's *Middle of the Night* (1956), Erik Moll's *Seidman and Son* (1962), Joseph Stein's *Enter Laughing* (1963), and Harold Rome's *I Can Get It for You Wholesale* (1963).[10] The fortunes and misfortunes of Jews in the entertainment industry furnished the subject of Herb Gardner's *A Thousand Clowns* (1962), Saul Bellow's *The Last Analysis* (1964), and the dramatization of Budd Shulberg's *What Makes Sammy Run*? (1964).

Problematic topics destined to develop into major themes began to appear. Intermarriage, depicted so lightheartedly in Anne Nichols's *Abie's Irish Rose* (1922), became for Jewish playwrights a topic to treat thoughtfully, if gingerly. Audiences found it difficult to reproach the lonely widower, played charmingly by Edward G. Robinson, who gambled on a few more years of happiness with a Gentile woman his daughter's age in Chayefsky's *Middle of the Night* (1956). Gertrude Berg, whose career began on radio in 1929, having long since convinced fans of her invincibility, hardly risked disillusioning them as the sympathetic widow who accepts a dashing Japanese suitor in Leonard Spigelgass's *A Majority of One* (1959). For all its improbabilities, Spigelgass's play boldly (eighteen years after Pearl Harbor) underscores parallels between people bereaved by wartime losses and points out analogues among Jewish, Buddhist, and Shinto mores.

Finally, there is the introduction of another troublesome issue that would inspire plays in the following decades—that of promising young Jewish men who, alienated from the values of their upbringing and rudderless, come to a sad end. The subject is early treated in S. N. Behrman's autobiographical *The Cold Wind and the Warm* (1959), and, more sensationally, in the play Meyer Levin adapted from his novel *Compulsion* (1957).

Levin aspired to be among the first Americans to write a play about the Holocaust, a subject which, once having made its way into the American Jewish creative imagination, eventually preoccupied it. An established fiction writer and journalist, Levin discovered Anne Frank's *Diary* while on assignment in Europe and quickly realized its dramatic potential. In a lamentable story of intrigue and Jewish infighting, Levin lost out to Hollywood scriptwriters Albert Goodrich and Frances Hackett.[11] Their version of *The Diary of Anne Frank,* which premiered in 1955, ran for 717 performances, and won the Pulitzer Prize and New York Drama Critics Circle Award.

Meyer Levin was not the only well-known American Jewish prose writer to whom the theatre beckoned between 1953 and 1964. Saul Bellow made his playwriting debut with the one-act *The Wrecker* (1956), in which tenants of a condemned building refuse to move before venting their rage on the walls that have witnessed their disappointments. It's a fascinating footnote to cultural history that when Bellow's only full-length play, *The Last Analysis,* was produced on Broadway in 1964, its author thought that what he labeled a farce would be better received than his contemporaneous novel, *Herzog*.[12] *Herzog* became one of Bellow's most celebrated novels; *Analysis* lasted for twenty-eight performances. In a perceptive *Herald Tribune* review, critic Walter Kerr faulted Bellow's "frightening naïveté," as a playwright, while hinting at what public expectations of Bellow, as a Jewish intellectual, must have been. Observing that "laughter *has* grown lame in a world resigned both to holocaust and to television" (TV is central to Bellow's play), Kerr wrote that of course Bellow "knows farce can no longer mean what it used to mean in a simpler and saner time."[13]

This was the era in which two of America's most celebrated Jewish playwrights departed from their customary cosmopolitanism to treat explicitly Jewish subjects. Lillian

Hellman wrote her only play about American Jewish life, *My Mother, My Father and Me* (1963), an absurdist adaptation of Burt Blechman's novel about a family as unhappy as it is implausible. In *Incident at Vichy* (1964), Arthur Miller addressed two daunting subjects: a roundup of Jews in wartime France, and the question of moral responsibility for evil. Hellman's play closed after seventeen performances. A frank experiment, it was an atypically frivolous play.

Incident at Vichy's modest run (ninety-nine performances) might be attributed to other commitments in the Lincoln Center repertory season. It is likely, however, that despite generally respectful reviews from clearly uncomfortable reviewers, audiences were disconcerted by the play's relentless questions about guilt and accountability, and by its brilliant redefinition of the Jew as "the man whose death leaves you relieved that you are not him. . . ." Again Walter Kerr's response was trenchant: "The matter," wrote Kerr, "is so recent and so serious, and we are all of us so engaged in it, that we scarcely dare acknowledge our dissatisfaction with its theatrical cloaking."[14] In 1964, Americans had neither the head nor the heart to confront the unprecedented issues raised by the Holocaust—unless they were packaged in the comfortable Broadway format cannily used by Goodrich and Hackett in *Anne Frank.*

"Alter's epoch" ends spectacularly with the premiere of *Fiddler on the Roof* in 1964. Its 3,242 performances established the long-run record it held until 1980. *Fiddler* signals a milestone in the popular acceptance of Jewish images in American theatre.[15] Although musical comedy admittedly has a wider box office appeal than straight drama, the acclaim won by this profoundly Jewish work suggests that the perception of Jews in America had undergone revision. The historical Jewish experience of vulnerability and uprootededness had come to be viewed as broadly representative. Joseph Stein, author of *Fiddler*'s book, attributed the pertinence of the Sholem Aleichem stories to the contemporary "breakdown of the traditional cultural forms and beliefs . . . under the buffeting of social change and hostile forces."[16]

II

The upheaval Joseph Stein refers to touched off pyrotechnics in the theatre. By the end of the period when plays like those mentioned above were delighting Broadway audiences, dramatic events of quite another order were taking place beyond the glow of the Great White Way. The political and social cataclysms of the sixties—the war in Vietnam, the civil rights movement, the assertion of ethnic pride, the emergence of the women's movement, and the steady inroads of cultural pluralism—would modify most of what characterized America at mid-century.

The theatre was profoundly re-formed as it reflected the disruption of the status quo. Powerful forces born in the sixties combined to fuel the explosion of American Jewish plays and playwrights that marks the century's last decades. The cultural revolution energized innovation and experiment. Everything expanded. New venues multiplied, as did playwrights, scripts, audiences, and, most critically, sources of support.

Chief among the transforming influences is the proliferation of noncommercial and experimental theatre that took root and flourished Off Broadway, ultimately spilling over into Off-Off-Broadway.[17] Animated by the Zeitgeist of the Age of Aquarius, Off Broadway grew into a worthy heir of the Little Theatre movement, whose influential successes in the teens and twenties mark the coming of age of the indigenous American stage.[18] The burgeoning of Off Broadway in the 1960s redefined American theatre, diversifying its goals and functions, enhancing its authority, and increasing the demands it made of its audiences.[19] In subsequent years, the role of Off Broadway has intensified enormously. By 1985, *Best Plays* observed that "Off Broadway was looking more and more like the major creative stimulus in the New York theatre, holding a virtual monopoly on innovation and generating a vigor essential to the survival of the fiercely commercial theatre uptown" (p. 20). Ten years later, *The New York Times*'s Frank Rich declared (though he was not the first to do so) that Broadway was "dead as a showcase for American drama." Rich based his autopsy largely on the decision of Neil Simon, Broadway's "most commercially successful writer for thirty years, [to defect] with his newest comedy to a small theater Off Broadway."[20]

There is no mystery about the appeal of Off and Off-Off-Broadway to people working in theatre in the turbulent sixties. Having plenty to say, bursting with a passion for performance and new ideas for using the stage, heady with the opportunity to pursue artistic, rather than monetary or even critical, success, they turned coffee houses, churches, fire stations, even old Second Avenue (once Yiddish) theatres into laboratories and greenhouses. There was a "found space" to express every point of view and an audience for every innovation.

The climate of openness favored an emerging pride in identity, particularly in ancestral roots. One result was the establishment of producing companies devoted to developing the work of specific ethnic and cultural groups. Among them were the Jewish Repertory Theatre and the American Jewish Theatre, about which more presently. That many of the pioneers of the Off-Broadway movement were Jewish—Judith Malina, Julian Beck, Joseph Chaikin, Richard Schechner, Charles Marowitz, Theodore Mann—is no surprise in light of the history of Jewish contribution to the making of American theatre. Among the playwrights who were nurtured in alternative theatres and whose work reflects their Jewishness were Rosalyn Drexler, Jules Feiffer, Israel Horovitz, Karen Malpede, Harvey Perr, and Susan Yankowitz.

In a figurative sense, the Off-Broadway movement covered the entire United States. The multiplication of professional regional theatres across the country, and of professional resident theatres at universities following the lead of Princeton, Michigan, and UCLA, provided vastly increased opportunities for play development. The statistics speak eloquently of the impact of decentralization on the repertoire and on audiences. In 1964–65, when the *Best Plays* yearbook initiated its Directory of Professional Regional Theaters, it reported 200 productions done by 26 companies in 25 cities. During the 1968–69 season, 37 groups in 35 cities mounted 279 plays, 153 of which were American works. Ten years later, 60 companies in 58 cities produced 490 plays, 281 American works among them.[21]

The expansion and professionalism of the regionals signify a revised American attitude toward theatre. As Ella A. Malin put it in 1965, the regionals represent "the slow but growing acceptance of theatre as a permanent cultural institution worthy of community support in much the same way as museums, libraries, and symphony orchestras."[22] Secretary of Labor Arthur J. Goldberg used the pages of *The New York Times* in 1961 to urge government support for the arts as essential to a free society. The National Endowments for the Arts and the Humanities were founded in 1965. Underwriting began to come from federal monies channeled to state subsidies, thence to arts councils, and from foundations, which followed the lead of such as the Rockefeller and Ford Foundations in supporting regional theatres. By the end of the sixties, critic Martin Esslin confidently included this country's stage among those in the West that regard live theatre as "a social necessity as distinct from a luxury industry confined to metropolitan areas."[23]

Over the last three decades, the regionals have contributed increasingly to the development and production of American Jewish plays. For example, Shirley Lauro's *The Contest* premiered at Houston's Arena Stage; Dick Goldberg's *Family Business* at the Berkshire Theatre Festival (Stockbridge, Massachusetts); Mark Harelik's *The Immigrant,* at the Denver Center Theatre Company; James Sherman's *Beau Jest* at Chicago's Victory Gardens Theatre. David Mamet's work has been nurtured by Chicago's Organic, St. Nicholas, and Goodman Theatres; Israel Horovitz refines his plays at the Gloucester (Massachusetts) Stage Company, which he founded in 1980. The Seattle Repertory Theatre has launched an impressive number of hits, including Wendy Wasserstein's *The Sisters Rosensweig* and Herb Gardner's *I'm Not Rappaport* and *Conversations with My Father*.

In addition to *Conversations,* three other plays in this collection got their start in regional theatres. Jeffrey Sweet's *The Value of Names* was commissioned by Actors Theatre of Louisville, Donald Margulies's *Sight Unseen* was commissioned by the South Coast Repertory (Costa Mesa, California), and Jon Robin Baitz's *The Substance of Fire* premiered at the Long Wharf Theatre (New Haven, Connecticut).

In addition to nurturing playwrights and launching new works into the repertoire, certain professional theatres across the country have cultivated an esprit de corps that has promoted American Jewish theatre in another way. Let Chicago's Second City exemplify a company that has served all three functions impressively. An improvisational theatre founded in 1959, Second City quickly became the forum for first-rate talent, converting into glorious irony the *New Yorker* put-down from which it had defiantly taken its name. The talent of some of its actors included playwriting: Shelley Berman *(First Is Supper)*, Joan Rivers *(Fun City)*, Elaine May *(Adaptation* and *Mr. Gogol and Mr. Preen)*. David Mamet, who as a teenager worked as a busboy at Second City, acknowledges the influence of the episodic format of the work he saw there.[24] At Second City, dramatists, actors, and directors—sometimes the roles were interchangeable—fed one another's creativity. The stimulation that began in Chicago spread to other venues and media (Second City's influence is strong in film and TV, as well as in the legitimate theatre). As Jeffrey Sweet points out in his book about Second City[25], "Jules Feiffer, Neil Simon, Herb Gardner, Wendy Wasserstein, and Donald Margulies have all cast Second City alumni in their plays. People write for the talent that is out there."

But at least as significant as American Jewish plays and players who came out of Second City is the unmistakably Jewish tone that it legitimized. Sweet notes the prevalence of scenes that "emphasized irony and skepticism, drew attention to ethical contradictions and lapses in the logic of authority figures. Conventional wisdom . . . was constantly being questioned and challenged. . . . This may not seem like such a big deal today, when much of mainstream popular culture has 'an attitude,' but coming out of Eisenhower's Fifties, with McCarthyism fresh in mind, the effect on contemporary audiences was bracing."

One easily recognizes in witty social satire and caustic comedy the characteristic stamp of traditional Jewish literature: the skepticism of those who view the establishment as outsiders, the defense the defenseless find in mocking the empowered. Like the merciless stand-up comics—Mort Sahl, Lenny Bruce—Second City artists figure among the heirs of Yiddish satirists and the irreverent early Jewish vaudevillians in America. In expressing Jewish distrust and ridicule of prevailing mores, these entertainers spoke for multitudes. They are a conduit through which brilliant comic impudence and rapier wit continue to enrich the American mainstream in all the performing arts.[26]

Yet another energizing current that refigured the substratum of American theatre was the "postwar revival of peoplehood."[27] The awakening of ethnic awareness and positive ethnic identity manifested itself in all the arts and prompted the establishment of a number of arts-supporting institutions.

Among them was the National Foundation for Jewish Culture, founded by the Council of Jewish Federations in 1960. Dedicated to "the enhancement of Jewish life in America through the arts and humanities," the NFJC has been an influential advocate of Jewish theatre. In 1980, the Foundation's newly formed Jewish Theatre Association convened the First Jewish Theatre Conference/Festival. Entitled "Exploring the Dimensions of Jewish Theatre," the four-day event revealed abundant, variegated evidence of widespread Jewish theatrical activity that surpassed its organizers' most optimistic expectations. Two years later, the NFJC was a co-sponsor of an international festival of Jewish Theatre at Tel Aviv University. The success of that event indicated that Jewish theatre in many languages has become an international phenomenon.

The National Foundation for Jewish Culture remains a major force in promoting Jewish theatre. It has supported translations and productions of Hebrew and Yiddish plays, subsidized the work of performers and consultants, sponsored new Jewish play competitions, and underwritten the publication of Edward A. Cohen's annotated catalogue *Plays of Jewish Interest* (1982).[28]

The most sustained theatrical activity taking place under the aegis of the NFJC is the energetic work of its Council of Jewish Theatres, whose "primary mission is the development and production of plays relevant to Jewish life and values." This network of some three dozen nonprofit producing companies across North America emerged in 1985 out of a restructuring of the Jewish Theatre Association. The Council brings together long-established companies, like Cleveland's Halle Theatre, running since 1951, with fledglings like Theatre Ariel, founded in Philadelphia in 1992. Virtually all the CJT affiliates are dedicated to developing new Jewish plays. So, for example, Barbara Lebow's *A Shayna Maidel* was launched when it won the Halle Theatre's Dorothy Silver competition; Chicago's National Jewish Theatre mounted the world premiere of Shelley Berman's *First Is Supper;* Detroit's Jewish Ensemble Theatre provided early support to Donald Margulies's *The Model Apartment* and produced the American premiere of Israeli playwright Motte Lerner's *Else, or Exile in Jerusalem.*

The same impetus that gave rise to the Council of Jewish Theatres inspired the founding in the 1970s of other performing companies dedicated to dramatizing the range of Jewish experience.[29] In 1974, two professional Jewish theatres were established in New York. Stanley Brechner's American Jewish Theatre has made an award-winning name for itself, not only with revivals of Yiddish classics, many in new translations (David Pinski's *The Treasure;* Peretz Hirschbein's *Green Fields),* but also in the development and production of new works. They have included the Israel Horovitz trilogy *(Today I Am a Fountain Pen, A Rosen by Any Other Name,* and *The Chopin Playoffs)* and Alan Brody's *Invention for Fathers and Sons*. Also in 1974, Israeli Ran Avni inaugurated the Jewish Repertory Theatre. In addition to producing Yiddish classics (such as Stephen Fife's new translation of Sholem Asch's *God of Vengeance*), the JRT regularly mounts European plays of Jewish content (Michel de Ghelderode's *Pantagleize,* John Galsworthy's *Loyalties).* With Edward M. Cohen, associate director through 1994, at their head, the JRT's playwrights-in-residence and writers' lab programs developed the work of many new dramatists.[30] A number of award-winning plays first staged at the JRT have gone on to healthy runs at commercial venues *(Kuni Leml, Crossing Delancey, Cantorial, Shmulnik's Waltz).*

Like all producing companies, Jewish theatres must overcome challenges to survival. Some succumb, but not without having enriched the repertoire. Elizabeth Swados's *Esther: A Vaudeville Megillah,* featured in this book, and Marilyn Felt's *Acts of Faith,* a play about an Arab hijacking, had their world premieres at the Mosaic Theatre during its tenure under Michael Posnick's direction at New York's 92nd Street Y in 1987–88.[31]

III

Within the climate favoring ethnic creativity of every sort, yet another stimulus animated American Jewish artistry. In terms of the off-stage forces that energized and shaped the postwar American Jewish repertoire, it is perhaps the prime mover. While revised attitudes toward ethnicity in general explain significant changes in public perceptions of Jews, the fundamental change took place in Jewish self-image.

In addition to social, cultural, and intellectual activities that brought Jews even closer to the mainstream (or the other way about), the impact of two historic events transformed the way American Jews saw and expressed themselves. The first was the dawning understanding of the devastation of the Holocaust; the second, the creation of the state of Israel.

For many American Jews too young or too disaffected in 1948 to be stirred by the implications of a Jewish state, the Six Day War in 1967 and the repeated performance of Jews as brilliant military strategists had far-reaching effects. Assessing the war's impact on identity, scholar Charles Silberman declared it "a watershed between two eras—one in which American Jews had tried to persuade themselves, as well as Gentiles, that they were just like everyone else, only more so, and a period in which they acknowledged, even celebrated, their distinctiveness.[32] Leonard Fein, longtime commentator on Jewish life, pointed out that for many Jews the Six Day War took on theological significance. Fein writes that the war propelled Israel to "the center of the Jewish religious consciousness and consensus. In a very precise way, Israel had now become the faith of the American Jew."[33]

To be sure, it took time for events of this magnitude to penetrate the American Jewish psyche sufficiently to inspire the creative imagination. However, we don't have to look back very far for evidence of how history fortified artists' self-confidence, newly uncontaminated by ambivalence about outsider status, and unconcerned about public rejection.

Consider, for example, the contrasting attitudes of two Jewish theatre artists working four decades apart. Deeply involved in Goodrich and Hackett's stage adaptation of the Anne Frank *Diary* in 1954, director Garson Kanin was especially anxious for the play to have the widest possible appeal. He believed that meant making it less terrifying—and less Jewish. Was it an accurate sense of audience or his own diffidence that made Kanin protest a scene taken directly from the *Diary*? Anne tells Peter, "We're not the only Jews that've had to suffer. Right down through the ages there have been Jews and they've had to suffer." Kanin objected to what he considered this "embarrassing piece of special pleading," pointing out to Goodrich and Hackett the importance of acknowledging that other people have suffered persecution because of their race or allegiances. Then he added, "The fact that in this play the symbols of persecution and oppression are Jews is incidental, and Anne, in stating the argument so, reduces her magnificent stature."[34]

Compare Kanin's fearful fastidiousness to the composure of Donald Margulies, whose plays are populated by unmistakably Jewish characters and situations. In the graceful prefatory statement he provided for this book, Margulies says, "When one writes about one's own people honestly and unflinchingly, one is writing about all people."

Although by the sixties, American Jewish playwrights had long since left behind the deliberate de-ethnicization of patently Jewish characters that had seemed prudent to some of their predecessors in the thirties and forties,[35] by today's standards of ethnic explicitness, even the most recognizable of the sixties voices sound muted. The only thing timid about Neil Simon's first comedy, *Come Blow Your Horn* (1961), was the nonspecific identity of its transparently Jewish protagonists. No such misgivings stay Simon's hand in his autobiographical trilogy, *Brighton Beach Memoirs* (1984), *Biloxi Blues* (1985), and *Broadway Bound* (1987). Similarly, nothing is made of the Jewishness of Murray Burns, the embodiment of dozens of Jewish TV writers (if not of Jewish fathers *manqués*) at the center of Herb Gardner's *A Thousand Clowns* (1961). Twenty-five years later, Gardner incarnated whole chapters of the realities and the myths of the American Jewish experience in Nat Moyer of *I'm Not Rappaport* (1986). If Paddy Chayefsky boldly transported audiences into an orthodox synagogue in *The Tenth Man* (1959), he nevertheless felt constrained, as mentioned earlier, to refer to features of the ritual by their English names. Ira Levin offered no such concessions in making the irresistible voice of a ghostly cantor chanting in Hebrew the dramatic center of *Cantorial* (1988).

A comparison of the plays in this book with those on similar subjects in *Awake and Singing* illustrates how the coming of age of American Jewish self-confidence has enabled artists to plumb dimensions of their identity. Where Isidore Solomon in *Welcome Stranger* (1920) and George Simon in *Counsellor-at-Law* (1931), who value their ethnicity, struggle for acceptance as Jews, Norma Teitel in Jeffrey Sweet's *The Value of Names* (1983) reserves the right to decide *how* her Jewish name and the famous Jewish parentage she is proud of will influence her professional life. Arthur Laurents's hypersensitive young GI in *Home of the Brave* (1959) is paralyzed by what he perceives as other people's anti-Semitism; David Mamet's veteran in *Goldberg Street* (1991) is, by contrast, acutely alert to his own conflicted reactions to the prejudice he experienced in the military; he admits his own complicity with the bias.

Those most traditional of American Jewish subjects—immigrant life, "making it" in America—treated with barbed humor by Aaron Hoffman (*Welcome Stranger,* 1920); with social and political overtones by Clifford Odets (*Awake and Sing,* 1935); and with sympathetic insight by Sylvia Regan (*Morning Star,* 1941)—are viewed no less tenderly, but with critical irony, in Herb Gardner's *Conversations with My Father* (1994).

One of the most compelling indications of the new self-assurance is the prevalence of plays about Jewish homosexuality. Almost totally absent from the early repertoire—Rose Franken's *Outrageous Fortune* (1943) is a notable exception—the subject is portrayed sensitively and with a candor that often admits humor, as here in William Finn and James Lapine's *Falsettoland* (1989).

Similar forthrightness and depth mark late-century dramatic depiction of Israel as a modern state whose politics and policies engage the passions of American Jewry. The sweetly innocent appreciation in Don Appell and Jerry Herman's *Milk and Honey* (1961) bears little resemblance to the clash of opposing American opinions about the policies of the Jewish nation in Allan Havis's *A Vow of Silence* (1994).

What a contrast in attitude is apparent between early dramatizations of Holocaust material, often more earnest than convincing in the effort to imagine the unimaginable, with those plays that draw confidently on what is genuinely part of the American Jewish psyche: understanding what it means *not* to have been personally involved, coping with the imperative to try to understand the experience of those who were. Emily Mann's *Annulla* (1988) captures the awe of that responsibility convincingly, largely by its unpretentiousness. In the last decades of the century, the Holocaust permeates American Jewish creativity. Even when the Shoah is not the subject of the work, it is a frequent theme, as here in Jon

Robin Baitz's *The Substance of Fire* (1991) and Donald Margulies's *Sight Unseen* (1992). A constant subtext, as in *Esther* (1988), where the biblical rescue from a planned genocide resonates with contemporary relevance, the Holocaust casts its shadow in *The Value of Names* (1986), *Conversations with My Father,* and *A Vow of Silence* as well.

The assurance and directness that typify recent dramatic treatments of unmistakably Jewish characters and subjects are accompanied by another late-century development. Dramatists' long-standing inhibition about appearing "too Jewish" has been replaced by their desire to explore what being Jewish means—especially being Jewish in America. What is particularly striking about this phenomenon is that it spans the generations. One might expect matter-of-fact explorations of Jewishness from a Tony Kushner or a Jon Robin Baitz, who, born in 1956 and 1961 respectively, have always known a pluralistic society that, as Leonard Fein puts it, "has permitted [Jews] both to be part of the larger society and to stand apart from it."[36] But what of playwrights like Neil Simon (born in 1927) and Herb Gardner (1934) who, as earlier indicated, abandoned their initial reserve and squarely addressed questions of Jewish identity and responsibility in what have turned out to be their strongest plays, *Broadway Bound* and *Conversations with My Father,* respectively. Or, to cite the most extreme example, take Ira Levin (born in 1929), whose plays and novels only occasionally deal with Jewishness. Yet in *Cantorial* (1988), Levin chooses to show how commitment to Jewish continuity and community gives new meaning to the life of a non-Jew.

But the theatre has no monopoly on Jewish self-expression. Late-century Jewish creativity in all the arts often grows out of the search for the implications of religious, cultural, or ethnic identity that earlier generations were given to taking for granted or soft-pedaling. Explorations of Jewishness lead to many forms of cultural expression in end-of-the-century America. This is where art historian Avram Kampf lives, organizer of a vast international exhibit, "From Chagall to Kitaj; Jewish Experience in Twentieth Century Art." Where a quartet of classical musicians led by Mark Ludwig seeks out and performs music composed in Theresienstadt. Where Steven Spielberg, wizard of megafantasy, realizes his full potential in filming the story of Oskar Schindler. Where the casts of TV series *(Thirtysomething,*

L.A. Law, The Commish, Seinfeld) include characters whose Jewishness is essential to their roles. It is, finally the place where artists find in their Jewishness the stuff of experimentation, be it the music of progressive bands like Ribot and Zorn's God Is My Co-Pilot; the dancing Hasidim of "Discipledom," choreographed by Amy Sue Rosen; or the one-woman-as-multiple-characters performances of Sherry Glaser and Lisa Lipkin.

IV

The abundance, diversity, and steady proliferation of American Jewish plays notwithstanding, some major themes and concerns are readily identifiable. I list them here, with a few examples and these reservations: I have tried not to be reductive; it is impossible to be exhaustive. What *is* unhappily too easy is eviscerating lively scripts by categorizing them. Classifying plays—for example, by subject—tends to obscure fundamental differences between them (e.g., sibling relationships are central to *The Sisters Rosensweig* and *A Shayna Maidel,* which are otherwise very different plays). In seeking to illustrate both range and variety, I have tried to include works that use the resources of the stage in new ways, for the vanishing sense of marginality has surely encouraged innovation. American Jewish playwrights, like their non-Jewish colleagues, have been moving away from the realism that has characterized this country's drama. The examples here include some as yet unpublished works.[37]

1. The Family. The term "Jewish family play" has earned generic status. Given the centrality of family in Jewish life, dramatists' partiality to the subject is easily explained, although, as a fleeting glance at Sophocles, Shakespeare, Pirandello, and O'Neill discloses, Jews have no corner on the subject. In the last four decades, however, the Jewish family play has undergone radical revision. Everything has changed: the kinds of problems families have, the frankness with which they are portrayed—even the definition of family.

Dissent between the generations springs from all the discontinuities of the nuclear age. Particularly conspicuous are disparities in the values cherished by each new generation. Parents no longer receive traditional deference—nor do they always deserve it. The irascible patriarch in Dick Goldberg's

Family Business (1976), embittered by the death of his wife in an accident with one of his sons, refuses to accept his four sons as the men they have become. In Woody Allen's *The Floating Light Bulb* (1982), a painfully shy youngster resists the efforts of both parents to remodel him. His philandering father wants to make him into a slugger; his alcoholic mother would make a performer of him. Loving parents send out mixed signals about self-sufficiency that confound their Harvard-educated daughter, struggling to find her own way, in Wendy Wasserstein's *Isn't It Romantic* (1983). The admirably responsible paterfamilias of Neil Simon's *Brighton Beach Memoirs* leaves his wife for another woman in *Broadway Bound,* pleading for understanding from his sons. They, meantime, have committed their own betrayal, selling comedy skits based on their family's idiosyncrasies. A wife cuts up her wedding gown for a Halloween costume in Donald Margulies's *The Loman Family Picnic* (1988), while her husband agonizes over bills for a pretentious bar mitzvah, which their son almost cancels when the rabbi refuses to explain his haftorah. Realism and fantasy intermingle freely in this play, which has four different endings.

In Alan Brody's innovative *Invention for Fathers and Sons* (1991), a middle-aged man coping ineffectively with his own troubled son has the opportunity everyone would welcome: He gets to say all the things to his dead father that were left simmering in silence during the older man's lifetime. The ironic title of Jules Feiffer's *Grown-Ups* (1982) refers to people who interrelate by hurting one another in childish ways. But they are benign by comparison with the unnamed cultural stereotypes in James Lapine's stylized *Table Settings* (1980), who actually do the spiteful things to one another that other unhappy families only fantasize. "Wife" in Lapine's play, described by "Mother" as "the ultimate shiksa," is a reminder that all members of the Jewish family are not Jews.

There are other permutations of the conventional Jewish family. In Harvey Fierstein's *Widows and Children First* (1979), the third play in *Torch Song Trilogy,* a gay man scandalizes his traditional mother when he adopts a gay teenager. She refuses to see that he is teaching the boy the values he had learned in his own childhood Jewish home. One of the achievements of William Finn and James Lapine's trilogy, *Falsettos,* is its portrayal of several kinds of family relationships in which characters are committed to others in gay and lesbian as well as heterosexual unions.

While domestic situations are not the focus of all Jewish plays about gay life (e.g., *Angels in America, Jeffrey*), they are significant enough to others to invite attention. For example, in Barbara Graham's *Camp Paradox* (1993, unpublished), a well-intentioned but overbearing Jewish mother holds forth from the wings, while center stage her emotionally needy adolescent daughter falls prey to the advances of her bunk counselor. The power of Larry Kramer's *The Destiny of Me* (1992) is attenuated because the play spews its anger alternately at the protagonist's contentious family relationships and the government's ineptitude in dealing with AIDS. Whether such scripts are suggesting cause and effect or casting blame seems less important than their insistence on yoking their Jewish protagonists' alternate lifestyle with their home life. Audiences viewing these Jewish home and gay scenes side by side on stage are led to conclude that they are equally influential in identifying and shaping the characters.

2. *Jewish Heritage.* A second major theme in the contemporary repertoire is the active appreciation of community, an organic concept that, rooted in family, expands to include peoplehood. For some playwrights, that means finding their subjects in traditional Jewish texts, sacred or secular. For others, it is a matter of connectedness to a chapter of Jewish history.

"I've always thought that the Jewish interpretations of the Old Testament were lively and rich with layers of meaning," writes Elizabeth Swados in her prefatory comments to her musical theatre work *Esther,* the first play in this book. Swados's affinity for biblical subjects also inspired *Song of Songs* (1989), *Jonah* (1990), and *Job: A Circus* (1992). Neil Simon too has been attracted to the Bible. His version of the Book of Job, *God's Favorite* (1974), struck one reviewer as "an uproarious morality play for the secular age."[38] Though not the first to incorporate Judaism anachronistically, Arthur Miller creates a Hebrew-speaking Lucifer (if not a Jewish play) in *The Creation of the World and Other Business* (1972).

Jewish folklore also inspires playwrights. Allan Havis completely reworks the legend of Adam's first wife as a cautionary, cryptic postmodern tale in *Lilith* (1990). In Norman

Lessing's winsome *36* (1985), three Hasidim succeed in finding a lost Lamed Vovnik in the person of a Polish electrician working in a Reform temple.

Other artists continue the tradition of reaching back to Yiddish classics. Nahma Sandrow, Raphael Crystal, and Richard Engquist's highly successful play with music *Kuni Leml* (1984), was based on the Goldfadn comedy *The Two Kuni Lemls.* Having cut his teeth on the French seventeenth century with a version of Corneille's *L'Illusion,* Tony Kushner turned for his next adaptation to the East European nineteenth century and Ansky's *The Dybbuk* (1994). Several Isaac Bashevis Singer stories have been refitted for the stage. *Yentl* (1977), written with Leah Napolin, benefits from its relevance to the women's movement; while *Teibele and Her Demon* (1978), a collaboration with Eve Friedman, charms precisely because it invites audiences into a fable that bears little resemblance to the real world. Singer's *Shlemiel the First* has had several dramatizations since 1974; in 1994, it became a hit for the American Repertory Theatre, which gave it a klezmer score. A Traveling Jewish Theatre, a San Francisco–based ensemble company, tours worldwide with its signature episodic programs that combine Jewish history, myth, folklore, poetry, mysticism, and music—e.g., *Coming from a Great Distance* (1979), *The Last Yiddish Poet* (1980).

It is not just in legends and tales that playwrights connect with their antecedents. Jewish history has inspired an enormous body of plays. It might be represented by two of its most popular subjects: the American Jewish past and the Holocaust.

Critical pronouncements to the contrary, tales of immigration, "making it" in the New World, and Depression woes are hardly passé, at least not in the theatre, as *Conversations with My Father,* the second play in this collection, forcefully illustrates. Despite what we know about the rigors of immigrant life, nostalgia for it is not dead, witness Alan Knee's portrayals of Lower East Side life at the turn of the century. Along with the hardships of the tenements and sweat shops, *Second Avenue Rag* (1980) reconstitutes a heady whiff of the spell cast by such Yiddish theatre stars as Bertha Kalish. In *Schmulnik's Waltz* (1985), Knee makes an authentic Jewish *tsimmes* from a recipe for romance concocted by Plautus and passed down through Rostand.[39]

Jewish dramatists also mine their personal histories. Neil

Simon begins his "BB Trilogy" with the bittersweet reminiscences of his fourteen-year-old persona coming of age in Brighton Beach in 1937. Mark Harelick's *The Immigrant* (1985) is accompanied, both in print and for production, by actual pictures of the events it recounts. *The Immigrant* tells the story of Harelick's grandfather's arrival in Galveston from Russia, and his ultimate success as a businessman and community leader in a small Texas town. Ellen Gould's one-woman *Bubbe Meises, Bubbe Stories* (1992) pays tribute to both of her grandmothers and the way in which their lives flow into hers.

By contrast, it is rare that American Jewish dramatists write about the Holocaust from personal knowledge of it. Despite the formidable challenge of revivifying the horror, the Shoah has inspired some superb drama—much of it from European playwrights who have the dubious advantage of intimacy with the intractable subject.[40] Nonetheless, there is an ever-expanding body of American Holocaust plays that polarize around three points of view.

Some works simulate Holocaust events. Arthur Miller's *Incident at Vichy* (1964) recreates the fear and suspense of the anteroom outside an interrogation chamber where rounded-up Jews await their fate. Harold and Edith Lieberman's *Throne of Straw* (1972) hews closely to the history of the Lodz ghetto under the monomaniacal rule of Chief Elder Mordechai Chaim Rumkowski. It asks audiences not to judge, but rather to consider what they might have done, faced with Rumkowski's "choiceless choices."[41] In *Hannah Senesh* (1985), scripted for one actor playing several roles, David Schechter and Lori Wilner used the poetry and diary of the eponymous Hungarian resistance fighter to dramatize her life and death. Joshua Goldstein's *Hate* (1993) is a one-act monologue in which the Führer's own words are used to reveal his ruthlessness and his increasing polish as a master orator.

Another group of plays deals with surviving the Holocaust. Barbara Lebow's *A Shayna Maidel* (1988) reunites two European-born sisters after the war. One, brought to New York as a child, was spared the Nazi terror experienced by her sister, who had been left behind. Alan Brody's *Company of Angels* (1990, unpublished), based on the real-life story of actress Rita Karpinowicz, shows actors emerging from the ashes to form a theatrical troupe that toured Displaced Persons camps before eventually migrating to Israel and the United States. In *Blue Light* (1994), Cynthia Ozick brings to America the death camp survivors she had created in her short story "The Shawl." Rosa and Stella are now plagued not only by memories, but by those who deny that the horror ever happened.

Finally, some of the most effective American Holocaust drama follows the lead set by Lenny Sack. She subtitles her performance piece *The Survivor and the Translator* "A Solo Work About Not Having Experienced the Holocaust by a Daughter of Concentration Camp Survivors" (1980). Storyteller Lisa Lipkin too weaves her experiences growing up as a child of survivors into *What Mother Never Told Me* (1993). Ari Roth's *Born Guilty* (1990) is based on Peter Sichrovsky's interviews with the children and grandchildren of Nazis, an endeavor which draws the journalist into the intersection of his own and his subjects' histories. It is notable that Arthur Miller's first published play explicitly about American Jews, *Broken Glass* (1994), portrays a Brooklyn woman literally paralyzed by the realization that she was totally uninvolved in Kristallnacht.

3. What It Means to Be a Jew. Distinct from drama inspired by playwrights' affinity with persons or events from the Jewish past is work that seeks to explore or illustrate Jewish values. That oft-used term is much easier to illustrate than to define. For many, responsible and authentic Jewish behavior is less a matter of what is Talmudically or Halakically prescribed than what Jews commonly recognize as ethical. The point was made by Arthur Miller in one of his earliest plays, *No Villain* (1936, unpublished). Its beseiged manufacturer hero refuses to join his colleagues' unsavory strikebreaking tactics, explaining, "Maybe it's honest for the steel companies to work this way, but I can't see that it's the way for Jewish men to act." It is as much a matter of ethos as of conscious religious observance that social responsibility and principled behavior, early established as stimuli and subjects of American Jewish playwriting, continue to inspire postwar drama.[42]

There are, for instance, works that focus literally on the search for justice in a courtroom setting. Both Donald Freed's *Inquest* (1969) and Emily Mann's *Execution of Justice* (1984) are crafted largely out of documentary materials of the cases they depict. *Inquest* reconstructs the trial of

Ethel and Julius Rosenberg, found guilty of espionage against the United States and executed in 1953. Freed's play posits that anti-Semitism was prominently involved in the Rosenbergs' fate. Mann paints from a wider palette in her punningly titled docudrama. Using court transcripts, news reports, and TV footage, she depicts the various shades of intolerance that stained the San Francisco trial of Dan White for the assassination of Harvey Milk, a Jewish homosexual, and George Moscone, the Mayor who had appointed Milk as city examiner.

Other works treat Jewish activism in the name of moral principles or human values. Corinne Jacker's *Domestic Issues* (1983) focuses on the maturing of an ex-terrorist trying to reconcile his guilt for former radicalism, his continued commitment to the purity of his cause, and his need to make peace with a world in which such action is no longer relevant. In Allen Havis's *Haut Goût* (1986), an American Jewish doctor has invented an infant formula intended for Third World use. Willing to put a prestigious practice on the line to serve his humanitarian goals, he falls victim to a Haitian dictator and is betrayed by his own government.

Jewish social responsibility is depicted in a wide range of contexts. In Leonard Spigelgass's *The Wrong Way Light Bulb* (1969), a young writer tries earnestly, though with limited success, to reconcile the multi-ethnic tenants of an inner city apartment house he's inherited. David Rush's *Elephants* (1985) lays bare the exigencies and guilt that distort the lives of a retired Jewish pharmacist and a bag lady to whom circumstances force him to sell stolen cocaine. Jon Robin Baitz's *Three Hotels* (1993) portrays the downfall of its protagonist, who buys ephemeral success in the corporate world at the expense of his family and his good name.

Works about blacks and Jews manifest both the ethics of responsibility and the parallels between disempowered, vulnerable people. Not all these plays convey the earnestness of Jewish involvement in the civil rights movement. Some, for instance, deal lightheartedly with evolving interracial friendships, like Howard DaSilva and Felix Leon's *The Zulu and the Zayda* (1966), set in South Africa, and Henry Denker's *Horowitz and Mrs. Washington* (1980), which takes place on Central Park West. Horowitz, victim of a stroke, a mugging, and racial bigotry is healed of all three by a formidable black nurse.

By contrast, an ugly animosity develops between black and Jew in *Trespassers* (1976, unpublished), which Martin Halpern adapted from Bernard Malamud's novel *The Tenants*. Halpern's very title announces his play's view of the place in society occupied by both its warring protagonists. A more nurturing association exists between the harried, arrogant black heavyweight prizefighter and his Jewish manager, empathetic but powerless against the flagrant prejudice his boss attracts, in Howard Sackler's Pulitzer Prize–winning *The Great White Hope* (1968).

Two more recent works examine the sometimes inharmonious companionship of blacks and Jews. Herb Gardner's *I'm Not Rappaport,* a Tony winner in 1987, portrays the association of two octagenarians who share a New York City park bench. Their past lives appear to have been entirely dissimilar (although it is hard to know if any of the fanciful curriculum vitae Nat Moyer lays claims to is true), and they are not exactly on good terms now. What allies them is serving as ill-equipped comrades in arms against the menaces of Central Park, and the infirmities and indignities of impoverished old age. A different set of circumstances forges the bond between black and Jew in Alfred Uhry's *Driving Miss Daisy,* the 1987 Pulitzer winner. The play traces the evolution over an historic quarter-century, 1948–73, of rapport between a strong-minded Southern widow and her self-respecting black chauffeur. What begins as a master-servant relationship grows into warm mutual reliance, devotion, and, at the play's poignant end, parity, as the two very old friends find comfort in supporting one another in "doin' the bes' " they can.

4. The Quest to Be a Jew. "Many things are possible in America," observes Leon Wieseltier, "but the singleness of identity is not one of them."[43] The theatre frequently serves as a forum for exploring some aspect of the complex, sometimes conflicting interrelation of that which is American and that which is Jewish.

David Mamet's two prematurely discouraged protagonists—they are in their early thirties—in *The Disappearance of the Jews* (1987) ruefully recall the opportunities they once saw open to them as Jewish Americans but didn't take advantage of. They lament thwarted youthful aspirations, failures they lay to drifting away from Judaism through intermarriage and assimilation. Wendy Wasserstein's three middle-aged *Sisters Rosensweig* (1992), like her twenty-something Janie Blumberg in *Isn't It Romantic,* are searching for authentic adult identities. The quest involves threading their way along paths deliberately distanced from the traditional values of the home they grew up in (and continue to value), and gravitating to opportunities open to bright, ambitious women to whom tradition offers few role models. In *Biloxi Blues,* Neil Simon's alter ego, Eugene Morris Jerome, cannot bring himself to emulate the stubbornly principled and defiantly Jewish Arnold Epstein. Craving the acceptance of their platoon mates, Eugene finds himself guilty of compromising his identity, of being, as he puts it, more Swiss than Jewish.

By contrast, a bar mitzvah boy in Israel Horovitz's *A Rosen by Any Other Name* (1987) enlists the help of his friends to dissuade his father from changing the family's conspicuously Jewish name. Though safe in Canada in 1943, Mr. Rosen, frightened by the news from Europe, seeks to deemphasize their ethnicity. Alison, the disaffected Jewish woman in the first of Ari Roth's interrelated one-acts *Proverbial Human Suffering* (1993, unpublished), reconnects with her heritage as the consequence of helping a dying Russian refusenik. In the second play, *Harlem Intifada,* Alison's Jewish loyalty is tested by a vigorous challenge from Palestinians protesting the visit of an Israeli poet to the New York campus where she teaches.

Playwrights use the stage to ask exactly what it takes to be a Jew. In Martin Halpern's *Last Wishes* (1983, unpublished), the bitter clash between the second wife of the dying Irving Rifkin and his sister—is he to have an Orthodox or a Reform burial?—raises a thorny, worthwhile question: In which part of his life was Rifkin truer to Judaism? Merle Feld's *The Gates Are Closing* (1988, unpublished) takes place in a synagogue on Yom Kippur, a venue in which it has in fact been performed. Ten congregants atone for sins easily recognizable as representative: a secret abortion; guilt over loyalties divided between Israel and the United States; the bitter confusion intermarriage has created around its progeny's bat mitzvah. Neo-Nazi Frank Collin's march in Skokie sharpens the identity of the intermarried protagonist of James Sherman's *The God of Isaac* (1982, unpublished), propelling him into an earnest (and comic) search for what it means to live as a Jew. In John Herman Shaner's *After Crystal Night* (1986), a Jewish Defense League–type organization makes a strong case against American Jews who "march and fight in every cause, except a Jewish cause," for fear of making themselves too conspicuous. The organization successfully enlists the activism of a highly assimilated businessman who, despite his all-American success and Beverly Hills refuge, has grown increasingly anxious about resurgent anti-Semitism.

Playwright and scholar David Cole views the exegesis of dramatic literature as a fertile bond between Jewish doctrine and the practice of theatre.[44] He puts his theories to the test in a Beckettian work, *The Responses* (1980, unpublished). Here an eminent rabbinical authority addresses inquiries about unresolved matters of law and practice sent him from all over the world, sometimes answering with riddles and unanswered questions of his own.

5. Israel. The Jewish nation is a momentous fact of life for American Jews. In life as in the theatre, however, Israel presents numerous problems. One may be overearnestnesss. For example, when Dore Schary and Amos Elon adapted Elon's biography of Theodore Herzl for the stage in 1976, reviewers tried hard to respect the work ("If good intentions could make good plays, 'Herzl' would be a work of great power," wrote Edwin Wilson).[45] Nonetheless, Israel figures more and more frequently in recent scripts, sometimes as subtext, other times as their explicit subject.

The former is illustrated by Donald Freed's *The White Crow* (1987), a play constructed of interviews between the imprisoned Adoph Eichmann and a German psychologist, clearly modeled on Hannah Arendt. An embodiment of the intelligentsia extirpated by the Third Reich, she tries to prevail on the Nazi to assess the humanity, rather than the legality, of his guilt. The implications of their encounters transcend the hermetic jail cell where they take place. Their significance is suggested by the play's subtitle, "Eichmann in Jerusalem," a reference to Arendt's vigorously disputed *New Yorker* essay of that title in which she originated the notion of the banality of evil.

Israel moves closer to the foreground in Gordon Rayfield's *Bitter Friends* (1988). The play depicts the divided loyalties of David Klein, an employee of the United States Defense Department. Convicted of passing secret military information to Israel, Klein is given a draconian sentence, life imprisonment. Though Rayfield denies any real-life references, his play inevitably rings echoes of the Jonathan Pollard case. In common with the works discussed in the last sections, *Friends* explores the difficulties inherent in acting on one's beliefs about what it means to be American and Jewish in our day.

A number of plays explicitly about the Jewish homeland are notably evenhanded in portraying Arab-Israeli relations. Marilyn Felt's *Acts of Faith* (1989) depicts both the tension and the need for mutual recognition between an American woman and the Shiite Arab who guards her during a hijacking. In Merle Feld's *Across the Jordan* (1991, unpublished), the relationship between an Israeli woman lawyer and her difficult Palestinian client, accused of terrorism, acquires depth as it is interwoven with the biblical story of Sarah and Hagar, both wives of Abraham. In addition to *Vow of Silence,* included in this volume, Allan Havis provides a forum for conflicting points of view in *The Road from Jerusalem* (1992, unpublished). The work depicts the fierce encounter of an American, a German, and a Palestinian forced together in a bomb shelter.

Elizabeth Swados's 1988 oratorio celebrates its title, *Jerusalem.* Its action follows a Child Traveler through the city shown as sacred to Christians, Moslems, and Jews alike, and wracked by contemporary strife. Swados has woven her own material together with folk and liturgical melodies of more than a dozen nations. Deliberately conflated images reinforce this internationalism; for example, the Rachael who weeps for her children is a Muslim mother lamenting her war dead. *Jerusalem,* which combines the poetry of Yehuda Amichai, the book of Jeremiah, and improvisational texts created by its original multi-ethnic LaMama cast, is a quintessential example of the phenomenon Robert Brustein was talking about when he observed in 1991, "Transcultural blending may be the most fully acknowledged artistic development of our time."[46] More pragmatically, Swados's *Jerusalem,* like the Felt, Feld, and Havis plays, recognizes that Jews are not alone in their zeal for Israel.

V

The plays that follow vouch for the robust health and multiformity of the late twentieth-century American Jewish repertoire. It is evident that the tradition pioneered in the

1920s by Aaron Hoffman and Elmer Rice has passed into clever and productive hands. Curious about how today's dramatists regard bringing Jewish subjects to the stage for general audiences, I invited the writers whose work appears here to comment on that question. Their responses, which precede their plays, are as varied as the works themselves.

Diversity of several kinds was an important consideration in compiling this anthology. With the playwrights, it was a matter of casting the net wide to bring together the already famous with those well on the way to establishing their reputations. In light of the enormous changes described in parts II and III of this essay, I sought dramatists whose work speaks to shifting outlooks on America, its theatre, and on writing about Jews.

The plays reflect a spectrum of issues that have preoccupied American Jewry in the last forty years of the century. They appear roughly in order of the events that inspired them, though in several cases history considerably antedates literature. That is most obviously the case with the first selection, which is based on the Book of Esther, believed to have been composed in the second century B.C.E. *Esther* is followed by plays about making it in America, the Holocaust, Jews in the U.S. military and in the arts, blacklisting, gay family life, AIDS, and that topic that transcends all chronology—intergenerational strife. The collection ends with a work representing the lack of consensus among American Jews on a matter that nonetheless unites them—concern with Arab-Jewish relationships in Israel.

The selections were made with the intent of showcasing the variety in dramatic styles that marks recent American Jewish playwriting. Continuity is of course as significant as experimentation, and it would be hard to find a better example of both—or a more fitting way to begin a volume of Jewish plays—than the first work, a thoroughly updated Purim play. Dating from the sixteenth century (perhaps even earlier), the Purim play is the forerunner of all structured Jewish theatre and the sole kind of playmaking accepted in the orthodox community. Elizabeth Swados's "vaudeville megillah" incorporates all kinds of transformations. They are appropriate both to the spirit of the holiday when, as she puts it, "anything is possible," and to the post-modern blurring of gender roles. Moreover, it is not only actors who slip in and out of their parts; members of *Esther*'s audiences also become actors in this roisterous celebration. And in using elements of vaudeville as her presentational style, Swados furthers a stage tradition in which Jewish entertainers early made their mark.

Like *Esther, Falsettoland* is almost entirely sung. It joins the Swados play in updating the traditions of Jewish activity in music and in humor. In addition, *Falsettoland* appropriates another established form, the coming-of-age play, to tell its radically unorthodox story. Its characters have the audacity to proclaim some well-kept secrets out loud: Jewish boys can't play baseball; everyone hates his parents. With winning frankness and charm, Finn and Lapine bring to the stage some of the most significant phenomena of our times: same-sex relationships, failed marriages, AIDS—and the stubborn inviolability of family love.

Realism is far from outdated; it is represented here by three scripts. Herb Gardner's *Conversations with My Father* varies the form with the onstage presence of Charlie, narrator and chorus, who also plays an active role in the plot. Having recounted or lived through his parents' experiences with the main forces that shaped American Jewish life in the first half of the century—immigration, memories of pogroms, wartime sacrifice, and the relentless struggle to make it—Charlie in turn has to mediate this heritage for his own son. Jeff Sweet's *The Value of Names* departs from its predominant realism only in the encounter between Leo and Benny, whose tone and rhythm often smack of a vaudevillian exchange. The scene, which fails to revive a once-warm camaraderie, echoes the equally insoluble differences between Benny and his daughter, Norma. Intergenerational dissent also plays an important role in Jon Robin Baitz's *The Substance of Fire*. More accurately, the first act of the play delineates the incompatible values that set the three Geldhart children against their imperious father, Isaac. Baitz breaks with conventional realism in the second act of the play, which, rather than developing the first act, in linear fashion, totally restructures Isaac's circumstances.

Emily Mann's *Annulla* innovates in several ways. The play's subtitle, *An Autobiography,* is to be taken literally. Mann, who has made a specialty of what she calls "theatre of testimony" in docudramas like *Execution of Justice* and *Still Life,* creates her script from her real-life protagonist's actual words. Like David Mamet's *Goldberg Street,* the second one-act play in this volume, *Annulla* is more than an intermittently punctuated monologue. In each case, the interlocutor's taciturnity belies her importance. *Annulla*'s second voice—Mann's own—is that of a young American Jewish woman seeking enlightenment about the fate of European Jews, which she and her family were spared. The daughter in *Goldberg Street* who serves as her father's confidante now has to cope with his confession of ambivalence about protesting anti-Semitism. Language works especially forcefully in both one-acts, though in antithetical ways. Mann's character is a fountain of words; Mamet's, characteristically, is terse and elliptical. It is hardly surprising that both scripts have lent themselves to production as radio plays.

Sight Unseen and *A Vow of Silence* break with other conventions. Donald Margulies defies chronology in *Sight Unseen*. The plot moves forward, then back, literally ending before it begins. The audience is left to reorder the scenes, making sense of them in a way consonant with other disconnections in the plot, not the least of which is the inconsistent behavior of its protagonist. In *A Vow of Silence,* Allan Havis also invites his audiences to arrive at their own conclusions, and not only about the Israeli-Palestininan conflicts in the play. The characters are as complicated as the situations in which they are placed; their motives are often inexplicable, occasionally contradictory, even self-defeating. The play intrigues precisely because its knotty problems suggest so many responses without authenticating any of them.

A number of factors other than the demonstration of various diversities determined the contents of this volume. Some were entirely practical: Were reprint rights available? Were several editions of a title already in print? Lacking the hindsight that made the choices for *Awake and Singing* more clear-cut, I was also guided by my own aesthetic judgment and delight meter. The recognition earned by a number of the plays only increased my admiration for them (*Sight Unseen,* an Obie winner, was nominated for all the major awards, including the Pulitzer, while *Conversations* and *Falsettos* won a clutch of Tonys, and *Substance of Fire* received two Lucille Lortel awards). Still, I empathize with the narrator at the end of a Samuel Beckett short story who says he could have told another tale, although in this case, an *additional* one, for there are enough wonderful contemporary plays to fill several anthologies.

The plays brought together here and in *Awake and Singing* exemplify the substance, insights, and pleasures of a major resource of the American theatre. The development of the American Jewish repertoire to its end-of-the-century preeminence reveals a good deal about the evolving place and perception of Jews in America. That is one reason the plays merit more critical attention. Another is their warm popular reception, no longer a mostly New York phenomenon, as the applause in Wisconsin, Idaho, and Alabama makes clear.

—Ellen Schiff

NOTES

1. Burns Mantle, Introduction, *The Best Plays of 1931-32 and the Year Book of the Drama in America* (New York: Dodd, Mead, 1937), viii.

2. Kenneth Tynan, "The Theatre," *New Yorker,* 14 Nov. 1959, 120.

3. Morris Dickstein, "Cold War Blues: Notes on the Culture of the Fifties," *Partisan Review* 41:1 (1974), 49.

4. Abraham J. Karp, "At Home in America," in Abraham J. Karp, ed., *The Jewish Experience in America,* v. 5 (Waltham: American Jewish Historical Society and New York: Ktav, 1969), xxxvi.

5. Stephen J. Whitfield, "Value Added: Jews in Postwar American Culture," in Peter J. Medding, ed., *A New Jewry? America Since the Second World War, Studies in Contemporary Jewry, An Annual, VIII* (New York: Oxford Univ. Press, 1992), 81.

6. Quoted by Theodore Solotaroff and Marshall Sklare, eds., Introduction, *Jews in the Mind of America* (New York: Basic Books, 1966), 4.

7. Robert Alter, "The Jew Who Didn't Get Away: On the Possibility of American Jewish Culture," in Jonathan D. Sarna, ed., *The American Jewish Experience* (New York: Holmes and Meier, 1986), 270.

8. Nessa Rapoport, "Summoned to the Feast," in Nessa Rapoport and Ted Solotaroff, eds., *Writing Our Way Home* (New York: Schocken, 1992), xxviii.

9. Ted Solotaroff, "The Open Community," in *Writing Our Way Home,* xx.

10. Nineteen-year-old Barbra Streisand made her show-stopping debut as Miss Marmelstein in *I Can Get It for You Wholesale*. Her electric talent and unabashedly Jewish persona rocketed her to stardom as Fanny Brice the next year in *Funny Girl* (1964). Credit is due Streisand for trumping prevailing notions of feminine beauty and winning popular acclaim for decidedly ethnic looks and demeanor.

11. The entire story is told in fascinating detail by Lawrence Graver, *An Obsession with Anne Frank: Meyer Levin and the Diary* (Berkeley: Univ. of California Press, 1995).

12. Keith Opdahl, "The 'Mental Comedies' of Saul Bellow," in Sarah Blacher Cohen, ed., *From Hester Street to Hollywood* (Bloomington: Indiana Univ. Press, 1983), 183.

13. Walter Kerr, "Bellow's 'Last Analysis'—Walter Kerr's Analysis," *New York Herald Tribune,* 2 Oct. 1964, *New York Theatre Critics Reviews,* XXV: 20, 206.

14. Walter Kerr, "Theatre: 'Incident at Vichy' Opens," *New York Times,* 4 Dec. 1964. *New York Times Theatre Critics Reviews,* XXV: 28, 116.

15. The accuracy of those images has been vigorously challenged by Yiddish specialists, among them, Joseph C. Landis. Landis argues that the musical thoroughly falsifies the original text, the world it depicts, and, most seriously, "Sholem Aleichem's sense of the moral code of his people." See his "Fiddling with Sholem Aleichem," *New York University Bulletin,* LXV, 20 (Spring 1965), 29–33.

16. Joseph Stein, *Fiddler on the Roof* (New York: Crown, 1964), 119.

17. In the 1965–66 *Best Plays Yearbook of the American Theatre,* editor Otis L. Guernsey, Jr., supplies these useful distinctions: "What is now being called off-off Broadway [is] the beehive of experimental play production put on, usually without such formalities as Equity contracts, daily performance schedules or invitations to be seen by critics. In the listing in this volume 'Broadway' is the collection of shows with Broadway union contracts, plus major repertory and visiting groups" in houses of 600 seats. " 'Off Broadway' is the collection of regularly-scheduled professional productions whose union contracts recognize their non-Broadway status with concessions" (p. 34).

18. See Dorothy Chansky, "Composing Ourselves: The Little Theatre Movement and the Construction of a New Audience Rhetoric, 1912–1927." Ph.D. dissertation, N.Y.U., 1996.

19. Let there be no misunderstanding that either Off Broadway or experimental theatre had their origins in the 1960s. The *Best Plays Yearbook* has included an Off Broadway re-

port annually since 1934–35, when it recorded foreign language productions, including those of the Yiddish theatre, as well as children's theatre, dance drama, and college plays. In the forties, the category begins to expand with the introduction of the work of new producing groups like the Associated Playwrights, alumni of the Theatre Guild's playwriting seminar. In 1953–54, Garrison Sherwood observed, "Off Broadway theatre has gone this year from the 'little theatre' class to big business," attributing its success to low ticket prices, more variety, and enhanced opportunities for theatre personnel (*Best Plays,* p. 356). By 1958, *The New Yorker* had hired a reviewer specifically to cover Off Broadway. And by 1981–82, *Best Plays* editor Otis L. Guernsey, Jr., predicted "Off Broadway could become the main event," basing his observation on the 1981–82 season in which "Off Broadway was the principal repository of American playwriting" (p. 31).

20. Frank Rich, "The Final Curtain?" *New York Times,* 30 Oct. 1994, sec. 4, 15.

21. I do not mean to imply that until the sixties, American theatre was synonymous with the New York stage and existed only there, though no one would deny New York's continued status as the center of American theatre. A more accurate picture is indicated by the coverage in the *Best Plays* yearbook. While for many years that authoritative annual had articles on theatre activities in Boston, Chicago, Los Angeles, and San Francisco, in 1961, Henry Hewes as editor expanded the year's overview to productions in Washington, Dallas, Houston, and Minneapolis-St. Paul. When Otis L. Guernsey, Jr., assumed the editorship of *Best Plays* in 1964, he added a Directory of Professional Regional Theatres, since a regular feature listing the seasons of the regional theatres coast to coast. Since 1976–77, the yearbook has also included summaries of new plays deemed outstanding by members of the American Theatre Critics Association, the organization of drama critics in all media dedicated to increasing "public awareness of the theater as a national resource."

22. Ella A. Malin, "The Season Around the United States, With a Directory of Professional Regional Theatres," in

Otis L. Guernsey, Jr., ed., *The Best Plays of 1965–1966* (New York: Dodd, Mead, 1966), 42.

23. Martin Esslin, "The Role of Theatre," in his *Reflections: Essays on Modern Theatre* (New York: Anchor, 1971), 211.

24. Samuel G. Freedman, "The Gritty Eloquence of David Mamet," *New York Times Magazine,* 16 April 1985, 51.

25. Jeffrey A. Sweet, *Something Wonderful Right Away* (New York: Avon, 1978). I am very grateful to Jeff Sweet for incorporating further observations about the Jewishness of Second City in his prefactory comments to *The Value of Names,* and have drawn heavily on that information in these paragraphs.

26. It would be irresponsible and ungrateful to observe how Jewish satire has infused popular culture without mentioning the work of Woody Allen, both in film and on stage, and that of Sid Caesar and the remarkable team of Jewish writers for his TV shows, who set standards for topical parody rarely equalled.

27. The phrase was coined by Allen Guttman, *The Jewish Writer in America* (New York: Oxford Univ. Press, 1971), 120–28.

28. The catalog contains capsule summaries of plays. Listings include works from the Dramatists Play Service and Samuel French catalogs, translations of Yiddish, Hebrew, and European plays, and unpublished works with the addresses of their authors or agents. It is available from the National Foundation for Jewish Culture, 330 Seventh Avenue, 21st floor, New York, NY 10001. A much-needed revised edition is planned for 1995.

29. Norman J. Fedder, who has pioneered energetically in the regeneration of American Jewish theatre, views its growth in a different context. "The year 1974," he writes, "might be considered the turning point in the revival of the religious theatre movement." "Beyond Absurdity and Sociopolitics: The Religious Theatre Movement in the Seventies," *Kansas Quarterly,* 1980, 123–31.

30. Five of them appear in Cohen's *New Jewish Voices* (Albany: SUNY Press), 1985.

31. Companies dedicated to American Jewish drama figure among many ethnic-specific theatres that blossomed in response to invigorating postwar opportunities and fertile grounding in multicultural vitality. Writing in the 1982–83 *Best Plays Year Book,* critic Mel Gussow remarked on the conspicuous role in New York theatre of Hispanic, Black, Greek, Irish, Jewish, and Asian American companies (p. 42).

Nor was this a uniquely New York phenomenon. In 1976, the American Theater Critics Association (see note 21) made its first award to an outstanding new play professionally produced outside New York. It is surely a reflection of the respect earned by ethnic drama that the winner was Wakako Yamauchi's *And the Soul Shall Dance,* an adaptation of an Asian American short story by Frank Chin.

32. Charles E. Silberman, *A Certain People: American Jews and Their Lives Today* (New York: Summit, 1985), 201.

33. Leonard Fein, *Where Are We? The Inner Life of America's Jews* (New York: Harper and Row, 1988), 19.

34. Quoted by Lawrence Graver, *An Obsession with Anne Frank,* 89.

35. See Introduction to *Awake and Singing: Seven Classic Plays From the American Jewish Repertoire,* xvi–xix.

36. Fein, 159.

37. The designation "unpublished" should be read only as a sign of the capriciousness that governs the publication of plays. Interested readers and theatres are urged to contact the authors or their agents. Most of the unpublished scripts mentioned here are by members of the Dramatists Guild, 234 West 44th St., New York, NY 10036; (212) 398-9366.

38. John Beaufort, "Neil Simonizing the Story of Job," *Christian Science Monitor,* 18 Dec. 1974. *New York Theatre Critics' Reviews,* XXXV:22, 147.

39. Asked what drew him to dramatize immigrant life, Knee, who was born in Manhattan in the mid-forties, explained that he wanted to go beyond the attitude of the milieu where he had been raised. He had been taught "Don't be obvious about your Jewishness, but never forget you're a Jew." It was in adapting *The Scarlet Letter* for TV that he observed that in the nineteenth century, Hawthorne had worked

through conflicting messages by going back to seventeenth-century Puritanism. Knee took the lesson to heart. That a Jewish playwright is inspired to return to his own origins by Nathaniel Hawthorne is a genuine "only in America" story.

40. Though the two fine collections in English of Holocaust plays are dominated by European scripts, each does include American works. *The Theatre of the Holocaust*, ed. Robert Skloot (Madison: Univ. of Wisconsin, 1982), contains Harold and Edith Lieberman's *Throne of Straw* and Shimon Wincelberg's *Resort 76*; *Plays of the Holocaust*, ed. Elinor Fuchs (New York: Theatre Communications Group, 1987), has James Schevill's *Cathedral of Ice*.

41. This apt phrase was coined by Lawrence L. Langer, eminent critic of Holocaust literature.

42. See the introduction to *Awake and Singing*, xviii-xix.

43. Leon Wieseltier, "Against Identity," *New Republic*, 28 Nov. 1994, 24–32.

44. David Cole, "Toward a Jewish Dramatic Theory," *Tikkun*, IV, 2 (1989), 26–28ff.

45. Edwin Wilson, "Herzl," *Wall Street Journal*, 2 Dec. 1976. *New York Theatre Critics' Reviews*, XXXVII:24, 101.

46. Robert Brustein, "The Use and Abuse of Multiculturalism," *New Republic*, 16 and 23 Sept. 1991, 31–34.

ESTHER

A VAUDEVILLE MEGILLAH

by

Elizabeth Swados

Elizabeth Swados comments:

I've always thought that the Jewish interpretations of Old Testament stories were lively and rich with layers of meaning. I wanted to see if I could create musical theater pieces that were Jewish in tone and lore, but secular enough to be attractive to audiences of many ages and faiths. Since I'd grown up singing *Amahl and the Night Visitors* and the *Messiah,* I wanted to try my hand at creating a more public version of certain Jewish holidays. I began with *The Hagaddah,* at Joe Papp's Public Theater, and my second project became *Esther*—a piece which started at the Public, then was performed at the 92nd Street Y in New York and went on to tour Italy, France, and Spain.

My Esther is a Jewish Mata Hari—a working wonder woman who gives up family and love to save her people. The production meant to reflect the madcap humor of Purim, and at the same time show the horrors of the deeds of the anti-Semite. And, since on Purim almost anything can happen, we wove many intricate magical illusions into the direction of the play. Therefore the piece has a shocking, drunken, mysterious change of mood and tempo.

EDITOR'S NOTE: This text has been given a lively dimension by the addition to song titles of descriptions of the wide range of musical styles applicable in production. These indications are largely the work of Laurie Wessely-Baldwin, who directed *Esther* in Washington and at its Canadian premiere in Toronto; they were edited and approved by Ms. Swados.

So that the reader can distinguish between lyrics and speeches, spoken lines are run on after the speaker, songs are set line for line below the singer. (This distinction is also made in Finn and Lapine's *Falsettoland*.)

Megillah is Hebrew for "scroll." The Book of Esther is the last of the five megillot in the Bible and perhaps the best known because of the merrymaking that accompanies its reading in the synagogue on Purim.

"Megillah" has also taken on the popular meaning of a long, detailed story.

Esther was first presented at the Mosaic Theater, 92nd Street Y, New York City on February 23, 1988 (Purim). The cast was:

KING AHASHUERUS	*Robert Ott Boyle*
MORDECHAI	*Peter Herber*
HAMAN	*Louis Padilla*
ESTHER	*Laura Patinkin*
NARRATOR—ETHYL	*Nancy Ringham*
NARRATOR—LUCY	*Frederique S. Walker*
MUSICAL DIRECTOR/KEYBOARDS	*Jonny Bowden*
DRUMS/PERCUSSION	*Jim Le Blanc*
STAGE MANAGERS	*Greg Johnson*
	Linda Carol Young

Directed by ELIZABETH SWADOS

All minor roles are to be shared ad libitum by all cast members. The major roles are not distinguishable at the outset, but evolve out of the "gaggle" of beggars that dominate the opening scene. The score identifications NARRATORS, COMPANY, and ALL are freely and interchangeably employed to designate choral or storytelling functions for the cast. All who perform the play may creatively adapt the execution of the material to the specific requirements of their production. The notations for the rhythm are intended as a stylistic guide for the drummer/percussionist, who should play, in addition to the standard drum set, an assortment of percussion instruments which may include bells, triangle, mark tree, wood blocks, finger cymbals, slapstick, small gongs, and other appropriate sounds.

ACT I

A company of six vaudevillians join in the telling of the tale of Purim. The story is told primarily through song and the overall presentation is concert-like, with all performers constantly present on stage. The action is further defined through on-stage costume changes and through the use of a variety of props, masks, and illusions.

The performers often engage in conversation with the audience and are free to ad lib in unscored sections, as vaudevillians would do. Some of the scripted material herein was developed in this manner.

The play begins as two well-dressed narrators begin entertaining ("warming") the audience. On cue they sing the opening songs and are joined by four beggars, who set about transforming the "nice" clothes of the narrators into "beggar's rags."

(Shoshanat Yakov—moderately slow, traditional sound)

NARRATORS:
Sho-sha-nat ya-kov,
Tza-ha-la,
Ve-se-me-cha,
B'ir o-tam ya-chad
Te-che-let mordechai.

Dai, dai, dai, dai, dai, dai, dai, dai, dai,
Dai, dai, dai, dai, dai, dai,
Dai, dai, dai, dai, dai, dai, dai, dai, dai,
Dai, dai, dai, dai, dai, dai.

(Narration 1—brightly)

Once upon a time
In a land far away
There lived a king
And his queen.
It would be impossible,
Perhaps improper,
To begin this story
Any other way.

For we are dealing here
With a marvelously simple,
Yet awe-inspiring fairy tale
Which manages to reassure
The child in each of us.

For at the very end of it,
All the ups and downs,
Good does vanquish evil
And joy does succeed sadness.

Everything in this story
Smacks of miracles.

For once it isn't difficult
To be Jewish.

COMPANY:
Ad-lo-ya-dah!
Ad-lo-ya-dah!
Ad-lo-ya-dah!
Ad-lo-ya-dah!

(Beggar's Song)

(During song, beggars convert narrators' costumes into beggars' rags.)

BEGGAR 1: *(In the audience.)*
Help me please,
I'm working my way

Through veterinary school,
Can you spare some change,
Can you spare some change,
Can you spare some change,
Can you spare some change?

BEGGAR 2:
I like your tie,
I used to have one like that,
I like your wife,
I used to have one like that,
Spare some change,
Can you spare some change,
Can you spare some change,
Can you spare some change?

BEGGAR 3:
Aunt Sadie's got shingles,
Uncle Morty's got mumps,
Got some money?
Got some money?
Can you spare some change,
Can you spare some change,
Can you spare some change,
Can you spare some change?

BEGGAR 4:
Help me,
I'm an African child.
Can you spare some change,
Can you spare some change,
Can you spare some change,
Can you spare some change?

4 BEGGARS:

Help	Help me please,	Aunt Sadie's got shingles,	I like your tie,
Me	I'm working my way	Uncle Morty's got mumps,	I used to have one like that,
I'm an	Through	Got some money?	I like your wife,

African child.	Veterinary school,	Got some money?	I used to have one like that,
Can you spare some change,	Can you spare some change,	Can you spare some change,	Can you spare some change,
Can you spare some change,	Can you spare some change,	Can you spare some change,	Can you spare some change,
Can you spare some change,	Can you spare some change,	Can you spare some change,	Can you spare some change,
Can you spare some change,	Can you spare some change,	Can you spare some change,	Can you spare some change,

(Repeat "Can you spare some change" section five times.)

NARRATOR: Tonight's the night when the rich get to be poor, and the poor get to be rich, and everybody gets to be Esther!

(Song of the Underdog—quickly)

It's always been the custom
That the poor entertain the rich.
They sing their lusty songs
And tell the poor man's joke.

The poor are so mysterious
That the rich would like to switch,
Parade around the square
Wearing the poor man's yoke.

COMPANY:
Here's to the underdog,
He comes up from the rear.
He gives the winner his run,
And causes the crowd to cheer.

Let's praise the underdog,
He drags his feet with such heart.
He fights as if he's going to win,
Though he was the loser from the start.

(Reggae.)

It's forever been the story
That the poor play for the rich,
And the rich pay to imagine that they're poor.

Let the smell of bread or coffee
Leak out through a crack,
There will be a beggar at your door forevermore.

It's theatrical tradition
That the powerful own the poor,
They buy up dreams like kids devour cake.

The poor will dance until they drop
To get through one more day,
And sell their precious dreams for their families' sake.

COMPANY:
Let's praise the underdog,
He comes up from the rear.
He gives the winner his run,
And causes the crowd to cheer.
Let's praise the underdog,

BEGGAR (Haman):
Aren't the poor
Lots of fun,
Flies on their eyes
Their noses run,
Persecution
Makes for wit,
The poor are so
Adept at it.
You give them bread
They sing their song,
Let's make a mess
And sing along,
How I love the poor!
How we love
The sad romance,

He drags his feet with such heart.

He fights as if he's going to win

Though he was the loser from the start.

The mother's wail
The tired dance.
Weeping tunes
And bloody faces,
Hooray for all
The dying races.
Like a circus
Full of fleas,
Let's applaud minorities,
How I love the poor!

ALL:
Let's praise the underdog,

(Foreign language ad libs between phrases: "Viva los publicitos!" "Lang leben zol dos folk!")

Let's praise the underdog,
Let's praise the underdog,
Let's praise the underdog!

NARRATORS: Tonight we shall tell tales. And nothing is more gratifying for a teller of tales than to bring people together . . . people of distant generations and contemporaries . . . Hassidim and philosophers . . . poets and dreamers . . . Jews and Christians . . . students and teachers . . . and Republicans! They are all prone to fall under the spell of certain words and they are intrigued by the density of certain silences. There is nothing like a good story.

BEGGAR (Haman): Let's get to the part where the Jews die!

(Narration 2—as before)

NARRATORS:
Once upon a time
In a land far away
There lived a king
And his queen,
It would be improper
To begin this story
Any other way.

COMPANY:
Adloyadah!

NARRATORS:
Well
Once upon a time
In a land far away,
There flourished a great community,
Though some of its men and women
And children too
Had been condemned to perish,
Luckily there lived a man,
A just man.
In their midst a man.

BEGGAR (Mordechai):
Just a just man.

BEGGAR (Esther):
And his niece
Or his daughter
Or his lover.

NARRATORS:
What does it matter?
The beat of his heart
Was the great woman,
The historical heroine
Esther.
She was so beautiful, and together they were able to avert a decree and save their people.

(We Will Witness Triumphs—fast driving rock tempo)

COMPANY:
We will witness triumphs,
Triumphs of faith and prayer
Over terror and cruelty.
Yesterday's victims
Emerge as today's victors
And power and glory will shift
From the haves to the have-nots,
From notables to simple people,
Everybody likes a happy ending.

(Out of tempo.)

COMPANY:
Ah—

NARRATOR 1:
Which explains the universal
Popularity of Purim.

COMPANY:
Ah—

NARRATOR 2:
Is that the reason for Purim's
Appeal and popularity?

COMPANY:
Mm—

2 NARRATORS:
In contrast to other holidays,
On Purim all we have to do
Is listen to a story
And get drunk,

COMPANY:
Mm—

2 NARRATORS:
And the more we listen
And the more we drink,
The better,

COMPANY:
And the more we listen
And the more we drink,
The better.

NARRATOR: *(Sermonizing, "gospel" style.)* Yes, Purim will be celebrated even after the coming of the Messiah, even after the redemption of all people, all nations, all men!

COMPANY: *("Gospel" style.)*
Amen.

BEGGAR (Haman): What are they saying, those stupid, sentimental, melodramatic, grandiose Jews! *(He sneezes.)*

(Narration 3)

NARRATORS:
Once upon a time
In a capital of an empire
That numbered a hundred and
Twenty-seven states,
There lived an old
And eternally bored
And boring king,
Ahashuerus.

COMPANY: *(Variously.) (Spoken.)*
A-ha-she-who-vous?
A house of various?

A-are you serious?
A-ha-ha-ha-ha!

KING: Who?

COMPANY: Ahashuerus!

KING: God bless you.

NARRATORS:
One day he had a vulgar
And not so very original idea
Of organizing
The largest dinner in history

KING: I was hungry.

NARRATORS:
Nothing but the best would be
Served to the most
Distinguished guests,
The most delicious dishes,
The best wines
And the highest quality entertainment.

KING:
Queen Vashti

COMPANY:
Please perform!

VASHTI:
No!

KING:
Queen Vashti!

COMPANY:
Please dance!

VASHTI:
No!

KING:
Queen Vashti!

COMPANY:
Show your talents please!

VASHTI:
No!

KING:
Queen Vashti, do a striptease!

(Out of tempo.)

VASHTI:
Are you crazy?

KING: *(Cursing ad libitum in "ancient tongue.")*
Sheh va-ke-te sheh-vaish-ta, sheh va-ke-te, etc.

(Queen Vashti's Song—à la Marie Antoinette)

VASHTI:
My father could drink
As much as you
And still he'd never
Do such a thing.
Oh, King, have pity
On yourself,
You disgrace!

My father could hold
Five times what you drink
And still he'd never
Think of this,
You insist on being
Stubborn and cruel,
You fool!

Oh, husband, think what you do
To the honor of the crown!
For one, crazed, moment
You'd drag me down!

My father could outdrink
You ten to one
And still he'd never
Do what you've done,
Humiliate his Queen,
To divert and entertain
You're a pig,
You're insane!

(Driving rock temp, à la Motown.)

No, no, I will not do as you say!
No, no, I will not compromise
Myself in any way!
No, no, I will not change myself
Into a rich man's toy!
Go find yourself some other game
You spoiled little boy!

No, no, I will not do as you say!

OTHER WOMEN:
As you say!

VASHTI:
No, no, I will not compromise myself in any way!

WOMEN:
No, no, no!

VASHTI:
No, no, I will not change myself
Into a rich man's toy!

WOMEN:
Won't be a toy!

VASHTI:
Go find yourself some other game
You

ALL THREE:
Spoiled little boy!

VASHTI:
My father loved his liquor just like you

WOMEN:
Just like you!

VASHTI:
But still he never asked me
To compromise like you do!
My father loved his liquor just like you

WOMEN:
Just like you!

VASHTI:
But still he never asked me
To compromise like you do!

VASHTI:
You pig!

WOMEN:
You pig!

VASHTI:
You fool!

WOMEN:
You fool!

VASHTI:
You pig!

WOMEN:
You pig!

VASHTI:
You fool!

WOMEN:
You fool!

VASHTI:
We're through!
I've had it with you!

(Narration 4)

NARRATOR:
Outraged by her refusal,
The King consulted with advisors on protocol,
Legislation, human rights and marriage counseling.

Never had anything like this
Happened to him before.

(Your Majesty, the Queen Is More Than Disobedient)

HAMAN: *(Not yet in full character.)*
Your Majesty, the Queen
Is more than disobedient,

COMPANY: *(With* HAMAN.*)*
Your Majesty, your wife
Is way out of line.

HAMAN:
Perhaps Queen Vashti
Is setting evil precedent
And unquestioned
Male dominance will decline.

COMPANY:
And other girls will
Follow her design

HAMAN:
Maids will henceforth
Maliciously malign
Their unsuspecting men.

KING:
I beg your pardon?

COMPANY: *(With* HAMAN.*)*
A man will lose
What makes a man
A man!

KING:
Huh?

COMPANY: *(With* HAMAN.*)*
We'll be a nation
Of eunuchs
In the end!

KING:
Oh no!
If a King can't keep
His Queen a proper slave

COMPANY:
A slave

KING:
How will the lower
Classes then behave?

COMPANY:
Behave?

KING:
If a Duchess clouts a Duke

COMPANY:
A Duke

KING:
For a fling that was a fluke

COMPANY:
Oh-hoo-hoo-hoo-hoo!

KING:
Or a Countess contradicts a Count
As to who is steed

ALL:
And who's the mount.

KING:
If a King can't keep his Queen
Obedient and mute

VASHTI: *(Bound and gagged.)*
Hm-mm-m-m-mm

(Out of tempo.)

KING:
Then I say, "No more chocolates."

COMPANY:
Let's execute!

KING: *("Ancient curse," as before.)*
Sheh va-ke-te sheh-vaish-ta, sheh va-ke-te, etc.

(Incidental music accompanies the action of VASHTI*'s execution and "floating head" ad libitum; music should be strange, otherworldly, etc.)*

(He's Forgotten Her—overdone Baroque recitative, then, kicks into tempo like James Brown)

NARRATOR:
The King has forgotten
Queen what's her name?

VASHTI'S HEAD:
Vashti!

NARRATOR:
The king wishes to announce
That he has completely forgotten
Queen what's her name?

KING:
I can't remember.

NARRATORS:
He's forgotten her,
So have we,
But he hasn't forgotten
That he needs a wife.
The king needs someone
At his side,
A woman, a female,
A wife, a pretty wife,
A beautiful wife.

NARRATOR: One who would take your breath away, take it away. Consequently, we are sponsoring a NATIONAL BEAUTY CONTEST!

NARRATORS:
Every single maiden
In this land
Must take part
In this contest,
How could you refuse,
How could you refuse,
How could you refuse,
You wouldn't dare!

NARRATOR: You don't dare. You don't think of it. After all, the prize is nothing less than an Imperial Crown, gold, jewels, crown-type things—A BEAUTY CONTEST!

(Several audience members and one company member are selected as "contestants" and are brought to the stage.)

(Skin Contest—fast reggae)

All right ladies,
Let's begin
With de skin contest.

Who's got de skin of a baby,
And who's got de hair of a lamb,
And who doesn't have any hair at all
And doesn't give a damn.

(Spoken.) Our fabulous King is looking for a beautiful girl, a virgin with no opinions, no bad habits, no strong needs, just a . . . beautiful body, a fabulous face, a moron in a dress that knows her place (you're a moron, but I don't like your dress) . . . etc. *(Monologue ad lib.)*

All right ladies
That's not all,
Come on forward,
Have a ball.

Who's got de dainty feminine feet,
That won't become bulbous in de heat.

(Beauty Pageant—ad libs welcome—underscored with generic cocktail music)

NARRATOR: *(To the "contestants.")* It's the King, don't get excited.

KING: Quite a crop!

NARRATOR: Time to meet our five semifinalists:

SEMIFINALIST #1, Miss Massapequa Persia. Miss Massapequa is the lovely Rifky Shimetz. For the talent competition, Rifky recited her recipe for blueberry buns while twirling two fire batons . . . let's hear it for Miss Rifky. . . .

CONTESTANT #2, Miss Paramus Mall. Miss Paramus Mall is the beautiful Helen Lumpkin. A past president of the Paramus Players, Helen starred in their all-Yiddish "Natalie Needs a Nightie." Her life goal is a scholarship to the Wilfred Beauty Academy . . . let's hear it for Helen. . . .

CONTESTANT #3, Miss Hebrew National Salami. Miss Salami is the lovely Rachel Shamsky. Miss Shamsky began her pageant career at the age of five when she was crowned "Little Miss Kosher Dill" . . . let's hear it for Miss Shamsky. . . .

CONTESTANT #4, Miss Bayonne. Miss Bayonne is the beautiful "Bubbles" Plotnick. "Bubbles" won our evening wear competition with a daring sequin babushka and an enameled bagel bracelet . . . let's hear it for Miss Bayonne. . . .

HAMAN: *(Grabbing the microphone.)* Give me that! I think it's time for our question-and-answer session, don't you? Come forward, please . . . Number One, what is your opinion of . . . the JEWS? . . .

(#1 Audience member's response, ad lib.)

Number Two, what is your opinion of the JEWS? . . .

(#2 Audience member's response, ad lib.)

(To Company member.) And you . . . what is your opinion of THE JEWS?

#3: They're great!

HAMAN: *(Scream and sneezing fit.)* Aaaaaaaaaaaaaaaaaa-aah!!!!

NARRATOR: Another beauty pageant scandal! I am so sorry. First Vanessa Williams poses nude for *Penthouse,* the Miss Minnesota gets caught shoplifting, and I don't even want to talk about Bess Meyerson. Then they fired Burt Parks, and now . . . this! *(Audience participants are returned to their seats.)*

(Skin Contest Reprise)

COMPANY:
Who's got de skin of a baby,
And who's got de hair of a lamb,
And who doesn't have any hair at all
And doesn't give a damn.
Let's give the King a Queen. *(Repeat three times.)*

NARRATOR: So, King, what did you think of our parade?

KING: *("Ancient curse.")*
Sheh va-ke-te sheh-vaish-ta, sheh va-ke-te, etc.

NARRATOR: Didn't any of these angels please you?

KING: They're all so bland and mediocre.

("Transformation trunk" is brought on stage.)

(A Mediocre Girl—moderate jazz softshoe)

NARRATORS:
A mediocre girl
Is always at her best.

KING:
I know, I know, and yet,

NARRATORS:
It was known that
The most beautiful girl
Of all was hidden.
Where was she hidden?
You will soon find out!

NARRATOR:
Imagine . . . a nice Jewish clapboard home in Soweto, Persia!

(Narration 5)

NARRATOR 1:
Once upon a time
In a land far away
There lived a humble Jew

NARRATOR 2:
And his niece or his wife
Or his lover or friend.

NARRATOR 1:
Who knows?

NARRATOR 2:
Her name was Esther.

NARRATOR 1:
And this humble
And ever so reverent Jew
Was devout and proud
Of his people

NARRATOR 2:
And worried about
The new prime minister
Haman.

HAMAN: *(Donning* "HAMAN" *costume for the first time, except for the hat.)*
Who was said to be anti-Semitic. *(He sneezes.)*

MORDECHAI: *(Assuming his character.)*
In Shushan a Jew walked humbly
And his name was Mordechai.

ESTHER: *(Assuming her character.)*
He raised the orphan Esther
And his name was Mordechai.

(Ah, Beloved Esther, You're Quite Grand—out of tempo)

MORDECHAI:
Ah, beloved Esther,
You're quite grand,
Didn't you know?

ESTHER:
Really?

MORDECHAI:
High society.

ESTHER:
Really?

MORDECHAI:
You're the best,
Didn't you know?

ESTHER:
Really?

COMPANY:
Real class!

ESTHER:
What's this about, anyway?

MORDECHAI:
You could be the beauty queen.

COMPANY:
Miss Persia, Miss Persia, Miss Persia!

ESTHER: I don't want to be Miss Persia. I don't want to be anyone's beauty queen. I just want to be with you.

SOLDIERS: *(At the door.)* Let us in! We hear the most beautiful girl in the kingdom lives here!

(Certainly, Certainly, Please Come In—very fast)

MORDECHAI AND COMPANY:
Certainly, certainly,
Please come in.
Wait just one moment!

*(*MORDECHAI *locks* ESTHER *in the "transformation trunk.")*

ESTHER:
La la la la la la la la la la
La la la la la la la la la.

MORDECHAI:
Now, what was it you wanted?

SOLDIERS:
Let us in!

MORDECHAI:
Certainly, of course,
Please be my guests.
Guests are always welcome
In a humble Jewish home.
Be my guests,
Feel at home.

Do you like my home?

COMPANY:
Good home!

MORDECHAI:
Do you like my floors?

COMPANY:
Good floors!

MORDECHAI:
Good walls.

Oh, sorry, no walls, but the nicest walls you ever saw before they fell in.

ESTHER: *(From inside the trunk.)*
I can't let them do this to you,
I can't let them kill you
Just to protect me!

MORDECHAI:
No you mustn't go with them!

ESTHER:
I can't let you die for me,
I will not let them kill you for me!
Let me out!
(Suddenly breaking into speech.) Wait a second! This is ridiculous! In the story I go to the King!

MORDECHAI: I changed my mind, you can't go!

MORDECHAI AND COMPANY:
Listen my friends,
Why be so sensitive
About an old trunk?
Let me do a puppet show.
How about a soft-shoe
With nobody?

MORDECHAI AND COMPANY:	SOLDIERS:
Listen my friends,	We are going to kill you!
Why be so sensitive	
About an old trunk?	
Let me do a puppet show.	And we are going to kill you!
How about a soft-shoe	
With nobody?	
Listen my friends,	
Why be so sensitive	And we are going to kill you!

About an old trunk,
About an old trunk,
About an old trunk,
About an old trunk!

MORDECHAI: This trunk's really nothing, it's just an old relic.

SOLDIERS: Open the trunk!

(Alternating.)

I will have you imprisoned!
I will have you tortured!
I will have you executed!

MORDECHAI: You can't have the trunk! And you can't have me! I'm a great ancient warrior! and what's more—

(Esther the Invincible—freely—an anthem)

ESTHER: *(Emerging as "Superwoman/spy.")* I am Esther!

Good-bye Mordechai,
Uncle, cousin, lover, patriarch.
I'm off to save the world
Like Noah with his ark.
I'm ripping off my wifely skirts
And the scarves around my head.
I'm marching like a soldier
To the bad King's bed.

(With a broad steady rock tempo.)

I am Esther the invincible,
I am braver than Eve.
I'm a lover like Sheba
With a knife up my sleeve,
But I do it for my people
And God alone,
I would trade in the glory
If I could go home.
I can't go home.

ESTHER AND VOICES:
I'm a pillar like Delilah,

I act sweetly, but
The moment the sun disappears,
I pull out my razor and I cut,
But I do it for my people
And God alone,
I would trade in the glory
If I could go home.
I can't go home.

ESTHER:
Oh, the woman that I am
Shall the win the prize of victory from above.
Maybe I will never be a mother,
I may have given up my love,

COMPANY:
But I do it for my people
And God alone,
I would trade in the glory
If I could go home.
I can't go home.

But I do it for my people
And God alone,
I would trade in the glory
If I could go home.
I can't go home.

(Oh My, This Is a Most Unusual Girl!—out of tempo)

KING:
Oh my!
This is a most unusual girl.
Poetry does not apply to her.

HAMAN:
I must admit she is unusual.

KING:
But she is beautiful, beautiful!
Come here child.
Be not afraid.
Why doest thou tremble?
Walkest closer to thy King.
What is that wetness upon thine eye?

Thou art beautiful,
Thou are ripe as a pomegranate!

*(*ESTHER *approaches* KING, *who says to her:)*

KING: Speak to me, child.

(Don't Tell Him You're a Jew—still out of tempo)

ESTHER:
I— *(Interrupted.)*

MORDECHAI:
Don't tell him you're a Jew!

ESTHER: *(Singing.)*
I—

MORDECHAI:
Whatever he may promise you

ESTHER:
I—

MORDECHAI AND COMPANY:
Don't tell him where you come from,

ESTHER:
I—

COMPANY:
Where you come from.

MORDECHAI:
Or who your relatives are.

ESTHER:
It's difficult to say, exactly . . .

MORDECHAI AND COMPANY:
Please keep your parents' faith
A secret safe from the villains.

HAMAN:
Speak up girl!

MORDECHAI AND COMPANY:
In the inner circle of the palace court,
Don't worship anymore.

ESTHER:
I—

MORDECHAI AND COMPANY:
Deny your past, forget your god,

ESTHER: It's lovely here.

MORDECHAI AND COMPANY:
Take on the gestures of a fraud.

ESTHER: It's really lovely here.

MORDECHAI AND COMPANY:
Don't reveal that you're a Jew,
Whatever the king may promise you,

KING:
It's yours!

MORDECHAI AND COMPANY:
Whatever he says.

KING:
You are the most beautiful creature
In the universe, Esther!

MORDECHAI AND COMPANY:	HAMAN:	ESTHER:	KING:
Lie to him.	You'd better not lie to him!	Lie to him?	
Mesmerize him.	Who are you?		You are so beautiful!
Disguise yourself		Help me!	
And save the truth	You'd better watch your step!	Help me!	
Don't betray us!	Something tells me you're a Jew!	When will someone help me!	You will be my wife.

KING: Sing me a song, sing me a love song. If your melodies are as beautiful as your face, I'll have a good time!

(Song of Songs—à la harp/rock)

ESTHER:
I am the rose of Sharon
And the lilly of the valley,
Of the valley.

My beloved is among you.
I sat down under his shadow
With great delight
And his fruit was sweet to my taste.

Oh, that he would have stayed with me,
Oh, that he would have comforted me
For I am sick of love,
For I am sick of love.

MORDECHAI:
The floor is dry with death,
My house is black with smoke,
There's broken glass and splintered wood,
I cannot mend it.

Our clothes are soiled and torn,
We are sick with hunger,
Esther's gone, the night is long,
And God is nowhere,
Esther's gone, the night is long,
And God is nowhere.
Where are you my beloved?

ESTHER:
I opened up to my beloved,
But my beloved was gone.

MORDECHAI:
The floor is dry with death,
My house is black with
smoke,
There's broken glass and
splintered wood,
I cannot mend it.

ESTHER:
I am the rose of Sharon
And the lily of the valley,
Of the valley.
My beloved is among you.

Our clothes are soiled and
torn,

I sat down under his shadow
With great delight

We are sick with hunger,

Esther's gone,
The night is long,
And God is nowhere,

Esther's gone,
The night is long,

And his fruit was sweet to
my taste.

Oh, that he would have
stayed
With me,

Oh, that he would have
comforted me
For I am sick of love,
For I am sick of love.

And God is nowhere.

KING: *(Lightly, in head voice.)*
Believe me dearest Esther,
This scepter and the homage fear inspires
Hold little charm for me.
The pomp and power
Is oft a burden to its sad possessor.

COMPANY:
What a poor king!

KING:
In thee, thee only do I find a grace.

COMPANY:
He violates her name!

KING:
How sweet the charm of loveliness and virtue.

COMPANY:
How would he know?

KING:
In Esther breathes the very soul of peace

COMPANY:
How would he know?

KING:
And innocence.

COMPANY:
How would he know?

KING:
Shadows flee before her,

She pours bright sunshine
Into days of gloom,
Believe me!

MORDECHAI:
Where are you my beloved?
We own so few precious objects
And they've all been stolen or spoiled.
Daylight brings fear,
Nighttime is freezing,
Purity is spoiled,
The wind song is sour,
I haven't seen a flower or a bird!
Esther's gone, the night is long
And God says not a word!
Esther's over there,

ESTHER:
Ah—

MORDECHAI:
Why should I care?

ESTHER:
Ah—

MORDECHAI:	ESTHER:
God is nowhere,	
God is nowhere,	I am sick of love.
God is nowhere,	
God is nowhere,	I am sick of love.
God—	

(Interrupting himself.) Excuse me! Excuse me, but this has to be a female's view of the story. I do not remember such grief on the part of Mordechai. He wanted Esther to be a beauty queen. He, as it is said, sent Esther to the King's palace so that she could be the first Jewish Mata Hari. He wanted the Jews to be strong, safe and powerful. He had a plan. His only concern was that she do her duty with the faithfulness and skill of a well-trained Jewish woman.

ESTHER: Excuse me! Isn't it like you to take the credit? Did you give me my figure, my voice? Did you design my costume? Is it your body that gets leered at and drooled over by His Majesty, the King of softness, His Highness the heavy thinker, Lord of indecision. Is it you who are in danger of being discovered as a Jew, as a tool for Mordechai, the Great? You're nothing but a pimp!

NARRATOR *(female):* Oh, I can't stand this. All our lives, when we were growing up, didn't we dress in little tutus with tin-foil crowns dreaming of "Queen Esther, Queen Esther"? But this is really a depressing story. This is no simple fairy tale. It's really a story of greed, violence, abuse, and bigotry, I hate this story! Why isn't it edited from the Bible? How could God let it be in His book?

NARRATOR *(male):* God had nothing to do with it, Honey.

NARRATOR *(female):* What do you mean, God had nothing to do with it?

MORDECHAI: It's true—God's name appears nowhere in the text.

NARRATOR *(male):* He refused to have anything to do with the Megilloth.

NARRATOR *(female):* Typical, typical. He creates misery, fear, loneliness, and near death and then blames everyone else for it.

NARRATOR *(male):* Rebbe Eliezar says that perhaps this is not a very important story and God had more urgent business elsewhere.

NARRATOR *(female):* How could anyone think that this is not an important story? Especially He, who creates all stories? Does He judge the plight of His people on a scale of one to ten?

NARRATOR *(male): (To the audience.)* Let's rate the books in the Bible. How many people think that Noah and the animals had it worse than my friend Mordechai and his girl, Esther? How about David? Solomon?

HAMAN: There's always Job. What a stupid, smelly, boil-infested Jew he was. *(Sneezes.)*

NARRATOR *(female):* How in good conscience could God turn his back on us? Stand us up? Not even send us flowers?

NARRATORS: *(Variously.)* Perhaps we should consult the audience. Do we have any Talmudic scholars here tonight?

Any rabbis? Cantors? Bartenders? Anybody have any education in the Torah? Anyone read the Cliff Notes?

ESTHER: Okay, okay! You go ahead and enjoy yourselves. While you talk, I have business. My people are going to be destroyed unless I act in the name of Justice. We've got to do something about Haman here. . . . Are you with me, Mordechai? What's the plan . . . ?

MORDECHAI: There's no plan. We'll just have to wait for something to happen.

(Cymbal crash.)

COMPANY: Looks like something's gonna happen!!

(Narration 6)

NARRATORS:
Sitting all night and all day at the gate,
Mordechai overhears a plot,
By two minor chamberlains,

COMPANY:
Bagathoos and Theodestes!

NARRATORS:
They wanted to kill the King.

COMPANY:
Oh, no!

NARRATORS:
Mordechai knew he must reveal this plan to Esther
For if the King were to die,
She would be in terrible danger
And all her people would perish.

KING: Bagathoos and Theodestes were eunuchs and everywhere you could recognize them because they rode . . . a eunuch cycle!

(Bagathoos Ought to Be King . . .—very fast)

BAGATHOOS AND THEODESTES:
Bagathoos ought to be King,
He should be King.

COMPANY:
He should be King!

BAGATHOOS AND THEODESTES:
Bagathoos ought to wear
The jeweled ring.

COMPANY:
The signet ring!

BAGATHOOS AND THEODESTES:
Bagathoos knows
What's right and wrong,
What's right and wrong,

COMPANY:
What's right and wrong.

BAGATHOOS AND THEODESTES:
Theodestes is
Smart and strong,

COMPANY:
He's very strong,
He's very strong!

BAGATHOOS AND THEODESTES:
Bagathoos will punch his King,
And shoot his king
And everything.
It's gonna be fine to be divine,

COMPANY:
It's gonna be fine to be divine!

BAGATHOOS AND THEODESTES:
It's gonna be fine to be divine,

COMPANY:
It's gonna be fine to be divine!

BAGATHOOS AND THEODESTES:
I'd like to see Ahashuerus
Hanging from a tower,

COMPANY:
Hanging from a tower!

BAGATHOOS AND THEODESTES:
I'd go to visit him every hour,

COMPANY:
Every hour!

BAGATHOOS AND THEODESTES:
I'd like to see him beheaded at his gate,
For his chopped head I'd salivate!

It's gonna be great to assassinate!
It's gonna be fine to be divine,

COMPANY:
It's gonna be fine to be divine!
Tra-la-la-la la-la,
It's gonna be fine to be divine!

(There's a Plot to Kill the King!)

MORDECHAI:
There's a plot to kill the king!
It's the two chamberlains,
Tell your husband to watch out
And tell him who told you,
But don't tell him why.

ESTHER:
Mordechai!

MORDECHAI:
Hurry up, hurry up or don't you care?

*(*MORDECHAI *first, joined by the* COMPANY, *and then the* KING, *sings the following in a round.):*

There's a plot to kill the king!
It's the two chamberlains,
Tell your husband to watch out
And tell him who told you,
But don't tell him why.

MORDECHAI:
Hurry up, hurry up, or don't you care?

ESTHER:
Why are you so official?
We planned this spying together.
Do not demean the one who knows you.

MORDECHAI:
You're looking fine, Queen Esther,
Your cheeks look healthy too.
Your eyes are full of fire.
Do not demean the one who found you

COMPANY:
Remember your people,
Remember their poverty!
Remember your people,
Remember their poverty!
Remember your people,
Remember their poverty!
Remember your people,
Remember their poverty!

(Esther's Prayer—rock ballad)

ESTHER:
You who know everything
Put eloquent speech in my mouth,
Before this lion, to change this man.
I hate this man, he is fighting You.
So there must be an end to him
And those who support him, he is evil.
Save me by Your hand and help me,
I, who stand alone.

I have no one but you,
I have no one but you,
I have no one but you,
I have no one but you.

Your slave has not eaten at his table,
Nor have I honored his feast,
Nor drunk the wine of his libations.
Two faces I have,
The mask of the Queen
And the Jew
Filled with fear.
Your slave has had no joy
From the day I was brought here,

Except in You,
Except in You,
Except in You,
Except in You,

MORDECHAI:	ESTHER:
You're looking fine Queen Esther,	Except in You,
Your cheeks look healthy too.	Except in You,
Your eyes are full of fire.	Except in You,
Do not demean the one who found you	Except in You,

COMPANY:
Remember your people,
Remember their poverty!
Remember your people,
Remember their poverty!

(Repeat ad lib, until interrupted.)

ESTHER: *(Interrupting.)* Hold it, now wait a second! Remember your people, don't forget your poverty. Fool the King, but not too well. If you're so smart, you be me. I'm sick of being Esther. I'd like to be Mordechai. Let me be a whining, pious, self-righteous, jealous prig, and you be Esther.

MORDECHAI: Okay!

ESTHER: Okay!

*(*MORDECHAI *and* ESTHER *change places.)*

(Your Majesty, There Is a Plot—much like a Gilbert and Sullivan patter song—brio)

MORDECHAI *(as Esther)*: *(In falsetto.)*
Your Majesty, there is a plot!

KING:
A what?

MORDECHAI:
A plot!

KING:
A what?

MORDECHAI:
A plot!
Your Majesty there is a plot!

KING:
A what?

MORDECHAI:
A plot!

KING:
A what?

MORDECHAI:
A plot!
Bagathoos and Theodestes, sir,

COMPANY:
Bagathoos and Theodestes, sir,
Bagathoos and Theodestes, sir,

KING:
Who?

MORDECHAI:
Huh!
Your chamberlains!

KING:
My chamberlains?

COMPANY:
Your chamberlains!

KING:
My chamberlains?

MORDECHAI:
Huh!
They want to take your kingdom from you.

KING:
But my goodness, why?

MORDECHAI:
Pure and simple evil, sire.
Cold ambition.

KING:
Cold amibition?

MORDECHAI:
Yes, dear sir, that must be why.

(Out of tempo.)

KING:
Who told you this?

COMPANY:
Huh!

MORDECHAI:
Mordechai!

KING:
Mordechai?
We must reward him.
Scribe!

SCRIBE:
Aahhh!

(Be-bop à la Elvis.)

KING:
Write his name in our diary now,
And take those eunuchs to the dungeon,
As fast as thy feet will allow.

SCRIBE: *(Surprised.)*
Yes, sir.

(Breaking out of tempo—a ridiculous fanfare.)

KING:
A decree has been issued.

SCRIBE:
A decree has been issued.

COMPANY:
A decree has been issued.

KING:
Executioners on the alert!

SCRIBE:
Executioners on the alert!

COMPANY:
Executioners on the alert!

KING:
Necks be noosed!

SCRIBE:
Necks be noosed!

COMPANY:
Necks be noosed!
Necks be noosed!

KING: *("Curse" as before.)*
Sheh va-ke-te sheh-vaish-ta, sheh va-ke-te, etc.

NARRATOR: And so, the eunuchs were executed.

KING:
Tell me once more the name of the man who saved me.

COMPANY:
Mordechai!

KING:
Thank you my darling,
Thank you so much.
Thank you dear Esther
You're good to touch

(Reaching for "ESTHER."*)*

MORDECHAI:
Aaaaaah!

ESTHER: Had enough?

(They switch again.)

KING:
Tell me once more the name of the man who saved me.

COMPANY:
Mordechai!

HAMAN: *(Donning three-cornered hat for the first time.)* Did I hear my name? I thought I heard my name!

(This Is the Moment I've Waited For—freely)

Jews cling like fleas,
Cower like women,
Smell like the dogs of the street.
They *speechh* in a tongue
That sounds like spit.
No matter how hard I try,
I can't understand it.
Jews!
(Spoken.) Once I'm in a powerful position, I'll address the Jewish problem and take care of it.

(Slow, broad rock tempo.)

This is the moment I've waited for,
An opening in the cabinet,
A chair that's close to the King's ear.
From there I will whisper certain facts,
To aggravate his stress and fear,
He'll grow to need me.

He'll grow to depend upon me
For each decision of his life,
I'll be his number one advisor
I'll overthrow that vicious wife.
This is my moment of stardom,
I hear the minstrels blow the call.
I'll be so crucial to his cabinet,
He won't need anyone at all,
Because he'll need me.

(Fast, driving, rock—double-time feel.)

I'll sanction immediate executions
Of Jews and Jews and more Jews!
The blood of the Jews will fill the rivers
And fill up the streets of the poor!
The King will find me a mirror,
I'll be his closest brother,

In his regal, lonely life.
I'll take his power bit by bit,
And overthrow that arrogant wife,
That Jewess!

(As before.)

This is the moment I've waited for,
An opening in the cabinet,
A chair that's close to the King's ear.
From there I will whisper certain facts,
To aggravate his stress and fear,
He'll grow to need me,
He'll grow to need me,
He'll grow to need me.

KING: Haman, could you come here please? A position has opened up and you are the man for the job. How would you like to be the new Prime Minister?

(Narration 7)

NARRATOR 1:
Haman the anti-Semite got his job
And what did Haman do?

NARRATOR 2:
He bought fancy clothes
And developed a walk
Of exaggerated grace.

NARRATOR 1:
He glutted himself on foods and wine,
Wore perfumes and glitter
And blinked all the time.
He tortured the Jews
With warnings and games and insults.

NARRATOR 2:
He condemned the Jews to death,
Told lies to the King,
Caused the King to hate
A poor and virtuous people
He'd never met.

2 NARRATORS:
Haman trailed Esther to catch her in a crime,
But luckily Esther caught him spying every time.
Haman threatened the Jews with a decree,
That they would die by a date decided by a lottery,
A lottery, a lottery,
And they'd be murdered instantly,
Instantly, instantly.

(Lottery)

HAMAN: *(To the audience.)* Hi, wanna help? I'm not a fascist, you know. I believe in democracy, so I'm not going to choose an execution date on my own, I'm gonna let you help me. Look, here I have a bag with some dates. My first date: February 14th, just so they can die with some loved ones! *(Boos.)* My next date is . . . Thanksgiving Day, just so they can have a nice roast before they go. *(Boos.)* . . . And my last date: Martin Luther King's birthday, just so you Jews don't have to feel alone. *(Boos.)* Now you pick and the day you pick, they'll die. Purim, after all, means "lottery" . . . *(Audience makes three selections. "Now" comes up each time.)* . . . I'm sorry, it says "now!" *(Three times.)*

NARRATOR: *(Blowing police whistle.)* Time out, Jews! You, I have a job for you. Do you think that political action means donating fifty dollars to charity? Or starring in a video singing a rock-and-roll song about peace? Do you think you can save your children, the environment, our planet, our souls from destruction by merely having good intentions? No! No! No! You must act. You must make sacrifice. Purim is the night which teaches us that we can change our destiny with courage, selflessness, and action. So if you believe that anti-Semitism is a bad thing . . . that this man Haman is a terrible destructive force, you can do something about it. And for a discount. True self-sacrifice at really low prices . . . We're passing out these gruggers to many of you in the audience and you're welcome to trade your ties, shoes, cars, stereos, trust funds, as a small contribution in exchange. Tips, though not mandatory, are a kind of obligation of heritage. *(Actors distribute gruggers to audience, but accept no money or gifts.)* Now, let's stop Haman! And we can do it with sound. On the night of miracles you can drown a murderer with noise. Shake those shakers when you hear Haman's name. Let's shake those shakers!

(Haman Rap)

Let us tolerate
A degree of undecorous
Conduct this evening
Which will be expressed
By the beating of Haman!

COMPANY:
Haman!

NARRATOR:
Every time we mention his
name, Haman,

COMPANY:
Haman!

NARRATOR:
Every time we read, Haman's

COMPANY:
Haman

NARRATOR:
Name we will beat him,
Haman!

COMPANY:
Haman

NARRATOR:
Every time we speak
Haman's

COMPANY:
Haman

NARRATOR:
Name we will beat him,
Haman!

COMPANY:
Haman!

NARRATOR:
Every time we sing Haman's

COMPANY:
Haman!

NARRATOR:
Name we will beat him,
Haman!

COMPANY:
Haman!

ALL:
Haman!
Beat him
Haman!
Haman!
Draw his face
And obliterate it
Haman!
Soles of the shoes

Stamp Haman out!
Haman!
Haman!
Clap our hands
At the mention of
Haman!
Hold up your hammers,
Bash out Haman!
Rip up a paper
With Haman's name!
Use a rattler,
Use a grugger,
Drown out Haman's name!
Huh! Huh!
Use a rattler,
Use a grugger,
Drown out Haman's name!
Huh! Huh!

FRENCH WAITER: *(Testing audience response to the word "Haman.")* Good evening, tonight we feature our special: an Asparagus Hollandaise Haman; a tip of Sole Flambé Haman with a tart, but peppy Haman Mousse. We have Haman-flavored pickled fishtail and a marinated Haman's oily artichoke salad au reservoir. For our entrées we feature Choke 'o Haman Beef à Spit, a frizzled filet with green Haman tussel, a fine lightly fried Haman poulet-pasta piggy, flecked with Haman frits and fits and a tuchas Pasta Ricco in mozzarella broiled, then baked Greco-Haman style. For dessert we will push our pastry cart featuring our prune raisin apple boysenberry bramble bush thorn snapper willow in an apple willow hummentaschen Haman, chocolate Haman gooseballs and a light orange-flecked cake with a frothy hazelnut frosting.

NARRATOR: That was really good. Now for the advanced round:

FARMER: I was working on the farm and I was pitching hay, man, and my boss comes up and says, "Hey, Ethel," and I say, "Hey, man, how's it going." He says, "Hey, I can' complain, 'cept Manny, he ain't doin' his job." I say, "Hey, Manny," you know Manny, hey, Manny, he's a careful sorta guy. Well, hell, my boss says, "I'd like to kick the hay outa Manny, you know." "Cool out," I said, "and help me pitch this here hay, man." "Aw, hey, man" says my boss, "I'm your boss." "Hell," I says, "you may be my boss, but you gotta help me pitch this hay, man."

NARRATOR: Thanks, that was great!

FARMER: Anytime, hey man!

(Half time.)

NARRATOR: Half time, but you can't go to the bathroom because we are giving out hamentaschen* and we have to collect your gruggers.

*(*COMPANY *leads audience in the singing of "Merry, Merry Be," interspersed with the routines "Kill Gumby" and "Knock the Head off Haman.")*

COMPANY:
Oh, once there was a wicked, wicked man
And Haman was his name sir.
He would have murdered all the Jews,
Though they were not to blame, sir.

Oh, today we'll merry, merry be,
Oh, today we'll merry, merry be,
Oh, today we'll merry, merry be,
And nasch some hamentaschen.

And Esther was the lovely Queen
Of King Ahashuerus.
When Haman said he'd kill us all,
Oh my, how he did scare us.

Oh, today we'll merry, merry be,
Oh, today we'll merry, merry be,
Oh, today we'll merry, merry be,
And nasch some hamentaschen.

But Mordechai her cousin bold said:
"What a dreadful chutzpah!"

******hamentaschen:* **Three-cornered Purim pastries, shaped to suggest Haman's hat, traditionally filled with prune or poppy seeds.**

If guns were but invented now
This Haman would I shoot, sir.

Oh, today we'll merry, merry be,
Oh, today we'll merry, merry be,
Oh, today we'll merry, merry be,
And nasch some hamentaschen.

("Kill Gumby": Lights dim. Actor produces clay "Gumby" statue which wears a "Haman"-style hat, sits it in centrally placed chair, and departs. Other actors illuminate statue with flashlights. Actor returns to smash "Gumby" with bowling ball. HAMAN *screams.)*

COMPANY:
The guest of honor he shall be,
This clever Mister Smarty,
And high above us he shall swing
At a little hanging party.

Oh, today we'll merry, merry be,
Oh, today we'll merry, merry be,
Oh, today we'll merry, merry be,
And nasch some hamentaschen.

("Knock the Head off Haman": HAMAN *is placed under a shroud so that only his head and what appears to be his hands are visible to the audience. The* COMPANY *distributes "Nerf Balls" to the audience, who attempt to pelt* HAMAN*'s exposed head.* COMPANY *then places jack-o'-lantern mask over* HAMAN*'s head in order to increase the size of the "target," and brings* HAMAN *downstage. The mask is removed and* ESTHER*'s head appears in the place of* HAMAN*'s.)*

Of all his cruel and unkind ways,
This little joke did cure him,
But don't forget we owe him thanks
For this jolly feast of Purim.

Oh, today we'll merry, merry be,
Oh, today we'll merry, merry be,
Oh, today we'll merry, merry be,
And nasch some hamentaschen.

ACT II

NARRATOR:
Act Two!

(Kee e-che-cha . . .—heavy and plodding)

COMPANY: *(Jews in prayer shawls demonstrating at King's "gate.")*
Kee e-che-cha
U-chal ver-ah-ee-tee
Bar-ah-ah a sher
Yim-tza et a-mee.

Kee e-che-cha
U-chal ver-ah-ee-tee
Bar-ah-ah.

MORDECHAI: *(In half time.)*
Kee e-che-cha

U-chal ver-ah-ee-tee

Bar-ah-ah.

(Narration 8)

NARRATORS:
Once upon a time,
In a land far away
There lived a King
And his Queen
And, as always happens,
There was also
A minority of men
And women who were
Terribly poor and persecuted.

And their humble leader,
Mordechai,

Put on his sackcloth,
Rubbed himself in ashes
And declared the fate
Of his people aloud in protest.

COMPANY:
Kee e-che-cha
U-chal ver-ah-ee-tee
Bar-ah-ah a-sher
Yim-tza et a-mee.

Kee e-che-cha
U-chal ver-ah-ee-tee
Bar-ah-ah.

MORDECHAI: *(In half time.)*

Kee e-che-cha

U-chal ver-ah-ee-tee

Bar-ah-ah.

(One Step Forward, One Step Backward—march with urgency)

ESTHER:
There is violence outside,
Your Majesty,
Our country's poor
Are pounding at your gate!

KING:
Yes-well-I-uh-
You-uh-yes-I-
Uh-we absolutely should,
No question.

HAMAN:
Don't waste your precious time
If the poor of this country are vermin!

ESTHER:
The feeling in the atmosphere,
Your Highness,
Is dark and quite foreboding.
Don't you think you ought to put
A stop to the violence at your gate?

KING:
Yes-well-I-uh-
I mean, you know
The Jews are gonna be
Killed anyway, right,

I mean, what's the point?
Haman says the Jews
Are gonna be killed anyway,
Right, I mean,
What do you think?

HAMAN:
Aaaaaaah!

KING:
Never mind what you think.
I'm sorry, no,
I only want to say
"What do you think?"

HAMAN:
Good thinking!

KING:
Ah—why not?
Of course, you're right.

ESTHER:	KING:	
My husband	Yes,	
Ahashuerus takes one	No,	
Step forward,	Maybe, I don't know.	
Then he turns around	Uh yes, uh no,	
And takes one step	Maybe,	
Backward.	I don't know.	
He can't decide which	Oh well,	
Way to go,	I'll see	
But he'll murder every	Maybe,	
Jew,	Me?	
'Cause that's what a	Uh yes,	
Good king	Uh no,	
Is supposed to do.	Maybe, I don't know.	
		HAMAN:
I can't understand	Oh well,	That's good

His patterns,	We'll see	Thinking,
He's unpredictable	Maybe,	Sir.
And dumb,	Me?	
And I have to mind	Uh yes,	What
Every word I say	Uh no,	A mind
Or else I could be hung.	Maybe,	You
My husband	I don't know.	Have.
Ahashuerus	Oh well,	Oh, I just love
Takes one step forward,	We'll see,	To hear
Then he turns	Maybe, me?	You talk,
Around and takes	Uh yes,	There's
One step	Uh no,	So much
Backward.	Maybe, I don't know.	I could learn.

HAMAN:
That's good thinking, sir.

KING:
What's good thinking, Haman?

HAMAN:
What you said before, Your Highness.

KING:
What did I say?

HAMAN:
Kill the Jews!

ESTHER:
No, don't kill the Jews!

HAMAN:
Come on, kill the Jews!

ESTHER:
Oh, no!

KING:
Go ahead, Haman,
Do as you please,
Get the Jews out of here.

ESTHER:
Oh, no!

KING:
Wait, Esther please!

HAMAN: Now I shall truly fulfill my destiny! I shall rise to power and humble the Jews! . . . There is nothing better than total humiliation!

(If My Pants Fall Down—chanted out of tempo, almost at a whisper)

FIRST JEW *(Mordechai):*
If my pants fall down,
If my pants fall down,
You can see everything,
You can see everything.
I don't care,
I've got clean underwear.

If my feet get tied,
If my feet get tied,
You go and run ahead,
You go and run ahead.
I'll hop,
I really don't mind.

SECOND JEW *(Narrator):*
If my arms get cut off,
If my arms get cut off,
You can have all the bread,
You can have all the bread,
I'll catch rain
With my head tilted back.

THIRD JEW *(Esther):*
If I fall from a tree,
If I fall from a tree,
I'll grab some rope or some twine,
Everything will be fine.
My neck may get a little sore,
What are necks for.

(Gently flowing.)

If my back gets broke,
If my back gets broke,

Just shift the weight of the rope,
Where there still are some bones
That are still in one piece.
It might not be fun,
But I'll get the job done.
By the way,
If my nose starts to run,
I agree there's no reason to wipe it.

FOURTH JEW *(King):*
If I trip on your boot,
If I fall on your sword,
Please don't stand on ceremony,
Don't bother helping me
Regain my dignity.
What's dignity?
My face is in the dirt,
But how much can dirt hurt
When you are half dead
Or probably full dead?
It isn't a matter of profile
Or high style,
It's fine to stay put for a while,
It's fine to stay put for a while.

(Moving forward.)

FIRST JEW *(Mordechai):*
If my pants fall down,
If my pants fall down,
You can see everything.
I don't care, it's all been seen
And I'll tell you
That even my bottom is clean,
At least my ass is clean,
At least my ass is clean!

(I Will Not Bow Down—heavy, chopped march)

HAMAN:
The King has commanded
That all people should bow down
And show me reverence,

Now Mordechai,
I've sewn a little idol here
On my costume,
Just because I know
You Jews like false idols.

I just want it clear
That each time you bow down to me,
You'll be worshipping
A couple of other gods too.
I knew that would please you,
I knew that would please you,
I knew that would please you!

(Bright reggae—using "Island" voices.)

MORDECHAI:
I will not bow down!
I will hold on!
Mordechaï is strong.
If I wait, Jah will come,
And Haman will be gone!

HAMAN:
Bow down,
Lie
Down,
Down,
Down
Sit,
Bow,
Lie,
Get
Down,
Get
Down,
Down!

NARRATOR *(Esther):*
He will not,
Bow down, no!
Don't bow down!
Don't bow down!
He will not
Bow down, no!
Don't bow down!
Don't bow down!
He will not
Bow down, no!
Don't bow down!
Don't bow down!
He will not,

COMPANY:
He will not bow down!

MORDECHAI:
I will not bow down!

COMPANY 1 & MORDECHAI:

He will not bow down!

COMPANY 2:

He will hold on!

Mordechai is strong.

If he waits, Jah will come

He will not bow down!

He will hold on!

He is strong.

ALL:
And Haman will be gone!

COMPANY 1 AND MORDECHAI:

He will not bow down!

He will hold on!

Mordechai is strong.

If he waits, Jah will come,

COMPANY 2:

He will not bow down!

He will hold on!

He is strong.

ALL:
And Haman will be gone!

HAMAN: We'll see who's ridiculous!

ALL:
If he waits, Jah will come,
And Haman will be gone!

HAMAN: You just made a fool of me!

ALL:
If he waits, Jah will come,
And Haman will be gone!

HAMAN: I hate you Jews!

ALL:
If he waits, Jah will come,
And Haman will be gone!

HAMAN: You just made a fool of me. I hate you Jews! *(Etc., ad libs. until cymbal crash interrupts.)* Let me explain myself: I'm not a bad man. Anti-Semitism is not an intellectual choice. It is the heroic duty of the superior man to rid the Earth of vermin in a natural, necessary evolutionary act. *(He snaps his fingers.)*

(Why Do I Hate This People . . .—dark ballad with a relentless beat)

Why do I hate this people?
Because they're all around,
Everywhere,
They litter the town,
Crowd the square,
They get in my way,
Spoil my day,
They plague me
Like uncollected garbage,
They don't go away.

I stroll to my left,
Turn to my right,
Some scrawny old Jew
Is always in my sight.
Their accents make my skin crawl,
I'm not fond of their children at all,
They scurry like rodents,
Buzz like flies,
And oh how they wail
When one of the die-yi-yi-s. *(À la "Jewish wail.")*

They're full of virtue
And generous deeds,
Their humanity
Suffocates me like weeds.
They're pushy and phony
And ugly with pride,
They'd drive any sensitive man
To Genocide!

(Spoken.) And I am fragile!

Why do I despise this people?
Because they stay with me,
Like a disease,
They refuse to crawl
On their knees,
They itch at me
Like some bees,

They plague me
Like Pharaoh's boils and locusts,
And they make me sneeze!

They're full of endurance,
Rock is their will.
Such insolence would drive
A good man to kill
And I am good,
And I'll be King,
And they'll be killed.

Why do I despise this people?
Because they grow at my feet,
Like thorny weeds,
They tickle and itch
And bite and sting.
They are so brave,
What a stupid thing!
No matter how I beat them,
They sing and sing,
And I will beat them,
And they will sing

Until I kill them!

(I Will Deliver—broad rock tempo)

NARRATOR 1 *(Mordechai):*
Children, children
Play and sing,
Do not think
What tomorrow will bring.

NARRATOR 2 *(Esther):*
Kinder, kinder,
Spielt und singt,
Fragt nischt vus
Der morgen bringt.

COMPANY:
Be not afraid of sudden terror
Nor of destruction,
For I am with thee.

Take counsel together,
Stand up to the word
And it shall be brought to naught.
Even in old age I am the same,
Even to gray hairs.

I will hear you,
I will carry
I will deliver,
I will hear you,
I will carry
I will deliver.

Be not afraid of terror
Nor of stupid violence,
For I am with thee
And thou art
With each other too.
Build strength together
And stand up to the evil word,
And it shall be brought down,
I promise you justice.
Even in old age,
Even as thy golden hairs turn gray.

I will hear you,
I will carry,
I will deliver,
I will hear you,
I will carry,
I will deliver,
I will hear you,
I will carry,
I will deliver.

(Al T'da-mi V'naf Shaych—chant intoned very softly under MORDECHAI*'s speech)*

NARRATOR:

Al t'da-mi
V'naf shaych,
L'hi-ma-lay-et,
Bet ha-me-lech,

MORDECHAI:
Perhaps you imagine that you, at any rate, are safe, and say to yourself that you need not pray. Know that if even

Mi-kol
Ha-ye-hu-dim.
Ki-im
Ha-cha-resh
Ta-cha-ri-shi
Ba-ayt ha-zot
Re-vach
V'ha-tza-la
Y'a-mod
La-ye-hu-dim
Mi-ma kom
A-sher
V'at u-vet a vi-cha
To-ve-do u-mi,
U-mi yo-dey-a
I'm l'ayt ka-zot
Hi-ga-at
La-mal-chut.

the foot of one Jew is injured, do not think that all the Jews shall escape. Do not fancy that you, of all Jews, shall be saved in the house of the King. Think not with thyself that thou shalt escape in the King's house more than all the Jews, for if thou hold thy peace at this time, then will relief and deliverance arise to the Jews from another place, but thou and thy father's house shall perish and who knows whether thou art come to royal estate for such a time as this.

MORDECHAI:
Speak up now!

COMPANY: *(In an urgent whisper.)*
Deliverance will come to the Jews from another place, but thou and thy father's house shall perish and you will have stayed in the royal estate for nothing!

ESTHER: *(Interrupting.)* Now wait a second, you pompous ass! Whose story is this? Are we not of the same blood? Have my eyes not seen the same suffering as yours? Who the hell do you think you are telling me how to behave as a serious, dedicated Jew? Listen, Mr. Talmudic Visionary, while you've been praying and moaning, I have been doing the footwork, you got that!? You know what a real miracle is, Mr. MordeCHAI!? It's good timing . . . knowing the exact moment . . . a miraculous tiny little second of historical good timing, during which Esther BABE here MAKES THE MOVE!

(For How Can I Endure—fast driving rock tempo, Tina Turneresque)

For how can I endure
The evil that shall come
Unto my people?

COMPANY:
Kee e-che-cha
U-chal ver-a-ee-tee.

ESTHER:
How can I endure destruction?

COMPANY:
Ver-a-ee-tee.

ESTHER:
How can I stand back
And watch my kindred suffer?

COMPANY:
No you can't!

ESTHER:
What do you think I am?
I'm nothing but your shield
And your soldier,

COMPANY:
Kee-e-che-cha
U-chal ver-a-ee-tee.

ESTHER:
Fighting to the death
For freedom!

COMPANY:
A-sher yim-sa,
A-sher yim-sa.

ESTHER:
What would I be
If I could tolerate
This poverty and terror?

COMPANY:
Kee e-che-cha
U-chal ver-a-ee-tee.

ESTHER:
Do you think that I am blind
To suffering?

COMPANY:
No!

ESTHER:
What grace could I enjoy
Watching the destruction
Of our children?

COMPANY:
Ah—

ESTHER:
What would you have me be?
I'm nothing but your shield
And your soldier,

COMPANY:
Kee e-che-cha
U-chal ver-a-ee-tee.

ESTHER:
Fighting to the death
For our people,

COMPANY:
Kee e-che-cha
U-chal ver-a-ee-tee.

ESTHER:
Fighting to the death
For our people,

COMPANY:
Kee e-che-cha
U-chal ver-a-ee-tee.

ESTHER:
Fighting to the death
For our people!

(Narration 9)

NARRATOR 1:
Now the King had made
A law that none of his
People should approach him
Whenever he sat on the throne
Unless he was summoned.

NARRATOR 2:
And round his throne stood men
With axes to punish anyone
Who approached the throne
Without being summoned.

COMPANY:
Huh! Huh! Huh!

KING:
The King himself,
However, as he sat
Held a golden scepter
Which he extended
To anyone
Whom he wished to save
Of those who approached him
Without being summoned,

NARRATOR 1:
And whoever touched it
Was out of danger.

COMPANY:
Huh! Huh! Huh!

KING:
Death to you
And death to you,
Hello, how are you?
Death to you.
Nice to see you,
Death to you,
How is the family?
Death to you!

NARRATOR: When the King saw Esther standing in his court, she miraculously obtained favor in his sight. *(*KING*'s scepter "miraculously" floats over to* ESTHER.*)*

KING:
What will thou, Queen Esther?
For whatever thy request,
Even to half the kingdom,
It shall be given thee.

ESTHER:
If I have found

Favor in thy sight,
And if it pleases the King,

(Spoken.) I'd like you and Haman to come to dinner.

KING:
A feast!

ESTHER:
A feast!

HAMAN:
A feast!

COMPANY:
A feast!

(King's Nightmare—out of tempo)

NARRATOR: That night the King, for the first time in his lazy, doleful life, found himself deprived of sleep and besieged by terrifying nightmares!

KING:
Aaah! I can't sleep!

ESTHER AND "VOICES": *(Mysteriously—as if there are many echoes.)*
You can't sleep!

KING:
What shall I do?

ESTHER AND "VOICES":
Why not call your scribe?

KING:
Scribe!

SCRIBE:
Waaaaaah!

ESTHER: Here is the story of a brave hero who saved a king long ago. Here is another brave man who was rewarded with the loyalty of the King. What have you done lately?

ESTHER AND "VOICES":
Remember Bagathoos and Theodestes?
They plotted against you!
Remember there was a man

Who informed against them
And saved you!

KING:
What are you saying?

SINGLE "VOICE":
Remember Bagathoos and Theodestes,
They plotted against you.
Remember there was a man
Who informed against them
And saved you!

KING:
What was that man's name?

ESTHER: *(Blues wail.)*
Mordechai!

KING: I never meant to be ungrateful. A busy man can just forget. What do you suggest I do, my darling Esther, the man's a Jew?

ESTHER:
Ask Haman!

(What Honor Should Be Done—a happy, absurd waltzing duet)

KING:
What honor should be done
To a person who the King
Wishes to honor?

HAMAN:
Great honor, sire,
Grand honor, sire,
Should be done
To the person who the King
Wishes to honor
(That's me!)

KING:
What specific honor
Shall the King honor
Upon the honoree?

HAMAN:
(Aside.) That's me!
(To King.) He ought to be bought
The finest of threads.

KING:
I have two golden robes
Draped over my bed.

HAMAN:
He ought to have a horse,
A slave with a horn,
Who washes and clothes him
And wakes him at morn.

KING:
That's easy enough,
Those honors shall be done
To the person whom I honor.

HAMAN:
(Aside.) And I am the one!
(Spoken aside.) Who would the king wish to honor more than me?

KING: Go and dress that Jew, Mordechai, and show him the honor you described so lovingly!

HAMAN:
Aaaaaaah!

NARRATOR 1: When Haman heard these words, he was greatly troubled. His countenance was changed ...

NARRATOR 2: ... his sight grew dim ...

NARRATOR 1: ... his mouth became distorted ...

NARRATOR 2: ... his thoughts confused ...

NARRATOR 1: ... his loins, languid ...

NARRATOR 2: ... and his knees knocked one against the other.

NARRATOR 1: He addressed the King.

HAMAN:
There are many Mordechais in the world.

KING:
I mean the Mordechai at my gate.

HAMAN:
There are many gates in the world.

KING:
I mean the gate where Mordechai sits.

HAMAN:
How am I to find this Mordechai's gate?

KING:
Haman, mind me before it's too late!

HAMAN: Of course, of course, I was just trying to be efficient.

(Singing.)

The clothes,
The horse,
The slave,
The bath,
Oh!

(This Is Really Unexpected—Russian two-step)

MORDECHAI:
Yes, over there,
Could you scrub me further down?
Strange how fleas
Love this part of town.

COMPANY:
Hey!

MORDECHAI:
Nice of you to
Clean my nails,
They get dirty from
Hauling all those pails.

COMPANY:
Hey!

MORDECHAI:
This is really unexpected,

I am out of breath.
Does this mean that I'm a Prince,
Or will you still put me to death,

COMPANY:
Will you still put him to death?
Gorbachov!

MORDECHAI:
Now that's a horse,
And those are boots,
Young man,
You have a knack.

COMPANY:
Vroshny!

MORDECHAI:
I beg your pardon,
I'm quite feeble.
Could I sit here
On your back?

COMPANY:
Borscht!

ALL:
This is really unexpected,
He is out of breath.
Does this mean that he's a Prince,
Or will you still put him to death,
Will you still put him to,

This is really unexpected,
He is out of breath.
Does this mean that he's a Prince,
Or will you still put him to death,
Will you still put him to,
Will you still put him to death?

(Mordechai's Parade)

KING: Haman, you said the honored man should be led around town. Where's Mordechai's parade?

NARRATOR 1: So Haman stooped down and Mordechai mounted by standing on his back, and he led him through the street where Haman lived. His daughter, who was standing on the roof, saw him . . .

NARRATOR 2: *(As* HAMAN*'s daughter.)* Who's that Jew? *(She sneezes.)*

NARRATOR 1: She thought the man on the horse was her father and the other man was Mordechai. She took a pot and emptied it on the head of her father . . .

NARRATOR 2: *(Laughs.)*

NARRATOR 1: He looked up at her. . .

HAMAN: Daughter?

NARRATOR 1: . . . and when she saw that it was her father . . .

NARRATOR 2: Dad!

NARRATOR 1: . . . she threw herself from the roof to the ground and killed herself.

*("*HAMAN*'s daughter" walks down the stairs screaming and throws herself on* HAMAN, *stunning him.)*

KING: I really liked that, can I try it?

NARRATOR: Sure.

NARRATOR 1: So Haman stooped down and Mordechai mounted by standing on his back, and he led him through the street where Haman lived. His daughter, who was standing on the roof, saw him . . .

KING: *(As* HAMAN*'s daughter.)* Who's that Jew? *(She sneezes.)*

NARRATOR 1: She thought the man on the horse was her father and the other man was Mordechai. She took a pot and emptied it on the head of her father . . .

KING: *(Laughs.)*

NARRATOR 1: He looked up at her . . .

HAMAN: Daughter?

NARRATOR 1: . . . and when she saw that it was her father . . .

KING: Dad!

NARRATOR 1: . . . she threw herself from the roof to the ground and killed herself.

(KING walks down the stairs screaming and throws himself on HAMAN, stunning him.)

(Haman's Putsch)

HAMAN: I think, sire, the Jews are causing grievous trouble in the land. They're spending all the money, spreading ill will against thee, and causing a general discontent towards thy kingdom!

KING: What would you do?

HAMAN: I will lay hand on their children first of all. Prepare them to die . . . all of them!

ESTHER: Lo Te'tzach et ami! You haven't seen anything yet!

(Who Eats Who—bright, lively tango)

Let's have a party
And you will be my guest.
I will serve you all your
Favorite foods
And Grant your strange requests.

COMPANY:
It's an old cliché,
You must fill up your man,
Slave over stoves
To cook what you can.

Why should I argue?
If it works, I'll be a winner.
Don't place bets
On who eats who for dinner.

(Brisk reggae.)

ESTHER:
Would you please come to my feast,
I've been simmering all week.
If you're curious about it,
Feel free to take a peek.

COMPANY:
It's an old cliché,
You must fill up your man,
Slave over stoves
To cook what you can.

Why should I argue?
If it works, I'll be a winner.
Don't place bets
On who eats who for dinner.

(Very fast samba.)

One!
Two!
One! Two! Three! Four!

ESTHER:
Let's have a party,
Wear your silks and crowns.
I will paint my face
And squeeze into a nightgown,
I'll keep the candle low,
I'll have the jester play the oud.
We'll keep the conversation
In a light and tickle-ish mood.

COMPANY:
It's an old cliché,
You must fill up your man,
Slave over stoves
To cook what you can.

Why should I argue?
If it works, I'll be a winner.
Don't place bets
On who eats who for dinner.

Don't place bets
On who eats who for dinner.

(Second Day of the Feast—exaggerated operatic recitative)

KING:
Haman and I love to
Drink with you, dear Esther.

NARRATORS:
This was the second
Day of the feast.

HAMAN:
I Must admit,
You stamp a fine vine,
Dear Esther.

KING:
Let me give you a little gift at least.
What is your request,
Queen Esther,

HAMAN:
That's extreme, sire.

KING:
And what is your desire?

HAMAN:
You've drunk too much!

KING:
Up to one half
Of my kingdom is yours,

HAMAN:
What!?

KING:
My heart is so on fire!
Oh, Esther!

HAMAN:
Oh, sire!

COMPANY:
And Esther answered.

(If I Have Found Favor in Thy Sight—solemn march with mounting urgency)

ESTHER:
If I have found

Favor in thy sight,
And if it pleaseth the King,
Let him give me my life,

KING:
Oh, Esther!

ESTHER:
And my people's lives.
For we have been sold,
I and my people,
To be killed and destroyed,
How can I hold my peace?

KING:
Oh, Esther,
Who's doing this,
Who is this man,
Who dares to hurt you?

HAMAN:
King, I'd like an audience,
Please may I have an audience?
King, I'd like to speak with you,
King, I'd like a word with you.
King, there's lots of rumors going around,
Your Majesty!

KING:
Who would hurt my Esther in this way?

ESTHER:	COMPANY:
Someone's trying to hurt us,	Hurt us!
ESTHER:	COMPANY:
Someone's trying to kill us!	Kill us!

MORDECHAI AND COMPANY:
The evil man, Haman,
Your guardian, Haman.
He wants to kill children,
He wants to kill children.
He wants to kill the Jews,
He wants to kill the Jews,
Your Majesty!

KING:
Who would hurt my Esther in this way?

ESTHER:
Someone's trying to hurt us,

COMPANY:
Hurt Us!

ESTHER:
Someone's trying to kill us!

COMPANY:
Kill us!

KING:
Haman!

COMPANY:
Haman!

KING:
Haman!

COMPANY:
Haman!

KING:
Haman!

COMPANY:
Haman!

KING:
Haman, how could you do this?

(HAMAN *shrugs.)*

KING:
I have to take a walk!

NARRATOR 1: Haman grew terrified before them, and the King, in his rage, went for a walk in the garden.

NARRATOR 2: Strong trees were felled in order to quell his anger . . . but to no avail.

HAMAN: Haman stood before the Queen to beg for his life, for he saw that he was about to feel the full measure of the King's wrath.

KING:
The King had too much wine to drink
And went for a walk in the garden.

COMPANY:
A walk in the garden.

HAMAN:
Haman is left alone with Esther.

COMPANY:
With Esther.

ESTHER:
He stumbles and falls on her.

COMPANY:
Stumbles and falls on her.

KING:
It was his misfortune
That Ahashuerus returned
Precisely at that moment.

COMPANY:
At that moment.

HAMAN:
Esther, cool, tells the king:

ESTHER: See, he wanted to seduce me behind your back.

KING: Aha! Execute him!

(Haman Rap reprise)

COMPANY:
Haman!
Beat him
Haman!
Haman!
Draw his face
And obliterate it,
Haman!
Soles of the shoes
Stamp Haman out!
Haman!
Haman!
Clap our hands
At the mention of
Haman!
Hold up your hammers,
Bash out Haman!
Rip up a paper
With Haman's name!
Haman!
Haman!

HAMAN: *(Out of character.)* But, wait a second! The accusation is false. Haman never meant to seduce Esther. He was a devoted father and a good husband . . . we know it from the text. Zarish, his wife was also his confidante . . . his ally . . . his advisor. He did nothing without consulting her, and Esther must have known that. So why did she compromise him?

(Out of tempo.)

ESTHER:
You anti-Semite!
I compromised myself,
And you,
And all of my people,
To see you dead!

NARRATOR: And what about the King? What happened to him?

KING:
Yes.
No.
Maybe,
I don't know.
All right,
We'll see.
Maybe.
Me. *(Removes crown.)*

NARRATORS: *(Variously.)*
What a strange man! He killed his wife, Vashti, because of his friend, Haman, and his friend, Haman, because of his wife, Esther. He desires Vashti, yet he kills her . . . he kills her and then he misses her. And look at the way he behaves toward the Jews. Based on rumors he orders their genocide, but based on love and a good dinner, he acquits them.

NARRATOR *(King, Out of character.)*: I just want to point out that the enemies are using the same arguments today. The enemies are using Haman's arguments. The situation remains precarious . . . AND . . .

COMPANY: . . . one must never rely on Kings and rulers. Their moods are too volatile.

(The following text is alternately chanted or spoken, as indicated, in rapid, continuous fashion like an incantation.)

(It Is the Duty Of a Man—chanted out of tempo)

It is the duty of a man to mellow himself with wine on Purim until he cannot tell the difference between . . .

Cursed be Haman,
Blessed be Mordechai.

It is the duty of a man to drink until . . .

Evil is good,
Good is evil.
Cursed be Haman,
Blessed be Mordechai.

Let the poor man eat, perhaps he will forget his poverty. Let the rich man drink, perhaps he will forget his wealth . . .

Blessed be wealth,
Cursed be poverty.
Cursed be wealth,
Blessed be poverty.

. . . and let the investigators and their investigations, the killers and their innocent victims, and the delvers and their delving, pass utterly from our memory . . .

Cursed be Haman,
Blessed be Mordechai.
Cursed be wealth,
Blessed be poverty.

. . . and the killers and their innocent victims, let them never come to mind.

(Narration 10)

NARRATORS:
Once upon a time,
In a land far away,
There lived enemies of the Jews
Who had their hatred turned on them,

And the Jews gained rule
Over those that hated them.

The scripture tells us
That Mordechai became
Great in the King's house,
And the Jews smote
All their enemies
With the stroke of the sword
And with slaughter and destruction.

COMPANY:
The ten sons of Haman
And five hundred men in Shushan!
Achim!
The ten sons of Haman
And five hundred men in Shushan!
Achim!

The Jews slew them
That hated them!
Seventy and five thousand!
Achim!
The Jews slew them
That hated them!
Seventy and five thousand!
Achim!

(Oh, Nations, Sing the Praise Of His People—militaristically)

MORDECHAI:
Oh, nations,
Sing the praise of his people,
For he will avenge the blood
Of his servants,
And he will bring
Retribution upon his foes,
And he will appease his land
And his people!
Let there be known among nations,
Before our eyes,

Revenge for your servants'
Spilled blood! *("Blood" on* MORDECHAI*'s hands.)*

NARRATOR: Time out! No, this is not good. It does not look good! Whose blood is this, is this your blood? Come, clean this up! It's not right to end a light and happy story with such anger and violence! No wonder God left his name off this book! Let us concentrate on Esther, the Beautiful . . . oi, oi, oi, Esther, a mishigina maidel. Let's concentrate on Esther the Beautiful. Let's consider her courage, her prophetic powers, her gracefulness, her piety. She kept kosher. She never looked at another man except Mordechai. A model of pure self-sacrifice. Let's end our story with the Great Queen Esther!

(Esther the Invincible reprise)

ESTHER:
Good-bye Mordechai,
Uncle, cousin, lover, patriarch.
I'm off to save the world
Like Noah with his ark.
I'm ripping off my wifely skirts
And the scarves around my head.
I'm marching like a soldier
To the bad King's bed.

I am Esther the invincible,
I am braver than Eve.
I'm a—

NARRATOR: *(Interrupting.)* No, no, no!! We cannot have a martyr, it's too Christian! This is supposed to be a happy story, a fairy tale with a happy ending. Why don't we have a wedding? In Scripture Esther is supposed to be young and beautiful, and Mordechai is strong and handsome, so, don't ask . . . you want to vote on the ending?

COMPANY: No!

NARRATORS: *(Variously.)* I'll tell you, I prefer drinking to voting. I drink to the miracle of liberation and the dream of freedom. What is Purim? A story about a conflict between good and evil? About fantasies or violence vanquished by prayer and commitment to truth and beauty?

Ultimately, Purim is not so much a tale about these things as it is a celebration of memory. Let us celebrate. Let us remember those who suffer. Let us remember every second of our tiny, but significant joys and let us grow generous and strong.

(Sing Unto the Lord a New Song—a broad rock anthem)

NARRATOR:
Let the enemies of joy be scattered,
As smoke is driven away,
So drive them away.
As wax melteth before the fire,
Let wickedness perish.

Let the people be glad,
Let them rejoice.
Let them make a joyful noise.

Let God be a father to the fatherless,
And a comfort to the widow.
Let the solitary find family.
Bringeth out those who are in chains,
Give the poor consolation,
And giveth the lonely company.

Lord, how long shall the wicked,
How long shall the wicked triumph?
How long shall they speak hard things?

COMPANY:
Lord, how long shall the wicked,
How long shall the wicked triumph?
How long shall they speak hard things?

NARRATOR:
Sing unto the Lord a new song,
Sing unto the Lord, all earth,
A new song, sing it loud,
Oh sing unto the Lord a new song.

COMPANY:
Sing unto the Lord a new song,
Sing unto the Lord, all earth,

A new song, sing it loud,
Oh sing unto the Lord a new song.

NARRATOR:
Let the sea roar,
And the fullness thereof,
The world
And they that dwell therein,
Let the floods clap their hands,
Let the hills be joyful together,
And the wicked
Shall no longer triumph,
And peace shall reign on earth,

COMPANY:
And the wicked
Shall no longer triumph,
And peace shall reign on earth.

NARRATOR:
Seek we this for thy people,
Go forth and speak of peace
To thy children.

COMPANY:
Seek we this for thy people,
Go forth and speak of peace
To thy children.

Sing unto the Lord a new song,
Sing unto the Lord, all earth,
A new song, sing it loud,
Oh sing unto the Lord a new song.

CONVERSATIONS WITH MY FATHER

by

Herb Gardner

By way of comment, Herb Gardner sent an essay called "Why I Write Plays," which appeared in the program of the Ahmanson Theatre (Los Angeles) production of *Conversations with My Father.* In it, he describes what a slow, terrifying business playwriting is. He dreams he is still working on a third act when he hears the "buzz of well-wishers and killers" in the "crisp opening night air of Bar Mitzvah and execution." The anguish of creation and meeting deadlines, and the risk of being misunderstood, make writing plays "an irrational act," which he loves but has trouble explaining. He says:

> How do I explain that I write plays, that I speak in the voices of other people because I don't know my own; that I write in the second person because I don't know the first; that I have been writing plays most of my adult life waiting to become both an adult and a playwright, and that it takes me so many years to write anything that I am forced to refer to myself during these periods as a playwrote?

Conversations with My Father was originally presented by the Seattle Repertory Theatre in April 1991.

The play was subsequently presented by James Walsh at the Royale Theatre in New York City on March 28, 1992. The cast was:

CHARLIE	*Tony Shalhoub*
JOSH	*Tony Gillan*
EDDIE	*Judd Hirsch*
GUSTA	*Gordana Rashovich*
ZARETSKY	*David Margulies*
YOUNG JOEY	*Jason Biggs*
HANNAH DI BLINDEH	*Marilyn Sokol*
NICK	*William Biff McGuire*
FINNEY THE BOOK	*Peter Gerety*
JIMMY SCALSO	*John Procaccino*
BLUE	*Richard E. Council*
YOUNG CHARLIE	*David Krumholtz*
JOEY	*Tony Gillan*

Directed by DANIEL SULLIVAN
Setting by TONY WALTON
Costumes by ROBERT WOJEWODSKI
Lighting by PAT COLLINS

CHARACTERS

CHARLIE
JOSH
EDDIE
GUSTA
ZARETSKY
JOEY, age 10
HANNAH DI BLINDEH
NICK
FINNEY THE BOOK
JIMMY SCALSO
BLUE
CHARLIE, age 11–13
JOEY, age 17

SCENE

The Homeland Tavern—also known as Eddie Goldberg's Golden Door Tavern, The Flamingo Lounge, and The Twin-Forties Café—on Canal Street, near Broadway, in Lower Manhattan.

ACT I

Scene 1: June 25, 1976, early evening.
Scene 2: July 4, 1936, early morning.

ACT II

Scene 1: July 3, 1944, early morning.
Scene 2: About seven that evening.
Scene 3: August 8, 1945, early morning.
Scene 4: October 15, 1965, early morning.
Scene 5: About eight weeks later, early morning.
Scene 6: June 25, 1976, early evening.

ACT I

SCENE: *The interior of The Homeland Tavern on Canal Street near Broadway in Lower Manhattan, June 25, 1976. Although the place is obviously very old, some attempt had been made at one time to give it an Old Tavern style in addition. The original patterned-tin ceiling is there, the pillared walls, the scarred oak bar, the leaded-glass cabinets, the smoked mirror behind the bar, the high-backed wooden booths with their cracked leather seats, the battered and lumbering ceiling fans; but someone has tried to go Old one better here, a kind of Ye Olde Tavern look—a large, dusty moose head has been placed above the mirror, its huge eyes staring into the room; an imitation antique Revolutionary War musket and powder horn hang on the wall over one of the booths, and over three others are a long-handled fake-copper frying pan, a commander's sword in a rusty scabbard, and a cheaply framed reproduction of "Washington Crossing the Delaware"; a large copy of the Declaration of Independence, with an imitation-parchment-scroll effect and a legend at the bottom saying "A Gift for You from Daitch's Beer," hangs on the back wall next to the pay phone, its text covered with phone numbers; a battle-scarred Old Glory print is tacked up over the yellow "Golden Door" of the entrance and a dozen copies of old oil lamps have been placed about the room with naked light bulbs stuck in them. But the genuinely old stuff is in disrepair—absent panes in the glass panels, missing slats in the booths, gaps in the ceiling design, blades gone from the fans, moth holes in the moosehide, dents in the pillars, the thick heating and water pipes acned by age and too many paint jobs—and the fake old stuff is just too clearly fake and secondhand, so the final effect of the place is inescapably shabby. Somehow, though, there is still something warm, colorful, and neighborhood-friendly about the place; you'd want to hang around in it.*

The bar runs along the left wall and the four booths run along the right, a few tables and chairs at center. The entrance is down left at the end of the bar, and on the wall behind the bar is a very large but not very good oil painting of four men playing poker and smoking cigars, one of them wearing a green eyeshade. Dozens of photographs of boxers and performers—the ones of Benny Leonard, Barney Ross, and Eddie Cantor are autographed—have been taped up around the mirror, as has the December 6, 1933, front page of The New York Times *heralding the end of Prohibition; a large photo of Franklin D. Roosevelt, a cigarette holder clenched in his broad smile, hangs in a fancy frame over the cash register. Against the wall up center is a glowing red, yellow, and orange Wurlitzer jukebox, Model 800, a beauty; to its left a door with a small circular window opens into the tiny bar-kitchen, and to its right a stairway leads up to the door of the apartment over the bar where a family once lived.*

At Rise: Before the curtain goes up we hear the zesty, full-spirited voice of Aaron Lebedeff, backed by a wailing klezmer band, singing the beginning of an old Yiddish music hall song called "Rumania, Rumania"; an invitation to the joys of food, wine, romance, friendship, dancing, and more food. The song speaks of Rumania, but it could be telling us about Odessa, Budapest, Warsaw, Lodz, Brody, the places of an older and better world that may never have existed but certainly should have.

LEBEDEFF'S VOICE:
"Rumania, Rumania, Rumania . . .
Geven amol a land a zise, a sheyne,
Ah, Rumania, Rumania, Rumania,
Geven amol a land a zise, a fayne,
Dort tsu voyen iz a fargenign,
Vos dos harts glust kentsu krign,
A Mamaligele, a Pastramile, a Karnatsele,
Un a glezele vayn, aaaaaaaah . . . !"

(Lebedeff's Voice and the bouncing Klezmer Band continue as the curtain goes up and we see that the Music is coming from the Jukebox; its pulsing colors and the glow from the open Apartment door at the top of the stairs are the only real light in the bar at first. It is early evening, June 25, 1976; no one onstage, the upended chairs on the tables and the dim, dust-filled light tell us that the place has been closed for a while. The music continues in the empty bar for a few moments.)

LEBEDEFF'S VOICE:
"Ay, in Rumania iz doch git,
Fun kayn dayges veyst men nit,
Vayn trinkt men iberal—
M'farbayst mit Kashtoval.
Hey, digi digi dam, digi digi digi dam . . ."

(A sudden rattle of keys in the entrance door and CHARLIE, *early forties, casually dressed, enters briskly, crosses immediately to the stairs leading to the apartment door, shouts up.)*

CHARLIE: *(Trying to be heard above the music.)* Josh! *(Opens jukebox, turns off the music, tries again.)* Josh!
JOSH'S VOICE: Yeah?
CHARLIE: It's five-thirty. *(He shifts his keys from hand to hand, glancing about the bar, waiting for* JOSH; *he clearly doesn't want to stay in the place any longer than he has to. He looks up at the moose for a moment, then raises his hand in farewell.)* Well, Morris . . . good-bye and good luck.

*(*JOSH, *about twenty, appears in the apartment doorway carrying an old folded baby stroller, an antique samovar, some faded documents, a few dusty framed photographs.)*

JOSH: Who're you talking to, Dad?
CHARLIE: Morris. Morris the Moose. We haven't had a really good talk since I was twelve. Find some things you want?
JOSH: *(Coming down stairs.)* Great stuff, Dad, great stuff up there. History, history. Grandma's closet, just the *closet,* it was like her own Smith*sonian* in there. *(Putting objects*

on table.) You sure you don't want *any* of this? *(Opens stroller, places it near bar.)* Look at this; perfect.

CHARLIE: Seems a little small for me, Josh. *(Reaches briskly behind bar for bottle of cold Russian vodka, knowing exactly where to find it, fills shot glass.)*

JOSH: Dad, believe me—some of the stuff upstairs, you really ought to take a look before I pack it up. Some extraordinary *things,* Dad—wonderful brown photographs full of people looking like *us*—some great old books, Russian, Yiddish—

CHARLIE: *(Briskly.)* It's all yours, kid. Whatever you can fit in your place. And anything down here; including Morris. Only the basic fixtures are included in the sale.

JOSH: *(Not listening, absorbed in documents.)* Perfect, this is perfect, one of Grandpa's bar signs—*(Reads from faded posterboard.)* "V.J. Day Special, the Atomic Cocktail, One Dollar, If the First Blast Don't Get You, the Fallout Will."

CHARLIE: *(Impatiently, checking watch, pointing upstairs.)* Josh, it's getting late; pick what you want and let's go.

JOSH: *(Reads from old document.)* "Declaration of Intention to Become a Citizen" . . . *Your* grandpa, listen . . . "I, Solomon Leib Goldberg, hereby renounce my allegiance to the Czar of All the Russias, and declare my intention to—"

CHARLIE: *(Cutting him off.)* Got the station wagon right out front; pack it up, let's move.

JOSH: I don't get it; only a month since Grandma died, why does the place have to be sold so fast?

CHARLIE: Leave a bar closed too long it loses its value. Customers drift away. That's how it works. Deal's almost set. *(Points upstairs.)* Come on, Josh, let's—

JOSH: I don't get it, I just don't get it . . . *(Going up stairs.)* What difference would another *week* make? What's the hurry, what's the *hurry* here, man . . . ? *(He exits into apartment.* CHARLIE *sits at bar; then looks up at moose.)*

CHARLIE: He wants to know what's the hurry here, Morris.

(Silence for a moment, CHARLIE *lost in thought; the jukebox glowing brighter as we hear the sudden sound of a full chorus and marching band doing a thunderous rendition of "Columbia, the Gem of the Ocean.")*

CHORUS AND BAND: *(From jukebox.)*
"Three cheers for the red, white and blue,
Three cheers for the red, white and blue,
The Army and Navy forever,
Three cheers for the red, white and blue . . ."

(All stage lights, one section after the other, coming up full now in strict cadence to the trumpets, drums, and chorus: the many fake oil lamps, the overheads, the bar lights, the dawn light from the street, all coming up in tempo to reveal an image of rampant patriotism only dimly perceived in earlier shadow—red, white, and blue crepe bunting hung across the full length of the bar mirror and on the back of each booth, and several dozen small American flags on gold-painted sticks placed everywhere about the room; the trumpets building, the ceiling fans spinning, as EDDIE GOLDBERG, *a man in his early forties who moves like an ex-boxer, bursts out of the kitchen, a swath of bunting across his shoulders, a batch of foot-high flags in one hand and an individual flag in the other, waving them all to the music. July 4th, 1936, and* EDDIE GOLDBERG *have arrived suddenly and uninvited—*CHARLIE *turning slowly from the bar to watch him.* EDDIE *wears a fine white shirt, black bowtie, sharp black pants, and noticeably polished shoes—an outfit better suited to an uptown cocktail lounge than to this Canal Street gin mill. He parks the batch of flags on a nearby table, drapes the bunting with a grand flourish across the stroller, sticks the individual flag onto the hood—all these movements in strict time to the powerful march music that continues to blare out of the jukebox, his spirits rising with the soaring finale of the record, circling the stroller once and finishing with a fancy salute to the* KID *within, kneeling next to the stroller as the record comes to a trumpet-blasting, cymbal-crashing end.)*

CHORUS AND BAND: *(Continued.)*
"When borne by the red, white and blue,
When borne by the red, white and blue,
Thy banners make tyranny tremble,
When borne by the red, white and blue!"

EDDIE: *(He points to the moose.) Moose.* See? See the nice moose? Moose, that's an easy one. An "M" at the beginning, "MMMM," and then "OOOO"; Moose.

Mmmmoooose. See the pretty moose? Just look at the moose. Moose. *(He waits. Silence from the stroller.)* Forget the moose. We'll wait on the moose. "Duckie." Hey, how about "duckie"? You had "duckie" last Saturday, you had it down cold. "Duckie." *(Reaches under stroller, takes out wooden duck, presents duck.)* Here ya go, here ya go; duckie. *Here's* the duckie. Look at that duckie; helluva duckie, hah? Hah? *(Hides the duck behind his back.)* Where's the duckie? You want the duckie? Ask me for the duckie. Say "duckie." *(Silence for a moment; he leans against the bar.)* You lost it. You lost "duckie." You had it and you lost it. Now we're losin' what we *had,* we're goin' *back*wards, Charlie. *(Starts to pace in front of bar.)* Kid, you're gonna be two; we gotta get movin' here. Goddamn *two,* kid. I mean, your brother Joey—your age—we had a goddamn conver*sationalist* in there! *(Silence for a moment.)* Charlie, Charlie, you got any idea how much heartache you're givin' us with this issue, with this goddamn vow of *silence* here? Six words in two years and now *gornisht,* not even a "Mama" or a "Papa." *(Grabs the batch of flags, starts placing one on each table about the room; quietly, controlling himself.)* Frankly, I'm concerned about your mother. Granted, the woman is not exactly a hundred percent in the Brains Department her*self,* also a little on the wacky side, also she don't hear a goddamn word anybody says so why should you want to talk to her in the first place—nevertheless, on this issue, my heart goes out to the woman. She got a kid who don't do shit. She goes to Rutgers Square every morning with the other mothers, they sit on the long bench there—in every stroller, right down the line, we got talkin', we got singin', we got tricks; in *your* stroller we got *gornisht.* We got a kid who don't make an *effort,* a boy who don't *extend* himself. *(Leaning down close to stroller.)* That's the *trouble* with you, you don't *extend* yourself. You never *did.* You don't *now,* you never *did,* and you never *will.* *(Suddenly, urgently, whispering.)* Come on, kid, gimme something, what's it *to* ya? I open for business in an hour, every morning the regulars come in, you *stare* at them; I tell 'em you're sick, I cover for you. It's July Fourth, a special occasion, be an American, make an effort. *(Grabs the duck off the bar, leans down to the stroller with it.)* Come on: "duckie," just a "duckie," one "duckie" would be a Mitzvah . . . *(Silence from the stroller; then the beginnings of a sound, barely audible at first;* EDDIE *leans forward, smiling hopefully.)* What's that? What . . . ? *(The sound grows louder, but there is no discernible word, and finally what we hear quite clearly is pure baby-babble, something like "ba-bap, ba-bap, ba-bap . . .")* Oh, shut up. Just *shut* up, will ya! If that's how you're gonna talk, then shut ya goddamn *trap*!

*(*EDDIE *turns sharply and throws the wooden duck violently across the room—it smashes against the farthest down right booth, barely missing* CHARLIE, *who has been seated in the booth, watching.* CHARLIE *turns, startled, as the pieces of the duck clatter to the floor.* EDDIE *strides angrily over to the bar and then behind it, turning his back to the stroller, starts to clean glasses from the sink and slap them onto a shelf as the baby-babble continues.)*

EDDIE: *(Shouting.)* The conversation is *over*, kid!

(The baby-babble stops abruptly. Silence for a moment.)

CHARLIE: *(To Audience; calmly, cordially.)* Duck Number Sixteen; other casualties this year include four torn Teddy bears and a twisted metal frog. *(Rising from booth, moving down towards us.)* "Gornisht"—in case it wasn't clear to you—means "nothing." "Gornisht *with* gornisht" being less than nothing. The only thing less than that is "bupkes," which is beans, and less than that is "bupkes mit beblach," which is beans with more beans. In Yiddish, the only thing less than nothing is the existence of something so worthless that the presence of nothing becomes more obvious. Which brings me to the story of my life . . . *(Shrugs, smiling.)* Sorry; I can't resist a straight-line, even one of my own. I just—I hear them coming. I am often criticized for this. Oh, but they are everywhere and always irresistible: there are people who are straight-lines—both my ex-wives, for example, and all of my accountants—days, sometimes entire years, whole cities like Newark and Cleveland—"What did you do in Newark last weekend? I dreamt of Cleveland"—and some lifetimes, whole lifetimes like my father's, are set-ups for punch lines. *(Moving towards stroller.)* That's me in the stroller there and, as you can hear, I *did* finally learn to talk—last year I even started using the word "duck" without bursting into tears— *(We hear the sudden sound of the* KID *crying; he leans down to stroller, whispers gently.)* Don't worry, kid . . . in just a few years they'll be telling you you talk too much.

EDDIE: *(Shouting.)* Gloria! *(Remains with his back to stroller, continues briskly cleaning glasses.)* Gloria, the kid! Change the kid! *(The* KID *is instantly quieter, comforted by the sound of his father's voice even though he's shouting.)* Gloria, the kid! Time to change him! *(Then, louder.)* For another kid! *(Turns towards stairway.)* Gloria, why don't you *answer* me?!

GUSTA'S VOICE: *(From upstairs, a strong Russian accent.)* Because I only been Gloria two and a half weeks . . . and I was Gusta for thirty-eight years; I'm waiting to recognize.

EDDIE: I thought you liked the name.

GUSTA'S VOICE: I liked it till I heard it hollered. Meanwhile, your wife, Gloria, she's got a rusty sink to clean.

EDDIE: Hey, what about the *kid* here? I gotta get the bar open!

GUSTA'S VOICE: *(Graciously.)* A shaynim dank, mit eyn toches ken men nit zayn oyf tsvey simches.

CHARLIE: *(To Audience.)* Roughly, that's "Thank you, but with one rear end I can't go to two parties."

EDDIE: English! English! Say it in *English,* for Chrissakes!

GUSTA'S VOICE: You can't say it in English, Eddie, it don't do the job.

CHARLIE: She's right, of course, English don't do the job. Sure, you can say "Rise and shine!," but is that as good as "Shlof gicher, me darf der kishen," which means "Sleep faster, we need your pillow"? Does "You can't take it with you" serve the moment better than "Tachtrich macht me on keshenes," which means "They don't put pockets in shrouds"? Can there be a greater scoundrel than a paskudnyak, a more screwed-up life than one that is ongepatshket? Why go into battle with a punch, a jab, a sock and a swing when you could be armed with a klop, a frosk, a zetz and a chamalia? Can poor, undernourished English turn an answer into a question, a proposition into a conclusion, a sigh into an opera? No. No, it just don't do the job, Pop. *(*EDDIE *flips a switch, lighting up the freshly* *painted entrance to the bar.)* Behold . . . the Golden Door—*(Taking in the bar with a sweep of his hand.)*—and here, "Eddie Goldberg's Golden Door Tavern" . . . formerly "Cap'n Ed's Place," "The Café Edward," "Eduardo's Cantina," and "Frisco Eddie's Famous Bar and Grill"; living above it are Gloria and Eddie, formerly Gusta and Itzik, their sons Charlie and Joey, formerly Chaim and Jussel—*(A sweep of his hand up towards the apartment doorway as* ZARETSKY *enters.)* and our boarder, Professor Anton Zaretsky—*(No matter how quietly or subtly, it is impossible for this old actor to come into a room without making an entrance—this same theatrical glow is true of his departures—proceeding purposefully down the stairway to the bar now, carrying his seventy years like an award, his unseasonably long, felt-collared coat draped capelike over his shoulders, his thin cigarette held elegantly, Russian-style, between his thumb and forefinger.)*—formerly of Odessa's Marinsky Theatre and the Second Avenue Yiddish Classic Art Players; now, in leaner times, appearing solo and at club meetings as *all* of the Second Avenue Yiddish Classic Art Players, some ascribing this to the Depression and others to the inconvenience of having to work on a stage cluttered by other actors.

(As ZARETSKY *arrives at the bar,* EDDIE, *without turning to him, and clearly enacting the ritual of many mornings, briskly pours half a tumbler of straight vodka, places it behind himself on the bar, still without turning, and quickly resumes his busy preparations.* ZARETSKY, *with a sweep of his arm and a sharp flick of his wrist, downs the vodka in one efficient swallow; he places the empty tumbler with a snap on the bar, pauses a moment—then lets go with a truly hair-raising, shattering, siren-like scream of pain. The scream, obviously part of the ritual, is in no way acknowledged by* CHARLIE, *the* KID *in the stroller,* EDDIE*—who continues with his back to* ZARETSKY*—or* ZARETSKY *himself. Silence again for a moment or two.)*

ZARETSKY: *(Elegant Russian accent, to* KID in stroller *and* EDDIE.) Chaim, Itzik, God had two great ideas: beautiful women, and how to drink a potato.

(He crosses briskly to his usual table at center, opens his newspaper—one of several Yiddish journals he carries with him along with an old carpetbag-style valise—and sits deep into his chair and a world of his own, encircled by his morning vodka and The Jewish Daily Forward; *all this as* CHARLIE *moves towards the stairway, looks up at apartment, continues talking.)*

CHARLIE: Very important distinction between living behind your store and living *above* it—two years ago we'd made the big move from "living in back" on Rivington to "living over" on Canal; surely goodness and mercy and the Big Bucks would soon be following us.

ZARETSKY: *(Not looking up from paper.)* For those interested, from today's *Jewish Daily Forward*, an item: "Yesterday morning in Geneva, Stefan Lux, a forty-eight-year-old Jewish journalist from Prague, stood up in the midst of a League of Nations meeting, pulled an automatic pistol from his briefcase, shouted 'Avenol, Avenol,' and shot himself in the chest. In his briefcase a letter to Secretary General Joseph Avenol stating that he has killed himself publicly to awaken the League's conscience to the plight of the Jews in the Reich." *(Silence; waits for response, then turns page.)* I thank you all for your attention.

EDDIE: *(Slaps the bar with his towel.)* O.K., Charlie, I know what's *up*, I know what you're doin' . . . *(Turns to stroller, smiling.)* And I *like* it! *(Approaching stroller with diaper and towel.)* You're *my kid* and you're not gonna say what you gotta say till you're damn good and *ready.* So I say *this* to you—don't let nobody push you around, and I include *myself* in that remark; got it? Because I would be tickled pink if the first goddamn sentence you ever said was: "Charlie Goldberg don't take shit from *no*body!" *(Taking dirty diaper out of stroller.)* O.K., now I see you got a hold of your dick there. This don't bother me, be my guest. There's many schools of thought on grabbing your dick, pro and con. Me, I'm pro. I say, go to it, it's *your dick.* What you hope for is that someday some kind person out there will be as interested in it as you are. What you got a hold of there is optimism itself, what you got there in your hand is blind hope, which is the best kind. *(Grips edge of stroller.)* Everybody says to me, "Hey, four bars into the toilet, *enough, forget* it, Eddie—a steady job tendin' *bar,* Eddie, maybe managin' a class place"—I say, "I don't work for *no*body, baby, this ain't no employee's personality; I sweat, but I sweat for my *own.*" *(Deposits slug in jukebox, making selection.)* And I ain't talking about no gin mill, kid, I ain't talkin' about saloons and stand-up bars—I'm talkin' about what we got *here,* Charlie . . . I'm talkin' about America . . . *(From the jukebox we begin to hear a full chorus and orchestra doing a gorgeous rendition of "America, the Beautiful," all strings and harps and lovely echoing voices.)* We give 'em *America,* Charlie—*(Takes in the place with a sweep of his hand as the music fills the room.)* We give 'em a moose, we give 'em George Washington, we give 'em the red-white-and-blue, and mostly we give 'em, bar none, the greatest American invention of the last ten years—*Cocktails*! *(He flips a switch, illuminating the entire bar area, the mirror glows, a long strip of bulbs running the length of the shelf at the base of the mirror lights up the row of several dozen exotically colored cocktail-mix bottles; he points at the stroller.)* O.K., *Canal* Street, y'say—that's not a cocktail *clientele* out there, these are people who would suck aftershave lotion out of a wet washcloth—*(Advancing on stroller as music builds.) Nossir!* The trick here, all ya gotta remember, is nobody's equal but *every*body *wants* to be—downtown slobs lookin' for uptown class, goddamn Greenhorns lookin' to turn Yankee—New York style American cocktails, Charlie! We liquor up these low-life nickel-dimers just long enough to bankroll an Uptown lounge—

CHORUS AND ORCHESTRA: *(A soprano solo rising delicately as* EDDIE *kneels next to stroller.)*
". . . Thine alabaster cities gleam,
Undimmed by human tears . . ."

EDDIE: *Yessir,* that's where we're *goin',* you and me; I'm lookin' *Up*town, kid, Madison, Lex—I got a *plan,* see, I'm *thinkin'*—*(Rising with the lush soprano.)* because there's only two ways a Jew *gets* Uptown; wanna get outa here, kid, you gotta *punch* your way out or *think* your way out. You're Jewish you gotta be smarter than everybody else; or cuter or faster or funnier. Or tougher. Because, basically, they want to kill you; this is true maybe thirty, thirty-five hundred years now and is not likely to change next Tuesday. It's not they don't want you in Moscow, or Kiev, or Lodz, or Jersey City: it's the earth, they don't want you on the *earth* is the problem; so the trick is to become necessary. If they need you they don't kill you. Naturally, they're gonna hate you for needing you, but that beats they don't need you and they kill you. Got it? *(His arms spread wide in conclusion.)* This, kid . . . is the whole story.

CHORUS AND ORCHESTRA: *(Full chorus and strings as the music comes to a lush finale.)*
". . . From sea to shining sea!"

ZARETSKY: *(Not looking up from newspaper.)* Itzik, the only Jew in this room being persecuted is two years old.

EDDIE: You, Actor; quiet.

ZARETSKY: Fortunately, he understands very few of your dangerously misguided words, Itzik.

EDDIE: *Eddie,* goddamnit, *Eddie*!

ZARETSKY: Please, enough; I am not feeling very vigorous this morning. You have kept an entire household awake all night with your terrible noises.

EDDIE: Terrible *noises*? I'm up all night doin' a complete refurbish on the place, single-handed, top to bottom; I don't hear no comment. *(Continuing work behind bar.)* Guy *lives* here should show an interest.

ZARETSKY: *(He puts down his paper; looks about, nodding thoughtfully.)* Ah, yes. Ah, yes . . . Tell me, Eddie; what period are you attempting to capture here?

EDDIE: Early American.

ZARETSKY: I see. How early?

EDDIE: Revolutionary *War,* shmuck. From now on this place, it's always gonna be the Fourth of July here. How about that moose?

ZARETSKY: *(Leans back, studying it.)* Ah, yes; the moose.

EDDIE: How's it look to ya?

ZARETSKY: Shocked. Completely shocked to be here. One minute he's trotting freely through the sweet green forest—next thing he knows he's staring out at a third-rate saloon on Canal Street; forever. Yes, shocked and dismayed to be here, in Early America. As am I, *Eddie. (He lifts up his newspaper.)*

EDDIE: *(Turns sharply from bar.) Greenhorn!* Greenhorn bullshit! You came here a Grinneh, you *stayed* a Grinneh. *Grinneh*—you were *then,* you are *now,* and you always *will* be! *(Leans towards him.)* I *hear* ya, what kinda *noise* is that? "I don't feel wery wigorous"—what *is* that? Ya don't have to *do* that, ya *know* ya don't, you could get *rid* of that. I come here after *you* did, listen to me. Check the patter. I read Winchell, I go to the movies, I know the score—

(During these last few moments, GUSTA *has entered from the apartment above and stopped about halfway down the stairs, her attention caught by the moose head; small, perpetually busy, near forty, she carries two large pots of just-cooked food, each about a third of her size.)*

GUSTA: Eddie, there's an animal on the wall.
EDDIE: It's a moose.
GUSTA: All right, I'll believe you; it's a moose. Why is it on the wall?
EDDIE: For one thing, it's a moose *head*—
GUSTA: Believe me, I didn't think the rest of it was sticking out into Canal Street.
CHARLIE: Hey . . . she's actually *funny* . . . *(To* EDDIE.*) Laugh,* will ya?
GUSTA: *(Crossing quickly to kitchen.)* My favorite, personally, was "Cap'n Ed's Place"; I liked those waves you painted on the mirror, and your sailor hat, *that* was a beauty.
EDDIE: *Captain's* hat, it was a *Captain's* hat—*(Quietly, to stroller.)* Why do I talk to her? Why? *Tell* me. Do *you* know?
GUSTA: *(Chuckling, setting pots down on stove.)* Meanwhile, I see so far nobody showed up for the Revolution.
EDDIE: Because we ain't *open* yet! *Eight* o'clock, that's the law, I stick to the rules. *(Points to framed Roosevelt photo.)* Like F.D.R. says, in that way he's got—"It is by strict adherence to the rules that we shall avoid descent to the former evils of the saloon."
GUSTA: *(Indicates F.D.R. photo.)* Look at that smile, the man him*self* is half-drunk mosta the time. Your Roosevelt, he says, "There is nothing to fear but fear itself." What, that's not *enough*?
EDDIE: Not another *word*—not another word against the man in my place!

GUSTA: *(Approaching stroller with bit of food on stirring spoon, singing softly, an old Yiddish lullaby.)*
"Oif'n pripitchok, brent a faieril,
Un in shtub iz heys,
Un der rebe lerent kleyne kinderlach
Dem alef beys . . ."

CHARLIE: *(At kitchen, inhaling the memory.)* That food . . . Brisket Tzimmes, Lokshen Kugel . . .

GUSTA: *(Sitting next to stroller, gently.)*
"Zetje kinderlach, gedenktje taiere,
Voseer lerent daw . . ."
(ZARETSKY starts to hum along with her.)
"Zogtje noch amol, un take noch amol,
Kometz alef aw . . ."

EDDIE: Hey, you people want lullabies, what the hell's wrong with "Rock-a-bye Baby"? A good, solid, American hit—

GUSTA: *(Softly, reaching spoon into stroller.)*
"Zogtje noch amol, un take noch amol,
Kometz alef aw . . ."

CHARLIE: *(Softly, kneeling near her.)* She's young . . . she's so young . . .

GUSTA: *(Smiling sweetly.)* Now sing along with me, darling; just "Alef aw" . . . *(Singing, CHARLIE behind her urging the Kid to respond.)* "Kometz alef aw . . . alef aw . . ." *(No response; she shrugs.)* A shtik fleysh mit oygen. *(Goes back to kitchen.)*

CHARLIE: My mother has just referred to me as "a piece of meat with two eyes."

EDDIE: That's why the kid don't talk, he don't know what *language* to speak!

GUSTA: *(Laughing to herself, stacking dishes on bar.)* Eddie, Ethel called me with two good ones this morning—I mean, *good* ones—

EDDIE: Not now, Gloria. Gimme the Specials. *(Turns to blackboard over bar marked "Today's Specials," picks up chalk.)*

GUSTA: So this old Jewish mama, lonely, a widow—her fancy son can't be bothered, sends her a parrot to keep her company—

EDDIE: The *Specials,* Gloria—

GUSTA: This is a five-hundred-dollar parrot, speaks six languages, including Russian and Yiddish—

EDDIE: The pots, the pots, what's in the *pots*?!

GUSTA: A week goes by, he don't hear from her, calls up, "Mama, did you get the parrot?" "Yes," she says, "thank you, Sonny; *delicious.*" *(Breaks up, laughing happily, turns heat down under pots.)* Eddie, you want the Specials?

EDDIE: *(To stroller.)* Come on, Charlie, *tell* me, why do I . . . ? Yeah.

GUSTA: O.K., in the big pot, Brisket Tzimmes with honey, carrot, sweet potato, a dash raisins.

EDDIE: *(Writing in bold letters on blackboard.)* "Mulligan Stew."

GUSTA: *(Removing apron.)* Next to it, still simmering, we got Lokshen Kugel with apple, cinnamon, raisin, a sprinkle nuts.

EDDIE: *(Thinks a minute, then writes.)* "Hot Apple Pie."

CHARLIE: *(Whispering.)* No, Pop . . . no . . .

GUSTA: *(Taking school notebook from shelf near phone.)* Now I go to Mr. Katz. Don't forget, in a half-hour, you'll turn me off the Lokshen please.

EDDIE: Twelve *years*—twelve years of English with Mr. Katz you're still sayin' "turn me off the Lokshen"!

GUSTA: *(Going to entrance door.)* It's not just English at the Alliance, we *discuss* things; politics, *Jewish* things.

EDDIE: Goddamn *Commie,* that Katz; he's open Washington's Birthday, *Lincoln's, now* he's teaching on July Fourth!

GUSTA: He's not a Communist; he's only an Anarchist.

EDDIE: What's the difference?

GUSTA: Louder, and fewer holidays. *(Breaks up again, laughing, opens door, waves to stroller.)* Bye-bye, Charlie, when Mama comes back we chapn a bisl luft in droysen, yes?

CHARLIE: *(To Audience.)* "Catch a bit of air outside."

EDDIE: *English,* for Chrissakes, *English*—

GUSTA: *(As she exits, laughing.)* "Delicious," she says, "delicious" . . .

EDDIE: *(Shouting at door.)* English— *(Turning sharply to* ZARETSKY.*)* English! The *two* of ya, the *mouth* on ya, kid's all screwed up, thinks he's livin' in Odessa; meanwhile ya give my *joint* a bad feel. Goddamn Jewish *newspapers* all over the place—what're we, advertisin' for *rabbis* here? *(Points to jukebox.)* Goodness of my heart I put some Jew music on the Box for ya—all I ask ya don't play it business hours or in fronta my kids. Next thing I know Jack says you're playin' "Rumania" straight through his *shift* last night. The two of ya, I swear, you're discouragin' the proper clientele here, and that's the fact of the matter. Jews don't drink; this a law of nature, a law of nature and of commerce. *(He slaps the bar with finality; then resumes his work. Silence for a moment.)*

ZARETSKY: *(Singing, from behind his newspaper, a thick brogue.)*
"Oh, Dan-ny Boy,
The pipes, the pipes are callin' . . ."

EDDIE: *(Leans forward on bar.)* Damn *right,* Mister—damn *right* that's who drinks! You can't sell shoes to people who ain't got no *feet,* pal!

ZARETSKY: *(Singing.)*
"From glen to glen . . ."

EDDIE: Hey, far *be* it! Far be it from me to discuss makin' a living! *(Coming out from behind bar.)* What's that foreign mouth been *gettin'* you, Zaretsky? A once-a-month shot in the Mountains puttin' retired Yiddlach to sleep with old Sholem Aleichem stories? *Pushkin* for the Literatniks? What? When's the last time you saw somebody in a Yiddish theater under a hundred who wasn't dragged there by his Zayde? Read the handwritin' on the goddamn *marquee,* amigo; it's *over.* Gotta give 'em what they *want,* see. That's the Promised Land, pal—find out what they want and *promise* it to them. *(Takes frozen vodka from under bar.)* Yessir— *(Pouring half glass; to stroller.)* A toast to that, Charlie!

CHARLIE: Pop never drank—except to propose a toast, and that toast was always to the same thing ...

EDDIE: *(Holding glass aloft, towards front door.)* The new place, Charlie . . . to today, the Openin' Day . . . I lift my lamp beside the Golden Door; bring me your tired, your poor, your drinkers, your winos, your alkies, your—

ZARETSKY: *(Lowers his newspaper.)* I knew a man once, Itzik Goldberg, with the colors of Odessa and the spirit of a Jew, and I saw this man turn white before my eyes, white as milk—Grade A, pasteurized, homogenized, American *milk*!

EDDIE: *(Softly, to stroller.)* Very sad, Charlie; a dyin' man with a dead language and no place to go. *(Downs vodka, turns sharply, shouting.)* Check me out, Actor—current cash problems I gotta *tolerate* your crap—soon as this place hits you're out on the *street,* inside a year you're sleepin' in *sinks,* baby; this is a *warning*! *(Slaps glass down.)*

ZARETSKY: *(Shouting, fiercely.)* And a warning to *you,* sir; I shall no longer countenance these threats!

CHARLIE: This exchange, a holler more or less, took place every day, except Sunday, at approximately seven-fifteen a.m. After which, they would usually— *(Sees his father pouring another vodka;* CHARLIE *is suddenly anxious.)* Oh, shit, another one . . .

EDDIE: *(Downs second vodka; then, quietly, to stroller.)* Hey, y'know, anything you got to say to me, nobody's gonna know, it's all strictly confidential. *(Takes small red ball from stroller, tosses it back in; pleasantly.)* There ya go, pick up the ball and give it back to Papa. *(Silence.)* Pick it up . . . *(A sudden, frightened whisper escapes him.)* Oh, kid, don't be dumb . . . you're not gonna turn out to be dumb, are ya? *(Pause.)* Those eyes; don't look at me like that, Charlie . . . *(Sits on chair next to stroller, gazing into it.)* You got your grandpa's sweet face, see . . . exactly, to the letter; the soft eyes and the gentle, gentle smile, and it scares the shit outa me. His head in the Talmud and his foot in the grave, the guy come here and got creamed, kid. Not you, Charlie; I'm gonna do good here, but you're gonna do better. There's two kinda guys come off the boat: the Go-Getters and the Ground-Kissers. Your grandpa, though a better soul never walked the earth, was to all intents and purposes, a putz; a darling man and a born Ground-Kisser. In *Hamburg,* in the harbor, we ain't even *sailed* yet and the kissing begins: he kisses the gang-plank, he kisses the doorway, he kisses the scummy god-damn *steerage floor* of the S.S. Pennland. Nine hundred miles we walk to get to the boat, just him and me, I gotta handle all the bribes. Ten years *old,* I gotta grease my way across the Russian Empire, he don't know how. *Fine* points, this is all he ever knew: *fine* points. *My* grandpa, one o' them solid-steel rabbis, gives Pop a sweet send-off back in Odessa: "Have a good trip, Solomon," he says: "eat kosher or die." So twenty-six days on the boat Pop eats little pieces of bread they give ya with kosher stamps on 'em and a coupla prayed-on potatoes; *I'm* scroungin' everything in sight to stay alive. *Fine* points! Pop loses thirty pounds, *he's* a wreck but the *lips,* the lips are in great shape, the lips are working! New York harbor, he's kissin' the deck, he's blowin' kisses to Lady Liberty, he's kissin' the *barge* that takes us to Ellis Island. On the mainland, forget it, the situation is turnin' pornographic. Twenty-eight blocks to his brother on Rivington—some people took a trolley, *we* went by lip. On Grand Street I come over to him, this little rail of a man, I say, "Get off your knees, Pop; stand up, everbody's *lookin',* what the hell're ya doin'?" Looks at me, his eyes are sweet and wet, he says, "It's God's will that we come here, Itzik. I show my love for his intentions . . ." *Fine* points! *(Suddenly rises, bangs his fist on the table next to him, showing the effects of his vodka.)* Goddamn *fine* points . . . *(Gradually turning towards* ZARETSKY, *who remains behind his newspaper.)* Opens a joint here on Rivington: Solomon's Tavern. The man is closed Friday night and Saturday by God's law and Sunday by New York's—the income is brought by Elijah every Passover. Comes Prohibition, he sticks to the letter; coffee, soda, three-two beer and no booze—every joint in the neighborhood's got teapots fulla gin and bourbon in coffee cups, we're scratchin' for nickels and lovin' God's intentions. A summer night, late, they come to sell him bootleg: two little Ginzos and this big Mick hench with eyes that died. "Oh, *no,*" says Papa the Putz, "not *me.* Against the *law,*" he says—he's *ed*ucatin' these yo-yo meat grinders, right?—he says he's callin' the cops and the Feds and he's goin' to all the local congregations to talk his fellow Jews outa buyin' or sellin' bootleg. "Do it and you're a dead Yid," says the hench. Pop don't get the message—no, he's got his *own* message now—in a week he hits every landsman's bar he can find, he's tellin' 'em they gotta respect where God has sent them; gets to five, six shuls that week, *three* on Saturday, he's givin' goddamn public *speeches* in Rutgers Square! A five-foot-six, hundred-and-twenty-pound Jew has selected Nineteen Twenty-one in America as the perfect time to be anti-gangster! What the *hell* did he think was gonna protect him? The *cops*? His *God*? By Sunday morning he is, of course, dead in Cortlandt Alley over here with his skull smashed in. They hustle me over there at seven a.m. to say if it's him; I know before I get there. When they turn him over I don't look—it's not the bashed-in head I'm afraid of; I'm afraid I'll see from his lips that with the last breath he was kissing the dust in Cortlandt Alley. *(Moving briskly up to bar.)* The *perfection* of it—his Jewish God had his soul and America had his heart, he died a devout and patriotic *putz*! *(Reflexively splashes vodka into his glass, downs it in a gulp, slaps glass onto bar. A moment; he chuckles.)* So he don't get thrown outa heaven, he gives two bucks to this place, the Sons of Moses, to guarantee his soul gets prayed for; for two dollars they send me a card every year for the rest of my *life* to remind me to light Pop's Yahrzeit candle and do the Kaddish for him; I can't get halfway through the prayer without sayin' "Go to hell, Pop." I look at the card, I see the alley. And wherever I live, the card comes. Wherever you go, they find you, those Sons of Moses. The putz won't leave me be. He wouldn't shut up *then* and he won't shut up now . . . he won't shut up . . . he won't shut up . . . he won't shut *up*—

(In one sudden, very swift movement, he kicks over the bar-table next to him, its contents clattering to the floor; CHARLIE, *taken completely by surprise, leaps to his feet in his booth as the round table rolls partway across the barroom floor.* EDDIE, *quite still, watches the table roll to a stop. Silence for a moment.* ZARETSKY *lowers his newspaper.)*

ZARETSKY: *(Raising his glass, proudly.)* To Solomon Goldberg . . . who I saw speak in Rutgers Square against drinking and crime to an audience of drunks and criminals. Completely foolish and absolutely thrilling. We need a million Jews like him. *(Downs shot, turns sharply.)* You came to the Melting Pot, sir, and *melted* . . . melted *away. (Slaps glass down.)*

EDDIE: *(Turns to* ZARETSKY; *quietly.)* Whatsa matter, you *forget*, pal? *(Moving slowly towards* ZARETSKY'S *table.)* Wasn't that *you* I seen runnin' bare-ass down Dalnitzkaya Street—a dozen Rooski Goys and a coupla Greek Orthodox with goddamn *sabers* right behind, lookin' to slice somethin' Jewish off ya? Only thirty years ago, you were no kid *then,* moving pretty good considerin'. Did they catch ya, pal? What'd they slice off ya, Zaretsky? Your memory? They held my grandpa down under his favorite acacia tree and pulled his beard out—his beard, a rabbi's honor—they're tearin' it outa his face a chunk at a time, him screamin' in this garden behind his shul, they grabbed us *all* there that Saturday comin' outa morning prayers. This chubby one is whirlin' a saber over his head, faster and faster till it whistles—I know this guy, I seen him waitin' tables at the Café Fankoni—"I'm takin' your skull cap off," he says to my brother Heshy; one whistlin' swing, he slices it off along with the top of Heshy's skull, scalpin' him. Heshy's very proud of his yarmulke, he's Bar Mitzvah a month before and wears it the entire Shabbes—he's got his hands on his head, the blood is runnin' through his fingers, he's already dead, he still runs around the garden like a chicken for maybe thirty seconds before he drops, hollerin' "Voo iz mine yarmulkeh? . . . Voo iz mine yarmulkeh?" The kid is more afraid of not being Jewish than not being alive. *(At* ZARETSKY*'s table, leaning towards him.)* My mother, they cut her ears off; her ears, go figure it, what was Jewish about *them*? Regardless, she bled to death in the garden before it got dark, ranting like a child by then, really nuts. The guy's caftan flies open, the one doin' the job on Ma, I see an Odessa police uniform underneath, this is just a regular beat cop from Primorsky Boulevard, and the waiter too, just another person; but they were all screaming, these guys—louder than my family even—and their women too, watching, screaming, "Molodyets!" "Natchinai!" "good man," "go to it," like ladies I seen at ringside, only happier, all screaming with their men in that garden, all happy to find the bad guys. *(Sits opposite* ZARETSKY.*)* This Cossack's holdin' me down, he's makin' me watch while they do the ear-job on Ma. "Watch, Zhid, watch! Worse to watch than to die!" He holds me, he's got my arms, it feels like I'm drowning. Since then, nobody holds me down, Zaretsky, nobody. I don't even like hugs. *(Grips* ZARETSKY*'s wrist, urgently.)* The October Pogrom, how could you forget? Livin' with us two *years* now, you don't even *mention* it. You wanna run around bein' Mister Jewish—that's *your* lookout—but you leave me and my kids *out* of it. *(Rises, moving briskly to bar.)* I got my own deal with God, see; Joey does a few hours a week o' Hebrew School, just enough to make the Bar Mitzvah shot—same with Charlie—I hit the shul Rosh Hashana, maybe

Yom Kippur, and sometimes Fridays Gloria does the candle routine; and that's *it.* You treat God like you treat *any* dangerous looney—keep him calm and stay on his *good* side. Meanwhile . . . *(Takes folded legal document from cash register, smiling proudly.)* Today, today the Jew lid comes off my boys. *(Striding back to* ZARETSKY*'s table, opening document with a flourish.)* Check it out, Anton, you're the first to know— *(Reads from document.)* "Southern District Court, State of New York, the Honorable Alfred Gladstone, presiding. Application approved, this Third day of July, of the year Nineteen Hundred and Thirty-six; Change of Family Name—" *(Holding document aloft.)* Yessir; so long, Goldberg; as of one p.m. yesterday you been livin' here with the *Ross* family—outside, take note, the sign says "Eddie Ross's Golden Door"; shit, I just say it out *loud,* I get a shiver. *(Sits next to* ZARETSKY, *pointing to photos over bar.)* "Ross," yessir—honor o' Barney "One-Punch" Ross *and* Mr. Franklin Delano Roosevelt, friend of the Jews, God bless 'im. *(Leans towards* ZARETSKY.*)* Goldberg sat down with ya, pal . . . *(Slaps table, stands up.)* but Ross rises. *(Striding briskly up towards bar.)* And he's got business to do!

ZARETSKY: *(After a moment, quietly.)* You didn't mention the feathers . . . *(*EDDIE *stops, turns to him;* ZARETSKY *remains at his table, looking away.)* All the goose feathers, Itzik. Three days exactly, the perfect pogrom; and on the fourth day, in the morning, a terrible silence and feathers everywhere, a carpet of goose feathers on every street. The Jews of the Moldavanka, even the poorest of them, had goose-feather mattresses and pillows; and this made the Christians somehow very angry. So from every home they dragged out mattresses, pillows, ripped them open and threw the feathers in the streets; thousands of mattresses, millions of feathers, feathers everywhere and so white and the blood so red on them, and the sky so very blue as only could be in Odessa by the sea. All beautiful and horrible like a deadly snow had fallen in the night. This is what I remember. In the big synagogue on Catherine Street they had broken even the highest windows, and these windows stared like blinded eyes over the Moldavanka. And below there are feathers in all the acacia trees on Catherine Street, white feathers in the branches, as though they had bloomed again in October, as though the trees too had gone mad. And crazier still that morning, waddling down the street towards me, an enormous fat man, like from the circus, laughing. I watch him, silent like a balloon on the soft feathers, into one empty Jewish house and then another he goes, growing fatter as he comes, and now closer I see the face of the Greek, Poldaris, from the tobacco shop, and he is wearing one atop the other the suits and cloaks of dead Jews. No, Mr. Ross, they didn't catch me, and no, I didn't forget; this morning even, the fat Poldaris follows me still, laughing, waiting for my clothes. *(Turns to* EDDIE.*)* A picture remains—a picture more disturbing even than the one of Eddie Cantor in black-face you have hung in my room. That first night I am hiding in the loft above the horses in the Fire Station and I see on the street below me young Grillspoon kneeling in the feathers before his house, his hands clasped heavenward, like so. He pleads for his life to be spared by five members of the Holy Brotherhood who stand about him—this group has sworn vengeance on those who tortured their Savior upon the cross, Grillspoon obviously amongst them, and each carries a shovel for this purpose. Now, a Jew does not kneel when he prays, nor does he clasp his hands, and it becomes clear that poor Grillspoon is imitating the manner of Christian prayer, hoping to remind them of themselves. The actor in me sees that this man is fiercely auditioning for the role of Christian for them—and these men for the moment stand aside from him, leaning on their shovels as they watch his performance. Presently, however, they proceed to rather efficiently beat him to death with their shovels. Talk about bad reviews, eh? *(Rises, takes a step towards* EDDIE.*)* Unfortunately, you have decided that the only way to become somebody in this country is first to become no one at all. You are kneeling in your goose feathers, Mr. Ross. *You,* you who profess to be such a violent Anti-Kneeler.

EDDIE: Go to hell, Actor. *(Turns away sharply, starts briskly stacking glasses behind the bar.)*

ZARETSKY: *(Moving steadily towards* EDDIE.) For God's *sake,* Itzik, they had to *take* your grandfather's beard and your brother's yarmulke—but what is yours you will *give* away; and like poor Grillspoon you will reap the disaster of a second-rate Christian imitation. And as a pro*fes-*

sional, I *swear* to you, Itzik—*(Bangs his fist on the bar)* you are *definitely wrong for the part!*

*(*EDDIE *wheels about sharply, about to speak—but* JOEY GOLDBERG *bursts in from the apartment above, speaking as he enters, cutting* EDDIE *off; a tough-looking ten-year-old, he bounds down the stairs, his Hebrew School books tied with a belt and slung over his shoulder, heading directly for his morning task—a tray of "set-ups" on the bar.)*

JOEY: Hey, sorry I'm late, Pop—

ZARETSKY: Jussel! A guten tog, Jussel!

JOEY: A guten tog, Professor! Vos harst du fun der Rialto!

EDDIE: *(Anguished, slapping bar.)* My God, they got *him* doin' it now too . . .

CHARLIE: *(Fondly.)* Hey, Joey . . .

JOEY: *(Passing stroller.)* How ya doin' kid?

CHARLIE: *(To Audience.)* Besides me, Joey loved only two things in this world: the New York Giants and the Yiddish theatre; for my brother had witnessed two miracles in his life—Carl Hubbell's screwball, and Mr. Zaretsky's King Lear.

JOEY: *(Carrying set-ups to center table, spotting valise.)* Hey, Mr. Zaretsky . . . we got the *satchel* . . .

ZARETSKY: Yes, Jussel—*(Grandly lifting valise)* today a journey to Detroit, in Michigan, there presenting my solo concert—"Pieces of Gold from the Golden Years."

EDDIE: Hey, Joey, I got the *moose* up, see—

JOEY: *(A quick glance at it.)* Yeah, great— *(To* ZARETSKY, *fascinated.)* "Pieces of Gold" . . . what's the lineup on that one?

ZARETSKY: *(Opening valise.)* The Program, as follows—

EDDIE: Joey, the *set*-ups—

ZARETSKY: *(His arms outstretched, setting the scene.)* A simple light—possibly blue—reveals a humble satchel, and within— *(*JOEY *and* CHARLIE, *their arms outstretched, saying the words with him.)* —a world of Yiddish theatre!

EDDIE: The set-ups, Joey—

*(*JOEY *continuing absently, sporadically, to place set-ups on tables, his gaze fixed on* ZARETSKY*'s performance.)*

ZARETSKY: *(Takes tarnished gold crown from valise, placing it on his head.)* To begin—

JOEY: The old guy with the daughters!

ZARETSKY: Der Kenig Lear, of course! *(Drops crown into valise.)* Three minutes: an appetizer. And then— *(Removes a battered plaster skull; studies it, fondly.)* "Zuch in vey, umglicklickeh Yorick . . . ich hub im gut gekennt, Horatio . . ." *(Briskly exchanging skull for an ornate dagger; a thoughtful gaze, whispering.)* "Tzu zein, oder nicht tzu zein . . . dus is die fragge . . ." *(Replacing dagger with a small, knotted rope.)* The bonds of Sidney Carton, the shadow of the guillotine . . . *(Looks up; softly.)* "Es is a fiel, fiel besera zach vus ich tu yetst, vus ich hub amol getune . . ." *(Swiftly replacing rope with the fur hat of a Cossack general.)* The "Kiddush HaShem" of Sholem Asch, sweeping drama of seventeenth-century Cossack pogroms; condensed. *(Drops Cossack hat into valise.)* When they have recovered—*(Places yarmulke delicately on his head; directs this at* EDDIE, *busy behind bar.)* Sholem Aleichem's "Hard to Be a Jew" . . . humor and sudden shadows. *(Removes yarmulke; his arms outstretched, grandly.)* In conclusion, of course, my twelve-minute version of "The Dybbuk," all in crimson light if equipment available; I play all parts . . . including title role. *(A moment; then he bows his head as though before a huge Jewish audience in a grand hall; he speaks quietly.)* I hear the applause . . . *(He looks out.)* I see their faces, so familiar . . . and once again I have eluded the fat Poldaris. He shall not have my clothes. *(Silence for a moment; then he picks up his valise, striding briskly to the front door.)* Give up my Yiddish theatre? No, Itzik, I don't think so. Yes, overblown, out of date, soon to disappear. But then, so am I. *(Turns at door.)* I go now to the tailor, Zellick, who repairs my robes for Lear. Good morning to you, Jussel; and good morning to you, Mr. Ross, and, of course, my regards to your wife, Betsy.

*(*ZARETSKY *exits;* EDDIE *instantly intensifies his work behind the bar;* JOEY *not moving, looking off at front door, still in awe.)*

EDDIE: *Fake-o,* Joey, I'm tellin' ya—fake-o four-flushin' phony. Man don't make no sense, any manner, shape or form.

JOEY: You should see the way he does that *Dybbuk* guy, Pop, he really—

EDDIE: Joey, the set-ups—what happened to the goddamn *set*-ups here! And the *mail,* kid, ya *forgot* it yesterday.

JOEY: *(Picks up books.)* Gonna be late for Hebrew, Pop, it's almost eight—

EDDIE: Then ya shouldn'ta hung around watchin' Cary Grant so long.

JOEY: Ten to eight, Pop, gotta get goin'—

EDDIE: Bring in the *mail* first, you got obligations here, Mister.

JOEY: *(Puts books down.)* O.K., O.K. . . . *(Passing stroller.)* He say anything today?

EDDIE: All quiet on the western front.

JOEY: *(Looking into stroller.)* Don't worry about him, Pop; look at the eyes, he's gettin' *every*thing. *(As he exits.)* He's smart, this kid; very smart, like me.

EDDIE: And modest *too,* I bet. *(Alone now; he pauses for a moment, then goes to the stroller, peers in thoughtfully.)* Everything?

CHARLIE: Every word, Pop.

EDDIE: *(Leans forward.)* Hey, what the hell're ya *doin'*? This ain't no time to go to *sleep.* You just got *up,* for God's sake— *(Shaking the stroller.)* Let's show a little *courtesy* here, a little common goddamn *courtesy. (Stops.)* Out. He's *out.* I either got Calvin Coolidge with his dick in his fist or he's *out*!

JOEY: *(Entering, thoughtfully, with stack of mail.)* Pop, the sign outside, it says "Ross" on it . . .

EDDIE: That's our new name, you're gonna love it; honor o' Barney himself. *(Takes mail, starts going through it.)*

JOEY: You mean not just for the place, but actually our new name?

EDDIE: All done; legit and legal, kid, Al Gladstone presidin'— *(Takes envelope from mail.)* Son of a bitch, the Sons of Moses, Pop's Yahrzeit again . . .

JOEY: So my name is Joe Ross? That's my name now? Joe Ross? Very . . . brief, that name.

EDDIE: *(Studying blue card from envelope.)* Fifteen *years,* they find me every time, it's the Royal Mounted Rabbis . . .

JOEY: Joe Ross; it starts—it's *over.*

EDDIE: Hey, *Hebrew* school—

JOEY: *(Suddenly alarmed.)* Jeez, went right outa my *mind— (Grabs Hebrew texts, races for door, slapping yarmulke on his head.)*

EDDIE: *Wait* a minute— *(Points to yarmulke.)* Where ya goin' with *that* on your head? What're ya, crazy? Ya gonna go eight blocks through Little Italy and Irishtown, passin' right through goddamn *Polack* Street, with *that* on your head? How many times I gotta tell ya, kid—that is *not* an outdoor garment. That is an indoor garment *only.* Why don't ya wear a sign on your head says, "Please come kick the shit outa me"? You put it on in Hebrew School, where it belongs.

JOEY: Pop, I don't—

EDDIE: I'm tellin' ya *once* more—stow the yammy, kid. *Stow* it.

JOEY: *(Whips yarmulke off, shoves it in pocket.)* O.K., O.K. *(Starts toward door.)* I just don't see why I gotta be ashamed.

EDDIE: I'm not askin' ya to be ashamed. I'm askin' ya to be smart. *(Sees something in mail as* JOEY *opens door; sharply.) Hold* it—

JOEY: Gotta go, Pop—

EDDIE: *Hold* it right there—

JOEY: Pop, this Tannenbaum, he's a killer—

EDDIE: *(Looking down at mail; solemnly.)* I got information here says you ain't *seein'* Tannenbaum this morning. I got information here says you ain't even headed for Hebrew School right now. *(Silence for a moment.* JOEY *remains in doorway.)* C'mere, we gotta talk.

JOEY: *(Approaching cautiously, keeping at a safe distance.)* Hey . . . no whackin', Pop . . .

EDDIE: I got this note here; says— *(Takes small pieces of cardboard from mail, reads.)* "Dear Sheenie Bastard. Back of Carmine's, Remind you, Jewshit Joe, eight o'clock a.m., Be there. Going to make hamburger out of Goldberger—S.D." Bastard is spelled here B-A-S-T-I-D; this and the humorous remarks I figure the fine mind of the wop, DeSapio. *(After a moment, looks up, slaps bar.)* And I wanna tell ya *good* luck, *glad* you're goin', you're gonna *nail* 'im, you're gonna *finish* 'im, you're gonna murder 'im—

JOEY: Wait a minute—it's O.K.? Really?

EDDIE: —and here'a couple pointers how to do so.

JOEY: Pointers? *Pointers?* . . . I need a *shot*gun, Pop; DeSapio's near twice my size, fourteen years *old*—

EDDIE: Hey, far *be* it! Far be it from me to give pointers—a guy got twenty-six bouts under his belt, *twelve* professional—

JOEY: Yeah, but this DeSapio, he really *hates* me, this kid; he hated me the minute he *saw* me. He says we killed Christ, us Jews.

EDDIE: They was *all* Jews there, kid, everybody; Christ, His mother, His whole crowd—you tell him there was a buncha Romans there too, makes him *directly related* to the guys done the actual hit!

JOEY: I *told* him that, Pop—that's when he *whacked* me.

EDDIE: And I bet you whacked him back, which is appropriate, *no* shit from *no*body, ya stuck to your *guns,* kid—

JOEY: So why're we hidin' then? How come we're "Ross" all of a sudden? *(With an edge.)* Or maybe Ross is just our *out*door name, and Goldberg's still our indoor name.

EDDIE: *Hey*—

JOEY: I don't *get* it, this mean we're not Jewish anymore?

EDDIE: Of *course* we're still Jewish; we're just not gonna push it.

JOEY: *(Checking watch.)* Jeez—three minutes to eight, Pop, takes five to get there, he's gonna think I'm chicken—*(Starts towards door.)*

EDDIE: *One* minute for two pointers; let 'im wait, he'll get anxious—

JOEY: He's *not anxious,* Pop, I promise ya—

EDDIE: Now, these pointers is based on my observations o' your natural talents: the bounce, the eye, the smarts—

JOEY: *(Protesting.) Pop*—

EDDIE: C'mon, I seen ya take out Itchy Halloran with one shot in fronta the Texaco station; who're we *kiddin'* here? Hey, I was O.K., but *you* got potential I *never* had.

JOEY: But Itchy Halloran's *my height, DeSapio's* twice my *size*—

EDDIE: *(Ignoring him.)* O.K., first blow; your instinct is go for the belly, right?

JOEY: *Instinct?* His belly is as high as I can *reach,* Pop—

EDDIE: Wrong: first blow, forget the belly. Pointer Number One—ya listenin'?

JOEY: Yeah.

EDDIE: *(Demonstrating, precisely.)* Considerin' the size, you gotta rock this boy *early* . . . gotta take the first one up from the *ground, vertical,* so your full body weight's in the shot. Now, start of the fight, right away, *imme*diate, you hunk *down,* move outa range; then *he's* gotta come to *you*—and you meet him with a right fist up *off the ground;* picture a spot in the middle of his chin and aim for it—*(Demonstrates blow;* JOEY *copies)* then comes the important part—

JOEY: What's that?

EDDIE: Jump back.

JOEY: Jump back?

EDDIE: Yeah, ya jump back so when he falls he don't hurt ya.

JOEY: When he *falls*? *Murder,* he's gonna murder me. Pop, Pop, this is an *execution* I'm goin' to here! I'm only goin' so I won't be ashamed!

EDDIE: There's only one thing you gotta watch out for—

JOEY: *Death,* I gotta watch out for *death*—

EDDIE: Not death . . . but there could be some damage. Could turn out to be more than one guy there, you're gettin' ganged up on, somethin' *special*—this *happens,* kid—O.K., we got a weapon here— *(Takes framed photo of boxer from wall.)* we got a weapon here, guaranteed. *(Hands photo to* JOEY.*)* What's it say there?

JOEY: *(Reading.)* "Anybody gives *you* trouble, give *me* trouble. I love you. Love, Vince."

EDDIE: O.K.; June four, Nineteen Twenty-one, I come into the ring against Vince DiGangi, they bill him "The Ghetto Gorilla"—a shrimp with a mustache, nothin', I figure an easy win. Five *seconds* into Round One comes a *chamalia* from this little Eye-tie—I'm out, I'm on the canvas, your Pop is *furniture,* Joey. I open one eye, *there's* DiGangi on his knees next to me, he's got me in his arms, he's huggin' me, he's kissin' my face, he loves me. I give him his first big win, his first knockout. I *made* him, he says, he's gonna love me forever. And he *does.* That's the nice thing about these Telanas, they love ya or they hate ya, but it's forever; *so, remember— (Leans toward him.)* things get outa hand, you got a group situation, somethin'—you holler "DiGangi è mio fratello, *chiamalo*!" *(Grips his shoulder.)* "DiGangi è mio fratello, *chiamalo*!" Say it.

JOEY: "DiGangi è mio fratello, chi . . . amalo!"

EDDIE: That's "DiGangi's my brother, *call* him!" *(Softly, awestruck, imitating their response.)* Whoa . . . DiGangi's the magic word down there, biggest hit since Columbus, lotta power with the mob. Perhaps you noticed, Big Vito don't come around here pushin' protection, whatever. This is the result of *one* word from Mr. Vincent DiGangi. *(Pats* JOEY*'s hand.)* Very heavy ticket there, kid, you don't want to use it unless the straits is completely dire. *(Slaps bar.)* O.K., ya got all that?

JOEY: *(Starting towards front door without much spirit.)* Yeah; take the first one up from the ground, jump back, and tell 'em about DiGangi if I still got a mouth left. *(As he passes stroller; softly, sighing.)* Well . . . here I go, Charlie.

CHARLIE: *(Speaking on behalf of the silent child.)* So long, Joey. Murder 'im.

*(*JOEY *stops at door; brushes off his shirt, stands up straighter, taller—then puts on his yarmulke.)*

EDDIE: What're ya doin' *that* for?

JOEY: This'll drive 'im crazy. *(Flings open door, darts off into street, racing past* HANNAH DI BLINDEH *and* NICK, *a matching pair of ragged, aging alcoholics who have been standing in the threshold; they are early-morning drinkers who have clearly been waiting at the door for the bar to open, anxious for their first shot of the day. We hear* JOEY*'s voice as he races down the street.)* They're here, Pop.

EDDIE: *(Looks up.)* Ah . . . Fred and Ginger. *(Checks pocket watch.)* Eight o'clock; on the button. Dance right in, kids.

CHARLIE: *(Gradually remembering, as they enter.)* Jesus, it's *them* . . . Of course, of *course* . . . no day could begin without them . . .

*(*HANNAH, *near sixty, Russian, and obviously sightless, wears faded, oddly elegant, overly mended clothing that may have been fashionable thirty years earlier.* NICK*'s bushy white beard and matted hair make it hard to read his age, anywhere between early fifties and late sixties depending on the time of day; he has a soiled, ill-fitting suit and shirt, what had once been a tie, a noticeably red nose, and a clear case of the pre-first-drink shakes. During the minute or so of*

CHARLIE*'s next speech,* HANNAH, NICK, *and* EDDIE *will go through the very specific steps of their morning ritual. Before they reach their assigned bar stools,* EDDIE *will have dropped a piece of lemon peel into a stemmed glass, filled it halfway with cold vodka and placed it in front of one stool, then snapped a neat row of three shot glasses down in front of the other, briskly filling each with straight bourbon. With due courtliness,* NICK *will escort* HANNAH *to the bar, pull out her stool for her, not sit till she is seated; then she will finish her vodka in three separate delicate sips, saying "Lomir lebn un lachn" before each, while in exactly the same tempo,* NICK *says "You bet" in response to each of her toasts and downs his row of bourbon shots, his shakes vanishing with the contents of the third glass,* HANNAH *finally sighing "Nit do gedacht" as she sets her empty glass down to end the first round; all this beginning and ending with the following speech,* CHARLIE *thoughtful, remembering, as he talks to us.)*

CHARLIE: Hannah . . . Hannah Di Blindeh—meaning Hannah The Blind One; I used to think Di Blindeh was her last name—and Nick; I didn't know his last name, a problem he often shared with me till his third shot of bourbon—

HANNAH: Lomir lebn un lachn—

NICK: You bet—

CHARLIE: Called "Nick" because, by his *sixth* shot, he believed—or would like *you* to believe, I was never sure which—that he was, in fact, Santa Claus; you can see the resemblance. In any case, this was an identity preferable to that of forcibly retired police sergeant; it seems that, in celebration of Repeal Day, Nick had managed to shoot out all the street lamps in front of the Twenty-second Precinct. He carried this famous Smith and Wesson with him every day to Pop's bar, which allowed them *both* to think of him as a kind of guard-bouncer for the place—God knows if he could still *aim* the damn thing, but Pop loved the street-lamp story and never charged him for a drink. Pop never charged Hannah for a drink either—

HANNAH: Lomir lebn un lachn—

CHARLIE: That's "May we live and laugh."

NICK: You bet—

CHARLIE: She'd been blinded somehow on the second day of the October Pogrom; Hannah didn't remember what she saw that second day, but what she heard still woke her up every morning like an alarm clock—

HANNAH: Lomir lebn un lachn—

CHARLIE: The noise didn't go away till she finished her first vodka.

HANNAH: *(Sets her glass down.)* Nit do gedacht.

CHARLIE: "May it never happen here."

NICK: *(Sets down his third shot glass.)* You bet.

HANNAH: *(Same Russian accent as* GUSTA, *as she "looks" about.)* Something different here, Itzik. I got a feeling . . . no more "Frisco Eddie's."

EDDIE: Right; I love ya, Hannah—it took *you* to notice.

HANNAH: "Frisco Eddie's"—gone. This includes the Chuck-a-luck wheel, Eddie?

NICK: Yeah, he's got a kinda . . . museum here now.

HANNAH: A shame; I *liked* that Chuck-a-luck wheel. But a museum, that's unusual. This could be something. The child, Eddie; he speaks yet?

EDDIE: Well, fact is—

HANNAH: *(Fondly.)* Vet meshiach geboyrn vern mit a tog shpeter.

CHARLIE: "So the Messiah will be born a day later."

NICK: You bet.

HANNAH: Gentlemen—today's Number: I am considering seriously, at this time, betting Number Seven-Seven-Six; this in honor of Our Founding Fathers. Comments, please.

NICK: Seven-Seven-Six it *is;* a fine thought, Hannah.

HANNAH: Next, we make the horse selections. You have brought the sheet, Nick?

NICK: *(Takes Racing Form from pocket.)* At the ready, darlin'.

HANNAH: Excellent. *(As* NICK *escorts her to their table.)* Until such day, which is likely never, they make a Braille Racing Form, you and me is buddies, Nick.

NICK: Longer than that, sweetheart, longer than that . . .

*(*FINNEY THE BOOK *suddenly bursts into the room—a tight, tiny bundle of forty-five-year-old Irish nerves under a battered Fedora, he heads straight for his special upstage booth near the wall phone. Usually anxious, depressed and fidgety, he seems in particularly bad shape today; the sound of nineteen-thirties Irish New York and the look of Greek tragedy.)*

EDDIE: Hey, Finney!

NICK: Mornin', Finn'.

CHARLIE: *(Fondly, as* FINNEY *enters booth.)* Ah, Finney . . . our Bookmaker In Residence; Finney The Book arrives at his office, ready to take bets on the Daily Number, and an occasional horse—early today but tragic as ever, having given up on the Irish Rebellion twenty years ago for a cause with even worse odds . . .

FINNEY: *(Slumps in booth.)* Oh, me friends . . . me friends . . . Nick, Eddie, Hannah . . . truly the Tsouris is on me this day!

HANNAH: Finney, darling . . . what *is* it?

FINNEY: What is it? What *is* it, y' say? It's the bloody July *Fourth,* is what it is! Every bloody Greenhorn from here to the river bettin' Seven-Seven-Six, every bloody Guinea, Mick, Jew and China-boy bettin' the Independence! *(Rising solemnly in his booth.)* "Finney, Finney," I say to m'self the dawn of every Fourth. "Finney, m'boy, stay in your *bed* this cursed and twisted day!"—and *fool* that I am, *ob*liged as I am t'me regulars, I hit the bloody *street*! It's me damned code of *honor* does me in! *(Shoves his hands deep into the pockets of his baggy suit jacket—we hear now the jingle and rustle of hundreds of quarters in one and hundreds of singles in the other.)* Four *hundred*—four hundred *easy* on Seven-Seven-Six and the mornin' still new yet! Seven-Seven-Six comes in, me entire Mishpocheh's eatin' *toast* for a year! *(Suddenly aware of the dozens of American flags about him.)* And what have ya got *here,* Eddie, me bloody *funeral* arrangements?! My God, man, the only thing missin's a bloody fife and drum to march me to me grave!

NICK: *(Pointing to phone.)* Well, you'd best start layin' off some bets then, Thomas—

FINNEY: Every damn Book in the *city's* tryin' to lay off the same bloody number, boy! Tom Finney, what's to *become* of ya? Finney, Finney . . . *(Suddenly turns to* EDDIE.*)* And while we're on it, Edward—even I do survive this day—I can't be givin' ya no more twenty for the use o' me booth; it's ten at best, here on.

EDDIE: What *is* this, *lep*rechaun humor? *(To* HANNAH *and* NICK.*)* Man's kiddin' me, right?—his own booth, his own personal *booth* nine till post time, *choice* location—

FINNEY: Edward, Edward, all me fondness, ya know damn

well I'm bringin' in more pony-people who drink than you're bringin' in drinkers who'll wager— *(Indicates stroller.)* Eight-to-one the boy don't say a word till Christmas. *(Heads briskly to phone.)*

EDDIE: The new *place,* I'm *tellin'* ya, it's all gonna turn around—

FINNEY: *(Grabs phone.)* Better start layin' off now or I'm surely gornisht in the mornin'. *(Dialing anxiously.)* Home of the bloody *brave* . . .

HANNAH: *(Handing quarter out towards him.)* Finney, darling; twenty-five cents on number Seven-Seven-Seven. May you live and be well.

FINNEY: *(Takes coin.)* Blessin's on ya— *(Into phone.)* Ah, now, is that me sweet Bernie there, the Saint Bernard himself? Finney here, and wonderin' would you care to take two hundred on— *(To the dead phone in his hand.)* Star-Spangled bloody Banner . . . *(Dialing again.)* Finney, Finney, you're sendin' an S.O.S. to a fleet o' sinkin' ships . . .

(He will continue, quietly, to call several more "Banks" through this next scene; the following dialogue between NICK *and* HANNAH *will happen at the same time as his call to Bernie.)*

NICK: *(Opens Racing Form.)* Where ya want to start: Belmont, Thistledown, Arlington Park . . . ?

HANNAH: I say Thistledown; why not?

NICK: Thistledown it *is* then. O.K., first race we got Dancin' Lady, four-year-old filly, Harvest Moon by Wild Time, carryin' one fifteen . . .

(They will continue, quietly and with great concentration, to pick horses for the next several minutes—both FINNEY*'s call to Bernie and their above dialogue happening at the same time as the entrance of two new customers:* BLUE, *followed a few moments later by* JIMMY SCALSO. BLUE *is large, Irish, about fifty, slow-moving, powerful, seeming at all times vaguely amused either by something that happened some time ago or something that might happen soon.)*

BLUE: *(Taps bar.)* You got Johnnie Red?

EDDIE: *(Pouring drink.)* Like the choice, *I* got it— *(Snaps it on bar.)* Now *you* got it.

*(*JIMMY SCALSO *enters a few moments later, sleekly Italian, just thirty, wiry, a smiler, wearing the kind of carefully tailored silk suit that demands a silver crucifix on a chain about his neck; he speaks and moves rapidly and surely but is still somehow auditioning for a role he hasn't gotten yet.* SCALSO *steps jauntily up to the bar, sits on a stool near* NICK *and* HANNAH; BLUE *takes his drink to a distant table, opens his newspaper.)*

SCALSO: You got Daitch on tap, fellah?

EDDIE: I got it; like the choice. *(Working tap spigot.) I* got it— *(Places full mug on bar.)* Now *you* got it.

SCALSO: New place, huh? I see the sign outside, "Opening Day." *(*EDDIE *nods pleasantly.)* I like the feel. Lotta wood; none of that chrome shit, shiny shit. And the lights: not dark, just . . . soft; like it's always, what? Evening here. *(Pause; sips his beer.)* So here we are, the *both* of us, huh?—workin' on a holiday. Ain't been on a vacation, when?—three, no four, *four* years ago. Four years ago, February. I take the wife and the kid to Miami. O.K., sand, sun, surf; *one* day, it's *over* for me, enough. I'm the kinda guy—

NICK: *(To* SCALSO, *quietly.)* Do you know who I am?

SCALSO: *(Ignoring him like the barfly he is.)* —kinda guy I am, I don't get the *point* of a vacation. You go, you come back, there you *are* again. I'm the kinda guy, I gotta be movin', workin'.

HANNAH: Give him a hint, Nick.

NICK: I give you a hint, "Ho, ho, ho."

SCALSO: They say, what?—"don't mix business with pleasure," right? Well, business *is* my pleasure, what can I tell ya? Second day in Miami, second *day,* I'm goin' crazy, I wanna get *outa* there.

NICK: *(Speaking confidentially, to* SCALSO.*)* You better watch out . . . you better not cry; better not pout, I'm tellin' you why . . .

SCALSO: Here in town, I'm up, a cup of coffee, a little juice, I'm outa the house—I can't *wait* to go to work. Saturday, *Sun*day, I don't *give* a shit. The wife says to me, "Jimmy, Sunday, we'll go to the park; you, me, the kid, we row a boat." I says to her, "Baby, I hate that shit, I'm *not* that kinda *guy.*" She says—

EDDIE: *(Leans towards him, quietly.)* Would you do something for me?

SCALSO: What?

EDDIE: Shut the hell up.

SCALSO: Huh?

EDDIE: Shut your goddamn face. Zip it up. Can it. Button the ruby-reds. Silencio. Got it?

SCALSO: Hey, Mister, what the hell kinda—?

EDDIE: You're boring. I can't stand it. It's killin' me. That moose up there, he's dead, it don't bother him. Me, while you're talkin' I got individual brain cells up here dyin' one at a time. Two minutes with you, I'm sayin' Kaddish for my brain. Shut up and drink your beer.

NICK: *(Confidentially, to* SCALSO.*)* I'm makin' a list . . . and checkin' it twice, gonna find out who's naughty and nice . . .

SCALSO: How come ya got a guy here half off his *nut*, and *I'm* the one ya—?

EDDIE: Because who he *thinks* he is is a hundred times more interestin' than who you *are*. You ain't just borin', buddy, you're a goddamn *pioneer* in the field.

SCALSO: Hey, I come in here for a beer, a little conversation, I don't expect a guy to—

EDDIE: You think the price of a beer you own *one minute* of my time? *(Leans close to him; calmly.)* O.K., I got two things I want ya to do for me. The first thing I want ya to do is go away, and the next thing I want ya to do is never come back. That's two things; can ya remember that?

SCALSO: *(Slaps bar.)* Place is open to the public, I got a right to sit here and drink my beer. Who you *oughta* be throwin' out is these two *drunks* here—

EDDIE: I got a private club here, pal. I got my own rules. You just had a free beer; good-bye.

SCALSO: This ain't no private club.

EDDIE: *(Indicating bar room.)* Right, this ain't no private club; but this— *(Takes billy club out from under bar; grips it firmly.)* this is a private club. It's called the Billy Club. Billy is the president. He wants you to leave.

*(*HANNAH *raises her head, listening;* BLUE *looks up from his newspaper;* FINNEY *turns from the phone, watching, tensely twisting his hat.)*

SCALSO: *(After a moment.)* Ya mean you're willin' to beat the shit outa some guy just because ya think he's *borin'*?
EDDIE: *(Taps the club.)* Right; self-*defense,* pal.

*(*SCALSO *suddenly starts to laugh, slapping the bar, enjoying himself.)*

BLUE: *(Puts his drink down.)* Come on, Jimmy; tell him, we got a long day comin'.
SCALSO: Hey, Blue, Blue, I like this guy, I like this guy . . . *I like this guy! (Still laughing;* EDDIE *regarding him stonily, tightening grip on club.)* You are *great,* Goldberg . . . you are *some*thin', baby . . . "A private *club,* the *Billy* Club" . . . great, great . . .
BLUE: *(Rising from table, impatient with him.)* Enough now; we gotta alotta *work* here, boy.
SCALSO: *(Still chuckling.)* Absolutely right, babe. Goldberg . . . Goldberg, Goldberg, *Goldberg;* you are cute, you are some cute Jew, you are the cutest Jew I ever saw. And tough; I never seen such a tough Jew, I include the Williamsburg Boys. *(*EDDIE, *his club at the ready, waiting him out.)* I'm Jimmy Scalso; maybe you don't hear, various internal problems, Vito had an appointment with the Hudson River, which he kept, Seranno gimme alla his Stops; bye-bye, Big Vito—bonjour, Jimmy. *(*EDDIE, *absorbing this, lowers club to his side.)* Y'know, I seen ya box, barkeep, Stauch's Arena, I'm sixteen—hey, Blue, this was *some*thin', The East Side Savage against Ah Soong, The Fightin' Chinaman—
BLUE: Move it along, boy; move it *along,* will ya?
SCALSO: Absolutely right, babe. O.K., business, Goldberg; Vito's got fifty-four Stops, fifty-three is solid—some reason he lets one of 'em slide; yours. I'm checkin' the books, ya got no cigarette machine here, ya don't got our *Defense* System, you got a Box should be doin' two and a half a month, you're doin' seventy. *Our* records, selected *hits, thirty* top tunes a month—you take only *two. (Points to jukebox.)* Blue, what's he *got* on there? *(Slaps himself on the head.)* Shit, where's my goddamn *manners*—Mr. Goldberg, this is Blue, for Blue-Jaw McCann; called such because the man could shave five times a day, he's still got a jaw turns gun-metal blue by evenin', same

color as the fine weapon he carries. A man, in his prime, done hench for Amato, Scalisi, Carafano . . .

*(*SCALSO *pauses a moment, letting this sink in.* EDDIE *puts his club down on the bar.* SCALSO *nods, acknowledging* EDDIE*'s good sense.)*

BLUE: *(Checking the jukebox.)* All right, he's got eight here by a fella, Leba—Leba—
HANNAH: *Lebedeff.* Aaron Lebedeff, the Maurice Che*valier* of the Jewish stage—
BLUE: Then there's a couple, a fella, Zatz, half-a-dozen Eddie Cantor, somebody Ukelele Ike, Jolson, Kate Smith, The U.S. Army Band, Irish Eyes—
SCALSO: *(His head in his hands.)* Stop, stop, stop, *night*mare, it's a *night*mare! Somebody *wake* me, I'm *dreamin'*! Goldberg, Goldberg, you're takin' the joie outa my goddamn *vie* here! *(Looks up mournfully, shouting.)* Whatta ya think ya *got* here, Goldberg, a *Victrola*? This is a *Box,* this is *our* goddamn *Box* here, *income, income.* Weird foreign shit, hundred-year-old *losers,* and mosta the plays is your own *slugs*! Where's the *hits,* where's— *(Stops himself; quietly.)* O.K., everybody calm down. A new day, a new dollar, right? *(Pacing, to* BLUE.*)* No Butts, no Defense, shit on the Box; Vito musta been crazy . . .
FINNEY: *(Whispering.)* Tell him, Eddie; DiGangi . . .
EDDIE: *(Whispering, sharply.)* Shut up.
SCALSO: *(Pleasantly, a man bestowing gifts.)* O.K., new deal, we start fresh—my true belief; everybody's happy. Goldberg, item one, comes tomorrow, A.M., cigarette machine—fifty-fifty split; Butts come certain sources, the price is hilarious. Item two: Angelo Defense System—I hear ya screamin': "Protection racket, ugly Italian behavior, get me outa here!" *(Softly, almost misty-eyed.)* My reply: au *contraire,* my darlin' Hebrew, a Wop and a Yid is one heart beatin' here. "Angelo Defense System": meanin' defense against every greasy hand wants *in* your satchel! The cops *alone,* whatta ya pay Christmas? Also Inspectors: Fire, Garbage, whatever—the Angel flies in. Figure what you save, one monthly shot to the Angel; words fail. *(Crossing up to jukebox.)* The Box; tomorrow, A.M., my people come, *out* goes the goddamn funeral music, the Memory Lane Losers, the Hollerin'

Hebes—*in* comes forty selected hits; once-a-week collection. Finney here, business as usual; already under the wing, a Defense System who I'm affiliated. *Finale:* same split like Vito on the Box, *plus* you got a one G advance from me on your end, good will, get acquainted, my pocket to yours, this very day. *(Strides back down to bar, takes neatly folded wad of hundreds from jacket, places it on bar in front of the silent* EDDIE, *sits on stool opposite him; then flatly, evenly.)* Now, some banana-nut reason, this deal don't appeal; need I mention, things happen. The Angel come down, fly away with the Liquor License, twenty, thirty days, outa business. Things break, toilets don't work, beer deliveries slow down— *(Suddenly smacks himself on the forehead.)* What the hell am I talkin'!? I gotta tell The East Side Savage birds-and-bees basics? You know the story. Gimme the Brocheh, baby; we go in peace. Whatta ya say?

(Silence; he waits for EDDIE*'s answer as does everyone else in the barroom. A thoughtful moment, then* EDDIE *picks up the wad of bills.)*

EDDIE: *(Turns to* HANNAH, *quietly.)* Hannah, how about you take Charlie into the kitchen, give him a little something to eat. Brisket's on your right, some Lokshen on the left. *(*HANNAH, *with some help from* NICK, *wheels the stroller into the kitchen and exits as* EDDIE *turns to* SCALSO, *continuing pleasantly.)* Fact of the matter, you first come in here, I figure you are definitely not with the Salvation Army; and this guy here, the bulge in the right jacket pocket is probably not his Holy Bible, I say to myself. *(*BLUE *chuckles softly,* SCALSO *smiles.)* I do *not* know you are a Seranno boy, got alla Vito's Stops now. *(He shrugs apologetically.)* Not knowin' this, I do the club thing for ya, kinda demonstrate my attitude and feelings how I run my place. *(A beat; then he tosses the wad of bills into* SCALSO*'s lap.)* Which remains the exact same. You're boring me to death, Ginzo. *(Continues calmly.)* I want your nose and your ass, and everything you got in between, *outa* my business. I don't want your cigarette machine, your records, your advice, and I want your goddamn Angel off my shoulder. I give you the same deal I give Vito on the Box, and that's *it.* And now I want you and your over-the-hill hench outa my joint instantaneous. Good-bye and good luck. *(He picks up the club, raps it sharply on the bar like a gavel.)* Conversation over; end of conversation.

*(*SCALSO *remains quite still,* BLUE *takes a small step forward from the jukebox,* CHARLIE *rises tensely in his booth,* FINNEY *is wringing his fedora like a wet bathing suit.)*

HANNAH'S VOICE: *(Softly, from Kitchen.)* Pogrom . . . pogrom . . . pogrom . . .

SCALSO: *(Points to his silver crucifix; quietly.)* This here J.C., my Pop give it to me; remind me of Our Savior, but mostly, he says, to do things peaceful before I do 'em hard; this has been my approach with you here. But you know what comes to me, I listen to you? Sooner or later, tough or chicken, lucky, unlucky, Jews is Jews. Ain't this the way, Blue? Ain't this the way? Goddamn *guests* in this country, they are—they're here ten minutes, they're tellin' ya how to *run* the place . . . *(He puts his hand on* EDDIE'*s arm.)* I pride myself, makin' friends with you Jews—but sooner or later, every *one* of ya—

*(*EDDIE *reaches forward, gets a firm grip on* SCALSO'*s crucifix and chain and pulls him across the bar with it, holding him firmly down on the bar.)*

EDDIE: You was holdin' my arm . . .

SCALSO: *(Struggling.)* Hey, my J.C., my J.C.—

EDDIE: You know us Jews, we can't keep our hands off the guy.

SCALSO: *Blue, Blue . . .*

*(*BLUE *thrusts his hand into his gun pocket,* NICK *turns to him;* FINNEY *races up stairs, hovering in apartment doorway.)*

EDDIE: *(Retaining firm grip on* SCALSO.*)* Here's the situation: Mr. Blue, whatever you got in mind right now, a fact for ya: Nick here, an ex-cop, got two friends with him, Mr. Smith and Mr. Wesson; there's some say his aim ain't what it used to be, but a target your size he's bound to put a hole in it somewheres; 'sides which, he don't care if he kills ya, he thinks Donder an' Blitzen gonna take the rap for him anyway. *(Lets go of* SCALSO, *holds his billy club high in the air; all in the room frozen.)* Scalso, any part of you makes a move on me, I bust it with Billy. This is the situation, both of ya. Stay and make a move; or go. *(Moving up to jukebox, watching them carefully.)* Meantime, while you're makin' up your mind, I got a need to hear one o' those Hollerin' Hebes; gonna play one of my records on my Box here . . . *(Quickly deposits slug, makes selection; turns to face them, his club at the ready.)* My personal suggestion, we go for a safe and sane Fourth.

*(*EDDIE*'s eyes dart from* SCALSO *to* BLUE, FINNEY *grips the edge of the apartment doorway;* BLUE, *his hand firmly in his gun pocket, looks over at* NICK, *sizing him up.* NICK, *still standing at the far end of the bar, slips his hand into the holster under his jacket, holds it there.)*

NICK: *(Quietly, to* BLUE.*)* I see you when you're sleepin', I know when you're awake; I know if you've been bad or good, so be good for goodness sake . . .

FINNEY: *(Whispering urgently to* EDDIE.*)* Just tell 'em about DiGangi; we stop all this, Eddie—

EDDIE: *(Quietly.)* Don't need him, I got it under control. This is *mine.*

(Suddenly, from the jukebox, we begin to hear Aaron Lebedeff's rousing rendition of "In Odessa" and its irresistibly danceable klezmer band backup; Lebedeff sings a dream of the old Moldavanka, inviting us to return to a world of swirling skirts, endless dancing, grand times till dawn in the shoreline cafés of the Black Sea and, of course, the food that was served there. NICK, SCALSO, FINNEY, BLUE, *and* CHARLIE *remaining quite still, the pulsing beat of the klezmer band filling the silence of this tense moment,* EDDIE *starting to snap the fingers of his left hand to the beat, the billy club still held high in his right, Music continuing to build through the scene.)*

LEDEDEFF'S VOICE:

"In Ades, in Ades, af der Moldavanke,
Tantst men dort a Palanez, mit a sheyn tsiganke . . ."

*(*SCALSO *rises suddenly from his bar stool, going to center of room, forceful, commanding, on top of it again.)*

SCALSO: *(Shouting, pointing fiercely at* EDDIE.*)* The man *marked* me, Blue; he put a *mark* on me! *(*BLUE *takes a step forward;* SCALSO *clenches his fists, ready to spring.)* O.K., school's in *session* now, barkeep; *lesson* time; Professor Blue and me, we gonna *teach* you something . . .
JOEY'S VOICE: *(Shouting, from street.)* Pop! Hey, *Pop*!

*(*ZARETSKY *suddenly bursts through the front door, his arm around a somewhat battered, bloody-nosed, but very proud* JOEY. *A man who knows how to make an entrance,* ZARETSKY *speaks immediately as he comes through the door, using the threshold as his stage; the* GROUP *remains frozen.)*

ZARETSKY: No, not since David and Goliath have I seen such! Yes, the child bleeds, but wait till you see what this *DeSapio* looks like—
JOEY: He went *down*, Pop, he went *down*— *(Indicating his bloody nose.)* I mean, later, he got *up*, but there was—
ZARETSKY: Please, Jussel, allow me—I come upon this child, familiar to me at a distance; opposing him, I tell you, a veritable *Visigoth* of a boy, he— *(His voice trails off; he becomes aware of the stillness in the room.)* I feel that I do not have the full attention of this group.
EDDIE: *(Quickly, quietly.)* Congratulations, kid. Go to Sussman's, pick up the bread order. Now.
JOEY: Pop, I gotta tell ya—
EDDIE: *Sussman's. Now.*
JOEY: Christ's sake, Pop—
EDDIE: *Now!*
JOEY: *(As he reluctantly exits.)* Christ's sake . . .

*(*ZARETSKY *sees the billy club in* EDDIE*'s hand, glances at the unfamiliar figures of* SCALSO *and* BLUE; EDDIE *remaining quite still, snapping his fingers as the music continues, swaying slightly to the beat.)*

EDDIE: Anton, we got a situation here.
SCALSO: *(Grips* BLUE*'s arm, urgently.)* Now, Blue, *now;* place is fillin' up. Look, Blue, man wants to dance; help

him dance, Blue—the feet, go for the feet. I want to see the man *dance,* make him dance, make him *nervous* . . .

BLUE: *(After a moment; his eyes fixed on* EDDIE.*)* Nervous? You ain't gonna make *this* boy nervous. This boy don't *get* nervous; which is what's gonna kill him one fine day. *(Pulls his empty hand sharply out of his gun pocket, his gaze never leaving* NICK *and* EDDIE.*)* Now *today,* Jimmy, here's how the cards lay down: what you got here is an ol' shithouse and a crazy Jew. Two and a half on this Box, boy? You give this Jew Bing Crosby in person, you give him Guy Lombardo appearin' nightly, he don't pull in more'n a hundred. Now, tell me, Jimmy-Boy, you want me to go shoot Santa Claus for a hundred-dollar Box?

SCALSO: *(Urgently, commanding.)* We gotta leave a *mark,* Blue, on *some*body, on *some*thing. Fifty-four Stops, this news travels; there gotta be *consequences* here, Blue, things *happened* here—

BLUE: *Consequences?* This Jew don't know consequences and don't care. Look at his eyes, Jimmy. He just wants to kill you, boy; don't care if he dies the next minute, and don't care who dies with him. Make it a rule, Jimmy-Boy, you don't want to get into a fight, weapon or no, with a man ain't lookin' to live. *(He turns, walks briskly towards front door.)*

SCALSO: *(Not moving, rubbing neck-burn.)* Things *happened* here, Blue—

BLUE: Seranno ain't gonna give a cobbler's crap about this place—fifty-three Stops to *cover,* Jimmy-Boy, let's go.

SCALSO: *(Silence for a moment; then, striding angrily towards* BLUE.*)* Hey, *hey*—how about you leave off callin' me "Jimmy-Boy," huh? How about we quit that shit, right?

BLUE: *(Patting* SCALSO*'s shoulder.)* In the old Saint Pat's, y'know, over on Prince, we used t'make you Guineas have mass in the basement. Biggest mistake we ever made was lettin' you boys up on the first floor. *(He exits.* SCALSO *remains in doorway, turns towards* EDDIE.*)*

SCALSO: *(Pointing, fiercely.)* O.K., now here's somethin' for *you* and *Billy* and the entire fuckin' *club*—

(But the Lebedeff music has built to an irresistible Freylekeh rhythm—irresistible, that is, to any triumphant Jew in the room—and Eddie, holding the billy club over his

head with both hands, begins to spin around the center table to the beat.)

EDDIE: Hey, Jimmy-Boy, you wanted to see the man dance ... he's dancin' ... *(Takes his handkerchief out of his pocket, extends it towards* ZARETSKY, *a gesture of invitation as old as the music he dances to.)* Hey, Actor, Actor ... come, come, this Ginzo loves dancin' ...

*(*ZARETSKY *joins* EDDIE *in perhaps the only thing they can ever agree upon, the pleasure of dancing to an old Lebedeff tune;* ZARETSKY *takes the other end of the handkerchief and, the handkerchief held taut between them over their heads, they dance aggressively towards* SCALSO, *their feet stomping to the beat,* SCALSO *backing away towards the door.* JOEY *suddenly bursts through the door just behind* SCALSO, *shouting at his back.)*

JOEY: DiGangi! DiGangi è mio fratello! Chiamalo! Chiamalo!

SCALSO: *(Surrounded by two dancing Jews and a screaming child; he shouts.)* Buncha crazy Hebes here ... !

*(*SCALSO *exits into the street.* ZARETSKY *and* EDDIE *triumphant,* ZARETSKY *swirling to the music,* EDDIE *beating out the rhythm fiercely with his club,* FINNEY *and* NICK *clapping to the beat,* JOEY*'s arms in the air, shouting.)*

JOEY: It *works,* Pop! The Di*Gangi* number; it works! It works!

EDDIE: Of *course* it works!

JOEY: *(Proudly.) Comes* to me, Pop, comes to me these guys don't *look* right, see—

EDDIE: Nobody messes with the Ross boys!

JOEY: Who?

EDDIE: Ross! Ross! Joey *Ross*—the kid who beat DeSapio!

JOEY: But I didn't *win,* Pop—

EDDIE: *(Prowling the room with his club, his tension unreleased by* SCALSO's *defeat.): Sure* you won, kid, we only got winners here, *winners ...*

ZARETSKY: *(Points challenging finger.)* So then, Itzik, I have seen you rise from your knees—something of your spirit has been touched today!

EDDIE: *(Fiercely.)* Only thing got touched was my goddamn *arm,* Actor.

HANNAH: *(Leaning out of kitchen.)* So, the coast, I am assuming, is clear?

EDDIE: Everything under control here, babe.

HANNAH: *(Standing in kitchen doorway.)* Gentlemen . . . I got big news . . .

ZARETSKY: What, Hannah?

HANNAH: Gentlemen . . . *the child has spoken!*

(The GROUP *cheers, but* EDDIE *cuts sharply through them.)*

EDDIE: *What?* What did he say . . . ?

(All fix on HANNAH *expectantly as* NICK *guides her down into the room.)*

HANNAH: Two statements, clear like a bell. The first, very nice, he touches my hand, he says, "Papa." *(All but* EDDIE *responding happily; he remains silent, quite still.)* The second statement, a little embarrassing to repeat . . .

EDDIE: *What,* Hannah . . . ?

HANNAH: A couple seconds later, he's got my hand again, this time a firm grip, he says—clear like a bell, I tell you—"No shit from nobody!"

*(*ZARETSKY *applauds lustily, shouting "Bravo,"* NICK *and* FINNEY *cheer loudly, waving their hats,* JOEY *leaps joyously in the air yelling "Hey, Champ";* EDDIE *remains silent, striding sharply away from the cheering* GROUP, *his club held tight in his fist.)*

EDDIE: *(Shouting, fiercely, above the* GROUP.*)* And no *exceptions . . . ! (Raising club violently over his head.)* No *exceptions . . .* no*body . . . ! (Smashing club down on center table) nobody . . . !*

(The GROUP *turns to him, startled, quite still, as* EDDIE *continues, out of control now, wildly, striking a chair, another table, killing them like Cossacks, shouting with each blow.)*

EDDIE: *. . . nobody . . . nobody . . . (Striking* CHARLIE*'s booth,* CHARLIE *rising to his feet, riveted.) Nobody! . . . (*EDDIE *freezes with this last shout, his club held high in the air, ready to strike another blow as . . .)*

THE CURTAIN FALLS

ACT II

Before the curtain rises we hear a full chorus and marching band moving up into a thunderous, rousing, next-to-last stanza of "Columbia, the Gem of the Ocean."

CHORUS:
"Three cheers for the red, white and blue,
Three cheers for the red, white and blue,
The Army and Navy forever,
Three cheers for the red, white and blue . . ."

At Rise: The blaring trumpets rise in pitch to herald the final stanza as the curtain goes up. CHARLIE *alone in the darkened bar—the dim, early evening light of the Present—seated exactly where he was at the beginning of the play, at the far end of the bar near the glowing jukebox, listening thoughtfully to the triumphant conclusion of the music to which* EDDIE *first burst into the room.*

CHORUS:
"Three cheers for the red, white and blue,
Three cheers for the red, white and blue,
Thy banners make tyranny tremble,
Three cheers for the red, white and blue . . ."

A cymbal-crashing, drum-rolling finale; CHARLIE *continues to look into the colors of the now silent jukebox for a moment or two, then turns to us.*

CHARLIE *(Indicating moose.)* Well—as Morris will tell you—the Golden Door Tavern did *not* get us Uptown; nor did Eddie Ross's Silver Horseshoe, the Empire State

Sports Club, or even Ed Ross's Riverview, motly because we didn't have one. *(Inserting slug in jukebox, making selection.)* But then came the summer of forty-four, the heyday of Café Society and, of course, its pulsating heart—Sherman Billingsley's Stork Club. *(With a sweeping gesture towards bar.)* Eddie's response was swift and glorious: Ladies and Gentleman, July Third, Nineteen Forty-four . . . the Opening Day of the Flamingo Lounge.

(A huge pink and crimson plaster-and-glass chandelier in the shape of a flamingo in flight—its spread wings, thrust-back legs and proudly arched head framed by several dozen glowing pink light bulbs—descends through the ceiling over the bar as we begin to hear the catchy bongo and trumpet calypso intro to the Andrews Sisters' recording of "Rum and Coca-Cola" coming from the jukebox.)

ANDREWS SISTERS:
"Out on Mandenella Beach,
G.I. romance with native peach,
All day long make tropic love,
Next day sit in hot sun and cool off, drinkin'—
Rum and Coca-Cola . . ."

(Music continuing, building, as lights come up full; it's exactly eight years later, about seven a.m. on Monday, July 3, 1944, and we see that the barroom has gone through a transition from general Early American to general Tropical Caribbean, the dominant theme, as always, being Gin-Mill Shabby. The Early American stuff remains but joining it now are coconut shell candle holders and plastic pineapples on each table, crepe paper leis hung about on hooks, an incandescent tropical sunset painting over the jukebox, brightly illustrated placards announcing various rum-punch drinks and their "Reasonable Introductory Prices" tacked up on the walls, running across the bottom of the mirror a red and white banner reading "Welcome to the Flamingo! Opening Day!" and over the door a painting of a flamingo with just the word "Lounge" under it. Eddie's usual Fourth of July bunting across the top of the mirror and small flags along the bar are in evidence, though the flags have not yet been put on the tables and booths. In addition, it is the summer of the Fifth Annual "Miss Daitch" Contest and a string of

six small posters, featuring a smiling head-shot and brief bio of each contestant, hangs across the right wall just above the booths; beneath these a bright banner states the Daitch Beer slogan; "There Is *a Difference and the Difference Is Daitch"; below that: "Vote Here for Miss Daitch, 1944," and next to the far right booth a ballot box and a stack of ballots. All this revealed as the music and* CHARLIE *continue.)*

CHARLIE: And tonight . . . the Victory Party, in honor of what we're all sure will be Joey's twenty-eighth straight win since he got his Amateur Card . . . *(As* JOEY, *almost eighteen now, enters from the kitchen with a tray of plastic pineapples, places them on tables, his boxer's authority and the tiptoe bounce of his walk distinctly similar to his father's.)* . . . twenty-three knockouts, six in the first three rounds, and four decisions. Got his A.A.U. card at fourteen—two years before the legal age—by using Vince DiGangi's son Peter's baptism certificate, so he's earned a very big reputation over the last four years for somebody called Pistol Pete DiGangi. *(*JOEY *turns, heading up to bar, the back of his jacket emblazoned with a "Pistol Pete" logo.)* I, of course, was known as the only kid ever to be knocked down by Cock-Eye Celestini—he being several years my junior, an infant really, and visually disabled—

EDDIE: *(Bursts in from the kitchen, delighted, waving a folded newspaper.)* Hey, ya see the ad in the *Mirror* this morning?—ya see that?—top of the *Card* tonight, Joey, top of the *Card.* "Bazooka-Boy" Kilbane, *no*body—goddamn *Main Event* even *with* this Mick bozo! This is because ya made a goddamn *name* for yourself, kid! *(He moves over to* JOEY, *the two sparring, jabbing, ducking, weaving about amid the tables now, clearly a morning ritual, as* EDDIE *continues.)* Let me tell ya about Kilbane's weak spot—his *body;* his entire body. Tonight's *pointer*? Bring some stamps with ya and *mail* the putz home! *(Indicates radio as their sparring continues.) Broad*cast—broadcast over the goddamn *air*waves tonight, Speed Spector him*self* doin' the blow-by-blow; *Spector.* Closin' the place up soon as the fights start, nobody in here unless by special invite; victory party, champagne, the works. I'd be at ringside, per usual, but I gotta hear this comin' outa the *Philco,* kid, I *gotta.* After, Spector always does an On-the-Spot with the Main Event Winner; gotta *hear* it, right? *(As their sparring ends,* EDDIE*—clearly outboxed and happily exhausted by* JOEY*—returning to set up bar.)* By the way, durin' the On-the-Spot, ya wanna drop a mention there's a new class place openin' on Canal, the Flamingo Lounge, this is optional— *(Suddenly slaps his head.)* Will you shut ya *trap,* Eddie?! This is *your* night, kid—don't *mention* me—what the hell am I *talkin'* about?! Would somebody *please* tell me to shut *up*?!

ZARETSKY: *(Entering from apartment.)* All right; shut up. *(Moving down to his usual table, folding back page of newspaper.)* For all assembled, I have here a certain item . . .

EDDIE: Shit, the Jew News . . .

ZARETSKY: Gentlemen, we have here on page twelve of *The New York Times,* amidst ads for Stern's Department Store and a Jewelry Consultant, an item, five sentences in length, which reports to us that four hundred thousand Hungarian Jews have thus far perished in the German death camps of Poland as of June seventeenth; and further, that three hundred and fifty thousand more are presently being deported to Poland where they are expected to be put to death by July twenty-fourth. *This* on page twelve; however— *(Turns to first page.)* we find here on the front page of this same journal, a bold headline concerning today's holiday traffic; I quote: "Rail and Bus Travel Will Set New July Fourth Peak." *(Neatly folding paper.)* I offer these items, fellow residents, for the news itself, also an insight into the ironic editorial policies of America's most prominent daily journal; owned, incidentally, by Jews.

*(*JOEY *has moved down to* ZARETSKY*'s table, clearly absorbed, as always, by* ZARETSKY*'s "Jew News.")*

JOEY: *(Quietly, studying newspaper.)* Jesus, the next three weeks . . . that's three hundred and fifty thousand in the next three *weeks* . . .

EDDIE: *(Turns sharply from his work behind the bar.)* Come on, Actor, the *truth*—what's it *say* there? That's another one o' those "Informed Sources *say,*" "Foreign Authorities *tell* us" goddamn stories, ain't it? If it's true, where's the *pictures*?! How come I never seen it in *Life* magazine?

How come I never seen it in the "March of *Time,*" they got *every*thing! *Winchell* even! How come *Roosevelt* don't mention—if F.D.R. *believed* all that he'd be doin' somethin' about it this *minute, guaranteed*!

ZARETSKY: *(Rising at his table.)* Itzik, you are a foolish tender of *bars*! *Election* year, he's *got* your vote already, he will not stir the *pot*! He will be silent, your Golden Goy. He listens, he hears the old and horrible songs—he knows that nobody believes the Jews are dying, only that somehow Jews are making millions from the war and want it. He will be quiet, Itzik, as quiet now as the Jews of page twelve!

EDDIE: *(Shouting.)* Do ya *mind,* Zaretsky? Do ya *mind* if we just let the guy go and win the goddamn *war*? Is that *O.K.* with you? The man knows what he's *doin',* pal—he does *now,* he always *did,* and he always *will.* Meanwhile, you breathe one *word* of that crazy shit durin' Joey's party and you're gonna see *my* twelve-minute version of "The Dybbuk"!

ZARETSKY: *(Slams his fist on the table.)* I *refuse*—I refuse, sir, to have a conversation of this nature with a man who has just spent the morning putting light bulbs in a huge pink bird! *(Turns to* JOEY, *suddenly pleasant, cordial; one of those instant transitions of which this old actor is very fond.)* I am off then to the home of the Widow Rosewald, who, among other favors, now repairs my robes for Lear, and kindly tolerates the aging process, both hers and mine. And, of course, my best with the Bazooka tonight. Bonne chance, Jussel, Joey, Goldberg, Ross, DiGangi—*(Patting his cheek.)* whoever you are. *(Striding to the front door.)* Don't worry, Itzik; tonight I shall sit quietly and cheer appropriately. In future, also, you will have less concern of my Jew News . . . as there are fewer and fewer Jews, there will be less and less news. *(He exits abruptly.)*

(Silence for a moment; EDDIE *continues busily setting up behind the bar,* JOEY *studies the newspaper article,* CHARLIE *absorbed, watching all this from near the jukebox and not his usual booth.)*

JOEY: *(Quietly.)* I think it's all true, Pop.
EDDIE: *(Distracted.)* What?
JOEY: What Mr. Zaretsky's tellin' us, Pop, I think it's all

true. It's *gotta* be—I mean, look at all the shit that's goin' on *here*.

EDDIE: Here is business as usual; maybe a little worse this summer.

JOEY: A little *worse* this summer?— *(Moving down towards him.)* Pop, *Brooklyn,* they hit two cemeteries in one *week*. You been on Rivington lately?—Jewish stars with swastikas painted over 'em, they're poppin' up on the walls like Lucky *Strike* ads. The Gladiators, the Avengers—*Boys'* clubs, they call 'em—they're on the prowl every night beatin' the crap outa Hebrew School kids. Grabbed a kid comin' outa Beth-El Saturday, ripped off his shirt and painted "Jew" on his chest, like maybe he *forgot*—you *hearin'* any of this, Pop?

EDDIE: *(Busily stacking glasses, his back to* JOEY.*)* It's not I ain't hearin' ya, kid; it's I *heard* it all already; been goin' on since before you was born. But this stuff *Zaretsky*'s talkin' about—not even in the old Moldavanka was there ever such.

JOEY: But if it's true—

EDDIE: If it's true then Uncle Nick's got his *sleigh* parked outside! It's all too crazy, kid, I'm tellin' ya. *(Turns to him.)* Now lemme *alone,* will ya—I gotta *open* here in twenty minutes! (JOEY *moving thoughtfully up towards phone,* EDDIE *glancing about.)* Shit, he ain't done the *setups* yet— *(Shouting.)* Charlie! Charlie, where are ya?! Charlie!

*(*CHARLIE *hears his name, tenses, looks up.)*

YOUNG CHARLIE'S VOICE: *(From apartment above.)* I'm in the studio, writing.

EDDIE: The studio. Is that the same as the toilet?

YOUNG CHARLIE'S VOICE: Sometimes.

EDDIE: *(Shouting.)* Charlie, *move* it, *now, pronto, down* here!

YOUNG CHARLIE: *(Entering from apartment.)* I'm coming, I'm in transit . . .

*(*YOUNG CHARLIE, *about eleven, concerned, thoughtful, and many worlds away, slouches down the stairs carrying a stack of loose-leaf pages and several pens;* EDDIE *leans towards him confidentially.)*

EDDIE: Charlie, I got this problem; see, until your book comes out and you become a millionaire, I figured I'd still run my little business here ... *(Shouting.)* so how about ya do the goddamn *set*-ups and help me *open* the place! The set-ups and the *mail,* Mister, you got obligations!

YOUNG CHARLIE: *(Quietly getting tray of set-ups from bar.)* I got the mail already, it's by the register.

*(*EDDIE *exits, briskly, to work in kitchen as* YOUNG CHARLIE *begins to go rather distractedly about the task of placing set-ups on two or three tables;* CHARLIE *watches him silently, intently, for a few moments, then ...)*

CHARLIE: Jesus, they were right, I *didn't* pick up my feet. *(Leans towards him.)* The shuffling, what's with the *shuffling* here? Straighten up, will ya? C'mon, Charlie, what happened to "No shit from nobody"?

YOUNG CHARLIE: *(A forlorn sigh, whispering.)* Oh-boy-oh-boy-oh-boy ...

CHARLIE: I don't get it, in all the albums I'm always *smiling* ... *(Nods thoughtfully.)* Yeah, but that's because they kept saying "smile" ... *(Following, close to him, gently.)* Don't worry, kid, you're gettin' out. *Outa* here. Sooner than you think. What is it, money? You need money? Bucks, Charlie, *bucks,* the bucks are on their *way* ... Oh, if I could just give you a coupla dollars, hand you a twenty, right now, a kinda loan, a ... *(During the above,* YOUNG CHARLIE *will have deposited several slugs in the jukebox, punched the same key several times and crossed over to the "Vote Here for Miss Daitch, 1944" display where he is now clearly entranced, as always, by the face of Miss Daitch Contestant Number Two, Peggy Parsons, and the biography beneath it; we begin to hear the Helen Forrest–Dick Haymes recording of "Long Ago and Far Away" from the jukebox, their voices drifting dreamily in the empty bar.)* Oh, my God ... Peggy Parsons ... *that's* it ... *(Turns to us, as it all comes back.)* The Miss Daitch Contest of Forty-Four, our bar has been selected as one of the officially designated polling places in the neighborhood ... *(Softly, from memory, as* YOUNG CHARLIE *studies bio.)* "Pretty, perky, pert Peggy Parsons, or 'Peggo' as she prefers to be called, plans to pursue an acting career in motion pictures ..." Peggo, Peggo ... To say that I had a crush on Peggy Parsons would be to say that Mao Tse-Tung had a crush on Communism; only the beginning of July and I had already cast over six hundred ballots in the Greater New York area. *(*YOUNG CHARLIE *sits in* CHARLIE*'s usual booth, starts fervently rewriting whatever is on his loose-leaf pages, all of it clearly inspired by occasional glances at Peggy; the music swells, filling the bar.)* Yeah, go with it, Charlie, this is it, it doesn't get better than this . . . *(Sits next to him in booth, leans close.)* Very important: love, Charlie, love does *not* make the world go round, *looking* for it does; this is important . . . Also very important, Charlie, in about ten years you're gonna meet a girl at the Museum of Modern Art, in front of the "Guernica"—let this painting be a *warning* to you—don't go out with this girl, don't even *talk* to this girl, by all means do *not marry this girl*—

JOEY: Hey, Charlie— *(Hangs up phone, comes down towards booth.)* Been settin' up tickets for the guys, everybody tells me—

YOUNG CHARLIE: *(Points to pages in Joey's pocket.)* Did you read it?

JOEY: Charlie, *listen,* word's out, the Avengers, the Gladiators, they're gonna be roamin' tonight, like Memorial Day, or maybe like the Jew Hunt on Pell Street—whatever, I don't want you walkin' over to Rutgers Arena by yourself tonight. Gonna work out with Bimmy, then I come *back* for ya—are you listening?

YOUNG CHARLIE: Yeah, after Bimmy's I go with you. Did you *read* it?

JOEY: Sometimes, I tell ya, it's like you're not *present* here—

YOUNG CHARLIE: *(Rising in booth.)* Did you read the *letter,* fa Chrissake!

JOEY: I *read* the letter, I *read* the goddamn letter! It's completely nuts and wacko. Also hopeless and dumb.

YOUNG CHARLIE: If you got a criticism, tell me.

JOEY: Charlie, number one: I don't *get* it— *(Indicating the Miss Daitch photos.)* These girls, they all got the same *smile,* the same *eyes,* the same *nose*— *(Pointing.)* C'mon tell me, what's the difference between Peggy Parsons . . . and "Lovely, lively Laurie Lipton" here?

YOUNG CHARLIE: The difference? The *diff*erence? Why am I discussing this with a boxer?

JOEY: I got to go to Bimmy's—

YOUNG CHARLIE: *(Holds up loose-leaf pages.)* Thirty seconds, Joey—the revised version; I changed key words.

JOEY: *(Leans against booth.)* Twenty.

YOUNG CHARLIE: *(Reads from pages.)* "Mr. Samuel Goldwyn, Metro-Goldwyn-Mayer Studios. Dear Sam: Enclosed please find photo of Peggy Parsons. I think you will agree that this is the outstanding exquisiteness of a Motion Picture Star. You may reach her by the Daitch's Beer distribution place in your area is my belief. If Motion Picture employment is a result you may wish to say to her who recommended her eventually. She or yourself can reach me by post at the Flamingo Apartments, Six Eighty-one Canal Street, New York City. In closing I think of you first-hand instead of Darryl or David because of your nation of origin Poland which is right near my father's original nation Russia. Yours truly, C. E. Ross." *(*YOUNG CHARLIE *does not look up from the letter, so concerned is he about his brother's response.* JOEY, *sensing this, sits opposite him in the booth.)*

JOEY: To begin with, that's an exceptionally well-put, well-written letter, Charlie.

YOUNG CHARLIE: I know what you're thinkin', but *wild things* happen out there, Joey; they're findin' stars in *drug*stores, *ele*vators—

JOEY: Right, and I'm sure the feeling you have for this Peggy is—

YOUNG CHARLIE: Peggo, she prefers to be called Peggo—

JOEY: Peggo, right—is genuine. So let's follow this through for a moment. Say, thousand-to-one shot, but Goldwyn, somebody in his office, sees the picture, say he gets a hold of her; say she's grateful, comes down here to Canal Street to see you, right?

YOUNG CHARLIE: Right, right.

JOEY: And you're eleven.

YOUNG CHARLIE: Joey, I'm *aware* that there's an age problem; I will *deal* with it.

JOEY: *(After a moment, quietly.)* Tell ya, sometimes, the similarities, you and Pop, it scares the shit outa me, kid.

YOUNG CHARLIE: *(Studying letter.)* Maybe "Dear Sam" 's too familiar; maybe "Dear Samuel" or "Mr. Goldwyn," huh?

JOEY: *(Pats his shoulder.)* Right; that'll do it. *(Rises, starts briskly towards front door.)* Gotta get to Bimmy, I ain't worked out since the Chocolate Chopper. *(As* EDDIE *enters, returning from work in kitchen to go to stack of mail behind bar.)* See ya before the fight, Pop; comin' back to pick up Charlie.

EDDIE: *(Looks up from mail.)* Hey, this kid tonight—an easy win, but the Bazooka's got a little weight on ya and I don't like his left—so go for the kill *early;* the *kill,* Joey. Remember, the boy is *nothin";* he is *now,* he always *was*—

JOEY: *(As he exits into street.)*—and he always *will* be!

CHARLIE: *(To us, from booth.)* Brother, brotherly, brotherhood: dynamite, powerhouse words, you could take them up off the ground like a punch; they meant—and still, now, at this moment, mean—Joey. However, take note, the only time Pop talks to me is when his prince is unavailable . . .

EDDIE: *(Behind bar, studying a letter.)* Charlie, the *set*-ups, what happened? (YOUNG CHARLIE *leaves booth to continue his task.)* You can stick the flags in the pineapples, O.K.? (YOUNG CHARLIE *carries flags and tray of set-ups to center table;* EDDIE, *still looking down at the letter, speaks quietly, solemnly.)* Charles . . .

*(*YOUNG CHARLIE *freezes at table.)*

CHARLIE: "Charles," in this household, is my criminal name.

EDDIE: Charles . . . I'm lookin' at a letter here from the Star of David School, Rabbi Rubin.

YOUNG CHARLIE: These flags, Pop, they don't fit into the pineapples . . .

EDDIE: *(Still looking down at letter, calmly.)* This is *some* letter, this letter. It's got my undivided attention.

YOUNG CHARLIE: Hebrew's been over a week now, Pop; it don't start again till—

EDDIE: *(Continuing calmly.)* Turns out it's been over for *you* a very long time now. About eight months, according to this letter. Also according to this letter there's been a lot of *other* letters. Says here, Rubin, "I had assumed from your past responses to my inquiries regarding Charles' religious training . . ." Turns out Rubin's been writin' to me, and I been *answerin'* him on this matter seven months now. Hey, I even got compliments on "the grace and wisdom of my remarks," says here. He *especially* likes the graciousness how I keep payin' him anyway even though you ain't goin' there no more.

YOUNG CHARLIE: Pop, how about we—

EDDIE: *(Still calmly, folding letter.)* Convenient for ya, you bein' the one gets the mail. Musta got distracted today, huh? Yeah. Bugsy Siegel don't get distracted, Frank Costello don't get distracted; Dillinger got distracted *once* . . . and now he's dead.

YOUNG CHARLIE: *(Moving towards bar.)* Pop, I gotta tell ya—

EDDIE: Charlie, look at my hands. Are ya lookin' at my hands?

YOUNG CHARLIE: Yeah.

EDDIE: What I'm doin' here is I'm holdin' onto the edge of the bar because if I let go I'm gonna beat the crap outa ya.

YOUNG CHARLIE: Here's what—

EDDIE: I'm here loadin' up shickers so you can hang out with God, twenty a month to the Star of David, hard cash, and you ain't even *there. (Quietly, in awe.)* While I'm *sayin'* it, I don't believe it. I don't believe that you're standin' there in front of me alive, I didn't kill you yet.

YOUNG CHARLIE: It was *wrong,* the whole *thing,* I *know,* but lemme—

EDDIE: My hands, they're lettin' go of the bar— *(Suddenly moving out from behind bar towards* YOUNG CHARLIE, YOUNG CHARLIE *backing up fearfully across the room, his hands raised, urgently.)*

YOUNG CHARLIE: I gotta tell ya *one* thing, Pop, *one thing*!

EDDIE: *(After a moment.) One* thing.

YOUNG CHARLIE: *(Keeping his distance; fervently.)* That place; you don't know what it *is* there, the Star of David. It's a terrible place. It's not even a Temple or anything. It's just this ratty place on Houston Street. This ratty room on the second floor of a building, two Rabbis in a room makin' a buck. Pop, I swear, God isn't there like you think.

EDDIE: He's *there,* kid. Take my word for it—

YOUNG CHARLIE: Over Pedro and Olga's *Dance* Studio? Two ratty guys with bad breath who throw chalk at your head and slam books on your hand every time you miss a trick? I mean real angry guys with bugs in their beards;

sometimes they just kick you in the ass on general principles.

EDDIE: Yeah, that's God all right; I'd know Him anywhere.

YOUNG CHARLIE: That ain't God, those guys—

EDDIE: Sure they ain't, I know that; but they're *connected.* That's the whole thing in life: *connections,* kid. *(Relaxes slightly, leans towards him.)* First thing, right off, I guarantee you, there's a God. You got that?

YOUNG CHARLIE: I'm with you on that. We only disagree on where He's located.

EDDIE: Hebrew School, He's located *there;* so you go back there. Sit. (YOUNG CHARLIE *sits obediently at center table;* EDDIE *sits opposite him.)* Because there's times—you're in trouble, you're really sick, and especially when you die, just before you die—you'll be glad you stayed in touch. That's the payoff. There's gonna be a time, guaranteed, you'll be grateful I made ya go, but the main thing is if ya don't go back I'm gonna kill ya.

YOUNG CHARLIE: I don't get it, Pop. Ma lights the candles Friday, starts the prayer, ya say, "Cut the shit and let's eat"; ya *never* go to Temple anymore, the *bar* was open last Rosh Hashana, ya—

*(*EDDIE *suddenly grabs* YOUNG CHARLIE *by the collar of his shirt with one hand and pulls him halfway across the table.)*

EDDIE: I stay in *touch,* Criminal! Look, you're makin' me grit my teeth! My goddamn *bridge* is crackin'! I stay in *touch,* Putzolla! Twenty a month to Rubin and the bandits so you should learn the worda the Torah and the worda God—

YOUNG CHARLIE: I can't breathe, Pop—

EDDIE: That's two shifts a month I'm puttin' out for God here exclusive, same like I done with Joey! Are you breathing?

YOUNG CHARLIE: *No*—

EDDIE: Then *breathe*— *(Lets him go.)* And I got married by a Rabbi, under God, twenty-five years and I stick! How *come* I stick? A woman, we all realize, is at this time a wacky person, nearly deaf; also a rough mouth don't encourage my endeavors whatever. *(Silence for a moment.)* This is currently. But there was occasions otherwise.

(Glances up at apartment door, then leans towards YOUNG CHARLIE; *quietly.)* You hearda the expression "raven-haired"? O.K., there's some girls got hair they call "midnight black," very beautiful, but it got no light in it, see. "Raven-hair" is like the bird, glossy, light come *out* of it, got its own light comin' out—this is what she had. First time I seen her she's runnin' down these steps to the beach, this hair is down to her ass, flyin' behind her like wings, her arms is out like she's gonna hug the entire Black Sea laughin' . . . *(Slaps the table.)* And then, Sonny-Boy, minutes, *minutes*—I swear to you, minutes after the Rabbi pronounced us the lights went out in her hair like somebody turned off a switch; and the mouth began. Continuing in this manner until she became the totally wacky deaf person we know in our home at this time; she is at this *moment* upstairs, stirring a pot, getting wackier and deafer. But I *stick*! *(Slaps the table again.)* That's my point, kid: I *stick*. Because there'll be a night one day when the heart attack comes and somebody'll have to call Dr. Schwartzman and the ambulance. And who will do it? The Wacky Ravenhead! In five minutes she covers a fifty-year bet! Why? Because I put my money on a good woman. Wacky and deaf; but good. There's a lot of people got this kind of arrangement. It's called a Coronary Marriage. And when you find a better reason for people staying together, let me know. Love; forget it. Who are they kidding? It won't be there when you get home and it won't call Dr. Schwartzman for you. *(Leans closer.)* Same with God. I *stick*. *I* stick and so will you. Because all God's gotta do is come through *once* to make Him worth your time. Maybe twice. Just one big deal and once when you die so you ain't scared shitless. *(Picks up letter.)* O.K., you hang in with Rubin till the Bar Mitzvah shot. Whatta we talkin' about?—a coupla years, tops, it's *over;* you're joined up with *my* Pop and *his* Pop and *his* and all the Pops back forever—you're covered, it's set, I done my job; then ya do whatever the hell ya want. *(Holds out his hand.)* Deal? *(A moment, then* YOUNG CHARLIE *shakes his hand;* EDDIE *rises, starts briskly back towards bar.)* C'mon, let's seal it. (YOUNG CHARLIE *follows him,* EDDIE *goes behind bar.)* Mine's vodka. What'll ya have?

YOUNG CHARLIE: *(Sits opposite him, elbows on bar.)* Let's see . . . you got lemon juice and seltzer?

EDDIE: Like the choice; *I* got it— *(A spritz, a splash, places it on bar.)* Now *you* got it. *(Pouring his vodka.)* Yeah, good; I think this was a good conversation.

YOUNG CHARLIE: Me too . . . I mean it ain't exactly Andy Hardy and the Judge, but it's somethin'. *(He laughs at his own joke; soon* EDDIE *laughs too, joining him, they "click" glasses.)* Boy, Pop, you're right—

EDDIE: *(Still laughing.) Sure* I'm right—

YOUNG CHARLIE: *(Still laughing.)* I mean about Mom, she sure is *some* wacky *deaf* person; I mean, she—

(A sudden, resounding smack in the face from EDDIE *sends* YOUNG CHARLIE *reeling off his bar stool, knocking him to the floor.* CHARLIE, *in his booth, holds his cheek, feeling the impact.)*

EDDIE: *(Shouting.)* You will not mock your mother! Even in jest!

YOUNG CHARLIE: *(Half-mumbling, still on his knees, his head still ringing, shocked and hurt at once.)* Hell with you, *hell* with you, don't make no sense . . .

EDDIE: *(Comes out from behind bar, thundering, pointing down at him.)* What's *that*? What do I hear?! Gypsies! Gypsies! The Gypsies brought ya! This can't be mine!

YOUNG CHARLIE: *(Scrambling to his feet, screaming.)* Oh, I wish to God they *had*! I wish to God the Gypsies brought me! I don't wanna be from *you*! *(Darting from table to table as* EDDIE *stalks him, the boy gradually rising to full, wailing, arm-flailing rage.) Nothin'* fits together, nothin' ya *say*! Goddamn switcher*oo* alla time! *Her? Her? You! You're* the crazy one, *you're* the deaf one, *you're* the one nobody can talk to! *(Whacking pineapples off of tables, wildly, screaming, pointing fiercely at* EDDIE.*)* Loser! Loser! Goddamn *loser*! You're a goddamn crazy *loser* in a goddamn loser *shit*house here!

*(*EDDIE *suddenly snaps, a moment of pure madness, races towards him, grabbing a chair, raising it over his head, clearly about to smash it down on* YOUNG CHARLIE; YOUNG CHARLIE *drops to the ground, his arms over his head,* EDDIE *lost in rage, all his enemies below him.)*

EDDIE: *(Roaring.)* You people . . . !

*(*EDDIE *freezes, about to strike, looks down, sees that it's* YOUNG CHARLIE*; he slowly lowers the chair, trembling with rage, looking at it, realizing for a moment what he was about to do, shaken, quite still; he tosses the chair to the ground.)*

YOUNG CHARLIE: *(Rises, unaware of what's happening to his father.)* Come on, great, let's see ya do the one thing ya *can* do . . . *(Shouting, his fists raised, holding his ground.)* No. No more hitting this year. This is *it* . . . Come on, come on, Pop . . . just one more move, I'm the perfect height; just one more move and I kick you in the balls so hard ya don't straighten up for a *month* . . . *(Full power now.)* One more move and it's right in the balls—right in the *balls,* Pop, I swear to God!

EDDIE: Swear to who?!

YOUNG CHARLIE: God! I swear to God!

EDDIE: *(After a moment, quietly.)* See how He comes in handy? *(A pause; then, still a bit shaken, covering.)* Well, I . . . I believe I've made my point. Sometimes ya gotta illustrate, y'know . . . for the full clarity of the thing. *(Sound of* GUSTA *approaching from the apartment above, humming a few phrases of "In Odessa,"* EDDIE *heading briskly back to bar, pulling himself together.)* Now you'll excuse me, I gotta open in five minutes. First day of the Flamingo Lounge.

*(*EDDIE *takes a quick shot of the vodka he left on the bar, erasing the episode, returning to work as* GUSTA *enters from the apartment carrying her usual two large pots of just-cooked food, humming brightly,* YOUNG CHARLIE *eventually retreating slowly, thoughtfully, to his booth and his loose-leaf pages.)*

GUSTA: *(Placing pots on kitchen stove.)* Today we got the usuals, Eddie—Mulligan Stew, Cottage Fries, General Patton's Pancakes, D-Day Dumplings—

EDDIE: General Patton's Pancakes, I forget—

GUSTA: Potato Latkes—

EDDIE: Potato Latkes, right—

GUSTA: *(Bringing plate of food to* YOUNG CHARLIE*'s booth.)*

Upstairs, simmering, I got for Joey's party tonight—it's just us, Eddie, I'll use maiden names—Kasha-Varnishkes, also Holishkes with honey and raisin.

EDDIE: Great, Gloria, great—

GUSTA: *(Starts back towards kitchen.)* Joey's boxing fight, I'll be upstairs; you'll inform me at knockout time, I bring down the food.

EDDIE: Don't worry, this guy won't *touch* him, Gloria—

GUSTA: This is how it is with me: I can't watch, so I can't listen either; it hurts.

EDDIE: *(Approaching her at kitchen doorway; quietly.)* Hey, for the party tonight, how about ya take the pins outa y'hair . . . let it, y'know, free.

GUSTA: I let it free it goes in the soup.

EDDIE: I mean, just loose, y'know, like flowin'.

GUSTA: Who's gonna *see*, Finney, Nick,—?

EDDIE: *Me, I'll* see it—

GUSTA: *(Suddenly.)* Eddie, there's a bird on the ceiling.

EDDIE: It's a *flamingo*.

GUSTA: All right, I'll believe you; it's a flamingo. Why is it on the ceiling?

EDDIE: Gonna be like a *symbol* for us, Gloria, for the place; like I was tellin' Joey: Borden's got a cow, Billingsley's got a stork, Firestone—

GUSTA: How much did the dopey bird cost?

EDDIE: It just so happens this hand-made, hand-crafted, sixty-eight-light Flamingo Chandelier is the only one of its kind in the world.

GUSTA: Two is hard to imagine. *(She goes to Kitchen stove;* EDDIE *continues, high with "Opening Day" fever.)*

EDDIE: Gloria, I'm talkin' to Joey this mornin', somethin' *come* to me—somethin' for the *place*, somethin' we never *tried* before—a *word, one* word, a magic word's gonna make all the difference!

GUSTA: Fire.

EDDIE: Advertising!

GUSTA: We'll burn it down and get the insurance. The moose *alone* puts us in clover. *(Exits deep into kitchen, out of sight.)*

EDDIE: *Advertising!* Advertising, kiddo! *(Exits into kitchen, pursuing her, inspired; we hear his voice from inside, his enthusiasm building.)* I'm talkin' about a small ad, classy, in there with the Clubs, Gloria—just a picture of a flamingo, *one* word: "*Lounge,*" under it; under *that* "Six Eighty-one Canal"—like everybody *knows* already, like it's *in,* Gloria—

CHARLIE: *(During above, rising from booth, moving towards kitchen.)* Leave her alone, Pop, leave her *alone,* it's never gonna *happen*—

EDDIE'S VOICE: Guy comes in here regular, works for the *Journal-American,* runs a heavy tab, I trade him on the *space,* kid—

CHARLIE: *(During above, louder and louder.)*—stop, we're never going Uptown; stop, *stop* driving us *crazy* with it, Eddie—this *bar,* this goddamn *bar*!

YOUNG CHARLIE: *(At booth, writing as* EDDIE*'s voice continues.)* "Dear Mr. Zanuck . . . it would not be perfectly candid of me if I did not frankly admit and advise you that I have just previously contacted Sam on this exact matter . . ."

CHARLIE: *(Turns, anguished, caught between the two of them.)* My God, you're just as crazy as *he* is . . .

YOUNG CHARLIE: *(Writing, his confidence building.)* ". . . I refer to the enclosed Peggy Parsons. We live in a competitive industry, Darryl, and I do not wish to keep this woman in a basket . . ."

(We begin to hear the sound of about twenty teenaged boys' voices, quite distantly at first, far down the street outside, singing happily, with great gusto; the sound of the voices and their song growing louder and louder, reaching a peak as we hear them pass the front door, then fading out as they continue along Canal Street; YOUNG CHARLIE *completely oblivious to this sound as he continues to write his letter,* CHARLIE *gradually caught by the sound of the boys' voices, the song drawing him slowly down to the front door as the passing voices reach their peak; all lights dimming far down now except for the remaining full light on* CHARLIE *at the front door, his face mirroring his almost forgotten but now vividly remembered helplessness and fear at the sound of the boys' voices and their song.)*

TWENTY BOYS' VOICES: *(To the tune of the Marine Corps Hymn.)*
"On the shores of Coney Island
While the guns of freedom roar,

The Sheenies eat their Matzo Balls
And make money off the war,
While we Christian saps go fight the Japs,
In the uniforms they've made.
And they'll sell us Kosher hot dogs
For our victory parade.
So it's onward into battle
They will send us Christian slobs,
When the war is done and victory won,
All the Jews will have our jobs."

(Sound of laughter, a crash of glass, then cheering as the boys' voices fade into the night.)

CHARLIE: *(Shouts towards the fading voices.)* If Joey was here . . . if Joey was here you'd never get away with it!

(The boys' voices are quickly obliterated by the sudden sound of a cheering crowd, raucous and enthusiastic, and the machine-gun voice of ringside sportscaster Speed Spector blasting out the blow-by-blow of a fight in progress, the tiny yellow light of the Philco radio dial popping on in the darkness and then glowing brighter as the cheering crowd, Spector's voice, and all the bar lights come up full to reveal that night's party and the party guests: HANNAH, NICK, *and* FINNEY, *gathered about the radio,* EDDIE *entering from the kitchen holding two champagne bottles aloft on a tray full of fancy glasses, a silk vest added to his usual Uptown bartender's white shirt and black bow tie,* ZARETSKY *entering somewhat later from the apartment above wearing an old but splendid smoking jacket and cravat for the occasion;* CHARLIE *remaining at front door looking off towards street,* YOUNG CHARLIE *no longer onstage.)*

SPECTOR'S VOICE: *(From Philco, breathless, one long sentence.)* . . . toe to toe and here they *go* fourth round another *fight* friends *first* three bouts waltz-time dancin' *darlings* number *four* we got a slammin' *slug* fest here Killer Kalish and Homicide Hennesy tradin' solid *body* shots insteada *party* favors here tonight forty-five seconds into frame *four* . . . *(*CHARLIE *being gradually pulled away from the front door by the much pleasanter memory of Spector's voice.)* . . . carryin' it to Kalish lightnin' *left* rockin' *right* a stick a stick a jab a hook hook hook roundhouse *right* Killer's outa *business* . . .

CHARLIE: *(To us, as Spector and cheering crowd continue.)* Well, they didn't call him Speed Spector for nothin', did they? And tonight we waited for *that voice* to talk about *my* brother. First, however, would be the usual pre–Main Event interview with Big Mike Baskin of Big Mike Baskin's Broadway Boys' and Men's Clothes, sponsor of the Tuesday Night Amateurs. We, of course, all knew him as the former Manny Buffalino of Buffalino's Grand Street Garments who gave a silver-plated watch to each of the winners . . . and a terrible headache to Pop.

SPECTOR'S VOICE: . . . whatta ya think about that whoppin' big *win,* Big Mike?

BIG MIKE'S VOICE: Spid, dis boy, alla tonight win' gonna get a sil'-plate wash froma Big Mike. Now, he don' like dis wash, he can hocka dis wash for fifteen doll'—

EDDIE: *(Entering with champagne.)* Can't stand the *mouth* on that greaseball— *(Turns radio volume way down; they all protest.)* Don't worry, Joey's bout ain't on for five minutes anyways—goddamn Steerage *Green*horn; twenty-six locations, man's sittin' on a coupla mil—*nobody* knows what the hell he's *talkin'* about! What's his *angle,* how's he *do* it—?

FINNEY: *(As* ZARETSKY *enters slapping* ZARETSKY *on back.)* Evenin', Mr. Z.; how's Show Business?

ZARETSKY: Mr. Finney; Abbott and *Costello* are in Show Business, Amos and even *Andy* are in Show Business, Franklin Delano *Roose*velt is in Show Business—

FINNEY: *(Pinching* ZARETSKY*'s cheek.)* Lost me bearin's, darlin', it's the joy of the night—

EDDIE: *(Placing bottles on center table.)* I say sixty seconds into Round One this champagne is pourin' and Gloria's down with the goodies!

HANNAH: And Nick wears the *shirt* tonight.

EDDIE: Great . . .

FINNEY: The shirt, of course . . .

HANNAH: The occasion demanded.

ZARETSKY: This then is a shirt of some significance, I assume.

NICK: Oh, ya might say. Ya might well say, Mr. Zaretsky. *(Opening old jacket to reveal a faded yellow shirt instead of his usual faded white shirt; there are dark brown stains on the shoulder and collar.)* For this then is the blood of Barney Ross, spilled the night he lost the World Welterweight to Armstrong, the greatest Losin' Win I ever saw.

EDDIE: Greatest Losin' Win in the history of the fight game.

FINNEY: Easy.

NICK: Second *row* we are, the four of us; May thirty-one, Nineteen Thirty-eight, Round Five, his legs said goodbye to the man, never to return in what was t'be the last bout o' Barney's life. Ref Donovan's beggin' Ross to let 'im stop the thing— "No," Barney says, through the blood in his mouth, "I'm the Champ, he'll have to beat me in the *ring* and *not* on a stool in m'corner!" There then come ten rounds of a horror ya never want to see again, but proud ya saw the once for the grandness that was in it, the crowd is quiet and many look away, but at the end the cheers is for Barney who lost his title and won his pride. *(Looking about at his friends.)* Which is why we call it, the four of us . . .

NICK, EDDIE, FINNEY: . . . the Greatest Losin' Win we ever saw!

HANNAH: In my case, heard.

FINNEY: It was in the Twelfth Barney's blood hit the shirt—

HANNAH: A thundering right from Armstrong, yes—

EDDIE: Ya *get* it, Actor—ya see why me and my boys are called *Ross* now?

FINNEY: *(Suddenly turns to radio.)* My God, the *fight*—

EDDIE: Oh, *shit—(He dashes to the radio, quickly turns up volume.)*

(We hear the sound of the cheering crowd as EDDIE *turns the volume up full, the sound building louder and louder as the crowd chants rhythmically;* CHARLIE *sits solemnly in his booth, nodding, remembering it all too well.)*

THE CROWD: Chicken *Pete* . . . Chicken *Pete* . . . Chicken *Pete* . . .

HANNAH: *(Confused, frightened.)* Chicken Pete, Nick? . . .

SPECTOR'S VOICE: *(Shouting above the chanting crowd.)* . . . Listen to *that,* Fans! *New* one on Old *Speed* here; got a referee, one fighter, whole crowd, packed Arena—*one* thing missing; the *other fighter*! Pistol Pete is *not* in that ring, *not* in the locker room, *no*where to be found, friends . . .

(All in barroom stunned at first; EDDIE, *the others, not moving, riveted by the information as it comes out of the radio; the sound of the chanting crowd building, filling the room.)*

SPECTOR'S VOICE: Ref Gordon tells me Pistol Pete's not in the *building,* no *message,* no *word; sounds* like the best explanation of this one's comin' from the crowd itself . . .

THE CROWD: *(Louder and louder.)* . . . Chicken *Pete* . . . Chicken *Pete* . . . Chicken *Pete* . . .

FINNEY: *(Bewildered, staring into radio.)* He didn't *show,* Joey didn't *show* . . .

(The sound of stomping and clapping joins the rhythmic chant of the crowd now as EDDIE *moves slowly out from behind the bar, carefully controlling his fear and confusion.)*

EDDIE: *(Quietly, evenly.)* He's hurt, he's hurt . . . out *cold;* he'd have to be out *cold* to stay away from that bout . . . he's hurt . . . *(Moving towards phone.) Bimmy's,* maybe somebody at Bimmy's, somebody knows . . .

ZARETSKY: He leaves with Chaim for the Arena, this is an hour ago . . .

FINNEY: I heard them Avenger boys was gatherin' on Pell . . .

HANNAH: Nit do gedacht . . .

NICK: *(Rising from stool.)* I go to the Precinct, get some of the fellahs . . .

EDDIE: *(Picking up phone.)* Yeah, yeah . . .

THE CROWD: *(Building to peak now.)* . . . Chicken *Pete* . . . Chicken *Pete* . . . Chicken *Pete* . . .

(The front door bursts open and JOEY *rushes in, followed by* YOUNG CHARLIE; *though somewhat shaken, there is something decisive, resolved in* JOEY *as he stands tensely at the center of the room, his "Pistol Pete" jacket gripped in his hand;* YOUNG CHARLIE, *clearly bewildered by the evening's events, stays close to his brother.)*

HANNAH: *(Trembling.)* Jussel, Jussel . . . ?

JOEY: *(Gently.)* Everything's fine, Hannah.

EDDIE: *(Starts towards him; quietly.)* Thank God, you're O.K. . . . you're O.K. . . .

JOEY: I'm not O.K. *(Races behind the bar towards the sound of the chanting crowd, snaps off the radio; the room is silent.)* I will be.

EDDIE: The *fight*, kid, the *fight* . . . what the hell *happened* . . . ?

JOEY: *(Slaps his jacket onto the bar, grabs up vodka bottle and shot glass.)* No more fights. No more fights, Pop. Not here. *(Fills his shot glass, downs it.)*

EDDIE: Not *here*? Not *here*? What the hell does *that* mean? I need some *explainin'* here, kid, I gotta—

ZARETSKY: Let him *speak*, Itzik.

JOEY: *(Quietly.)* Pop, this mornin', workin' out with Bimmy—

EDDIE: To*night*, kid, I wanna know about to*night*—

JOEY: *(Continuing, firmly.)* This mornin', workin' out with Bimmy, we're skippin', we're sparrin', my mind ain't there, Pop. I'm doin' math. Three hundred and fifty thousand Jews in twenty-one days, comes out seventeen thousand five hundred a day, *this* day, today—

EDDIE: A buncha crazy *stories*, Joey, I told ya— *(Wheeling on* ZARETSKY.*) You*, it's you and your goddamn *bull*shit—

JOEY: *(Moving towards him.)* Please, ya gotta be quiet, Pop. That's maybe two thousand just while I'm workin' out. Seventeen thousand five hundred a day. No, it's impossible, I figure; Pop's *right*, it's nuts. I keep punchin' the bag. I come back to pick up Charlie, we're headin' over, not seven yet; then I hear people hollerin', I look up, I see it. Top of the Forward Buildin', tallest damn buildin' around here, there's the *Jewish Daily Forward* sign, y'know, big, maybe thirty feet high and wide as the buildin', electric bulbs, ya can see it even deep into Brooklyn, *forever*, Pop. What they did is they took out the right bulbs, exactly the right bulbs, gotta be hundreds of 'em, so instead of "Jewish Daily Forward" the sign says: "Jew is For war"; it's goddamn blazin' over the city, Pop, and Charlie and me start runnin' towards it, we're still maybe eight blocks away, we're passin' alotta people and kids on Canal, pointin' up, laughin', some cheerin', "Son of a *bitch*, son of a *bitch*, we fight the *war* and the Jews get *rich*," a guy grabs my arm, smilin', musta seen me box, guy my age, he says, "Pete, Pete, let's go get us some Yids, Pete!" and I know that second for sure they are doin' seventeen thousand five hundred a day, somewhere, seventeen thousand five hundred a day and I'm a guy spends his time boppin' kids for a silver-plated watch from Big Mike, hockable for fifteen dollars; right now I wouldn't hock me for a dime. Point is, I'm goin' in, Pop. I'm gettin' into this war and I need your help, now. *(*EDDIE *is silent.)* Army don't register me till next month, then it could be a year, more, before they call me. *Navy,* Pop, Navy's the game; they take ya at seventeen with a parent's consent. Eight a.m. tomorrow I'm at Ninety Church, I pick up the consent form, you fill it out, sign it, ten days later boot camp at Lake Geneva, September I'm in it, Pop. Korvette, destroyer, sub-chaser, whatever, *in* the goddamn thing.

EDDIE: *(After a moment.)* Your mother will never—

JOEY: I just need you, Pop. One parent. One signature. *(Silence for a moment.)* Do me a favor; take a look outside. Just turn left and look at the sky.

(During JOEY*'s story,* HANNAH *has moved instinctively closer to* NICK*, holding his arm;* ZARETSKY *rises.)*

ZARETSKY: Come then, Itzik.

*(*EDDIE *turns towards the door;* ZARETSKY *crosses to the door, exits into street, followed after a moment by* EDDIE *and then* FINNEY*;* NICK *starts to go but* HANNAH *whispers fearfully to him.)*

HANNAH: Stay with me, Nick. They'll look, they'll describe.

NICK: *(Embracing her.)* Sure, darlin', sure . . .

(Silence for a few moments; CHARLIE*, in his booth, watching the two boys.)*

YOUNG CHARLIE: You didn't tell me that part . . . about goin' in. You didn't mention that.

JOEY: It come to me, Charlie.

YOUNG CHARLIE: *(Urgently.)* Lotta guys to fight *here,* y'know, the Avengers, the Gladiators; ya don't have to go all the way to *Europe,* ya—

*(*EDDIE *enters, crosses slowly to bar, sits on stool; he is followed by* FINNEY, *and then* ZARETSKY, *who remains at doorway looking out into street.)*

FINNEY: *(To* HANNAH *and* NICK.*)* Hangin' over town like a second bloody moon, it is.

EDDIE: *(After a moment, slapping bar.)* Get me the goddamn paper, I sign it *now.* Go down to Ninety Church Street, wake the putzes *up,* bring me the form and I sign it now. All I ask, kid, you're over there, you kill a couple for your Pop, *per*sonally. *(Starts towards* JOEY; *fiercely.)* Kill 'em, Joey, *kill* 'em. *Show* 'em, kid, show 'em how a Jew fights.

JOEY: *(Grabs* EDDIE*'s fist, holds it proudly in the air.)* And in this corner, wearin' the green trunks—The East Side Savage!

(All cheering, patting JOEY *on the back, except for* ZARETSKY *and the two* CHARLIES.*)*

YOUNG CHARLIE: *(Looking anxiously from one to the other.)* Everybody goin' so *fast* here, so *fast*—

NICK: Try to get home for Christmas, kid—

YOUNG CHARLIE: They got *reasons,* y'know, why they don't take guys till they're eighteen, they got—

JOEY: *(Turns to* ZARETSKY, *who has remained silent at front door.)* You're *with* me, aren't ya?

ZARETSKY: *(After a moment.)* Yes . . . *yes,* were I your age— *(*JOEY *rushes forward, embraces him.)*

EDDIE: *(Holding champagne bottle aloft, rallying the* GROUP.*)* Hey, hey, *hey*—we still got a *party* goin' here—a *better* one—goddamn Warrior's *send*-off we got here! *(Pops cork at center table as all gather round, except for* YOUNG CHARLIE, *who moves slowly over to his usual booth, sits near* CHARLIE.*)* First-class Frog juice we got here—*I* got it— *(Pouring for* JOEY *first.)* Now *you* got it, kid— *(As he pours for the others.)* Hey, this ain't just Bazooka Kil*bane* goin' down—I'm talkin' about the whole goddamn Nazi-Nip *War* Machine here! *(Raising his glass.)* To the Winnah and still Cham*peen*!

HANNAH: *(Raising her glass.)* So what's wrong with the Bounding Main?

NICK: *(Raising his glass.)* Right! To the Navy!

FINNEY: *(Raising his glass.)* To the Navy and Victory!
ALL: *(Loudly, raising glasses.)* The Navy and Victory!

(They click glasses just as GUSTA *enters from the apartment above carrying a large tray of party food; starts down stairs, confused, seeing* JOEY *among the* GROUP.*)*

GUSTA: The boxing-fight, Joey, you won already? Nobody informed me. *(They all turn to her, their six glasses held aloft, poised; she stops near* JOEY.*)* Ah, no marks; good. O.K., party treats— *(Goes briskly to down left table, a distance from the* GROUP, *starts taking dishes from tray, placing them on table, her back to them; they all remain quite still, watching her.)* First, of course, basics: we got Kasha Varnishkes, we got Holishkes, special for Mr. Zaretsky we got Kartoffel Chremsel with a touch apple . . .
HANNAH: *(Quietly.)* Eddie signs a paper, Gusta, Joey goes to war.
GUSTA: *(A pause; then she continues briskly.)* We got Lokshen Kugel, we got a little Brisket Tzimmes with honey, special for Charlie we got Cheese Blintzes, a side sour cream . . .
JOEY: *(Softly, moving towards her.)* Ma, did you hear that, Ma . . . ?
GUSTA: And special for Finney and Nick—why not, I was in the mood—we got Mamaligele Rumanye with a smash strawberry.
JOEY: Ma . . .
GUSTA: *(A moment; she turns to him.)* I hear everything, Sonny. You got some good news for me? *(Looks over at the* GROUP.*)* I hear it all. It's just that twenty years ago I started making selections. *(Walking slowly towards the* GROUP.*)* You see, if I listened, I would want to speak. And who would hear me? Who would hear me? Who would *hear* me?

(She slaps EDDIE *hard across the face. A beat; we hear the sudden sound of a full marching band and a male chorus doing a blasting, drum-rolling, lusty-voiced rendition of "Anchors Aweigh" as all lights fade quickly down on the frozen Party Group and the still figures of* GUSTA *and* EDDIE, *music continuing at full volume.)*

MALE CHORUS:
"Anchors aweigh, my boys,
Anchors aweigh,
Farewell to college joys,
We sail at break of day, day, day, day . . ."

(During CHARLIE*'s next speech the pulsing jukebox lights will come up again and with them the half-light in which we will see only* EDDIE *and* YOUNG CHARLIE *remaining onstage and making those changes in the barroom that would have occurred during the thirteen months till the next scene begins:* EDDIE *solemnly draping a length of black ribbon about the frame of the grinning F.D.R. photo, then proudly hanging a map of the Pacific Theater of War over the jukebox, happily placing several blue and white Service Stars about the room, including one over* JOEY*'s boxing photo, finally exiting into kitchen;* YOUNG CHARLIE *will take down the Miss Daitch Display—being careful to keep the Peggy Parsons photo which he stores, among other treasures, in the hollow seat of the booth he and* CHARLIE *usually use.* CHARLIE *will have moved down towards us only a moment after the blackout on the Party Scene, humming a few phrases of "Anchors Aweigh" along with the jukebox, then speaking immediately to us during the action described above.)*

CHARLIE: Joey called the shot exactly: September, he was in it—desperately trying to promote his way onto a Convoy-Korvette in the European Theatre, he ended up on a destroyer in the Pacific and, as Joey pointed out, the only dangerous German he ever got to face was our dentist, Dr. Plaut—but he was *in* it; and, finishing ten weeks of gunnery school in four, he became quickly known aboard the destroyer Campbell as "The King of the Twin-Forties"—double-mounted anti-aircraft machine-guns in a swiveling steel bucket operated by a gunner and an ammo man—*(Here replicated by* YOUNG CHARLIE *holding two broom handles atop a spinning bar stool.)* Yes, Joey was proud and brave and good and strong—but mostly, he was *gone. (*YOUNG CHARLIE *puts on the "Pistol Pete" jacket* JOEY *left on the bar, his posture noticeably straightening.)* He was gone and *I* was here, the house was mine. I was *it:* star of the show, Top of the Card, the Main Event. Civilians look for job openings in wartime . . . and there was an opening here for Prince.

(CHARLIE turns to center as lights come up on YOUNG CHARLIE alone onstage, seated comfortably on bar stool, his feet up, legs crossed at the ankle, on bar, gazing critically at the huge painting of the Four Poker Players over the bar mirror. Sound of Harry Truman's voice fading up with the lights as "Anchors Aweigh" record ends on jukebox.)

TRUMAN'S VOICE: . . . on Hiroshima, a military base. We won the race of discovery against the Germans. We have used it in order to shorten the agony of war, in order to save the lives of thousands and thousands of young Americans. We shall *continue* to use it until we completely destroy Japan's power to make war . . .

EDDIE: *(Bursts in from kitchen.)* The Atomic Cocktail, Charlie! *(Holds aloft two large containers of freshly mixed cocktails.) Two* kindsa rum, light *and* dark, shot o' grenadine—pineapple juice and coconut cream, give a kinda Tropical-Pacific feel. *(Sets containers and handmade placard on bar.)* Whatta ya think, kid?

YOUNG CHARLIE: *(Still looking at Poker Picture, thoughtfully.)* That's a terrible painting, Pop.

EDDIE: *(Reads from placard—he's illustrated it with a classic mushroom-cloud Hiroshima photo from a newspaper.)* "Atomic Cocktail—One Dollar—If the First Blast Don't Get You, the Fallout Will." How about that, Charlie?

YOUNG CHARLIE: *(Squints at Poker Picture.)* Not only poorly painted, but look at all the *room* it takes up.

EDDIE: What?

YOUNG CHARLIE: This painting here, Pop; it's no good.

EDDIE: What're ya talkin' about? This here's a hand-painted oil picture, seven feet by *six,* fits *exact* over the mirror. This is an original by goddamn Lazlo *Shim*kin; run up a big tab, gimme the picture on a trade-off. Got any idea what this thing's *worth* today?

YOUNG CHARLIE: Nothin', Pop.

EDDIE: Listen, Putz, this picture been sittin' up there since a year before you was *born.* You seen it every day o' ya *life*—all of a sudden it's no *good*?

YOUNG CHARLIE: Yes; strange, isn't it?

EDDIE: *(Quietly.)* I gotta open the bar in twenty minutes;

otherwise I would immediately take the picture out in the alley and burn it. Only thing I can suggest to you in the meantime, Charlie, is that you *spend the rest of your goddamn life lookin' the other way*! *(Leaning towards him.)* Gypsies! Gypsies! The *Gypsies* left ya at my *doorstep*! *This* can't be *mine*! Before this personally autographed Lazlo *Shim*kin picture goes, *you* go. *(Points.) Feet* off the bar, and finish the set-ups.

ZARETSKY: *(Entering from apartment above.)* Ah, I sense artistic differences in the air.

YOUNG CHARLIE: *(Starts working on set-ups.)* 'Morning, Mr. Zaretsky.

ZARETSKY: Chaim, you have not yet, I trust, fetched the mail? *(*YOUNG CHARLIE *shakes his head.)* Good then, it shall be my task. I expect today a cable from Buenos Aires, in Argentina, where still exist two hundred thousand speakers of Yiddish, there confirming my appearance, a full three weeks of concerts; my first since the War. *(Starts towards front door.)*

YOUNG CHARLIE: *(Impressed as always.)* Hey, Argen*tina* . . . Great.

EDDIE: *(Stacking glasses.)* Three weeks without ya, Anton; breaks my goddamn heart. Don't worry, babe, we'll keep y'room *just* the way ya left it.

ZARETSKY: Unfortunately. *(Opens front door.)* A room in which, for twelve years, sunlight has appeared almost entirely by metaphor. *(Exits into street. Silence for a moment.)*

EDDIE: *(His back to* YOUNG CHARLIE, *busily stacking glasses.)* O.K., just for laughs, Putz, what's so ugly about that picture?

YOUNG CHARLIE: For one thing, the light, Pop . . . *(*EDDIE *squints at the painting.)* It's all like . . . flat, see. It's like the light is coming from *every*where, y'know, so it's not really—

EDDIE: Yeah, right, O.K., good this come up. This stuff about where the light's comin' from, also these here poems and stories you been writin'. Take a for-instance— *(Takes folded piece of loose-leaf paper from cash register.)*—this poem ya give me Father's Day.

YOUNG CHARLIE: Did ya like it? Ya never mentioned—

EDDIE: Sure, sure. *(Hands it to him, sits at their usual center table.)* Do y'Pop a favor, O.K.? You read this to me, then

I'm gonna ask ya a question. *(*YOUNG CHARLIE *hesitates for a moment.)* Go ahead.

*(*YOUNG CHARLIE *starts to read as* ZARETSKY *returns with the mail, places all but a few pieces on bar, listens attentively to poem.)*

YOUNG CHARLIE: *(Reading.)* O.K. . . . "Father of the Flamingo; by C. E. Ross: . . . He leadeth them beside distilled waters, he restoreth their credit; and if they be Mick Shickers, he maketh them to lie down in dark gutters. And yea, though I may walk through the valley of the shadow of Little Italy, I shall fear no Goy or evil sound, 'cause my Pop has taught me how to bring one up from the ground."

ZARETSKY: *(Applauding.)* Bravo, Chaim; bravo! *(He exits upstairs, continuing to nod his approval for the work of a fellow artist.)*

EDDIE: O.K., very nice. *(Leaning forward, pleasantly.)* O.K., now all I'm askin' is a truthful answer: who helped ya out with that?

YOUNG CHARLIE: Nobody, Pop. I mean, it's a Twenty-third Psalm take-off, so I got help from the *Bible*—

EDDIE: I *know* that, *besides* that—the thing, the *ideas* in there, how it come together there—you tellin' me nobody helped ya out on that, the *Actor, no*body?

YOUNG CHARLIE: Nobody, Pop.

EDDIE: *(He pauses, then indicates the chair opposite him;* YOUNG CHARLIE *sits.)* O.K., there's times certain Jewish words is unavoidable, I give ya two: Narrishkeit and Luftmensh. Narrishkeit is stuff be*yond* foolish—like what?—your mother givin' English lessons, this would be Narrish-work. Now this Narrishkeit is generally put out by Luftmensh—meanin', literal, *guys* who live on the *air*—from which we get the term "no visible goddamn means of support." Poem-writers, story-writers, picture-painters, we got *alotta* 'em come in here; what ya got is mainly y'fairies, y'bust-outs and y'souseniks—a blue *moon,* ya get a sober straight-shooter, breaks even. *(Slaps the table.)* Now, I'm lookin' at this poem two months now, besides takin' note, numerous situations, how you *present* y'self, kid—first-class, flat-out *amazin',* this poem. *(*YOUNG CHARLIE *smiles happily,* EDDIE *taps his son's head.)* It's goddamn Niagara *Falls* in there—now all we gotta do is point it the right way so ya can turn on a coupla *light* bulbs with it. The *answer*? Head like yours, ya know it already, don't ya?

YOUNG CHARLIE: *(Confused but flattered.)* No; I don't, Pop.

EDDIE: I speak, of course, of the legal profession! Brain like that, how you get them words together, I'm talkin' *Up*town, Charlie, I'm talkin' about the firm o' Ross, Ross, Somebody and *Some*body; you're gonna be walkin' through places the dollars stick to your *shoes*, y'can't *kick* the bucks off. Hey, looka the experience you got already, huh?— *(Rises, arms wide, delightedly struck by the perfect illustration)* —twelve years now you been pleadin' cases before the bar!

*(*EDDIE *laughs happily at his joke, slapping the bar,* YOUNG CHARLIE *laughing with him, their laughter building with the sharing of the joke,* CHARLIE *joining them.)*

CHARLIE: *(Chuckling.)* Not bad, not bad; one for *you*, Pop . . . *(Suddenly frightened, remembering; he shouts.)* *Now*—it was *now*—

(We hear GUSTA *scream from upstairs—a long, wrenching, mournful wail, like the siren of a passing ambulance—even at this distance, a stairway and a closed door between them, the sound permeates the barroom. Then silence;* EDDIE *and* YOUNG CHARLIE *frozen for a moment, then both racing towards the bottom of the stairs. Before they can reach the first step, though,* ZARETSKY *enters at the top of the stairs from the apartment above, closing the door quietly behind himself.* EDDIE *and* YOUNG CHARLIE *remain quite still, several feet from the stairs;* ZARETSKY *takes a step or two down towards them.)*

ZARETSKY: The telegram I opened was not for me, Itzik. It is for you and Gusta. Jussel is dead. He was killed two days ago. The first telegram says only *(He reads.)* "The Secretary of War desires me to express his deep regret that your son, Petty Officer Second-Class Joseph Ross, was killed in action in defense of his country on August sixth, Nineteen Forty-five." *(A moment.)* Gusta stays upstairs; she requests to be alone for a while. *(*EDDIE *and* YOUNG CHARLIE *remain standing quite still at the bottom of the* *stairs, their backs to us, not a tremor, their emotions unreadable.)* There is more; shall I go on? *(*EDDIE *nods.)* Enclosed also, a cable, this from Captain Nordheim of the destroyer Campbell. He begins: "The fanatical suicide attack which caused the death of your son . . ."

*(*CHARLIE*, downstage, continuing the cable from memory now as* ZARETSKY *continues reading, inaudibly, on the stairs behind him.)*

CHARLIE: ". . . is tragically consistent with the desperate actions of our enemy at this time of their imminent surrender. On the morning of August sixth a force of eight Zeros descended upon the St. Louis and the Campbell at one-minute intervals; the sixth and seventh of these craft being destroyed by Petty Officer Ross from his forward forty-millimeter position, the eighth now aimed directly for his battle station. With ample time to leave his position for safety, your son, to his undying honor, remained at his weapon, as determined to destroy the target as was the target to destroy his battle station. As recommended and reviewed by myself and the Secretary of the Navy, it has been deemed appropriate to recognize his selfless valor by awarding the Navy Cross to Petty Officer Second-Class Joseph Ross. In addition, I have respected your son's prior request to be buried at sea, the Kaddish being read by an Ensign Sidney Berman for the name of Jussel Solomon Goldberg, also by the same request."

(Starting with the first line of the above speech, the action will begin to move forward in time behind CHARLIE *to the evening of the next day, the first of the seven days of Shiva, the family's mourning period—daylight giving way to night outside and near-darkness in the bar as* CHARLIE *speaks,* ZARETSKY *slowly folding the cable, putting on a yamulke, and then joining* YOUNG CHARLIE *behind the bar where they drape a large piece of black cloth over the long bar mirror; their movements—and those of the others during this transition—are deliberate, trancelike, ritualized, as though to the beat of inaudible music. During the draping of the mirror,* GUSTA *will have entered from the apartment, her head covered with a dark shawl, carrying a tray of pastries and* EDDIE*'s black suit jacket; she places the tray on the cen-*

ter table, drapes the jacket over a chair next to it, then places a piece of black cloth over JOEY's *Navy photograph above the jukebox as* EDDIE, *who has remained quite still at center, slowly puts on his jacket, then sits at center table, blankly, looking off, as though in a dream.* YOUNG CHARLIE *comes up behind* EDDIE, *delicately places a yarmulke on his father's head and then one on his own as* NICK, HANNAH, *and then* FINNEY *come quietly through the front door, wearing dark clothes, each bearing a box of pastry, moving slowly, silently, through the half-light of the barroom;* GUSTA *embracing* HANNAH, *the two women holding onto each other for a few moments before* NICK *leads* HANNAH *gently away to their table and* GUSTA *sits at the center table near* EDDIE. *After saying the last few words of the memorized Nordheim cable,* CHARLIE *pauses a moment, then turns to look at* EDDIE, *who remains quite frozen, listless, on his chair.* HANNAH *and* NICK *at their usual table now, holding hands,* FINNEY *in the shadows of his booth, his head bowed.* CHARLIE *moves close to* YOUNG CHARLIE *and* ZARETSKY *now; having lit the seven-day memorial candle and placed it on the far left table, the old man and the boy sit near its glow, leaning towards each other in quiet conversation.)*

CHARLIE: I'd never said the Mourner's Kaddish before; I knew what the Hebrew words meant—but suddenly that morning in the synagogue it made no sense to me; here in this ancient, ancient prayer for the dead was not a reference, not a phrase . . . not a word about death.

ZARETSKY: *(Leans towards* YOUNG CHARLIE, *answering his question.)* It's not *about* death, Chaim; we have here a prayer about faith only, absolute faith in God and his wisdom. *(Closes his eyes.)* Listen, the music of it, "Yisgaddal v'yiskaddash shmey rabboh . . ." You praise God, "B'rich Hu": "blessed be He; blessed, praised, glorified, exalted . . ."

EDDIE: *(Quietly, almost to himself, still looking off.)* It's like the Mafia, Charlie . . . It's like talkin' to a Mafia Chief after he does a hit, ya kiss the Capo's ass so he don't knock *you* off too: "Hey, God, what a great idea, killin' Joey Ross. Throwin' my cousin Sunny under a garbage truck—I thought *that* was great—but havin' some nutso Nip drop Joey, this is you at the top of your *form,* baby . . ." *(*GUSTA *rises slowly, staring down at him.)* Oh, yeah, magnified and sanctified be *you,* Don Giuseppe . . . *(*GUSTA *turns sharply, walks quickly to the stairs and exits into the apartment;* EDDIE *barely glancing at her, continuing louder now, all in bar turning to him.)* Hey, Charlie that's *it* for Hebrew School. Over and *out,* kid. I hear ya go *near* the goddamn place I bust ya in the chops . . . *(Rises, pulls off his yarmulke, then yanks off* YOUNG CHARLIE*'s.) Hell* with the Bar Mitzvah; I'm takin' ya to Norfolk Street and gettin' ya *laid* that day . . . *(As* EDDIE *continues, louder, his rage growing, we begin to hear* GUSTA *singing the old Yiddish lullaby we heard in Act I, distantly, gently, from upstairs.)*

GUSTA'S VOICE: *(Singing.)*

"Oif'n pripitchok,
Brent a faierel,
Un in shtub iz heys . . ."

(Continuing softly through the scene . . .)

EDDIE: . . . Three years Joey put in, the prayers, the bullshit, the Bar Mitzvah shot, the goddamn criminal *con* of the whole thing. I *knew* it— *(Shouting, striding fiercely to bar, tearing black cloth off of mirror.)* I *told* ya, I knew it all *along* it was a sucker's game! You *watch* me, alla you, *tonight* I go to Beth-*El,* I go to the *East Window* because this is where God's supposed t'hear ya better—and I tell 'im, I tell the Killer Bastard—get *this,* God, I ain't a *Jew* no more! *Over,* pal! Fifty years of bein' a Jew Loser; *over,* baby! *Take* 'em, take the *resta* them, they're *yours—you* chose 'em, *you* got 'em—

YOUNG CHARLIE: *(Quietly.)* Shut up . . .

EDDIE: —every *God*-fearin', *death*-fearin', scared-*shit*less *Jew*-creep is *yours*—but not *Eddie,* not—

YOUNG CHARLIE: Shut up, will ya? *(He rises.)* You really gonna blame this on *God,* Pop? Really? This is what you *wanted,* Pop: Mr. America, the toughest Jew in the Navy, and you got it; only he's dead. Every *letter, twice* on the phone with him I heard ya—"Kill, kill, *kill* 'em, kid!" Same as you screamed in the *ring.* And you want *God* to take the blame for this? *(Pointing fiercely, tears in his eyes.)* All for *you,* Pop, the Ring, the Twin-Forties, he was fightin' for *you.* "Kill 'em, kid! *Get* 'em!" No, Pop, no, not *God,* not *God*—you, it was *you,* it was *you,* Pop. *(He races quickly up the stairs, crying, exits into apartment, slamming the door behind him.)*

(Silence for a moment, even GUSTA*'s distant singing has stopped.* EDDIE *goes quickly up the stairs to the door.)*

EDDIE: Listen to me, kid; ya got it all wrong, I straighten it out for ya . . . *(He tries to open the door, but it has clearly been locked from the inside; he leans closer, raises his voice a bit, trying to talk to* YOUNG CHARLIE *through the door.)* Listen to me, Charlie; it's just my wacky Pop, see. Just my wacky Pop all over again. *Fine* points; it's the goddamn *fine* points, kid—*(Louder, almost cracking, his rage holds him together.)* He *knows* this Nip Fruitcake is comin' right *for* 'im, but he stays there behind his gun, because he *thinks* he's *supposed* to! It's my Pop all over again, pal—*fine* points; goddamn fine points! Wacky, the *both* o' them . . . *wacky* . . . *(Silence. He tries the knob again.)* Come on, kid; open up. *(One bang on the door; sternly, evenly.)* Hey, Charlie; open up. *(Silence.)* Let's move it, Charlie; let me in. *(Starts banging more forcefully on door.)* Let me in, Charlie; let me *in* there . . . *(Now wildly, fiercely, pleading, pounding with all his strength, the door shaking from his blows.)* Charlie, Charlie, let me *in,* let me *in*! *(Both fists together now, pounding rhythmically, shouting with each blow.)* Let me *in,* let me *in,* let me *in* . . .

(He continues banging on the door, his shouting almost like a chant now; NICK *and* FINNEY *rise as though to come to his aid;* ZARETSKY *remains on his wooden box, his head bowed, intoning loudly above the din.)*

ZARETSKY: "Yisgaddal v'yiskaddash shmey rabboh . . ."

(A sudden silence, a sharp drop in light, they are all quite still, frozen silhouettes in the dim remaining glow; CHARLIE *alone in a small spotlight at right, caught by the moment.)*

CHARLIE: *(Turns to us; softly, a plea.)* I didn't mean it, I just . . . I mean, I was *twelve* at the time, very upset, a *kid* . . . I was just . . . ya know what I mean?

(The sudden sound of Lyndon Johnson's voice fills the stage, his echoing drawl offering the promise of the Great Society as EDDIE, ZARETSKY, HANNAH, NICK, *and* FINNEY

exit into the shadows of the bar, the Flamingo Chandelier rising into the darkness above it, CHARLIE *moving slowly down center as this part of his past disappears behind him.)*

JOHNSON'S VOICE: Is our world gone? We say farewell. Is a new world coming? We welcome it. And we bend it to the hopes of Man . . .

CHARLIE: *(Turns to us, brightening.)* Amazingly . . . amazingly, life went back to normal after Joey died—Pop quickly resumed living at the top of his voice and the edge of his nerves, battling with Zaretsky in the mornings and me in the afternoons and re-naming the bar "Big Ed's Club Canal." My next bout with Pop—oh, there were a few minor exhibition matches about leaving home at seventeen, not going to law school, not visiting often enough—but our next *real* bout was more than twenty years later. October fifteenth, Sixty-five; I remember exactly because it was the morning the Vatican Council announced that the Jews were no longer responsible for the death of Christ . . . *(As he continues, an older* GUSTA, *her raven hair streaked with gray, enters from the kitchen in the dim half-light behind him, carrying a tray; she will move briskly from table to table as he speaks, clearing away the many plastic pineapples and coconut shells, eventually disappearing back into the kitchen.)* By then I had become one of the blue-moon Luftmenshen who had *made* it in the Narrishkeit business. This, starting at the age of twenty-*three,* by knockin' out almost one novel a year. The most familiar to you, from the early Sixties, would be *Over at Izzy's Place,* the first of the "Izzy" books, eight and still counting, three best-sellers by then, vast areas of virgin forest consumed by paperback sales, undisputed Middleweight Champ at thirty-four, I had become . . . unavoidable. And so had Izzy. Izzy, tough but warm, blunt yet wise, the impossible and eccentric Bleecker Street tavern-keeper who won not only your heart in the final chapter, but the Mayor's Special Cultural Award that year for "embodying the essential charm and excitement of New York's ethnic street life." *(Shakes his head, smiling.)* Unavoidable, that is, to everyone but Pop. Hard to take it personally, he never read anything longer than Winchell's column or the blow-by-blows in the *Trib.* We were down to maybe four or five visits a year by then—the first half of each being consumed with how long it'd been since the last one and the second half with contractual arrangements for the next—and we didn't meet at the usual family weddings and Bar Mitzvahs because Pop would never again enter a synagogue or any place that resembled one . . . *(Lights coming up slowly on the bar as he continues;* GUSTA, *who has returned from the kitchen, sits alone now at the center table, businesslike, in charge, wearing glasses, checking a stack of bills, as* CHARLIE *moves about her in the empty barroom indicating the places where The Regulars once sat.)* Hannah was gone by then, and Nick too; I never did learn their last names. Finney—old, but sharp as ever—smelled O.T.B. and legal lottery in the wind and was now taking Temperature-Humidity Index bets at a Kosher delicatessen in Boca Raton. Mr. Zaretsky died in January of sixty-one, just a week before his ninety-third birthday, during the closing moments of a concert for the Y.M.H.A. of St. Louis, in Missouri, performing his twelve-minute version of "The Dybbuk"; passing away in crimson light, playing all parts . . . including title role. *(Moving down behind* GUSTA*'s chair as she continues busily checking bills.)* I called Mom every Sunday to hear her two jokes of the week, but this last call was different—Pop'd had a mild heart attack in sixty-four from which he'd quickly recovered, but now she said something had "gone wrong with the health"; I asked for more details but she was already into her second joke by then— *(Sound of* EDDIE *laughing loudly from the kitchen as though at what* CHARLIE *has just said; morning light starts to stream in from outside as* GUSTA *rises with her stack of bills, exits briskly up the stairs into apartment.)* —so I came down early the next morning to check it out myself, and found him, as always, in better shape than *I* was . . . *(*EDDIE *enters from the kitchen, chuckling happily at something on the front page of* The New York World-Telegram*;* EDDIE, *though twenty years older, seems spry enough as he walks down towards the far right booth, sharply opening the paper to read the rest of the front-page story that amuses him so much; the front page faces us now and we see a huge banner headline which states: "Vatican Absolves Jews of Crucifixion Blame."* CHARLIE *turns to him.)* Pop . . .

EDDIE: *(Glances up from paper, pleasantly.)* Hey . . . it's *him. (Returns to paper.)* How ya doin', kid?

CHARLIE: Fine, fine; I'm—

EDDIE: How'd ya get in?

CHARLIE: I got my key. Listen, Pop, I was . . . uh . . . in the neighborhood, stopped by . . .

EDDIE: *(Sits in booth, still reading paper.)* In the neighborhood?

CHARLIE: Yeah right . . . *(Approaches booth, indicating headline.)* Well, I see you've gotten the big news, Pop.

EDDIE: Winchell had it two days ago. Just sent the Pope off a telegram on the matter; here's a copy. *(Hands him piece of note paper.)*

CHARLIE: *(Reading.)* I don't think they just hand telegrams to the Pope directly, Pop; especially ones that say, "Thanks a lot, you Greaseball Putz."

EDDIE: Well, let's see, must be what?—four, five months now since you last—

CHARLIE: Let's skip that one this time, O.K.? Mom tells me we got a health problem here.

EDDIE: *(Slaps table, laughing.)* I don't believe it. I don't *believe* it. Six *months* ago I say I'm not feelin' so good, she decides to hear it *now.* That listening thing she does—I'm tellin' ya, kid, it's wackier than ever—the woman hears less and less every week and what she *does* get comes to her entirely by *carrier*-pigeon. *(CHARLIE smiles; EDDIE rises from booth.)* Old news, kid, I'm fine now; looka me. *(Demonstrates a boxing combination.)* Looka me, huh? Also the place is a hit, Charlie; just happened the last few months. Hey, not *giant,* but a hit. *(Chuckles, pointing upstairs.) She* did it; the Wacky One. Turns out, right near here, starts out a whole new neighborhood, "HoHo"—

CHARLIE: That's "SoHo"—

EDDIE: *(With a sly wink.)* I'm tellin' ya, kid, *Ho*Ho—wall-to-wall Luftmensh, blocks and *blocks* of 'em, doin' nothin' but Narrishkeit, and they got these *galleries* here, hustlin' the Narr for 'em; *bucks,* Charlie, bucks like ya wouldn't believe—and all from this Narrishkeit done by these Luftmensh livin' in these Lufts around here.

CHARLIE: Lofts, Pop.

EDDIE: And the *rent* for these Lufts—I'm talkin' *Vegas* money, Charlie. Anyways, maybe five months ago, a coupla these Narrishkeit hustlers come in here, they're havin' some o' the Mulligan Stew—they go *crazy* for it—

CHARLIE: I don't blame them—

EDDIE: Next thing I know we got a goddamn *army* o' these Narrishkeit people with the fancy Lufts comin' here, they're gobblin' up everything in sight, they love the stuff and they love Mama—under the original *names,* the Varnishkes, the Holishkes—they come in strangers, they go out grandchildren. I put up a new sign outside, musta seen it, "The Homeland"—I up the prices a little, we're a *hit;* not a cha*malia,* but we're doin' O.K. Your Mom done it. *(Sits at center table.)*

CHARLIE: She mentioned something about hiring a waitress, but I had no idea— *(Sits opposite him.)* —this is *great,* Pop.

EDDIE: Yeah, so how *you* doin'?

CHARLIE: Well, I'm workin' on a new—

EDDIE: Hey, I seen ya on the TV last week.

CHARLIE: Oh?

EDDIE: Yeah, you was gettin' some prize for something', the Mayor was there.

CHARLIE: Right.

EDDIE: Yeah, I seen ya on the TV. You come in old.

CHARLIE: Old?

EDDIE: Yeah; I mean, you're a young fellah, but on TV you come in old.

CHARLIE: Pop, do you happen to recall *which* prize it was and *what* I got it for?

EDDIE: It was one o' them "Dizzy" books.

CHARLIE: "Izzy," Pop, *"Izzy"*—

EDDIE: Maybe it was the tuxedo.

CHARLIE: The tuxedo?

EDDIE: That made you come in old. Yeah, that's what it was.

CHARLIE: O.K., Pop, I'm glad you're feeling well, and I'm delighted about the place. *(Rising to leave.)* Now I gotta—

EDDIE: O.K.; give my regards to . . . to . . . uh . . .

CHARLIE: Allison.

EDDIE: What happened to Sally?

CHARLIE: We were divorced three years ago. As you well know.

EDDIE: *(Hits his head.)* Of course. Of course. Hard to keep track, alla them—

CHARLIE: Pop, I've only been married twice, Sally and *Karen—*

EDDIE: Better catch up; that puts you two behind Rita Hayworth. So what's with this . . . uh . . . ?

CHARLIE: Allison. You've had dinner with her twice. Last time for three hours. She told you she was editing a book that proved Roosevelt did nothing for the Jews during the War. You broke two plates and walked out. She thought you were cute.

EDDIE: *(After a moment.)* Shit, *marry* that one.

CHARLIE: *(Starts towards door.)* O.K., I really gotta—

EDDIE: Right; hugs to Sarah and Josh—hey, Josh; where's my Josh? Been a coupla *months* now—

CHARLIE: He was hanging around here entirely too much, Pop, it was—

EDDIE: We talk things *over,* we *discuss* things—

CHARLIE: Pop, he's the only ten-year-old at Dalton who drinks his milk out of a shot glass.

EDDIE: *(Laughs happily.)* A *pisser,* that kid; goddamn *pisser—*

CHARLIE: *(Opens door.)* Right; see ya around—

EDDIE: *(Quietly.)* O.K., them books, I read one. *(*CHARLIE *turns at door, his hand on knob.)* Well, not *read;* I give it a skim. The first one. *(Chuckling.)* That's some *sweet*heart, that guy. Who *is* that guy? The bartender with the two sons, comes from Russia; who *is* that sweetie? Got *all* sweeties in there, y'sweet blind lady, y'sweet ex-cop, y-sweet bookie—*three* pages, I got an attack o' diabetes.

CHARLIE: Pop, if I told the truth they'd send a *lynch* mob down here for ya.

EDDIE: Always glad to see new customers, kid. This guy in the book, supposed to be a Jewish guy, right? What kinda Jew is that? Don't sound like no Jew *I* ever heard. Could be anything—Italian, Irish, some kinda Chink even. *(Turns to newspaper.)* Well, what the hell, regardless, I wanna wish ya good luck with them "Dizzy" books.

CHARLIE: Izzy! *(Closes door, turns to him.) Izzy, Izzy, Izzy.* As you know damn *well.* O.K., that's it. No more, Pop, that was *it.* I am never playing this fucking game again; it's *over. (Moving towards him.)* Izzy? You don't like him? Not Jewish enough for ya? He's *your Jew,* Pop, you made him up. He's *your* Jew, and so am I; no history, no memory, the only thing I'm linked to is a chain of bookstores. Vos *vilst* du?—that's Yiddish, Pop; it means "What do you *want*?" God bothered you, we got rid of him. Hugging bothers you, we do not touch. Here I am, Pop, just what the Rabbi ordered; only now you don't like it; now you don't want it. Vos vilst du, Goldberg? *(Leans towards him at table.)* That prize you don't know the *name* of for the books you never *read*—I *won* it, Pop, *me*, the *air*-person, I *did* it— *(Bangs fist on table, shouting.)* —right here at this bar, everything you *asked* for. I am an honest-to-God, red-white-and-blue, *American fucking millionaire.* A *mil,* Pop, a *mil,* a *bundle*! And I never sleep, only in moving vehicles. I hail a cab to take a nap; I work, I work, there's like a fire in me and I don't know where it is so I cannot put it out. And the fire is you. I *did* it, Pop. I won. K.O. in the first *round.* Vos *vilst* du, Papa? Vos *vilst* du fun mir? What do you fucking *want*?

(Silence for a moment. EDDIE *remains quite still.)*

EDDIE: *(Quietly.)* You shouldn't use "fuck" in a sentence, Charlie, you never put it in the right place. You don't blow good, kid, never did; ya don't have the knack. Another item: I listen to ya, I don't like the scorin' on this bout. How about *I* get credit for all the hits and *you* get the credit for bein' a nervous nut. *(Rises from chair, his old energy.)* What're you, goddamn Zorro the Avenger? What? You lookin' to come back here with your empties and get a *re*fund? I didn't *order* this item, you ain't a *cake* I baked. I wasn't just your *Pop,* or Joey's neither, I'm Eddie; for this I take all blame or commendations. Nothin' else. I lived in *my* time, now you gotta live in *yours,* pal, and you can't send me the goddamn bill. Give it *up,* kid, give it the hell *up.* Give yourself a rest, you'll waste your life tryin' to catch me, you'll find y'self twenty years from now runnin' around a cemetery tryin' to put a stake through my heart. Sure I screwed up; now it's *your* turn. Yeah, let's see what *you* do when you look at Sarah or Josh and see *your* Pop's eyes peekin' out at ya; or worse, your *own.* Let's see what ya *do,* kid. *(Turns, starts towards bar.)* Meanwhile, currently, I admit I give ya a hard time—but, frankly, I never liked rich kids. *(He stops, stands quite still; speaks briskly.)* O.K., conversation over. End of conversation. See ya around; good-bye— *(Grips* *back of chair, staggers, as though about to faint, whispering.)* Shit, here we go again . . . *(He suddenly falls to the ground, the chair clattering down with him.)*

CHARLIE: *(Rushing to him, breathless.) Pop,* Jesus . . . Pop . . .

EDDIE: *(Almost immediately, sitting up.)* It's O.K., it's O.K., get me a vodka . . .

CHARLIE: *(Helping him up.)* Pop, I thought you—

EDDIE: *Vodka,* get me a vodka— *(*CHARLIE *races behind the bar;* EDDIE, *standing now but still a bit unsteady, leans on the table for a moment.)* O.K., O.K. now. Comes, then it goes. *(Walking slowly to bar.)* Comes, then it goes. Fine now. Perfect. *(*CHARLIE, *behind bar, quickly pouring a glass of vodka, handing it out to him—but* EDDIE *grabs the bottle and takes a long swig directly from it.)* Excellent. Excellent. *(Sets bottle down on bar, renewed. Silence for a moment.)* O.K., I conned ya, Charlie . . . I got this heart thing; special disease named for some goy, Smithfield. Your Mother says right off, "How come you got Smithfield's Disease and he don't got yours?" Don't care how old the joke is, what the occasion, she tells it. Turns out that wasn't no heart attack last year, it was this Smithfield number. The valve closes up, you keep fallin' asleep, fallin' over— *(Pulls wheelchair out from behind far end of bar.)* I'm supposed to sit in this thing a lot because I keep droppin' alla time. What kills you is these embies—

CHARLIE: *(Quietly.)* I think that's . . . that's embolus, Pop . . .

EDDIE: *(Moving wheelchair down left.)* Right. Anyways you can shoot off these embies anytime. They go all over the joint. Musta shot one off four weeks ago, I'm all screwed up, I go in for these tests—turns out I'm the proud owner of a new, fully automatic *Smithfield.* Knocks you off in like six months or maybe next Tuesday. So— *(Sits down in wheelchair.)* —good ya stopped by, we do a wrap-up shot, I got a *job* for ya—

CHARLIE: *(Sits next to wheelchair.)* The doctors, they're *sure*?—I mean, I can get you—

EDDIE: Minute I get the news I got only one item concerns me, see; I go down to Barney's Tattoo Parlor on Mott, take care of it right off, goddamn relief. Looka here— *(Rolls up both sleeves,* CHARLIE *comes closer to look at the two tattoos.)* One says "Pistol Pete," see, nice gun picture there, and this one here—

CHARLIE: *(Reading elaborate red and blue tattoo on* EDDIE*'s left arm; confused.)* "King of the Twin-Forties." I don't—

EDDIE: *(Triumphantly.)* Hebrew *law,* Charlie—one of the oldest—you can't get buried in *any* Jewish cemetery if you got tattoos! Twenty *years,* kid, I ain't had to be no kinda *Jew* at *all*—coulda ended up gettin' *Kaddished*-over, full-out ceremony, then gettin' stuck in some sacred Jew-ground with a buncha Yiddlach for *eternity*! *(Quietly, glancing upstairs.)* She ain't to be trusted on this issue; since Joey, the woman is a goddamn religious *fanatic*—candles, prayers, every weird little holiday— *(Leans towards* CHARLIE, *grips his arm.)* So, here's the job, Charlie—*any*thing goes wrong, I want your personal guarantee—

CHARLIE: Of course, Pop—

EDDIE: *(Hands him card from wallet.)* Here's where ya put me, kid; place in Queens, no religions whatever, no gods of any type.

CHARLIE: It's done.

EDDIE: Because the woman, I'm tellin' ya, she's got her eye on this spot in Brooklyn where they planted the Actor. Woman thinks dyin' is movin' to the *suburbs,* wants us all *together* there—me, her, Ethel, and *Zaretsky*! Can ya *picture* it, Charlie?—me and Zaretsky, goddamn *room*mates *forever*! Wouldn't get a minute's rest. 'Specially *now,* what I know *now* . . . *(He looks away. Silence for a moment.)*

CHARLIE: *What?* What do you know now?

EDDIE: *(Pause; a deep breath, plunges in.)* O.K.—*day* before he goes to St. Louis, the man gets a flash he's gonna kick it, makes out a will. Man is ninety-goddamn-*three,* he's first makin' out a will. Brings a lawyer over here, *also* about a hundred and eight, Ruskin, used to do all his business when he had the New Marinsky on Houston, wants me and Finney to witness, sign the will. I look it over, I see two things—first, I'm not in it; second, whatever he's got is goin' to the State of Israel . . . whatever he's *got* bein' one million, five hundred thousand dollars and change. A mil and a half, Charlie; the man was sittin' on a *mil* and a *half.* And this Ruskin almost as rich; *Ruskin,* with an accent on 'im made Zaretsky sound like George M. *Cohan*! They sell this Marinsky dump for bupkes back in Twenty-eight; they parlay the bupkes into a fortune, they was good at *business, American business,* and the rest he got from them goddamn *concerts,* Charlie! *(A pause; he rubs the arm of the wheelchair.)* I made Finney promise to zip it; I never told you, Gusta, nobody . . .

CHARLIE: Hey, far as me and Joey were concerned, you were always the *boss* here; wouldn't've made any difference—

EDDIE: A mil and a *half,* Charlie—he's livin' in that little room, takin' shit from me—

CHARLIE: He *loved* it here, Pop—he even liked fightin' with *you,* he—

*(*CHARLIE *stops in midsentence, aware that* EDDIE *has started to nod off to sleep . . .* EDDIE *suddenly hits the arm of his wheelchair, forcing himself awake.)*

EDDIE: *(Outraged.)* A *millionaire,* Charlie! Workin' in a loser language! He did everything *wrong*—and he was a hit! Can you make *sense* of this, Charlie? *Zaretsky,* why *him*—why *him* and not *me*? And, you'll forgive me—I wish ya all the best— *(Gripping* CHARLIE*'s arm.)* —but why *you,* ya little Putz, you with your goddamn *Narr*ishkeit—why *you,* and not me? Why? *(Starting to become drowsy again.)* Surrounded by goddamn millionaires here . . . Can you make *sense* of this . . . the bucks, what happened? The Big Bucks, why did they avoid me? Wherever I was, the bucks never came, and when I went to where the bucks were they flew away like pigeons . . . like pigeons in the park . . . *(His head nodding forward, drifting off.)* Got this dream alla time I'm at Ellis Island, only I'm the age I'm now. Old days, you had a disease, they wouldn't let ya in. They mark on your coat with chalk, "E" for eye, "L" for lung, and they send ya back. In the dream, I got an "H" for heart and they won't let me in . . . they won't let me in, Joey . . . *(He falls deeply asleep in the wheelchair. Silence.* CHARLIE *leans anxiously towards him.)*

CHARLIE: Pop . . . ? *(Touches his arm gently.)* Pop . . . ? *(Silence again.* CHARLIE *rises, carefully turning the wheelchair around so that* EDDIE*'s sleep is not disturbed by the morning light that comes in from the front door.* EDDIE *remains with his back to us; during this next scene we will not see his face except perhaps for brief glimpses of his profile.* CHARLIE *speaking to us as he turns the* *chair.)* Six weeks later one o' them embies shot off into the left side of Pop's brain, paralyzing his right arm and leg and taking away his ability to speak. *(Opening small side table on arm of wheelchair, placing pad and pencil on it.)* Two weeks back from the hospital he had somehow taught himself to write almost legibly with his left hand—according to this terrific speech therapy lady I went to, this meant he could eventually be trained to speak again. But all he was able to produce were these unintelligible, childlike noises, and he refused to see anyone, no less try to *speak* to anyone, including Gusta. He closed "The Homeland" down and sat here. Ten days, like this. On the eleventh day, armed with some hints from the speech therapist, I came down to take a shot. *(To* EDDIE*:)* Delighted to see me, huh? *(*EDDIE *shakes his head angrily.)* And you're thinkin' what's the sense of trying to learn how to speak again because you figure you *can't,* also why torture yourself if you ain't gonna live that much longer *anyway,* right? *(*EDDIE *points with his left hand as though to say* "You *got it,*" *then does a powerful "Go away" gesture.)* Right. And there's these clear pictures in your head of all the words you want to say and your mouth just won't do the job, right? *(*EDDIE *does not respond. Then, after a moment, he nods "Yes.")* O.K., now I don't know *how* this works or *why* this works, but there's a thing you're capable of right now called "automatic speech." As impossible as it must feel to you, you are capable, right now, of saying, distinctly as *ever,* certain automatic phrases—ends of songs, if I do the first part, a piece of a prayer, something. And, thing is, you hear yourself *do* that and that'll get you to want to work at the whole talkin'-shot again, see. *(*EDDIE *scribbles something on the pad on the arm of his wheelchair, hands pad to* CHARLIE.*)* "Go *away. Stay* away." Pop, I gotta try the number here. C'mon, gimme a chance . . . (CHARLIE *leans forward, singing softly:)* "Oh beautiful for spacious skies . . ." *(Pause, no response.* CHARLIE *tries again.)* "Oh beautiful for spacious skies, for amber . . ." *(Silence for a few moments; then very suddenly, sharply.)* You got some ice-cold Daitch on tap, fellah?

EDDIE: *(Suddenly.) I* got it, now *you* . . . got it. *(*EDDIE *realizes what he has just done.* CHARLIE *smiles. Silence for a moment;* EDDIE *appears to be chuckling softly.)*

CHARLIE: Well, now. Shall we proceed, sir? *(Silence for a moment.* EDDIE *turns away; then looks at* CHARLIE*; he nods.)* O.K., now we got some pictures here . . . *(Takes a stack of eight-by-eleven-inch cards out of an envelope.)* Objects, people, animals, O.K.? Double item here, see; there's a picture of the thing and then the word for it printed underneath. You go for either one—word or picture, and *say* what it is. Be patient with yourself on this, O.K.? *(*EDDIE *nods.)* O.K.; animals and birds. *(Looks through cards, stops at one; smiles.)* Yeah, here's a good beginning . . . *(He turns the card around; it is a full-color illustration of a duck.)* "Duck." We'll start with "Duck."

*(*EDDIE *does not move, there is a long silence. Then* EDDIE, *rather forcefully, raises his left arm, the middle finger of his hand jabbing upward, giving* CHARLIE *"the finger."* EDDIE *continues to hold his hand up firmly; the lights come down, one single light remaining on "the finger."*

CHARLIE: *(Turns to us.)* Well, there it is, my last image of my father: his memorial, his obelisk, his Washington Monument. *(He moves across towards his booth at far right, the light gradually dimming down on "the finger" during his next speech; only a small spotlight on* CHARLIE, *the rest of the stage is near-darkness.)* He died about seven months later; by then he was talking, even hollering, and terrorizing his third speech therapist. *(We hear the distant sound of a Cantor singing a phrase of the Kaddish, rising then fading, as the barely visible shape of the older* GUSTA *comes out of the kitchen; she rolls the wheelchair off into the shadows as* CHARLIE *continues.)* Bicentennial's next week, two hundred years since America was born and, two days later, ten years since Pop died. I wish I could tell you that he won my heart in the final chapter, but he did not. I light his Yahrzeit candle every year, though, and say the prayer; I figured Mom would appreciate it. *(After a moment.)* It's a month now since *she* died, joking as she closed her act. "I'm thinking of becoming a Catholic," she says, that last night. "And why's that, Ma?" I say, feeding her the straight-line like a good son— *(With* GUSTA*'s accent.)* "Well, Sonny, I figure better one of *them* goes than one of us." *(Takes keys from jacket.)* I miss her, of course; but I will not miss this place. *(A beat.)* Pop got his wish, of course; I buried him in this aggressively nonsectarian joint called Hamilton Oaks out in Queens. However, one of the reasons I never forget his Yahrzeit is that every year, a week before the sixth . . . *(He takes the familiar blue and white card out of his jacket.)* this card comes from the Sons of Moses to remind me. For fifty bucks he got them to find me for the *rest of my life.* Los Angeles, *London,* the Virgin fucking *Islands,* they *find* me, those Sons of Moses . . .

(The sudden lights of the Present—the early evening light of the beginning of the play—come up in the barroom as CHARLIE *holds the card up and crushes it fiercely in his hand; he tosses the mangled card on the floor and strides angrily towards the bar, the old stroller once again down left, his rage building as he slams noisily about behind the bar looking for his glass and vodka bottle.)*

CHARLIE: The old switcheroo—the old switcheroo every time! Never made any *sense, never*—his *head,* his *head,* it was *steeple*chase up there, the goddamn *roller*-coaster—*(Bangs his fist on the bar.) None* of it, nothing he said, *none* of it fit together—*none* of it—*still* doesn't—son of a bitch—

JOSH: *(Entering briskly from the apartment above, carrying two cartons; brightly.)* Dad . . . Dad, I've been thinking, how about—why don't we *keep* this place and just get somebody to *run* it for us; y'know, a manager, we'll find a good manager. We *keep* it, Dad, we keep it just the way it *is*; I'll help out, weekends, every summer, maybe even—

CHARLIE: *(Fiercely, wildly, shouting.)* I *told* you, we're *selling* it, we're selling it, you don't *listen*—

JOSH: *(Startled.)* I just—I just thought maybe we could—

CHARLIE: *(He smashes his fist on the bar, coming quickly out from behind bar towards Josh.)* It's *gone, over,* outa *my* life, outa *yours, over, over*— *(*CHARLIE*, blindly, violently, his fist raised, advancing on* JOSH, JOSH *backing fearfully away across the room.)*—you don't *listen,* you *never did*—you don't *now,* you never *did,* and you never *will*—

*(*JOSH *is trapped against one of the booths, startled, frozen.* CHARLIE *stops, stands quite still, trembling with his*

own rage; then gradually begins to focus on his son's frightened eyes.)

CHARLIE: *(Lost, whispering.)* Josh . . . sorry, I was . . .

*(*JOSH *backs away towards the front door, warily, as though from a stranger.)*

JOSH: *(Softly.)* You get yourself together, O.K. . . . ? I'll wait in the car, O.K. . . . ?
CHARLIE: Josh, I'm sorry . . . I was . . . see, I was . . .
JOSH: You get yourself together, I'll be in the car . . .
CHARLIE: *(Moving toward him, his hand up.)* Josh, what happened, let me explain . . .

(But JOSH *has gone out into the street with his cartons, the door closing behind him.* CHARLIE *stands exhausted at the center of the room, looking at the door; silence for several moments. He turns, looks about at the bar for a moment, sees the crumpled Sons of Moses card on the floor; he picks it up, studies it thoughtfully, then starts straightening it out as he walks slowly towards the bar. We begin to hear the violin introduction to Aaron Lebedeff's recording of "Rumania" from the jukebox, and then Lebedeff's rousing voice.)*

LEBEDEFF'S VOICE:
"Rumania, Rumania, Rumania . . .
Geven amol a land a zise, a sheyne . . ."

(As CHARLIE *reaches the bar and sits on one of the stools, the old bar lights fade quickly up, the colorful lights of the Thirties and Forties, and* EDDIE *enters briskly from the kitchen, the younger* EDDIE *with his fine white shirt, black bow tie, and sharp black pants;* EDDIE *goes directly behind the bar, takes a glass and a bottle from the shelf, pours with his usual flourish and sets a drink down next to* CHARLIE; CHARLIE *looking down at the card as the Lebedeff music fills the room,* EDDIE *leaning forward with his hands on the bar, looking at the front door, waiting for customers, as . . .)*

THE CURTAIN FALLS

GOLDBERG STREET

by

David Mamet

In the essay, "The Decoration of Jewish Houses,"[1] David Mamet discusses the paradoxical commitment of American Jews to equal rights and full respect for every group except their own. Jews are proud to be citizens of a country that can take seriously the presidential aspirations of an African American—even one given to expressing anti-Semitic sentiments. Yet, Mamet observes, Jews view the possibility of a Jew making a run for that office as "irrelevant and ridiculous." He adds, "As it seems to us faintly ridiculous that we might want in our cities major thoroughfares called Birnbaum or Schwartz."

Goldberg Street focuses on flagging Jewish self-esteem in the face of anti-Semitism in the combat military, an arena where, ironically, impartial recognition of merit and self-respect based on performance seem especially warranted.

[1] In *Some Freaks* (New York: Viking, 1989), 7–14

Goldberg Street was first presented live on WNUR Radio in Chicago on March 4, 1985, with the following cast directed by David Mamet:

Mike Nussbaum
Susan Nussbaum

A man and his daughter talking.

MAN: Goldberg Street. Because they didn't *have* it.
They had *Smith* Street—they had *Rybka* Street.
There was no Goldberg Street.
You can keep your distance and it's fine.
If a man is secluded then he feels superior. Or rage. But where's the good in that?

DAUGHTER: There is no good in it.

MAN: I'm not sure. And I'm not so sure. But sometimes . . . *(Pause.)*
And sometimes, also—you must stand up for yourself. Because it is uncertain . . . what we're doing here.
And masses of *people* do now this and now that; and *at the moment* you might say "this seems wrong," or "this seems attractive."
Popular delusions warp . . . you cannot say they are the product of one man.
Some men like hunting. I enjoy it myself.
Some men like to kill.
Many have killed. Many would say this is not a bad thing.
But they know it is.
Which is not to say they have not enjoyed it.

MAN: A man would *wish* . . . *(Pause.)*
A man would wish someone to inform him . . .
I, if I may say, this is a good example—I am not mechanical but if something is broken and I *must* fix it there comes a point at which pride *in myself*—for the alternative is to say that I am not a man, or that I am an impotent

or *stupid* . . . or, in some way unable to do those things many have done . . .

At one point I would say: "It now is mine to fix it."

When it's up to *me*—if there is no one there . . . then I *will* fix it—for it isn't hidden.

So with problems . . . those things where one *cannot* refer to someone.

At some point. One must say: *I* am the . . .

DAUGHTER: . . . the authority.

MAN: . . . the, *loneliness* that that entails, of course . . . and who would be so droll as to form a religion on ethical principles? *(Pause.)*

And one is alone.

And *so* one is . . .

And so what.

From *that* one may say "well, then I can proceed . . ."

Lost in the wood you must say "I am lost."

DAUGHTER: You killed the deer.

MAN: The man in *Bregny* . . . *(Pause.)*

Men hunted them with automatic weapons.

Which is not a sporting way and it is not an effective way.

Because you can't *aim* them, truly . . .

DAUGHTER: . . . because they jump.

MAN: They *do* jump. And . . . you can aim the first shot, of course . . .

But we were taught to fire them from the hip. Held on the sling to give it tension.

And they *hunted* them, and, as you couldn't aim your shot, the animal, hit badly . . .

Ran.

Died.

Left a blood trail, but they couldn't follow it.

Or wouldn't.

Although they were country boys.

And, I'm sure . . . revered life.

Loved hunting . . .

. . . anyway

(Pause.)

They couldn't read a compass.

In Arkansas one time we were lost. The leader asked if anyone could read a compass. We'd all heard the lecture.

I said, well, I'd never *held* one, but I heard it, I supposed I . . . took it. Read it. Followed the map.

Led us back to camp. It was easy enough. None of it was difficult.

And they put me in for the Unit. When they asked for volunteers.

Which may have been a joke. It was a joke. For anti-Semitism in the army. Then. Even now . . . *(Pause.)*

Even for, and especially then which I see as . . .

If you look at the world you have to laugh. They scorned me, as I assume they did, for those skills they desired to possess. And it was funny I had them.

To them. Lost in the woods. It seems simple enough. If you just take away the thought someone's coming to help you. *(Pause.)*

DAUGHTER: You never see them?

MAN: No, although we were close. In a way. Over there. Where would we . . .

I have no desire to go down south. *(Pause.)* To go visiting at all.

DAUGHTER: You went to France.

MAN: I did. It was the Anniversary. I wanted to see.

DAUGHTER: What did you see? *(Pause.)*

MAN: People. *(Pause.)* I saw the town.

DAUGHTER: Had it changed?

MAN: No. It hadn't changed. Just as the world has changed. *(Pause.)*

DAUGHTER: I heard they saw you.

MAN: Yes. They saw me. There's always someone there.

Laying flowers—it's right by the cliff. I mean the cliff is right beside the road. They . . . *(Pause.)*

DAUGHTER: They knew you.

MAN: I was . . . no, they didn't know me. They saw someone standing . . . *(Pause.)*

A man spoke English. He went in the pub. He must have said, he said something like "one of them's come back." And, in the cemetery . . . they came over there.

DAUGHTER: You were reading the stones?

MAN: They're crosses, really . . . *(Pause.)* Yes. I was looking for the names.

DAUGHTER: Did you find them?

MAN: I thought that I would not remember them. I . . . but I . . . *(Pause.)*

People from the pub came out. *(Pause.)* They said, "You were here."

Yes. We wept.

Patton slapped that Jewish boy.

They said . . . *(Pause.)*

DAUGHTER: They remembered you. *(Pause.)* They remembered what you'd done.

MAN: They sent me for a joke. Because I read the compass. I was glad to go. I knew they thought me ludicrous. Our shame is that we feel they're right. *(Pause.)* I . . . have no desire to go to Israel. *(Pause.)* But I went to France.

ANNULLA, AN AUTOBIOGRAPHY

By
Emily Mann

Emily Mann comments:

It is a rare opportunity for a writer to be asked to go back to his or her first play and confront it anew, some twenty years later, as it is for me with *Annulla, An Autobiography.* I wish to thank Ellen Schiff for asking me to look again at a piece that is in every way seminal to me as a writer. It has been said: "A writer always writes the same play." True or not, I started here and every play since owes its life to this source.

A Love Letter to Mother

Special thanks to the remarkable Timothy Near

Annulla, An Autobiography was presented from March 20 through April 7, 1985, at the Repertory Theatre of St. Louis. Timothy Near directed. The set and costumes were designed by Arthur Ridley and the lighting was by Max DeVolder. The cast:

ANNULLA	*Jacqueline Bertrand*
YOUNG WOMAN'S VOICE	*Jennifer Russell*

The play was presented at the New Theatre of Brooklyn, starring Linda Hunt and directed by the author in the fall of 1986.

An earlier version of the play, *Annulla Allen: Autobiography of a Survivor (A Monologue),* premiered at the Guthrie Theatre's Guthrie 2 in 1977, in a production directed by the author and starring Barbara Bryne. The production was remounted for the Goodman Theatre the next year, and later recorded for Earplay.

PLAYWRIGHT'S NOTE: For the most part, these are Annulla Allen's own words told to me during the summer of 1974 in London, and my own words told to Timothy Near over a decade later.

During the voice-overs, lights change and Annulla continues her activities. In Ms. Near's production, the sound of a ticking clock accompanied the young woman's voice.

CHARACTERS

ANNULLA ALLEN: 74 years old, Eastern European. Tiny. She never walks, she runs.
YOUNG WOMAN'S VOICE: Early 30s. American.

TIME: Teatime.
PLACE: Annulla's North London kitchen.

The play takes place in ANNULLA*'s North London kitchen. It is clean but untidy. A mammoth manuscript covers the kitchen table stage center. It is half typed/half written, and in terrible disorder.*

The room is still. It is teatime. The kettle whistles on the stove.

YOUNG WOMAN'S VOICE: In 1974, the summer I left college, I went to England. That is where I met Annulla. Annulla is the aunt of the woman who was my roommate in college and is my dearest and closest friend. We got a grant to do oral histories of her family, a fascinating family, and I was going on that trip to find my grandmother's village, in Poland. My mother's mother's village—Ostrolenka. We went first to London, Irene and I, and at that time she said to me, "Emily, before we go to Poland you must meet my father's sister, my aunt, my Aunt Annulla."

She lived in a flat in Hampstead heath. We went for a visit. We went for tea.

(ANNULLA *enters, carrying packages, crosses to the stove.)*

ANNULLA: Oh! How do you do? I am so sorry I am late. Oh, this kettle. Excuse me. I have just to put these packages down. *(She puts them down on table.)* I would have been earlier but I had to go shopping for my sister, Ada. She was hit by a milk truck six months ago. She says to me, "I will stay crippled for life now because you have no time for me." Pah! I am really very glad you came here for tea today, really. I expect it's because you have heard about my play.

Here it is. It is called *The Matriarchs.* I have boiled it down to just over six hours, but they tell me it has to be a bit more condensed, but you know I am a woman who has never any time. *(Crosses to cabinet and things fall out.)*

Oh, really this is too much! Oh, I am always doing things like this when I have visitors.

Oh, really, You know, my life is in terrible disorder. And this is so tragic, really, I have so much to do.

Do you know, my brother who is a very eminent biochemist is always reproaching *me* about not being hygienic enough. "Don't you know there is bacteria there?" *(Indicating pot.)* He says this is *poison.* Tea! Only metal is good. If you have tea in an old china cup and you put more in after six hours, this is dangerous. I never knew I lived dangerously. *(Sips.)* Ach! This tea is terrible.

But, do you know, I think I will someday commit suicide. My sister thinks that I should be at her *beck* and *call* since her accident. I am a woman who never has any time.

If you ask me what I am doing one day, I could not explain. Do you know, I don't know what I am doing? I remember when I was eleven, I felt already adult, we went on holiday to Heist, the whole family—the five children, the father and the mother, and the governess. And on the train, a man talked to us, to the children, and then said to my mother, "I am telling you, Madame, one day you will conquer the world with your children." He was so impressed. I was eleven, Ada was nine-and-a-half, Czecha was thirteen or fourteen, Nunu was sixteen, Mania was . . . I don't remember. But that man was so impressed. He was an intellectual. "One day you will conquer the world with your children." We didn't conquer the world yet.

But can you imagine that family! Czecha was a concert pianist at the age of eleven, Ada was . . . a young ballet star. Mania was . . . Mania—och. You don't need to know about Mania. She's a happy woman. Married. Lives in Israel now. Very boring. Nunu was in Vienna teaching medicine as a young teenager. And then came the war. You know, he is a very eminent biochemist. Everyone was convinced that he would win the Nobel Prize. Then the

Nazis destroyed his laboratory in Vienna in 1938 and he had to flee.

Yes, I can tell you what it was like to live always in the shadow of tyrants. I have seen firsthand men's barbarism taken to his extreme with Hitler. You know, I just bought this Solzhenitsyn's *Archipelago*. You know, those of us who lived through it are not shocked by the Stalinists. It is common knowledge to us the barbarism of these men. If there were a global matriarchy, you know, there would be no more of this evil. I have all the answers in my play! I wanted to read you some of my play. The pages are not numbered. Just before you came I dropped it . . . It's all out of order. It's too much of a mess now, maybe later I will read parts of it to you.

VOICE: I needed to go to someone else's relative in order to understand my own history because by this time my only living relative of that generation was my grandmother—my mother's mother—and she had almost no way to communicate complex ideas. She'd lost her language. Her first languages were Polish and Yiddish, but when she went to America she never spoke Polish again. My grandfather spoke English at work, but at home they spoke a kind of Kitchen Yiddish together—certainly not "the language of ideas." Her children first spoke Yiddish, but they wanted to become American, so as soon as they went to kindergarten, they only spoke English. So in the end, she read a Yiddish newspaper but spoke in broken Yiddish–half Yiddish, half English. She had *no fluent language*. This isn't uncommon among immigrants of her generation.

So I went to Annulla, who had the language.

ANNULLA: You know, it is funny, the police, you know—from immigration—they came to see me in London asked me where I came from. I said, "L'vov, Galicia." He said, "Where?" I said, "Don't you know? It was Austria when I was born, and then it was Poland. Now it is Russia." "But," he said, "where was Poland before?" He didn't even know there was no Poland in 1900. I say this to you gently, but I want you to know that I mean it. How can people change if they don't know what happened? It is like in psychoanalysis. You must know what happened to you. Do you know, some people do not remember their childhoods at all? I remember almost nothing of my childhood, but I had such an unhappy childhood I want to forget it.

But I must tell you, I have been lucky in my life. I was telling my niece that I was pretending to be an Aryan all the time I was in Germany. I was like the horseman. Do *you* know this fable by Heine? No? Then I must tell you. A man, riding a horse at night, a cold foggy night, is riding with no direction. He is riding for miles and can't get to the place he wants to. And in the morning, when the first light arrives, he realizes he was riding all night on the thin ice of the Bodensee and he didn't know it. And he was lucky, nothing happened to him. That is how I felt in Vienna when my husband was in Dachau. Either or. Either they will find me out and kill me or I would survive. It was the only chance. I was really ignorant of the horror that could befall me because I had to be. My cousin did the same thing in Poland, but she was found out. She knew it was her only chance—she was looking also very un-Jewish—and someone gave her away. An anti-Semitic Pole, and she was sent to Auschwitz . . . They did not take the women on that first raid when my husband was taken. They took only the men. They made a raid of all Jews in Vienna and took all the men away in 1938, the Night of Broken Glass. You have heard about this . . . ? Krystallnacht. The SS came to our house. I can't remember it was so fast. And they were so crude! This Solzhenitsyn says in his book, this *Gulag Archipelago,* and I quote: "That's what arrest is: it's a blinding flash and a blow which shifts the present instantly into the past and the impossible into omnipotent reality." *(Throws books down.)* And that is how it was.

They never found out that I am Jewish. They thought that I am Czech because of my accent, you see. And, in Vienna you had hundreds of thousands of marriages between Aryan women and Jews. And the Viennese Jews, and my husband was Viennese, never married the Polish Jews. So they never suspected. And, of course, I was so beautiful they couldn't believe I could be a Jew. And I was so cheeky with them. I must tell you this story . . . There was this Gestapo man at headquarters—I knew there was one chance to save my husband's life—get the rubber stamp on this document so he could leave the camp. The man said to me, "*Waren helfen Sie disen Jude?* Why are you helping this Jew?"

He wanted to show me what a big powerful man he was—of course, I had flirted with him a little to get my way. He said, "You just go upstairs and ask for the rubber stamp." So I went upstairs to that office and said, "Mr. So-and-So downstairs told me to tell you to give me that rubber stamp on this document." He said, "Are you Aryan?" I said, "Yes." And he gave it to me. This is how I went along.

Of course, I had no papers. I remember I went shopping into a Jewish shop one day. And they waited for me outside. They wanted to hang on me the placard for Aryan women who still shopped in Jewish shops. I tell the man that I am Jewish. I wasn't afraid then. Because it was *before* my husband was taken. He said *(Does loud voice.)*, "I don't believe it! Show me your passport!" I said *(Looks indignant.)*, "If I were not Jewish I would show you my passport. But I am a Jew and you took away all our passports." So he let me go. This was a very interesting time, living in the shadow of the Nazis. My son, though, he got such a trauma from this experience. He was taken by friends when he was eight years old to Sweden. And then it was too dangerous for him. He couldn't get back. And I couldn't get to him. But I knew by 1939 . . . I knew it was safer for him to stay there. In Sweden. Oh, this time away from him. It was a great grief. He grew up without me. They sent me a photo of him at school. Curly red hair. Fat little cheeks. A little Jewish boy, the only one. He looked out at me from that picture—"Mummileh, I am so lonely."

(Sips tea.) Ach! This tea should be a farce. I go on and on. It is not me who is interesting, it is my play. You know, it tells how there would be no more tyrants if the women ruled the world.

VOICE: We sort of knapsacked our way around London. We were still the knapsack generation. You know, skinny, tanned and freckled from too much hitchhiking, T-shirts, T-shirts with no bras, jeans and sandals, frizzy wild hair, uh-smoking constantly. You get the picture.

We were ecstatic to be in England. As a child I had traveled with my parents all over the world but had never gone to Ostrolenka. We had never gone to Poland. When

I asked my grandmother about it she'd say, "Why do you want to go there? They killed us there. Why— what do you want to know about that place?" But now I was on my own. I was young— And I wanted to know.

ANNULLA: You know, I knew what went on in Dachau. In 1938 I knew. My husband wrote me every month a letter. He was very sick when he was there—his legs swelled up. My friends who survived said he looked like an elephant. But it was because of the Nazis that he survived. B&M is the first antibiotic invented. They tried the drug on the prisoners because they dared not experiment on the Aryans. They tried it on the Jews first, you see? And they saved my husband's life. Can you imagine? There are times when I feel grateful for the strangest things. Do you know what I mean? Have you also?

Do you know I went to Dachau? For a visit. Yes. I did. It was the worst day of my life. You see, I was so indifferent to what would happen to me. One day, some man from the Gestapo came to see me and said, "I am going to buy your house. I will give you so-and-so marks for it. You have to sell it to me." I said, "But my husband is in Dachau." And he said, "Well, you'll have to get his signature." So I went to Dachau. I took a train from Munich to Dachau, spent the night in a hotel . . . can you imagine, a Jewish woman in Dachau in 1938 and I took a room in a hotel! The cheek.

And this solicitor who worked in the Dachau camp. He came back and told me, "I spoke to your husband . . . and got the signature. I'll tell you something. But it is confidential and *really* I am not allowed to tell you, but I will tell you. Your husband *will* come out . . . before the end of the year." And do you know, he came out on the thirty-first of December? Yes, you see, they were moved by the many steps I had taken. They couldn't understand. They asked me why do you not leave this Jewish husband? They asked me in Vienna, they asked me in Munich—I did not say it was because I am also Jewish. I said, "Because I love him."

You know, I got only inside the perimeter of Dachau. I saw through the barbed wire fence, but I did not see my husband—they told me later, the survivors, that they called my husband the saint. He gave the prisoners the strength to live. Oh, he was a good man, my husband. He was not very bright, I must tell you, but he was so kind, so tender. You know, I loved him very much. Those thirteen months while he was in Dachau and I was alone were horrible.

But this is when I became political. It was rage at what was happening, you know, and nobody did anything about it. Everyone, especially Americans, ask why? Why, if you *knew*, did no one *do* anything about it? Well, I will tell you. I don't think *you* would have done anything about it either. That is normal human nature. That you don't do anything about it. That is what is appalling about human nature. But I have found the solution for everything in my play. If the women with their hearts would start thinking, we could change everything within a year. But the women are not taking action. And that is the trouble.

Here I will read a bit. Oh, really I can't find anything, it is all out of order. Ah! here is the beginning. Oh, no, what, what, what? Ah, here is something. No, it is really not applicable. Excuse me. I have to start skinning this chicken for Ada's dinner. *(Starts making chicken soup.)*

I shall send this play off to the producers after I have edited a bit more, but I am a woman who never has any time, and sometimes I don't know why I bother.

VOICE: Well, who knows if she would ever have been a writer or not, she was constantly interrupted—she was an immigrant from the earliest time in her life. She left L'vov in Galicia in her early teens, where her first language was what? Polish? Right. Then German. And then—and then Ukrainian. Then French with her governess, also Ruthenian, she spoke Ruthenian because the peasants who lived in the Carpathian Mountains near her summer home spoke Ruthenian. Then she went to Vienna, where she started using her German. Then to Germany. From Germany to Italy in her thirties. She learned Italian, and then escaped to England. Her seventh language is English. She loved England. And she thought it was "*the* civilized place to live." Prides herself on the fact that she has perfect English, which we know, of course, she doesn't. And then she tries to learn how to write in her seventh language . . .

ANNULLA: *(Skinning chicken.)* But I can understand you women not being able to take action when you feel a great grief. During those thirteen months when I was alone, posing as an Aryan every day, I lost myself. I couldn't work. I got those crying fits. You know, they are called *schreikrampf,* screaming spasms. I suddenly screamed without any reason. I would be doing something normal, something ordinary, like ironing a shirt, and then suddenly I would get this screaming fit. That grief was so deep. Because I never believed that he would come back. I met him on the stairs. I was in a coffeehouse in Vienna with some other women. They telephoned me to the coffeehouse and said, "Come quickly, there is news from Gustav." They did not want to shock me too much by telling me he had come back.

So I came up the stairs, and he came towards me down the stairs. You know, I was stunned! I was standing there, I couldn't move. I didn't believe my eyes. I thought I would never see him again. But my husband was such a good soul with such a mild nature that not even the Nazis could have harmed him. It is six years since he died and there are times I feel how long it has been since I saw him. You know, if his mother had not died from cancer, we would have never have got married. He had a slight Oedipus condition, my husband. When his mother died, she died a year before we got married, he felt suddenly completely lost. I married him, you know, only because I got so bedazzled by sex. And at this time, you couldn't sleep with a man like now. That was not done. Not in our circle. That is why I couldn't write my thesis. I was too absentminded, distracted by this sex. In Vienna, don't forget the men were all killed off in the First World War. There was one man to ten women in the 1920s. "So, all right," I said, "I'll marry him." He was very nice to me. As he always was. And he was very tender . . . And he wanted to get married by hook or crook. So, I got married. Just got married to get married. Then he grew on me. I fell in love gradually. And I loved him very much. Afterwards. Because I didn't know him. You know, we knew each other only four weeks when he proposed to me. And you know, there was a thunderstorm when he proposed to me. We were on the street, and I said, "Yes, all right, I'll marry you." And, there was this thunder and I got terribly frightened. Oh, my father wanted me to get married. I was a terrible nuisance at home. I was twenty-eight, I hated my mother. She hated me. It was high time I got married. And, how I resented my father. He had a compassion, a burning compassion for suffering, but he was very indifferent to his children. I liked him, but he didn't notice me. Actually, I pitied him because he had too many commitments. You see, he had a whole family who relied on him to support them. Ach, we were a tragic family. My mother often said, "We are like the Strindberg families . . ." Do you know Strindberg? Where everybody is at odds with everybody else. Fantastic. Such tension. *The Road to Damascus* is a fantastic drama. You know, Strindberg is not appreciated in America. They like Ibsen. They play him on and on. But really there is very little in it. Ah, but Strindberg . . . You know why they can't play it? Because there are no actors of the stage who can play these people. It's like *Faust* by Goethe. All those tormented souls. Americans can't play this.

I wanted to be an actress, you know. I went for an audition—to the Vienna State Theatre—and the director said to me: "You might be quite good, you know, but you are much too small for the stage."

Ada is a Strindberg character. In Vienna she danced on the stage, the Viennese ballet. She was good, nothing special, but she was good. You wouldn't want to meet her . . . You know, ballet bores me to extinction. *(Puts chicken in pot.)*

When I went to Vienna I wanted to work, to really take a job. And do you know they shooed me out? Do you know why? They found out my father was a millionaire. You know how? My father offered for sale to some other firm something or other. And this firm where I was working wanted to buy it, so they asked me. Are you any relation to Simon? I said, "Yes, that's my father." The next day they gave me notice. I am always connected to the wrong people. *(Puts lid on pot.)*

But you know, then I went back to making my thesis, and I passed all my seminars and at last I thought I would settle down to do something *useful,* and then I got married! I wouldn't have finished that thesis anyway. It was on that Gautier. You probably never even heard of him. Very boring. So, I got married and my father died on the first day of our honeymoon. We left on the twenty-first of April and he died on April twenty-third at six o'clock in the morning. But do you know, from that day on, my mother became the best of mothers, and I became the best of daughters. Because we didn't need each other any more. We no longer lived in the same house. *(Gets onions.)* Ach, you know I *abused* my mother. I called her names. I was so bitter about her. My mother was a tyrant. She wanted everyone to be according to her image. She couldn't stand otherwise. That is why my older sister, Czecha, was the way she was. I had a stronger personality than my sister. I could survive it. My sister could not survive it. They call it now schizophrenia is a person who tries to live in an unlivable world. And that world was unlivable for my sister. And she escaped from it, through schizophrenia.

My mother was a very bad mother really. She didn't take any notice of the younger children. Only Nunu and Czecha. They were her darlings. We got pushed away with nannies, with *Kindermadchen.* We never saw our mother and father. We were deprived children, completely deprived of love. *(Chops onions.)*

You know, my father moved from L'vov to Vienna so that Czecha could be analyzed by Freud. In the end it was Adler who treated her. But she saw a few times Sigmund Freud. Oh yes—we're quite an interesting family.

When we moved back to the house in L'vov, Galicia, the three small children lived downstairs with our French governess and the others lived upstairs. Only I and Ada went to the same school. To a Catholic nun's school! We had to go to prayers every morning and kneel down. They didn't allow the Jewish religion there. But they accepted us. You know, they were fond of us, the Catholics. This is unusual, especially in L'vov where anti-Semitism was horrid. *(Puts onions in pot.)*

VOICE: On our way to Poland, after we left Annulla, we visited Irene's uncle, who lived alone in a castle on the Rhine. A Catholic who had been a high ranking member of the Reich, he'd gotten the Jewish members of his family out of Germany, but had remained a lawyer to Adolf Hitler during the war.

When we arrived, he sat us on wooden chairs in an empty room. He spoke to Irene in German. Later that night, Irene told me what he'd said to her: He said, who are you to judge me? I wanted to live. You would have done the same thing.

We left early the next morning.

ANNULLA: You know, when Ada left Vienna, she came to live with me and my family in London after the war in 1949. It was a terrible time. I gave her the bedroom. My husband slept in the dining room. I slept in the small room; my son was in the living room. I was so unhappy I got cancer. The doctor told me: happy people do not get cancer. Ada is very difficult to put up with. Where are the carrots?

We have never been on very good terms with one another; I take care of her only out of a sense of duty. She was a very spoiled girl. She married that man only because he was very good-looking. Really good-looking. *(Washes and scrapes carrots.)*

They met each other by him putting an advertisement in the paper that he was looking for a good-looking girl who can act, and he is a producer of Sasha, the only film company in Vienna. Ada went to see him for an audition. It turned out later that he was a *friend* of someone's at Sasha, and he gave him the room to interview people. He was a cheat. But Ada fell in love with him . . . a very unsavory business, I can tell you.

I wrote her letters every day. Ada, I warn you, don't marry that man. He's taking advantage of you. He wants your money. He has no job, he will never have a job, he embezzles money, and he lives in your flat. *(Chops carrots.)* He still lives in her flat with another woman which belongs to Ada which my mother left her when she went back to Poland. Ada could stay because she was married to an Aryan. We couldn't stay. So my mother went to Poland with my older sister where they were killed; they were shot by the Nazis, my mother and Czecha, before they got to the concentration camps. And Ada was left with the flat. And this man took it over and threw her out of it. We tried to get her a divorce after the war. We told Ada, "Look, go into the flat and claim your conjugal rights and your flat." And she said, "I'm not going to. I'm afraid of him." And that was that. She never wanted a divorce really, I think. She couldn't get married anymore. Ach, she had a very bad life. I don't think any man she was ever with really cared about her.

You know, it's difficult not to call Ada gruesome. She's terribly gruesome. A terribly gruesome person. She loves children, you know. She has missed something in life.

Some women are not suitable to be mothers, but she is. And that is the tragedy of it. You see, every time she would have no fathers for her children. So she had to get abortions. For a time, she lived with a Rumanian in the country. I never met him. She still writes letters to him. Or to his family. I think he died. I posted a letter just last week. I think she still loves him. He left her for a servant. And she can't see why. After all, she was forty-two or forty-three when she met him. And when she tells you this story she says, "How can a man with his culture get himself a servant girl?" She couldn't understand that this servant girl attracted him immediately. She wouldn't understand that . . .

You know, my husband knew nothing about sex when I married him. He was thirty years old; he came to sex late in life, too. And he was wonderful. I remember he used to come home from work to have lunch with me in the first years we were married, and you know, I don't think he once had time for a meal. You know, I think for some it is better to be older. All of these young people are so impatient. And then they get bored so fast. My niece, though, is different. She has a lot of boyfriends. Intellectuals, athletes, politicians. Very good-looking. Do you know she is very politically aware for her age? She says that when I was in Berlin in 1919 there were huge workers' riots. You know, I was so frivolous that I can not even remember that. All I remember is that everyone spoke Russian to me. You know why, of course. There were one hundred thousand Russian emigrés from the revolution in Berlin. This is where I met the Pasternaks. I lived with Lydia, Boris's sister, during the Second World War in Oxford. Lydia is a wonderful woman. She has a Russian soul. But she never had any hope for my Women's Party. It was wartime, of course, and she was sure we would lose the war. Everyone thought we would lose the war in 1941. But even now, she cannot talk about politics. She lives like it is still *Dr. Zhivago*. I cannot talk to her at all anymore. But when I met them in Berlin, it was an interesting time. Of course, there were so many refugees and Jews there, the anti-Semitism didn't become obvious until they didn't accept us at university. This happened to a lot of Jews. You see, I started following the lectures. And after two or three months, they told me they had rejected my application because I was a foreigner. Do you know what my passport was? Ukrainian. Yes, I was Ukrainian for one year. You see, when the Russians had that war with Poland in 1918, they made Galicia a state of its own in the Ukraine. And since I was born there, I got a passport from them, the Provisional Ukrainian Government, which was established by the Communists. And with that passport I went to Berlin. Of course, they didn't accept me. My father had applied for Polish citizenship in 1918 because he had all his estates in Poland. He had to become Polish. The Poles were completely disorganized still. They were only one year old. There was no Poland before. But really I did not want to become Polish. The Poles butchered Jews, they always have. Everyone says: but if you speak Polish, you should want to become a Pole. But I say: no. This didn't matter to me. My mother tongue may have been Polish but I also spoke Ukrainian because the peasants spoke Ukrainian. They couldn't speak Polish. And, of course, I spoke German. *(Puts vegetables in pot, stirs.)*

Oh, that makes me think—I must tell you—I met a man in Switzerland last February. I was having coffee in a restaurant. He sat at my table only because everything was occupied, so it appeared. He started speaking German to me. He said, "You are not Swiss, are you?" I said, "No, I am not." He said, "What are you? You sound, what, Russian?" I said, "No, I am not Russian either." He suddenly started talking Russian to me. So I answered in Ukrainian because I could understand what he was saying but I couldn't speak the Russian. "You are not from Russia. You are from the Ukraine." I said, "Yes." Then he went on speaking Russian very fast to me. And I couldn't understand a word. So I think he thought I was a Russian spy. *(Puts lid on pot.)* Speaking of spies. You know, I was photographed *(Phone rings.)* coming out of the tube—oh—here at Swiss Cottage station—excuse me.

Hello, what? Oh, really. This is too much. Oh, no, I'll bring you my bread. Oh really—no! All right, all right. *(She hangs up.)*

That was my sister. I will commit suicide. She can do everything for herself. Now she rings me she hasn't any bread. I come back at four o'clock. Now she rings me at five she hasn't got any bread. I told her, "I'll give you my bread." "No, I don't eat your bread. It must be Farmhouse or Sunblest."

Ada is impossible! She wants me to sacrifice my life for her now that she is sick. *(Adds spices to pot.)*

VOICE: Annulla arranged for us to meet Ada. I remember we came to tea one day and Ada was at Annulla's, sitting regally at the dining room table, her blond, blond hair done up in a French twist—exquisitely dressed, with her leg elevated on Annulla's best pillows—a little princess even in her seventies; and Annulla was serving her in an absolute rage.

ANNULLA: You know, they thought she would never walk again. The first day when I asked the doctor, he said she would be here for a very long time. Well, Ada decided it would not be a very long time. She simply started getting out of bed. She has a colossal willpower when she wants to . . . But Ada is a flighty woman.

While she was living with that husband of hers, she was pregnant by another man whom I knew. And she had to have an abortion. Ada told me her husband never found out why she was ill, but I knew. That other man proposed to me, I want you to know, to go over the border illegally. I was alone in Vienna. My son was already in Sweden. My husband had already left for England in April because the visa came. I had no visa, no place to go. The Nazis had taken my place already in Vienna. I was with Ada in the flat that husband of hers has now. "Look," this man said, "I'm going illegally over the Czech border. Why don't you come with me?" He was a Jew, by the way, who dared to wear the swastika, so he wasn't molested. I lived the same life he did—we both passed for Aryans—but I didn't wear the swastika. This is the man that made Ada pregnant. The cheek of that man. He lost a job when the Nazis came. I can't remember what. He was some sort of intellectual . . . Ada made a human being out of him. He wasn't a *very* human being, but he was a normal man. That is to say, he wasn't mad. He lived on the earnings of a woman who was a cello player. She had a child by him, and they lived together and he wasted her money, spending her money on cardplaying at night. He was a terrible, terrible man. I got out without him. I went with my typewriter to Italy. I just crossed the border myself. They tried to stop me. I said, "Leave me alone. I'm writing a novel."

Then I was getting on the boat to go to England and they stopped me again. I *threw* my typewriter at the man—I was in such a rage. I got to England.

You know, I wanted to tell you: you Americans are not unresponsible for the Nazis, you know. And the English and the French. What they did to Germany, no country could take. The Germans are a very proud people and I am not surprised. It cost five million marks in 1923 for a loaf of bread. People used to go to bakeries with wheelbarrows full of money that was as valuable as rubbish. And it was not just the Depression. It was the reparations, that Treaty of Versailles. This is one of the reasons a Hitler could come about. And the stupid French. The French were responsible for it too. They said the Germans started the war. All right, but so in 1917, we didn't have anything to *eat.* I had a friend, an Aryan friend at school. She was fifteen years old and looked like a girl of eight: because she had nothing to eat. Terrible injustice was done to people in Europe by those countries. Of course, we were a wealthy family, we didn't starve; but these people did. And the blockade. No food could come through. The anti-Semitism, this is complicated, but you know anti-Semitism has been ingrained in the German culture for the longest time. You know, I had a cousin of my uncle—a businessman. He saw he could buy whole buildings for practically nothing in 1923. So he did it. He bought up all these poor people's homes. For nothing. He was rich. They were starving—they had nowhere to live. And he was a Jew, so . . . People needed a catchword, you know, for the misery, and the Jews were the obvious target. They always are. I cannot even talk to you about the death camps . . . this whole affair, this whole Hitler affair . . . this whole war, made me start thinking about my Women's Party. I didn't know that people were so evil until I saw it with my own eyes. I didn't believe it that people could be so evil.

I started thinking of founding my Women's Party as early as 1939. You know, I don't think very much of your America. You may think of founding a political party, but you need a lot of money to found a political party in the United States. You don't here. You can start a party like the Liberals. You know what one of them did? He went on television. Did you see this? And said, "Every person who voted Liberal (eight million voted Liberal in the last election) should send me a pound." And I sent him a pound to the House of Commons. And what do you think? I got a letter which cost three pence to post, and the secretary, and the paper to write on, and how much does he have left of the pound I sent him? This time I am going to send him two pounds.

Excuse me, I must start cleaning up for Ada's dinner. *(Turns on radio.)*

Ah—Heifitz. *(Pause.)*

VOICE: I have a sense from my—both my father and mother—a sense of responsibility, history. Of course, I am the daughter of an historian, but I think most Jewish children do have this. I look at those old family pictures that people will look at and I know who everyone is. I know where they lived. I know the towns. I know every face. *(Pause.)*

The Nazis came into Ostrolenka and they said they wouldn't harm people if they would point out the Jews. So the neighbors who'd lived side by side with them for ever and ever, harmoniously, saved their own lives, I guess, and pointed everyone out. They were all herded into the town square. My great-grandfather unfortunately was a much-loved elder of the community, so he was . . . you know . . . taken by the beard and made to eat grass before they killed him and then the entire community was shot. And my mother remembers when my grandmother got the letter in America—telling her . . .

ANNULLA: Do you know that during the war people did nothing. They saw evil all around them and they didn't do anything. Of course, a Marx could have inspired people to make a revolution. It has to be a Marx. *(Packs up dinner.)*

But do you know that all of the main revolutions ended up with things becoming as they were before? Look at the French Revolution, how many people they sent to the guillotine and what happened after that. Look at the Russian Revolution. Look at any revolution you like. Everything gets worse. I have a special chapter in my play for the Chinese. They are not human anymore. It is my intuition only. I know nothing of what goes on inside China. But the Western people don't even see that Mao has made the Chinese not human anymore. They have been completely brainwashed. They are like you put on a tape recorder. And this cheek of that Mao! He entertains your Nixon. He was in Peking and they entertain him. Did you see this on television? With this ballet of a capitalist landlord and this girl. And this girl *shoots* the capitalist! This is tact for you. This is tact, and poor Nixon has to smile. This is politicians. And do you know on the corners of the street in Peking there are schoolchildren while the workers are going to work, they read aloud Chairman Mao's thoughts? To the workers who pass them . . . They are brainwashed from *cradle* to *grave*. They cannot think anything for themselves.

Don't you have any women in America who can *talk*? You have a lot of millionairesses in their own rights in your country, my brother tells me. Widows. They must give this money for the party!

How many women do you have in your Congress? This is disgraceful. Have you no women who can rouse people? My play—I hope you like it—is not silly. Ada dragged me to Brecht's *Arturo Ui*. I was outraged. This moronic man, this Brecht, makes Hitler *funny*! Did he think no one in the audience had lived through it? You know, Brecht had not. He was in Hollywood. To make Hitler into a gangster, *this* shows ignorance. To make Nixon into a gangster, this I can understand. But anyone who had lived through Hitler would not do this.

But you Americans with your capitalism. It is a terrible, terrible system. Communism would be a better system if it had any humanity in it, if they could combine freedom and communism. But they cannot seem to do it. I don't know why; communism is better in the book . . .

If I had not been an alien, I would have started my party. You see, only women know mother-love. It is the most powerful response in the world of a positive kind. Men have strong feeling too, but they are violent. They should not be allowed to rule. A woman's *natural* instinct is loving. Oh, I go on and on. It will be clear when I finish my play. Oh, I don't know what I am doing. I would have started my party here, but you could not believe the anti-foreign feeling here in England . . . My husband came to England first. I couldn't get a visa. I had to get a domestic servant card from my cousin. She sent me a visa to Italy. You see, they wouldn't let anyone in who didn't want to work, the English. They didn't like aliens. They still don't like aliens. And when I hear that standard phrase: "Don't tell bad things about Churchill. Be grateful he saved you from Hitler!" He did not want to save us from Hitler. He wanted to have domestic servants. I worked as a domestic servant for three months and then I took a job as a children's maid in Oxfordshire with a gentry family. And only because my husband joined the English forces could I get permission to drive a lorry.

I wanted to join the ATS—the Women's Auxiliary Territorial Services. They were crying out for drivers because hardly any girls knew how to drive at that time. And I came with my international driver's license and said, "I would like to join the ATS. I would like to join as a driver." "Oh, no," they said, "You are an enemy alien!" I said, "I am not an enemy alien. I have been cleared because my husband is in the British *army.*" They said, "You are still a foreigner. You can only be an orderly." That means scrubbing floors. I said. "Thank you very much. I'd rather not join." *(Annulla sits in easy chair.)*

VOICE: We got to Ostrolenka. My grandmother had drawn us a map. She marked where the family store had been, the synagogue— She wanted us to find the graves. Well, we got to the town—followed the map—we found the store, but it wasn't a store anymore. The synagogue had been destroyed, never rebuilt. There was no Jewish graveyard. We went to the town hall and asked for the family records. We were told that there was no record of any of the names we asked for. There were no records. No trace. Nothing.

ANNULLA: *(Turns on light.)* You know, my husband did not come back from Dunkirk. This was when my first neurosis came. My husband, you should have known him. He was the slowest man on earth. He missed all the boats. Everyone else was back on the sixth of June in 1940 except him. He didn't come back. I thought the worst that could, happened. He had already been in Dachau. He was a traitor, you see. They would have eaten him alive. I don't know what they would have done. I wrote a letter to Anthony Eden—he was Secretary at the time. I said, "Where is my husband? If he falls into German hands, you can't imagine what will happen to him." And he wrote back, "He is not in German hands. He will come back. His unit is still in the harbor." So Gustav came back on the sixteenth of June. But this ten days was such a horror that two months later, I got this anxiety neurosis.

This was not the screaming. Anxiety neurosis is a terrible illness. You are afraid, but you do not know what you are afraid of. You can't eat, you can't sleep. I saw letters upside down, I had illusions. It is horrible. A doctor saw me and said, "No, she is not mad . . . it is a delayed reaction, an anxiety from those ten days." But do you know, my son arrived on the sixteenth of April 1942, and from that day on, the neurosis had gone. And the first words he said to me, I will never forget . . . He came running up to me, "Mummileh, Mummy have you grown small? You are very small." He forgot that he had grown four years. He was eight when he left and almost twelve when he returned. He's very tall now. I did not see him for four years. Oh, that time was a great grief. I don't think anyone who has not gone through this experience can really understand. My dreams. I always dreamed that Gustav was in a cage behind bars and he was telling me, "I am not in Dachau. I am dead. Don't you know. I am dead." I kept dreaming this over and over again. Do you have recurring dreams? Isn't it horrible? It was the worst time of my life, but it was like the year after my husband's death. You know, at his funeral I screamed again, just as I had when he went to Dachau. Now I knew he would never come back.

VOICE: My mother looks more beautiful and more alive than she's ever looked. She said such an interesting thing to me. She said, "I feel like I've finally figured out how to live and it's going to be over." And I know what she means. I remember being with her at her mother's funeral. And the tears just welled up in her eyes. And she said, "I can't believe it went by so fast." She was putting her mother into the ground, and she remembered sitting in the kitchen and talking to her about—you know—baking bread; five years old, remembered the smell, remembered every single moment of it and all of a sudden sixty years had passed. Her mother's life was over. And she looked at me and said, "There's no time."

ANNULLA: I have so much time now, I am alone. I write all of the time. That is why I wake up every day. Ada is a terrible nuisance . . .

Do you know, when my son was born, I sobbed uncontrollably. Every woman has this love in her. It may be sleeping but it can be awakened. I sobbed and sobbed when they gave him to me. The doctor said to me, "Why are you crying?" I said, "Because I am happy." He said, "People who are happy do not cry." I said, "I do."

But after all this—after Dachau, after Dunkirk—do you know how my husband died? He was sitting here, in the kitchen watching me fry an egg like I always did for him. I turned around to look at him and he had fallen over . . . dead. Yes . . . so . . . *(Gets up, crosses to table. Looks at manuscript.)* It still needs some minor editing.

Excuse me, I have to go. I have to take dinner and Sunblest bread to Ada. *(Puts on coat.)*

VOICE: I came back to America just before my grandmother died. I told her we went to Ostrolenka. I think she actually was glad. I tried to get into Bucovina where my father's family came from, but it's no longer in Austria, it is in Russia and they wouldn't let us in. My family names on my mother's side are: Brum, Blum, Schleifer, Zimyevsky, Blut, and Simon.

There is a wonderful fairy tale about a young girl who loans her relatives to another young girl who doesn't have any. You see? It's been fourteen years since I visited Annulla.

ANNULLA: I am so glad you could come to see me today. Really. But *it went by so fast.* Do you know, *everything* has gone by so fast . . . Thank you . . . It was so nice to meet you. Good-bye.

VOICE: Good-bye.

ANNULLA: Good-bye.

*(*ANNULLA *exits.)*

THE VALUE OF NAMES

by

Jeffrey Sweet

Jeffrey Sweet comments:

My mother is Jewish, my father isn't. I wasn't bar mitz-vahed. In fact, I had no religious instruction at all. (Some years ago, when I was hired by a sitcom to write an episode with a Hanukkah theme, I had to buy books from the local Judaica bookstore.) Nevertheless, when, as a teenager, I en-countered Jules Feiffer, Herb Gardner, Mort Sahl, Lenny Bruce, Paddy Chayefsky, and Philip Roth, the inflections and cadences and music of their work struck a responsive chord in me.

I felt a similar identification when I first saw Chicago's Second City comedy troupe—an identification so strong that I devoted four years to researching and writing a book called *Something Wonderful Right Away*, an oral history of that company and its predecessor, the Compass Players. These improvisational theatres produced some very talented non-Jewish actors and directors, but with an alumni list that in-cluded Viola Spolin, Paul Sills, Mike Nichols, Elaine May, Shelley Berman, Barbara Harris, Bernie Sahlins, Paul Mazursky, Alan Arkin, Joan Rivers, Robert Klein, and Gilda Radner (among many, many others), there is little question as to which cultural influence was most heavily reflected on their stages.

Second City got its name from a *New Yorker* piece that portrayed Chicago as condemned to be forever on the other side of the cultural window—outside, nose pressed against the glass. By appropriating what was intended to be an insult as the name of the company he founded, director Paul Sills made a point of pride out of outsider status. I think being outsiders—by virtue of being Chicagoans and (mostly)

Jewish—gave the gang at Second City a double advantage in making theatre, particularly theatre with a social or satiric bent.

Undoubtedly, part of their appeal to me was that, because of my parentage, I, too, have always felt like an outsider. I feel least Jewish when with Jews, and most Jewish with non-Jews. I may not have a home in either house, but I am blessed with the offers of guest bedrooms in each. This split cultural personality has sometimes led me to treat the same themes from different cultural perspectives in different plays: for instance, *The Value of Names* is my Jewish father-daughter play, and *Porch* is my WASP father-daughter play.

Names was written when I was a member of the New York Writers Bloc, a group of writers, actors, directors, who met weekly to read and discuss new material. Though way too young for the part, the Bloc member who regularly read Benny as this play was being built—and whose voice inevitably influenced the way I wrote the character—was Donald Margulies. *The Value of Names* was written on a commission for Actors Theatre of Louisville. The director of the original production there and of a subsequent production at Hartford Stage was Emily Mann. It is a particular satisfaction to share this binding with Donald and Emily.

The Value of Names had its first public performance on November 4, 1982, at the Actors Theatre of Louisville. Emily Mann directed a cast which included:

BENNY	*Larry Block*
NORMA	*Robin Groves*
LEO	*Frederic Major*

The Louisville version was produced at the Victory Gardens Theatre, Chicago, on March 30, 1983, directed by Sandy Shiner, with the following cast:

BENNY	*Shelley Berman*
NORMA	*Jill Holden*
LEO	*Bryne Piven*

The play opened at the Hartford Stage Company on February 10, 1984, directed by Emily Mann and featuring:

BENNY	*Larry Block*
NORMA	*Robin Groves*
LEO	*Alvin Epstein*

The Value of Names was produced at The Vineyard Theatre, New York, on June 1, 1989. Directed by Gloria Muzio, the cast included:

BENNY	*John Seitz*
NORMA	*Ava Hadda*
LEO	*Stephen Pearlman*

TIME: Early 1980s
PLACE: Malibu

The set is a patio high up in hills over Malibu. Upstage is BENNY SILVERMAN*'s house. It is the house of someone very comfortably off. The patio may be entered either through a door from the house or through a gate that leads directly from the road.*

At rise: BENNY *has an easel set up and is painting the view from his patio. He is in his late sixties or early seventies and appears to be in fine health.* NORMA *is in her early twenties. A few seconds of quiet, then he speaks—*

BENNY: Does it sound too Jewish?

NORMA: *(To audience.)* No, hold on. First, a couple of things you should know: It's 1981. A patio up in the hills overlooking Malibu. Over there, the Pacific Ocean. Next to me, my father. On the whole, I have less trouble with the Pacific.

BENNY: *(As in "Are you finished?")* OK?

NORMA: Sure. Go ahead.

BENNY: Does it sound too Jewish?

NORMA: Pop—

BENNY: You're changing your name. Stands to reason there's something about the one you've got you don't like. Or maybe find inconvenient.

NORMA: *(To audience.)* I should have known he'd take it like this.

BENNY: Could put you at a disadvantage. A name like Silverman. Some parts—the casting directors won't even look at you. I know. Say, for instance, they do a new version of *The Bells of St. Mary's.* Casting people see the name Norma Silverman, what are they going to say? "Nope, don't call her. A person obviously without nun potential. Get me an O'Hara or a Kelly. Get away with this Silverman." And there goes your chance to play Ingrid Bergman. Of course, Bergman, too, is a name that's a little suspect.

NORMA: Pop—

BENNY: But then, one look at her, that question's laid to rest. Even if she did play Golda Meir once. One look at that nose of hers. That was not a Jewish nose. But then—thanks to the magic of science—who can tell from a nose?

NORMA: Of course.

BENNY: I could show you Horowitzes and Steins and Margulieses with noses on them look like they belong to Smiths. Very funny seeing a Smith nose on a Horowitz. Or a Horowitz nose on a Smith, although this is rarer.

NORMA: They don't transplant noses.

BENNY: You want to know why?

NORMA: *(With a sidelong look to the audience.)* OK, why?

BENNY: Run the risk of the body rejecting. Sure, it's a big problem. Heart transplant, kidney transplant—the body sometimes says, "No, thank you. Take it away." A case like that, all that happens is maybe someone dies. But a nose transplant—could you imagine the humiliation if that happened? Walking down the street, maybe you hiccup, a slight tearing sensation, and suddenly there's a draft in the middle of your face. You look down on the pavement, see two dainty nostrils staring up at Heaven.

NORMA: Are you finished?

BENNY: Are you?

NORMA: With what?

BENNY: This nonsense. This changing-your-name nonsense.

NORMA: It's not nonsense. I'm going to do it.

BENNY: Fine. So do it. So what do you want from me?

NORMA: I don't want from you. I just thought I should tell you.

BENNY: OK, you've told me. So what do you want me to say? You want me to say congratulations? Like you're having a baby—congratulations? You're having a new name—how wonderful! And who's the father of this new name? I know who the father of the old name is. I see him sometimes on the Late Show.

NORMA: OK, Pop.

BENNY: It's not OK. But never mind, we won't talk about it.

NORMA: Fat chance.

BENNY: So what else is new? A sex change?

NORMA: It doesn't have anything to do with Jewish or not Jewish.

BENNY: What *has* it to do with?

NORMA: You.

BENNY: Oh. *I'm* the "to-do-with"?

NORMA: Here we go.

BENNY: *I'm* the reason you're changing your name?

NORMA: Do you want me to explain now? Or shall I give you a little room for a tirade?

BENNY: What tirade?

NORMA: The tirade you're gearing up for.

BENNY: Who, me?

NORMA: I wish you'd understand.

BENNY: What's to understand? You're changing your name. You're changing your name because it's my name. This makes me feel instantly terrific and wonderful. It makes me feel how glad I am to have my daughter's love and respect. How fulfilling it is to be a parent. How worth it all it's all been. Would you like a little coffee?

NORMA: Look, every time I've ever done anything, every time I've ever been reviewed, they always put in that I'm your daughter. My name is not Norma Silverman. My name is Norma Silverman Benny Silverman's daughter.

BENNY: So what are you trying to do—convince people you're the product of a virgin birth?

NORMA: I'm very proud of being your daughter. But I would like, for once, when I got on a stage, for them to see me. Not just see you in me. There's a comparison implied there. "Is she as good as . . . ?"

BENNY: Aren't you?

NORMA: I don't think I should have to fight that. You really don't want to understand, do you?

BENNY: Who put you up to this?

NORMA: What?

BENNY: This is your mother's idea, isn't it?

NORMA: No.

BENNY: I recognize the style.

NORMA: What do you mean?

BENNY: Right after the divorce, she got her driver's license changed back to her maiden name. Sarah Teitel. And her checking account and her magazine subscriptions and all the rest. Sarah Teitel. Didn't want to be known by her married name anymore, thank you very much. Oh no. Said she wouldn't use it ever again. You know what I did? I made the alimony checks out to "Mrs. Benny Silverman." Would have loved to see her face when she had to endorse them.

NORMA: She didn't have anything to do with this.

BENNY: Maybe not, but she didn't tell you no.

NORMA: Actually, she told me you'd probably scream your head off, but she understood.

BENNY: That's generous of her.

NORMA: She respected my decision. Because that's what it was, Pop—my decision. She didn't enter into it. It's something I decided to do by myself, for myself. It's what I wanted.

BENNY: Fine—you wanted, you got.

NORMA: You know something—if you look at it the right way, it's a compliment.

BENNY: It is?

NORMA: If you look at it the right way.

BENNY: Let's hear this right way.

NORMA: Never mind.

BENNY: No compliment?

NORMA: Help.

BENNY: First it's out with the name, then it's good-bye compliment. Beats me why I should give you a cup of coffee.

NORMA: I don't want a cup of coffee.

BENNY: I can understand that. If I were you, I'd have enough trouble sleeping at night.

NORMA: *(Referring to the painting.)* I like it.

BENNY: Do you know anything about art?

NORMA: Do I have to know something about art to like it?

BENNY: If you knew something about art, you'd be able to appreciate the shadings, the nuances—all the really subtle reasons why this is lousy.

NORMA: One of the things I love about you is this terrifically graceful way you have of accepting compliments.

BENNY: I like my compliments honest.

NORMA: What's not honest? I said I like it. I *do* like it. I didn't say that it's good.

BENNY: Oh, so you *don't* think it's good.

NORMA: Obviously I'm not entitled to think it's good *or* bad. I'm not even entitled to like it. So what *am* I entitled to? Statements of verifiable fact only? OK, a statement of verifiable fact: You are painting a painting, and it's sitting on an easel.

BENNY: Thank you, I'm flattered.

NORMA: And what would be so terrible if I liked it?

BENNY: Anybody can like. To like doesn't take any great skill, any great powers of discernment.

NORMA: I see. Only people with certifiably elevated taste are entitled to like something.

BENNY: Do you know what Monet or Chagall would say if they saw this?

NORMA: What?

BENNY: "Benny, stick to your acting."

NORMA: So why don't you?

BENNY: I like it.

NORMA: *You* like it?

BENNY: Yeah.

NORMA: I thought you said it's lousy.

BENNY: It *is* lousy.

NORMA: It's lousy but you like it.

BENNY: It's *because* I know that it's lousy I can like it.

NORMA: Come again?

BENNY: I don't pretend it's good. I don't delude myself. All I can say is that standing here, doing this, I enjoy myself. It doesn't have to be good for me to enjoy myself.

NORMA: Someone should make you a ride in an amusement park.

BENNY: You really like it?

NORMA: Yes.

BENNY: When I finish, it's yours. I hope you treat it better than other things I've given you. Like my name.

NORMA: OK, Pop—

BENNY: *(Referring to a playscript near her.)* I've read this script of yours.

NORMA: I didn't write it.

BENNY: Well, you're going to be in it.

NORMA: That still doesn't make it mine.

BENNY: It makes you associated with it.

NORMA: As in guilt by association?

BENNY: Who said anything about guilt?

NORMA: Your tone does. You don't like the play.

BENNY: It's OK for what it is. Are you really going to take off your clothes?

NORMA: Not clothes. Just my top.

BENNY: Your top isn't clothes?

NORMA: I'm not taking off my clothes, plural. I'm taking off a piece of clothing, singular.

BENNY: A piece of clothing singular, that covers up parts of you, plural.

NORMA: It's not a big deal. A lot of plays these days call for it.

BENNY: That excuses everything.

NORMA: I didn't realize there was anything to excuse.

BENNY: It's your business.

NORMA: It is, you know.

BENNY: You knew what was in the script before you signed the contract?

NORMA: Of course.

BENNY: It's your business. It's not my ass people will be looking at.

NORMA: It's not my ass either.

BENNY: Just your boobies.

NORMA: That's right.

BENNY: I never had to do that. Of course, who would pay to see my boobies? Or my ass, for that matter?

NORMA: Who knows, somebody might.

BENNY: Nobody I'd want to meet.

NORMA: I knew you were going to pick up on that. Out of everything in the script, that was the one element you were going to bring up.

BENNY: You like this play?

NORMA: I like it very much. I like my part very much. I feel very lucky to have landed it.

BENNY: All right.

NORMA: It's my business?

BENNY: Who else's?

NORMA: Not yours?

BENNY: Never.

NORMA: Well, I'm glad we got that settled.

BENNY: There was never any issue.

NORMA: Could have fooled me.

BENNY: And your mother?

NORMA: What about her?

BENNY: She doesn't have any opinion?

NORMA: All she wanted to know was if it's in—

BENNY AND NORMA: *(Together.)* —good taste.

BENNY: Of course, I'm used to a different kind of play. The kind with ideas and metaphors.

NORMA: I think this play is metaphoric.

BENNY: There is nothing metaphoric about an attractive young woman with her top off.

NORMA: That moment you keep harping on is about vulnerability.

BENNY: In your mind it may be about vulnerability. Maybe in the playwright's mind. In the audience's mind it will be about tits. The women out there will be thinking, "Gee, I couldn't do that. Well, maybe I could do that. But how many Margueritas would it take?" Meanwhile, the guys in the audience will be thinking— Well, you *know* what they'll be thinking. And their wives will know what they're thinking. And the women will look at their husbands like they're saying, "Yeah, and what are you gawking at?" And the guys will go, "Hey, I'm not gawking." And the women'll go, "Oh, yeah, right." And the guys will go, "Hey, but it's OK: this isn't tits, this is art. I'm having a catharsis here. Swear to God." You're up there acting your heart out, in the meantime, they've forgotten your character's *name.*

NORMA: Could be the audience is more sophisticated than you think.

BENNY: Don't believe me then.

NORMA: It's not a question of my believing you or not. I believe that you see things the way you see things. I just don't. But things have changed in the theatre since you got started. I know it's hard to believe, Dad, but Clifford Odets is dead and gone.

BENNY: Clifford Odets? He was dead and gone even before he was dead.

NORMA: Maybe you'd like to recommend a good hotel.

BENNY: Hotel, for what?

NORMA: To stay in.

BENNY: You don't like the bed in your room?

NORMA: The bed's fine.

BENNY: I should hope so. The mattress was rated a "best buy" from *Consumer's Union.* What are you talking about, a hotel? What have I got a house with three bedrooms for, so that you can pay money to strangers to sleep someplace?

NORMA: Look, the next few weeks aren't going to be easy

for me. It's a new script, and what's undoubtedly going to happen is that, after I've finally memorized the lines, they're all going to be changed on me during rehearsal.

BENNY: That goes with the territory.

NORMA: What I'm concerned about is what goes with *this* territory. Staying here.

BENNY: A nice view of the Pacific where occasionally a whale swims by, spouts off.

NORMA: And you.

BENNY: I don't swim anymore.

NORMA: You do your share of spouting off.

BENNY: That's me—Benny the whale.

*(*BENNY *laughs and goes back to his painting.)*

NORMA: *(To audience.)* I was fifteen years old, pushing a shopping cart at the A&P, when I found out what he'd been through. There were two people standing on line ahead of me, so I checked out the magazine rack to see what I could waste a few minutes with. And there was a caricature of my father grinning out at me from the cover of *TV Guide*. At the bottom it said, "Benny Silverman of *Rich But Happy*." That was the name of the situation comedy he played a crazy neighbor on—*Rich But Happy*. So, of course I'm eager to see what it has to say about him. Maybe he'll mention me or Mom, though at that point they'd been divorced already ten years or so. So I'm standing on line at the A&P, smiling, reading about how he's buddies with all the technicians on the set, about a practical joke he played on the producer once, about how the younger actors on the show revere him as a comic genius, and so forth and so on. And then there was this classic *TV Guide* transitional sentence. Something about—"But Benny Silverman still has vivid memories of the black days when his chief concern was not fine-tuning a laugh but fighting for the right to practice his craft." This was followed by how he was named in front of the House Committee on Un-American Activities. And how he had been subpoenaed to appear, and how he did appear but did not cooperate. And then, years of not being able to find work. I was in the middle of this when it was my turn at the checkout counter. I paid for the groceries, and I took them home and dumped them on the kitchen table. And I asked my mother whether it had been by planning or oversight that nobody had ever told me a word about it.

BENNY: Planning. I asked her not to.

NORMA: Why?

BENNY: It happened before you were born. It had nothing to do with you. Why should you be bothered by it?

NORMA: You expected me never to find out?

BENNY: What did it matter whether you found out or not?

NORMA: If it didn't matter, why keep it from me?

BENNY: You were a kid. Your mother and I figured, between homework and puberty, you had enough to handle. What did you need to know about something that took place years before you were even conceived?

NORMA: It might have helped me to understand you better.

BENNY: Understand what?

NORMA: Why you are what you are. Why you do what you do.

BENNY: You expect to understand all that? Nothing like modest ambitions.

NORMA: I had to go to the library, for God's sake. I had to look up your name in indexes. I had to *read* about you.

BENNY: Well, at least some good came of it. It was always murder to get you to crack a book.

NORMA: Can I ask you something?

BENNY: No. What is it?

NORMA: There was another book I found, on political theatre. And there was a picture. A photo of the Labor Players—

BENNY: *(Correcting.)* The *New* Labor Players.

NORMA: Maybe seven or eight of you in the picture. And standing next to you is Leo Greshen, and your arm is around his shoulder.

BENNY: That was a fake arm. They touched that arm into the picture.

NORMA: He was a friend of yours.

BENNY: He gave that appearance for a while.

NORMA: So what did he say?

BENNY: Look it up. The transcript's public, it's easy to find.

NORMA: I don't mean his testimony. I mean what did he say to you?

BENNY: Why you want to dig into this is beyond—

NORMA: Did he call you afterwards? Try to explain?

BENNY: Not afterwards, before. Squealer's etiquette. Sort of like an arsonist calling up ahead of time. "Hello, I'm going to burn your house down. Thought you might like to know." Only instead—"Hello, I'm going to burn your career down." "Thanks a lot, Leo. Hope to return the favor someday."

NORMA: But he was a friend. Didn't he give you reasons?

BENNY: Oh, everybody knew the reasons why. He had the prospect of directing his first picture, and he didn't want this to blow it for him.

NORMA: He said this to you? That was why he was going to testify?

BENNY: Did you know "testify" and "testimony" come from the same Latin root as "testes" as in "balls"? I'm not making this up. In Rome, if you wanted to make a big point that something you said was true, when you said it, you'd grab your balls. Which is why I don't think what he said to the Committee really qualifies as testimony. How could it? The man had no balls to grab.

NORMA: I shouldn't have had to find out that way—reading it in a book.

BENNY: "Find out." You talk as if you'd uncovered something shameful.

NORMA: Being ashamed of something is one reason why someone may keep something secret.

BENNY: I was not ashamed. I *am* not ashamed. Perhaps I had a very good reason for not telling you.

NORMA: Such as what?

BENNY: To protect you.

NORMA: To protect me from something you weren't ashamed of. Sure, that makes sense.

BENNY: Do you remember the Epsteins?

NORMA: The Epsteins?

BENNY: The Epsteins, the Epsteins.

NORMA: Why?

BENNY: Do you?

NORMA: I think so.

BENNY: They lived in your Aunt Bertha's building.

NORMA: All right, yes, I remember the Epsteins. So?

BENNY: All right. One night, your mother and I were at the Epsteins'. Ten-thirty, eleven o'clock, their daughter Becky comes in. She's coming home from a date with someone her parents don't approve of, which is to say someone who isn't Jewish. An argument starts. Didn't they tell

Becky not to see him? She doesn't care what they told her. She has a mind of her own, her own life to lead, she'll make her own decisions, etc. If she wants to go out with him she'll go out with him, and it's just too damn bad if her parents don't like it. And it keeps going like this, back and forth, more and more heat and passion and arm waving. Finally, her mother cries out, "This is what I survived Buchenwald for? For a daughter with a mouth like this?" I shudder to think how much time that girl probably ended up spending on a psychiatrist's couch.

NORMA: So you think they shouldn't have told her?

BENNY: I think it's not right to bludgeon other people with your suffering.

NORMA: There's a difference between bludgeoning and telling.

BENNY: There's a difference between everything and everything else. You can draw distinctions till you're blue in the face.

NORMA: Don't dance away from me like that. We're talking about something here.

BENNY: All right, so I was a little overprotective. When did this become a felony? But what did you learn that was so valuable? That some son of a bitch, in order to save his own ass, got up in front of some other sons of bitches and said he'd seen me a handful of times in the same room with another group of sons of bitches.

NORMA: And you didn't work for years after that.

BENNY: This was all way before you were born. Do you ever remember going to bed hungry because I couldn't provide? No. So it didn't touch you. So why are you complaining? Are you complaining because you didn't have pain? Or are you complaining because the pain you did have isn't the pain you wanted to have? Maybe you can give Becky Epstein a call, see if she wants to trade. Or maybe she'll give you the name of her shrink. You can go lie on his couch and complain about how awful I was that I didn't lift up my shirt and show you ancient scars.

NORMA: Just because I didn't know about it doesn't mean that it hasn't touched me.

BENNY: Enough already. Are we going to go over all this again? *(A beat.)* So, what name now? So when I look in the program I know which one is you.

NORMA: Norma Teitel.

BENNY: Teitel? *(NORMA nods.)* I should have guessed. You sure this wasn't your mother's idea?

(A beat.)

NORMA: Hey, are you glad I'm here?
BENNY: How could you doubt?

(They both smile. During NORMA's following speech, BENNY hauls his easel and canvas and paint into the house. He is back on the patio at the conclusion of the speech.)

NORMA: *(To audience.)* And you know something? We get along OK for a little over a week. And the play's coming along well, too. And then our director has a stroke. They take him off to the hospital, where they tell us the prognosis is, thank God, good. But that leaves us without a director. The producers call a hiatus for a couple of days so they can put their heads together and come up with a new director. And then I get a call and they tell me who they've decided on. And that their offer has been made and accepted. I tell them I have some problems with their choice. I explain why. They say they hope I will stay with the show, but that I have to decide quickly. "Think about it seriously," they say. I promise I will. And then I tell Pop.
BENNY: Do you tell me because you want my advice?
NORMA: I tell you because I think you should know. I mean, it's partially for your sake I'd be doing it. If I did it.
BENNY: Quitting?
NORMA: Yes.
BENNY: Well, it *is* your decision.
NORMA: I know.
BENNY: I will only say one thing, and this is not to in any way influence your decision, but—if you were to stay with the play, I wouldn't be able to go to it.
NORMA: You hate him that much?
BENNY: I used to go to see his stuff. And when it was good work, I'd be angry. And when it was bad or flopped, I'd get satisfaction. And then I thought to myself, "What am I doing to myself? I mean, this is stupid. I've got myself to the point where I'm happy about bad work and miserable about successes." I was letting the guy twist me into

knots, plus a percentage of my ticket money was going into his pocket so that I was paying for him to do this to me. So I stopped. I don't go to see his stuff, I don't go to see the stuff of some of the others. And do you know something? The world doesn't end because I miss a play or a movie.

NORMA: So there are people whose work you won't go to see.

BENNY: I think that's what I said.

NORMA: Because of their political beliefs?

BENNY: Because of the way they *expressed* these beliefs.

NORMA: I guess you wouldn't work with them either.

BENNY: No, I wouldn't.

NORMA: When you were on *Rich But Happy,* did the issue ever come up? Was there ever a time when the producer wanted to hire one of these guys that you wouldn't work with?

BENNY: No, they knew not to do that.

NORMA: They knew there were certain people you didn't want hired.

BENNY: They were sensitive to the way I felt.

NORMA: Was there a list?

BENNY: What?

NORMA: Of people you wouldn't work with. Did you write up a list?

(A beat.)

BENNY: Cute.

NORMA: Well, I'm your daughter.

BENNY: What you're describing is not the same.

NORMA: You weren't hired, and you turned around and saw to it that other people weren't hired.

BENNY: There's a difference. There's a distinction.

NORMA: I'm sure there is.

BENNY: To anybody with a pair of eyes in her head.

NORMA: Explain the distinction to me.

BENNY: I don't have to defend myself to you.

NORMA: All right.

BENNY: What—do you think I should forget? Would you expect me to work with, for instance, a Nazi?

NORMA: Nazi?

BENNY: You know from Nazis, don't you? They're the guys

who had the franchise on swastikas before the Hell's Angels. Let's say I'm in a movie, OK? I'm going to do a scene with this guy. While we're waiting to shoot, we're sitting around, we're kibbitzing. I tell an anecdote. He laughs and says, "You know that reminds me of something funny that happened when I was in the S.S."

NORMA: Right.

BENNY: So according to you what I should say back is, "Hey, Fritz, want me to cue you on your lines?"

NORMA: Why is it whenever you get mad, you reach for a Nazi?

BENNY: What are you talking about, "reach for a Nazi"?

NORMA: You do, you know.

BENNY: You make it sound like a soft drink. "Worked up a thirst? Reach for a nice, refreshing Nazi!"

NORMA: It's like a conversational pre-emptive strike. Whenever you don't agree with me, it always comes around to Nazis or anti-Semitism. First is my name too Jewish. Then it's Becky Epstein and the Holocaust. And now, even this, in come the jackboots again.

BENNY: "Even this"? What "this" are you saying "even this" about?

NORMA: McCarthyism, the blacklist—

BENNY: And you don't think that was anti-Semitism? Look at who was on the Committee. Martin Dies. Harold Velde. Karl Mundt.

NORMA: Oh come on, everybody with a German name isn't an anti-Semite. Besides which, there were a lot of people on the Committee who weren't German.

BENNY: That's right, Nixon isn't German. And we all know what a warm feeling he has for people of—how would he put it?—Hebraic persuasion? And as for the guys he and his buddies went after—

NORMA: All Jews, right?

BENNY: Let's just say you wouldn't have had trouble raising a minyan. Oh, and the fun the Committee had with the Jewish names! You can't tell from reading the transcripts—how they punched them, mispronounced them, tried to make them sound sinister and alien. "Carnovsky, Papirofsky, Ruskin." Ever hear anything so suspicious in your life? And did they have a field day with the ones who had *changed* their names! "You call yourself 'Holliday' but your real name, the name you were born with is what? 'Tuvim.' " As if they were talking to a criminal trying to hide something. You're going to tell me that wasn't anti-Semitism?

NORMA: That's not my point.

BENNY: Oh, I know what your point is.

NORMA: I never said you should work with Nazis.

BENNY: So, it's OK with you if I don't? I mean, you won't disapprove if I turn down a contract to co-star with Dr. Mengele?

NORMA: There *is* a difference between Mengele and Nixon.

BENNY: You're absolutely right—one murdered Jews, the other only made it hard for them to eat.

NORMA: OK, go ahead, twist everything.

BENNY: And you weren't twisting? That comment about my having a list?

NORMA: I was just raising what I thought was an interesting question.

BENNY: I was kept from working because some of the views I used to have suddenly weren't popular anymore. If I prefer not to work with people who kept me from working or gave support to people who kept me from working, I think I'm within my rights.

(He exits into the house.)

NORMA: Pop . . .

(She follows him off, hoping to calm him down. A second after she exits, LEO *enters. Like* BENNY*, he is in his late sixties, early seventies. He looks around the patio. He knows he is trespassing, but he is mentally prepared to face whoever might come out and face him. He is "casing" the place, when* NORMA *returns to the patio. Initially, due to where he stands, she doesn't see him.)*

LEO: Miss Teitel?

(Startled, she turns to look at him.)

NORMA: You're Leo Greshen.

LEO: *(With a smile.)* Guilty. I thought, rather than ring the doorbell, I'd just come around. I hope you don't mind.

NORMA: They told you.

LEO: Our beloved producers? Yes. At first, I couldn't figure it out. They said your father was somebody I used to know and that that was the reason why. And I kept thinking, "Teitel. When did I ever know a guy named Teitel?"

NORMA: My mother's name.

LEO: You changed it from Silverman?

NORMA: Yes.

LEO: Benny must love that. Why?

NORMA: Personal reasons.

LEO: You and he have a falling out?

NORMA: No.

LEO: OK.

NORMA: This is his house. I'm staying here.

LEO: Point taken.

NORMA: I shouldn't have said anything to them.

LEO: Them meaning our producers?

NORMA: I shouldn't have told them.

LEO: What then? Just walked out without warning?

NORMA: Of course not. I haven't decided to leave. All I said to them was that I was thinking about it. It didn't occur to me that they'd tell you.

LEO: Not to mention my popping up unannounced.

NORMA: There's the telephone.

LEO: True, but I've heard that the view here is terrific.

NORMA: Yes, well, there it is.

LEO: Very pretty.

NORMA: The blue part is the Pacific.

LEO: Somehow I never could live in L.A. Oh, I usually have a good time here. But I'm really a lazy bastard at heart, and this climate would probably aggravate that. Too easy to forget that time is passing when there's basically only one season. You're from the East, too, aren't you?

NORMA: New York.

LEO: Sure, you know what I mean. Every three months, you've got another season kicking you in the ass, telling you that the meter's ticking. One moment you're trying to find your sandals, the next you're digging galoshes out from the closet. Keeps you alert. *(A beat.)* Is he here?

NORMA: Inside. Probably taking a nap.

LEO: Ah. *(A beat.)* Did he ask you to drop out?

NORMA: No.

LEO: But he's not terribly happy about it. About the idea of you working with me.

NORMA: Did you think he would be?

LEO: How is he anyway?

NORMA: Fine.

LEO: He's a talented man, your father. We did a lot of work together.

NORMA: I know.

LEO: He told you?

NORMA: Not really. I did some reading.

LEO: Reading?

NORMA: Yes.

LEO: What did he do—hand you a bibliography and tell you there'd be a quiz?

NORMA: There are certain things he just never talks about.

LEO: And I'm one of those things. Right. *(A beat.)* You know, there were once these two guys named Stalin and Trotsky. They were both bigwigs in the Russian revolution.

NORMA: You don't have to patronize me, Mr. Greshen. I do know who Stalin and Trotsky were.

LEO: In my experience, that puts you firmly in the minority of the people your age. Their idea of history is when the Beatles first appeared on Ed Sullivan. Anyway, as you apparently know, after Lenin died, Stalin took over and tossed Trotsky out of Russia. Parenthetically, Trotsky was later murdered with a pickaxe. One of these days Brian de Palma will make a movie about this. Anyway, if you were an earnest young student of history while Stalin was in power—at Moscow U., say, or Petrograd Prep—you would have searched in vain to find any mention of Trotsky's part in the revolution in the state-approved texts. In the jargon of the time, he became a nonperson.

NORMA: Your point is?

LEO: Your father has the making of a fine Stalinist historian. Never talks about me at all, hunh?

NORMA: A little—recently, when I asked him. But not very much. The subject's painful for him, I guess.

LEO: Believe it or not, there was a time when he didn't hate my guts. But I don't imagine that was in your reading.

NORMA: You were both members of the New Labor Players.

LEO: Actually, I was one of the founders. A fellow named Mort Kessler was one of the other actors. He also wrote a lot of stuff. That's how he got started as a writer. Anyway, one day he brought in this piece—it was about St.

Peter and about how two or three fat-cats con their way past him into Heaven. *(Remembering title.)* "Capitalist Heaven"—that's what we called it! Well, of course, as capitalists always did in our subtle little plays, they set up an exploitive society—turned the poor cherubim into wage slaves in the harp factory, clipped their wings, etc. Anyway, we didn't have a St. Peter, and somebody knew your father. They had seen him do imitations or something at a party. So I met him. He was working in the garment district. I suggested he might have more fun earning next-to-nothing with us than earning almost-next-to-nothing hauling around big rolls of fabric. He believed me. And that's how he became an actor. He was a terrific St. Peter. Who would have guessed he would end up in a swanky place like this? Talk about Capitalist Heaven.

(A beat.)

NORMA: Did you want to see him?
LEO: I came out to see you.
NORMA: Yes, but this is his house. You must have known there was a reasonable chance of running into him.
LEO: I'm not afraid of that.
NORMA: I didn't say you were.
LEO: I'd like you to stay with the show.
NORMA: Have you seen any of my work?
LEO: The producers seem to think you're good.
NORMA: But you've never seen me do anything?
LEO: Nope.
NORMA: If I were to leave, it wouldn't be difficult for you to find someone else.
LEO: That's true.
NORMA: There are lots of good actresses.
LEO: A dozen or so at least.
NORMA: It might be easier for you.
LEO: Thank you for your concern, but I think I could bear up. I long ago accepted the fact that Mother Teresa would beat me in a popularity contest.
NORMA: I don't see why it would be worth it to you.
LEO: Why is your understanding so important?
NORMA: Because, if I were to stay, I'd like to know on what basis.
LEO: That you do your job. What other basis is there? You

fulfill a contract that was negotiated in good faith. Or don't you think you can play the part?

NORMA: I can play it.

LEO: It's not unheard of for an actor to come up with a convenient excuse to leave if he thinks he's out of his depth.

NORMA: I can play the part.

LEO: I believe you. Now, as for me, you acknowledge that I probably can do that job I've been hired for. True?

NORMA: Yes.

LEO: Then isn't that all we need be concerned about?

NORMA: I should just do my work and go on about my business.

LEO: It's called a professional attitude.

NORMA: You wouldn't be trying to prove something to my father?

LEO: What would I be trying to prove?

NORMA: You can't tell me the fact that I'm his daughter doesn't enter into this somewhere. Let's face it, I'm being kind of difficult here. And it's not as if I have any real reputation or name that you should have to put up with it.

LEO: Wait a second. Do you want me to fire you?

NORMA: I didn't say that.

LEO: What do you want?

NORMA: Mr. Greshen, I happen to believe I'm good at what I do. I happen also to have a well-known father who's also an actor.

LEO: That can be an advantage.

NORMA: It's an advantage I don't want. Whatever my career is, wherever it goes, I want it to be on the basis of what I do myself. One of the real kicks of getting this part was that they hired me without knowing who my dad is. I mean, they hired *me*.

LEO: I understand.

NORMA: Well, now I get the feeling that it's because of him you want me to stay.

LEO: Isn't it because of him you're thinking of leaving?

NORMA: Those are two separate issues.

LEO: I don't think so.

NORMA: But it *is* because of him you want me to stay. At least partially.

LEO: If you've got to know, it's because I don't like being walked out on. All right? *(A beat.)* Jesus, even if I *didn't* know you're Benny's daughter, I'd probably guess. You're a lot like him, Miss Teitel. By the way, that's a compliment.

*(*BENNY *enters. At first,* NORMA *sees him and* LEO *doesn't. Then* LEO *senses his presence and turns around.)*

BENNY: Very difficult to nap. All this back and forth outside my window.
LEO: Hello, Benny.
BENNY: She's right, you know.
LEO: Oh?
BENNY: If you think you're going to prove something to me—
LEO: No?
BENNY: You proved all that you had to prove to me a long time ago. That fabulous phone call.
LEO: The book is closed, hunh?
BENNY: That's the way it is.
LEO: You know, I've got an Aunt Sadie, still has my cousin Ernie's baby shoes. A friend of mine, he saves matchbooks from restaurants. But you—you collect old injuries.
BENNY: A shame, isn't it?
LEO: I think so.
BENNY: A shame and a waste. You feel sorry for me.
LEO: I do.
BENNY: I am touched by your concern.
LEO: I can tell.
BENNY: No, really. It comes a little late. But what's thirty years in the grand scheme of things?
LEO: I've always been concerned.
BENNY: " 'I weep for you,' the Walrus said, 'I deeply sympathize.' " You know, I believe him. I believe his tears are genuine. I have my doubts about the Carpenter, but the Walrus is a feeling man. Or as feeling as a Walrus can be. You, too, Leo.
LEO: Same old Benny.
BENNY: Some people are born walrus, some people achieve walrus, and some have walrus thrust upon them. You can't blame the people who are *born* walrus. After all, that's all they know. But the ones who *choose* it—
LEO: It's all nice and simple for you, isn't it?
BENNY: Why don't I throw you off my patio?
LEO: Maybe you don't want to.

BENNY: Why wouldn't I want to?
LEO: It's been almost thirty years.
BENNY: You say that as if there's a statute of limitations.
LEO: *Are* you going to throw me off your patio?
BENNY: I'm thinking about it. *(A beat.)* You want a beer?
LEO: Couldn't hurt.
BENNY: *(To* NORMA.) You want to bring this bastard a beer?
NORMA: What about you?
BENNY: Why not?

*(*NORMA *exits.* LEO *sits.* BENNY *picks up a bowl of chips, offers him some.* LEO *takes a few.* BENNY *grabs some chips for himself and sits. For a while, they sit and munch chips in silence. Then—)*

LEO: She looks like her mother.
BENNY: We're divorced.
LEO: I heard. I'm sorry.
BENNY: She isn't. She's a very happy divorcée. She's told me so herself. *(A beat.)* So you're coming back to the theatre. What happened? The movies go sour on you?
LEO: The movies are going fine. As a matter of fact, in a couple months I start a new one.
BENNY: But you're directing this play.
LEO: I wasn't aware of any rule that if you do one you can't do the other.

*(*NORMA *returns with two beers. She hands one to* LEO *during the following. He nods thanks.)*

No, the producers were in a bind. They needed a director. They talked to my agent. The timing worked out OK. I read the script.

*(*NORMA *now hands* BENNY *his beer.)*

BENNY: You like it?
LEO: It's a little lighter than I usually do, but I thought it might be fun to direct.
BENNY: Fun to look at my daughter's chest?

*(*NORMA *wishes the ground would open up.)*

LEO: Hunh?
BENNY: The scene she takes her top off.
LEO: Oh that.
BENNY: Yes, that.
LEO: I told the playwright I want to cut that. I don't like naked actors on the stage. Distracts from the play.
BENNY: Oh.
LEO: You don't agree?

(BENNY shrugs, but he sends a pointed look in NORMA's direction.)

NORMA: I think I'm going to take a drive.
BENNY: Where to?
NORMA: Nowhere in particular. Just a drive. Things to think about.
BENNY: I see.
NORMA: Besides, you probably want to be alone, right?
BENNY: *(Not replying to her line.)* Will you be gone long?
NORMA: I don't know.
LEO: I'm glad I had a chance to meet you, Miss Teitel.
NORMA: Mr. Greshen.

(She exits.)

LEO: You should let her do the play, Benny. It's a good part. People will notice. She'll be on her way. *(BENNY laughs.)* What?
BENNY: Good thing you didn't say that in front of her.
LEO: What?
BENNY: About my "letting" her. She would have laughed in your face.
LEO: Is that so?
BENNY: The idea that I have anything to do with what she decides.
LEO: Not a thing, hunh?
BENNY: Do you think I "let" her go into acting?
LEO: No?
BENNY: If you knew how hard I tried to keep her out of this business. And you can see how successful I was.
LEO: She never consults you.
BENNY: Who's around to consult? This is the first time

we've actually laid eyes on each other in almost two years. She's in New York, I'm here.

LEO: And the telephone hasn't been invented.

BENNY: Why should she care about my opinion?

LEO: *(Anticipating* BENNY *saying this—)* You're just her father.

BENNY: What do you think? She does your show, I'm going to cut her out of my will?

LEO: Apart from everything else, whether or not the show does well, I think she'd find it a valuable experience.

BENNY: You want me to tell her that? You want me to put in a good word for you, Leo?

(A beat.)

LEO: When's the last time *you* did a play?

BENNY: Half dozen years ago.

LEO: Which?

BENNY: *Front Page.*

LEO: Who'd you play?

BENNY: Pincus.

LEO: Remind me.

BENNY: The little schmuck with the message from the Governor.

LEO: Bet you were good.

BENNY: Me? I was terrific.

LEO: Not a big part, though.

BENNY: It was one of those all-star casts. Limited run.

LEO: Ah.

BENNY: I did it for the fun of it.

LEO: Was it fun?

BENNY: Sure.

LEO: So why not anything since?

BENNY: Wasn't *that* much fun.

LEO: Oh.

BENNY: Besides, nobody's sent me a script I really wanted to do in a long time. God, the things they call musicals these days! Most of them seem to be about some kid screaming how he wants to be a star. I've also been sent a lot of plays about people dying. You think they're trying to tell me something? Sometimes you get an adventurous blend of the two—about celebrities who die. From what I can tell, nobody's writing about anything anymore but show business and cancer. As if there were a difference.

LEO: You don't think you're overstating the case?

BENNY: Not by much, no.

LEO: You could always revive "Capitalist Heaven."

BENNY: At least that was about something.

LEO: Yeah, about twenty-five minutes.

BENNY: You didn't think so at the time.

LEO: At the time was at the time.

BENNY: What a way with words you have!

LEO: We were talking about you doing a play.

BENNY: Why should I haul my ass down to some drafty theatre eight times a week? It's not like I need the money.

LEO: That I noticed. *(Referring to the house.)* Is the inside as nice as the outside?

BENNY: You'll have to take my word.

(A beat.)

LEO: When did you start painting?

BENNY: How do you know I'm painting?

LEO: I could pretend to be Sherlock Holmes and say it's the smudge of blue on the side of your thumb.

BENNY: Did Norma tell you?

LEO: Nobody told me. I saw.

BENNY: Saw what?

LEO: One of your paintings.

BENNY: Where?

LEO: I was at someone's house. There was a picture on the wall. A view from this patio.

BENNY: I paint it a lot. Monet had water lilies and haystacks. Silverman's got smog.

LEO: Anyway, I told him I liked it, and he said you painted it.

BENNY: He?

LEO: Mort Kessler.

BENNY: I didn't know you and Morty were in touch.

LEO: More than in touch.

BENNY: Oh?

LEO: We get together whenever I'm out here. Or he gives me a call when he's east. Sure.

BENNY: From what happened I wouldn't say it was all that sure.

LEO: Oh, we patched all that up a long time ago.

BENNY: Patched it up?

LEO: There was a fund-raiser. Somebody did a dinner in their home, for the farmworkers, I think. One of those, I don't know. As it happened, Morty and I found ourselves seated near each other. He pretended I wasn't there for a while. Then I remember some woman walked by with impossibly blond hair. Well, the lady I was with made some comment like, "Do you believe that hair?" And Morty said, "Hey, I happen to know her mother was a natural fluorescent." I laughed. He looked at me. You can't ignore a man who laughs at your joke, right? And we started talking, and before the evening was over we were friends again.

BENNY: He never said.

LEO: Probably thought it would upset you.

BENNY: Why should it upset me who he chooses for friends? Just surprises me a little, that's all.

LEO: Like I said, we patched it up.

BENNY: He always did have a forgiving streak. You know, a couple weeks ago, I even heard him say something nice about his third wife.

LEO: He didn't forgive me. I didn't ask him to forgive me. I don't ask anybody to forgive me.

BENNY: He may have done it without your asking. Without your permission. He's got a sneaky side.

LEO: I don't think so. I don't think forgiving had anything to do with anything. I think he just put it aside. Somewhere along the line, he must have weighed things in the balance—

BENNY: And put it aside.

LEO: Yeah.

BENNY: First he weighed it, then he patched it, then he put it aside. Where? In storage?

LEO: In the past, where it belongs.

BENNY: Well, he never told me.

LEO: He knows you had strong feelings.

BENNY: I still do.

LEO: I guessed as much. But I suppose you're entitled.

BENNY: Thank you.

(A beat.)

LEO: So, how are you feeling?
BENNY: How am I feeling about what?
LEO: The question is health, Benny, not opinions.
BENNY: I'm feeling fine.
LEO: You've recovered.
BENNY: What am I supposed to have recovered from?
LEO: Morty said something about you in the hospital.
BENNY: Oh, that. Nothing dramatic. Just a little prostate trouble.
LEO: How much is a little?
BENNY: It got to the point where it was taking more time for me to pee than to prepare my taxes. The doctor kind of thought maybe we should do something about that. So did my accountant.
LEO: So you went to the hospital. How was that?
BENNY: Not too terrible actually.
LEO: Did they knock you out?
BENNY: No. They gave me a spinal. That just anesthetizes you from about the navel down. The upper part stays wide awake. As a matter of a fact, they asked me did I want to watch?
LEO: And?
BENNY: I took a pass.
LEO: If you could take a pass, you wouldn't have needed the operation.
BENNY: Anyway, I said no, thanks, my idea of entertainment was not to watch them drill for oil in my privates. So they put up a sheet to block the view, and they called in a Roto Rooter man. A few hours, and that was it.
LEO: So it was all right.
BENNY: All right? What are you talking about? Better than all right! Fantastic! Really, Leo, you should give it a try.
LEO: I mean it healed nicely. No complications.
BENNY: Such an interest you take! What—you want to make an on-site inspection?
LEO: Maybe some other time.
BENNY: Nope, you had your chance. For awhile there I had to avoid orange juice, grapefruit juice, pineapples—
LEO: Why?
BENNY: Citric acid, you know. Stings like crazy.
LEO: Right.
BENNY: But it's fine now.
LEO: Well, that's good news.

BENNY: Jesus.

LEO: What?

BENNY: I remember when we used to talk about girls and the revolution. Now—

LEO: You want to talk about girls, I'll be glad to talk about girls.

BENNY: Morty keeps you posted on my health.

LEO: He doesn't hand me bulletins or anything, but I like to keep track of the old gang.

BENNY: You heard about George.

LEO: I saw it in the *Times*. Christ, every morning, opening the God-damned *Times* to find out who I've survived.

BENNY: I know.

LEO: You went to the funeral?

BENNY: They didn't have a formal funeral. There was a kind of memorial thing.

LEO: What was that like?

BENNY: Sort of fun actually. Everybody got up, told stories.

LEO: *(Laughing.)* Oh?

BENNY: No, the clean ones.

LEO: Must have been a short memorial.

BENNY: They read some from his file. You know, he got the stuff the F.B.I. kept on him under the Freedom of Information thing.

LEO: Sounds like a lot of laughs.

BENNY: Did you ever hear about when he was in the army?

LEO: I know that he was in the army—

BENNY: About when he was in the hospital in the army?

LEO: Wait a second? About the F.B.I. agent?

BENNY: Came to question the other guys in the ward about him—

LEO: I've heard it, yeah.

BENNY: Didn't recognize him. Gave a testimonial to his own—

LEO: Yeah, I heard it.

BENNY: They asked him his name—

BENNY AND LEO: Jake Barnes.

BENNY: You heard it.

LEO: I heard it.

BENNY: You ever send for your file?

LEO: What for?

BENNY: To see what they said about you.

LEO: What for?

BENNY: I sent for mine.

LEO: To see what "they" said about you?

BENNY: What are you smiling about?

LEO: You remember the end of the second part of *Faust*?

BENNY: It doesn't spring to my lips, no.

LEO: Goethe.

BENNY: All of a sudden this is *G.E. College Bowl.*

LEO: He talks about "the Eternal Feminine." The last line is something about constantly pursuing "the Eternal Feminine."

BENNY: So?

LEO: So, instead of "the Eternal Feminine," for you it's "the Eternal They." "They" do this, "they" keep you from doing that. Always "they."

BENNY: Not always, Leo. Sometimes it's "you."

LEO: So you sent for your file.

BENNY: I sent for my file.

LEO: Anything interesting?

BENNY: Great nostalgia value. Lists of the petitions I signed, the magazines I subscribed to. Some bastard even showed up at one of the benefits I performed at. "Subject performed allegedly humorous routine—"

LEO: "Allegedly humorous." He said that?

BENNY: Fucking critics, they're everywhere. You remember—just after Sarah and I got married, I had to go out of town on that tour?

LEO: *Native Son,* wasn't it?

BENNY: Probably. Anyway, Sarah was doing real well in radio then, so she didn't go out with me. So we wrote each other a lot. Some of it was kind of personal stuff.

LEO: You mean love letters?

BENNY: Well, yeah, I guess you could call them that. Anyway, I'd lost the originals a long time ago in one of our moves. But, like I say, I had the F.B.I. send me my file, and they must have kept a mail cover on us, because there they were—all the letters I'd lost. A lot of them anyway.

LEO: They Xeroxed your letters?

BENNY: Xeroxed? In nineteen forty—

LEO: Right.

BENNY: No, someone actually typed them up. Probably anchored them with a book or something so they'd lie flat, be easier to type from. You know Sarah's handwriting—probably had to hire a cryptographer to decipher. Sarah and I were waiting for the final divorce papers when I got that file from the Feds.

(A beat.)

I almost sent her copies.

LEO: *(Gently.)* Almost?

BENNY: What purpose would it have served? It was all over between us by then.

LEO: Benny, what happened?

BENNY: Well—

LEO: The two of you—I've never seen a couple like—

*(*BENNY *suddenly realizes how close he's gotten to the old friendship. He forces himself to pull back.)*

BENNY: No, I'm not going to talk about that.

LEO: If there's something you want to—

BENNY: Not with you.

(A beat.)

LEO: OK.

BENNY: Anyway, I get some satisfaction out of knowing that the S.O.B. who typed that all up is probably dead now.

LEO: Or maybe having a prostate operation of his own.

BENNY: He should only have it done without a spinal.

(A beat.)

How's your beer?

LEO: Fine.

(A beat.)

I was given an honorary degree, you know. Last spring.

BENNY: In what—communications?

LEO: A doctor of letters, actually. Avery College, New Hampshire. For my body of work. That's how they phrased it. Sounds cadaverous, doesn't it? "Here lies Leo Greshen's body of work." I had to laugh when I was told. But I said sure. Sure, I'd be honored to be honored. And, generous fellow that I am, I say I'll throw in a seminar on directing or some damn thing. They couldn't be happier. I'm met at the airport. I have dinner with a bunch of deans and professors and nice faculty wives, faculty husbands, whatever. Some nice stroking. Springtime in New Hampshire. Who could object to that? So I'm scheduled to speak to this media studies class. The guy who runs the class introduces me. My pictures, the plays I've directed, blah, blah, blah, and would you please welcome. Applause. All very nice. He asks me questions. I answer. I make jokes. He tosses in a quip or two like a regular Dick Cavett. Everything's bopping along well. About forty-five minutes of this, he says he's going to open the floor to questions. Four or five hands shoot up. I see this one intent kid off to the side, near the window. Skinny kid with eyes like lasers. I look at him and I know he's going to ask it. I just know it. But my friend, the would-be Dick Cavett, calls on some girl who asks me how it was to work with so-and-so, and I tell an amusing story and everybody laughs in the right place except for the kid with the laser eyes. I've barely finished my amusing story when his hand shoots up again. The professor again chooses another hand. Bearded kid wants to know if I story-board when I'm in pre-production. I tell another amusing story. Soon as I'm finished with that one, again that kid's hand shoots up. Again my host chooses another hand, but I interrupt him. I say, "Wait a second. There's a young man over there by the window seems to have something urgent to ask. Yes, son, what is it?" Yes, son, I'm thinking, go ahead and prove how brave and liberal you are. Nail me in front of all your nice classmates and your nice teacher on this nice, nice campus in New Hampshire. "Yes, son," I say, "what's your question?" He doesn't disappoint. No sooner has he said the magic words "House Committee on Un-American Activities" than my friend the professor interrupts, says that we are not here to discuss that. "We are here to discuss Mr. Greshen's art, Mr. Greshen's craft. We are here to learn what we can from Mr. Greshen's years of experience in the theatre and film. Politics has nothing to do with it." And he asks if there are any other questions. I answer two more, and my friend the professor wraps it up by thanking me on behalf of the class for my generosity and candor. Applause. My host and I go to the faculty lounge. He buys me a drink and tells me that he's sorry about the boy's rudeness. Apparently that boy has a habit of stirring things up. And that was why my friend hadn't wanted to call on him. He was trying to protect me. Seems like this kid had circulated a petition calling on the college to rescind the honorary degree. That it would not redound to the school's credit to honor a stoolie. This was not quite how my friend put it, but that was the jist of it. So there was a ceremony, I got my degree, shook a lot of nice hands, and went home. And all through this I was thinking of how I should have answered the little bastard.

BENNY: And what would you have said?

LEO: That he hadn't earned the right to ask me that question. He hadn't earned the right to brandish his moral indignation in my face.

BENNY: That's a nice snappy reply. Maybe you'll have another opportunity to use it.

LEO: Oh, I don't lack for opportunity. Even after all these years, it knocks with regularity. I'm constantly being offered forums for public confession. Really, it's very touching to know how many people are concerned about my moral rehabilitation. So eager to help me get this awful weight off my shoulders. This one woman—from some French film journal—for some reason I agreed to be interviewed for an article she was writing on my films. Turned out to be structuralist bullshit. Anyway, in the middle of it—here we go again. To be fair, we'd had a bottle of wine and we were getting along. Anyway, I informed her as affably as possible that I really didn't want to get into that subject. And she leaned forward and took my arm with that easy familiarity that a shared bottle of wine can encourage, she took my arm and looked into my eyes and said, "But Leo . . ." Not "Monsieur Greshen" but "Leo," right? "But Leo," she said, "you will feel—how do you say it?—the relief, no?"

BENNY: And you don't think you'd feel relief?

LEO: Benny, please. To step into a mess of dog shit once—that's something that can happen to anybody. To intentionally step into the same dog shit again—

BENNY: What dog shit is that?

LEO: Look, I've been through this before. "Leo, get up, get it off your chest. You'll feel better, swear to God." All I had to do was submit to a nice dirty ritual of public cleansing. Did you read the Navasky book?

BENNY: I glanced at it.

LEO: Well, I think a lot of it is doubletalk. But he got that part right. The ritual part. Get up in front of the Committee, admit your errors. Prove how repentant you are—*demonstrate* your sincerity by naming a few names, you'll emerge redeemed, rehabilitated. Decent American folks will be happy to shake you by the hand, slap your back, let you do your work. Now, though, different political truths are operative, as the saying goes. Now I'm told that I bought the moral equivalent of a pig in a poke. I got myself the wrong brand of cleansing and rehabilitation. There's a new improved formula. Yes, there is! This season, if I want to be cleaner than clean, I'm supposed to get up and say I done wrong when I said I done wrong before. I'm supposed to do a *mea culpa* over my other *mea culpa.* Only instead of doing it in front of a mob of congressional Neanderthals, I'm supposed to confess to someone like Navasky or that French structuralist or that kid at Avery College. And after I choke out my apology, Navasky, on behalf of his enlightened readers, will dispense absolution. "Go and sin no more." In my book, it's the same damn ritual of public cleansing, only some labels have been changed to conform to the spirit of blacklist chic. Well, like I say, I stepped into that shit once. I'm not doing it again. Not even for you, Benny. And believe me, you're about the only reason I'd think of doing it.

BENNY: Sounds like you've got this all thought out.

LEO: It's not like I haven't had the time.

BENNY: Just one problem, Leo. When you called me up that night, you didn't call me because you thought you were right. You called me because you felt lousy about what you were going to do.

LEO: Benny, I never claimed to feel good about it.

BENNY: But you did it.

LEO: Only a fool fights the drop.

BENNY: You want to translate?

LEO: You've seen enough cowboy movies. If the bad guys have got the drop on you, it's crazy to draw on them. You're only going to get gunned down. Can't fight if you're dead.

BENNY: So now we're cowboys?

LEO: Thank you for taking what I have to say seriously.

BENNY: Seriously, OK: Leo, not only did you not fight the drop, you helped the bad guys gun down some good guys. What would the kids in the balcony say if Roy Rogers shot Gabby Hayes?

LEO: Bad guys, good guys—

BENNY: It's your analogy.

LEO: I said nothing about good guys.

BENNY: Oh, I see: there were no good guys?

LEO: Present company excepted, of course.

BENNY: No good guys. Well, that makes it nice and convenient, doesn't it? If everybody's equally scummy, then the highest virtue is survival. That must make you pretty goddamn virtuous. You should write a book about your philosophy, Leo. Really. I've got the title for you: *Charles Darwin Goes to the Theatre.*

LEO: Being a victim doesn't automatically entitle you to a white hat, Benny. It's that old liberal impulse—romanticize the persecuted.

BENNY: What the hell would you know about liberal impulses?

LEO: Hey, I've got my share of them.

BENNY: You—a liberal? Don't make me laugh.

LEO: I sure wouldn't want to do that, Benny—make you laugh.

BENNY: Maybe you're a checkbook liberal. You send in contributions to those ads with pictures of kids starving in South America, a couple bucks to the A.C.L.U.—

LEO: More than a couple of bucks, but never mind—

BENNY: More than a couple? Well, hey, that changes my opinion completely.

LEO: I'll tell you where I part company with a lot of them, though. I won't romanticize. Just because someone's a martyr doesn't make him wise and good and pure. Sure, I sent in money to Joan Little's defense fund, but that doesn't mean I'd trust her to baby-sit my grandchildren.

BENNY: The guys the Committee went after weren't accused of murder, just of having believed in something unpopular. And the ones who wouldn't buckle under—out with the garbage.

LEO: Which is exactly what they did to each other when they were members of the Party. Those bastards were always browbeating each other, excommunicating each other for not embracing "the correct revolutionary line." Do you remember when the Party endorsed Henry Wallace for President? Lenny Steinkempf got up in a meeting, said he thought it was a crappy idea. So what did the Party do? They threw him the fuck out. And after *they* threw him out, his *wife* Elaine, being a loyal Party member, *she* threw him out. As far as I was concerned, facing the Committee was an exercise in déjà vu. Believe me, Nixon and Mundt could have taken lessons from some of those old Commies. I wasn't about to put my dick on the block for any of those guys. Why should I keep faith with them when they couldn't keep faith with themselves?

BENNY: The point wasn't to keep faith with *them.* Leo, don't you remember anything about how or why we put together the New Labor Players?

LEO: Oh, for Christ's sake!

BENNY: For Christ's sake what?

LEO: *(Laughing.)* Benny, you aren't seriously going to hit me with the New Labor Players?

BENNY: And why not?

LEO: All that agitprop bullshit, the slogans, screaming our lungs raw—

BENNY: Worthless?

LEO: Not worthless, exactly—

BENNY: Then *what,* exactly?

LEO: All we ever did was play to people who felt exactly like we did. Invigorating—sure. Fun—absolutely. And a great way to meet girls. But don't try to tell me we ever accomplished any great social good. I doubt that we ever changed anybody's mind about anything.

BENNY: That's how you measure it?

LEO: You measure it differently?

BENNY: Seems to me there's some value in letting people know—because they laughed or maybe cheered at the same time as a bunch of other people—letting them know they aren't alone. That there are other people who feel like they do.

LEO: Maybe we should have broken out some red pom-poms while we were at it.

BENNY: Pom-poms?

LEO: Hey, if you're going to cheerlead, you should have pom-poms. "Give me a P, give me an R, give me an O, give me an L!"

BENNY: Leo—

LEO: *(Continuing.)* "Whattaya got? Proletariat! Whattaya got? Class struggle! Whattaya got? Dialectical materialism! Rah, rah, rah!"

BENNY: Some terrific joke, Leo. Very funny.

LEO: What's funny is you telling me this stuff.

BENNY: What's funny about that?

LEO: You think I don't know my own spiel when I hear it?

BENNY: Your spiel?

LEO: Of course my spiel. "Class consciousness is the first step. Through theatre we give dramatic form to our lives and hopes and so create our identity and the identity of our community." You like it? I've got another three or four hours of this. Rousing stuff, hunh?

(A beat.)

BENNY: Yeah, I thought so.

LEO: Oh, I convinced myself pretty good, too. But I'm not a twenty-two-year-old kid anymore, and neither are you. And I'm not going to let you get away with pretending that "Capitalist Heaven" and the rest of it was any great golden age of drama. Face it, Benny, it was amateur night.

BENNY: I'm not talking about how sophisticated or how professional. Leo, what I'm saying is that when we started, all right, we may not have had much polish or technical expertise, but we did have a sense of purpose. There was a *reason* I started acting. There was a *reason* Mort Kessler started writing. There was a *reason* you started directing. And then came a point you gave up your reason so you could keep on directing.

LEO: Maybe directing *was* my reason.

BENNY: What—directing anything?

LEO: Of course not.

BENNY: You say of course not, but I don't take it for granted that there are things you wouldn't direct. Before the Committee—yes. But after?

LEO: So all of a sudden I'm a whore. Of course, it isn't whoring to do some dumb-ass sitcom. What was it called—*Rich and Happy*?

BENNY: *Rich But Happy*.

LEO: I stand corrected. Truly edifying, uplifting stuff. My God, in the old days, if somebody had told you that's what you'd end up doing! *Rich But Happy*. I mean, back then just the *title* would have made you gag!

BENNY: I had to live.

LEO: So did I, Benny. So did I.

BENNY: But if I did crap—and God knows I'm not holding up *Rich But Happy* as an example of high culture—but if I did crap, I didn't destroy other people to do it.

LEO: I don't happen to think that the work I did after that *was* crap. As a matter of a fact, a lot of it was damn good.

BENNY: If you do say so yourself.

LEO: You're going to tell me that it wasn't? Oh, I know this riff. If a guy's politics aren't approved, aren't correct, then he can't be any good as an artist. I bet you're one of those people who think God took away Frank Sinatra's voice as a punishment for voting Republican.

BENNY: I'm not talking party affiliation—

LEO: I know what you're talking about: In order to be an artist, you've got to be a certified good guy.

BENNY: Being a *mensch* enters into it, yes.

LEO: And if he isn't, you feel cheated. Shortchanged. Well, if art by bastards upsets you so much, you should drop everything right now, go into your library, and toss out anything you have by Robert Frost. Now there was a world-class shit! And how about Ezra Pound! And let's not bring up Wagner!

BENNY: I don't have any Wagner in my house.

LEO: No? Well now *there's* a brave stand! My hat's off to you, Benny! Keep those doors guarded. Be vigilant! Hey, you can't be *too* careful. I mean, you never know when somebody might try to sneak the fucking *Ring Cycle* into your house without your knowing it, right?

BENNY: This I'm enjoying—you linking arms with Wagner!

LEO: Tell me something, if you found out that Charles Dickens shtupped ten-year-old boys, would that make him any less of a writer?

BENNY: Well, it sure as hell would make a difference in how I read *Oliver Twist*.

LEO: Whatever you or anybody else thinks about me as a person, I did good work, Benny. Not just before. After, too.

BENNY: I wouldn't know about after. I didn't see most of it.

LEO: Well, you missed some good stuff. If you don't want to take my word for it, you can take if from the critics. You can look on my fucking mantel in New York at the prizes and the plaques—

BENNY: I'm sure they would blind me.

LEO: They mean something, Benny, even if it's fashionable to sneer at them. They mean that a lot of people thought that the work was good.

BENNY: And that's important to you.

LEO: Yes, it is.

BENNY: You like having the good opinion of others.

LEO: Is that a crime?

BENNY: No, I don't think it's a crime. I like it, too. I'm just sorry to have to tell you that you haven't got my good opinion, Leo.

LEO: And I'm sorry to have to tell you I don't give a damn.

BENNY: Then why are you here?

LEO: Because I don't want your goddamn daughter walking out of my goddamn play.

BENNY: Fine, you told her that. So why are you still here?

LEO: Because I'm a masochistic idiot!

BENNY: What, you expected me to throw my arms open?

LEO: No.

BENNY: Then what?

LEO: Damn it, Benny—thirty years! It's been more than thirty years! We're going to start *dying* soon! ***(A beat.)*** While there's still a chance.

(A beat.)

BENNY: Leo, you got a car?

LEO: Yeah. Why?

BENNY: Let's say for the sake of argument there's someplace you want to go. So you go to your car, put the key in the ignition—nothing. It isn't working. But there's this place you want to go. You want to go there real bad. You take a look in my garage, what do you know?—I've got a car. A car in good working condition. It's got a few years on it, but it runs fine. We're talking about a respected make. So you ask me, can you take my car? I say no, I'm sorry, I've made plans, I need it. You tell me about this place you want to go, how important it is to you to get there. I say I'm sorry, but no, I can't let you have my car. What do you do? You take it anyway. Now what do you figure I do in a situation like this? Call the cops, of course. Give them your description and the license number, they take off after you. What happens if they catch you? You end up being charged with grand theft auto. All right, you didn't steal my car. But there *was* someplace you wanted to go, and the only vehicle you could get your hands on was something else that belonged to me. *(*NORMA *has entered during the above. Neither* BENNY *nor* LEO *betrays any notice of her presence. Which is not to say that they don't know she's there.)* Something that belonged to me, something that belonged to Morty, something that belonged to a few other guys. I don't know how you did it with them, but I get the famous phone call. You call and tell me what you're going to do. You cry about the pressure. You tell me how much getting to this place you want to go means to you. You want me to tell you, "Sure, Leo, go ahead. Take it for a drive. Barter it for the good opinion of a bunch of cynical shits. Buy yourself a license to work." But it doesn't play that way. I say no. And the next day, you go into that committee room, and you use it anyway. The difference between that and you taking my car—my car you can return. *(A beat.)* Leo, I'm not Morty Kessler. I won't put it aside. I'm sorry. *(A beat.)* Norma, Mr. Greshen dropped by to ask you about his show. Why don't you tell him what you've decided? *(A beat.* NORMA *doesn't respond.)* Norma?

(A beat.)

LEO: Miss Teitel, I would appreciate it if you would call me later.

*(*NORMA *nods.* LEO *exits. A beat.)*

NORMA: OK, I think I've got it now.
BENNY: What is that?
NORMA: Why you didn't throw him out before. All these years, you've been thinking, working up what you would say if you ever met him again—
BENNY: Who wanted to meet him again?
NORMA: I'm saying "if."
BENNY: I did my best to make sure that wouldn't happen.
NORMA: I'm sure you did.
BENNY: I gave up my favorite Chinese restaurant. A place I

knew he sometimes ate. Never went back. Last thing I wanted was to see him.

NORMA: Last thing, hunh?

BENNY: If you'll have the stenographer read back the transcript, I think you'll see that's what I said.

NORMA: I know you said it—

BENNY: But you—with your years of wisdom and experience—you see the deeper truth, is that it?

NORMA: Maybe *at first* you didn't want to meet him again—

BENNY: Oh boy, here we go—

NORMA: Maybe in the beginning—

BENNY: I can see where all this is heading. I didn't, but really underneath it all, I did.

NORMA: After all, you had the speech ready. What good is a speech if you don't give it?

BENNY: And there it is, folks—my soul naked and quivering.

NORMA: Then why did you come out in the first place? If you knew who I was talking to—

BENNY: This isn't a Chinese restaurant. This is my patio. I won't stop coming here.

NORMA: That's not what I'm saying.

BENNY: Oh, you grant me the right to step out on it if and when I please?

NORMA: Sure, and it pleased you to do it then because he was out here.

BENNY: I should hide inside?

NORMA: Nobody said anything about hiding.

BENNY: What about Leo? It sure pleased *him* to barge in here uninvited.

NORMA: We're not talking about him.

BENNY: No? Oh, I see, *you're* setting the agenda here. The topics of discussion. Sorry, Mr. Chairman.

NORMA: Mr. Chairman?

BENNY: Mr. Silverman, you aren't being cooperative. If you would please answer the question. Did you or did you not know that the American Committee for Spanish Freedom was a Communist front organization?

NORMA: Pop—

BENNY: And just exactly who was present that night in Mr. Kessler's house?

NORMA: If you can't tell the difference between me and the Committee—

BENNY: The tone is similar, believe me.

NORMA: You're misunderstanding—

BENNY: I don't know what you think you're accusing me of—

NORMA: I'm not accusing you—

BENNY: No?

NORMA: I'm not disagreeing with anything you said to him.

BENNY: Then what? That I said it at all?

NORMA: Never mind.

BENNY: What—are you afraid I lost you your job?

NORMA: No.

BENNY: That's it, isn't it?

NORMA: The job isn't yours to lose.

BENNY: Right. Your decision.

NORMA: That's what he said.

BENNY: And you can take it from me, he's a man to be trusted. Yes, sir.

NORMA: I just hope you got what you wanted.

BENNY: And what might that be?

NORMA: I don't know. Satisfaction?

BENNY: No way to get satisfaction.

NORMA: Then why do it?

BENNY: Sometimes you do a thing because you've got the right to do it. Or don't you think I have the right?

NORMA: Of course you've got the right. And I've got the right to do some things, too.

BENNY: Like to judge me, my behavior? Well, I beg to differ, kiddo. You haven't earned it.

NORMA: Oh, so it's like with the painting. I don't have the proper background, so I can't appreciate it. Because I didn't suffer through the blacklist, I can't have an opinion.

BENNY: Have any opinion you want, but don't expect me to get all worked up about it.

NORMA: No, of course not. Who the hell am I, anyway? If I happen to think that walking around spitting battery acid at the world is no kind of a life—

BENNY: I don't have to listen to this.

NORMA: Pop, he did a shitty thing to you. No argument. But after all of these years, to let it keep eating at you, to let it take over your life—

BENNY: "A shitty thing." Your command of the language— "A shitty thing." Like maybe he stole a girl from me or got drunk and peed in my swimming pool. It goes beyond. You think something happens and that's it, it's over with? That it's gone and remote because you can stick a date to it and a lot of calendars have been tossed out in the meantime? All those books you've read, all that time in the library, you still don't understand a thing. *(A beat.)* I was an actor. Basic to being an actor is the fact that you can't do it by yourself. It's not like plumbing or fixing shoes or painting a picture. You've got to do it *with* other people in the *presence* of other people. If someone does something to cut you off from them, you're not an actor anymore. I don't care what you call yourself or what you put on your resumé, you're not. You can't grow, you can't develop. You're not allowed to be what you could. You aren't even allowed to be who you are. You're an exile. Not just from your profession, your business. You're an exile from yourself. That's what Leo did to me when he said my name. This charming fellow with all of his stories and his reasons. Sorry, yes. I'm sure he is. But that's what he did.

NORMA: And that's what you want me to do to myself. Because you couldn't work, you want me to refuse to work. Doesn't what you were saying apply to me as well? About needing other people to be an actor? You were entitled to work. Aren't I entitled, too? Or am I supposed to give up my entitlement because I'm your daughter?

BENNY: But with *him*.

NORMA: Since when do you have to like everybody you work with?

BENNY: Fine, you want the part, you keep the part. It's your decision.

NORMA: Pop—

BENNY: No, I think it's a terrific career move. And as far as your not liking him goes, I'll bet you get past that. I'll bet you two get along great. After all, so much in common: He steals my name, you throw it away.

NORMA: What do you want? You want me to blacklist myself?

BENNY: I want you to go ahead and do what you're going to do and spare me the hypocrisy of pretending that you give a good goddamn about what I want.

*(*BENNY *exits. A beat.* NORMA *turns to the audience.)*

NORMA: That afternoon, I move to a motel. We go back into rehearsal a couple days later, a couple weeks later we open. True to his word, Pop doesn't come to the opening. The next day, I drive over to see him.

*(*BENNY *enters with brushes and paint, goes to the easel. He begins to work. A beat.)*

BENNY: The reviews?
NORMA: Mostly good.
BENNY: What about for you?
NORMA: Also good.
BENNY: Congratulations.

*(*NORMA *takes out a program.)*

NORMA: Something I want to show you.
BENNY: What is it?
NORMA: The program.
BENNY: What about it?

*(*NORMA *opens it to a specific page, hands it to him.)*

NORMA: Here.
BENNY: Your bio? I'm familiar with your credits.
NORMA: I added a line to the end.

(A beat. BENNY *looks at it, reads.)*

BENNY: "Norma Teitel is the daughter of actor Benny Silverman." *(He hands the program back to her.)* It's not enough.

(A beat. She stands there as he goes back to painting. The lights fade on them.)

FALSETTOLAND

by
William Finn and
James Lapine

William Finn's remarks begin with a comment about the entire trilogy, *Falsettos,* of which *Falsettoland* is the middle play:

I was struggling with the concept of what a man is, trying to write—in the first show, *March of the Falsettos*—a "how-to manual" on how a man should behave.

The opening number, "Four Jews in a Room Bitching," is almost a Platonic concept of the perfect musical! With this song, what I was trying to say to audiences is that what you're going to see is not going to be like any other Jewish musical you've ever seen before. This is going to be a musical about angst and identity and community (which others have been), but told in a way that embraces modern Jewish diction (which other musicals have not).

I'd always thought that Jews were both smart and funny. What I wanted to write was something representative in that the characters were all smart and funny and in predicaments that let them use their intelligence and their sense of humor to their advantage. By incorporating bar mitzvahs and other Jewish things, I wasn't consciously trying to be "Jewish," but rather, to discuss what manliness is. The bar mitzvah is natural because it's a rite of manhood, and Jason proves himself adult by making the decision he makes.

Some gay audiences respond to it very positively; others think it's not gay enough, a criticism I really don't understand. It's not pedagogical; it's heterogeneous and inclusive, rather than homogeneous and exclusive. And even when the incidents aren't exactly Jewish, the tone of the play very much is.

For Arthur Salvadore

Falsettoland opened at Playwrights Horizons in New York City, under the artistic direction of Andre Bishop, on June 28, 1990. The cast was as follows:

MARVIN	*Michael Rupert*
TRINA	*Faith Prince*
JASON	*Danny Gerard*
WHIZZER	*Stephen Bogardus*
MENDEL	*Chip Zien*
DR. CHARLOTTE	*Heather MacRae*
CORDELIA	*Janet Metz*

It subsequently moved downtown to the elegant, newly restored Lucille Lortel Theatre on September 16, 1990. It was produced by Maurice Rosenfield and Lois F. Rosenfield, Inc., with Steven Suskin in association with Playwrights Horizons and by special arrangement with Lucille Lortel. It was directed by James Lapine. The set was designed by Douglas Stein; the costumes were by Franne Lee, the lighting by Nancy Schertler, and the sound by Scott Lehrer. The musical direction and arrangements were by Michael Starobin. The stage manager was Kate Riddle.

Opening

When the audience enters, they see a huge, three-dimensional "1981" on stage. Two huge flashlights—the kind used to land planes at airports—are seen at the back of the stage behind the numbers. We cannot see who is manipulating them, but the lights are slowly prescribing the dimensions of the stage. Then the flashlights are turned into the eyes of the audience.

MENDEL: *(Acting as our tour guide.)*
Homosexuals.

(He searches the audience for them.)

Women with children.

(Ditto.)

Short insomniacs.

(He shines the lights on his face.)

And a teeny tiny band.

(He shines them on the band upstage. The band area lights up and the band waves.)

Come back in,
The welcome mat is on the floor.
Let's begin.
This story needs an ending

(MARVIN *enters.)*

Homosexual.

(Light on MARVIN.*)*

Father with children.

(JASON *enters.)*

One bar mitzvah that
Is scrupulously planned.

*(*WHIZZER *and* TRINA *enter, followed by everyone else.)*

ALL:
Lovers come and lovers go.
Lovers fight and sing fortissimo.
Give these handsome boys a hand.
Welcome to Falsetto—

MEN:	DR. CHARLOTTE:	TRINA AND CORDELIA:
—land!	Nancy Reagan—	Ooooh.
		WOMEN:
		Meanest and thinnest of the First Ladies—
		Moves into the White House.
MEN:		
Yabba dabba		It's the eighties.

ALL:
Yabba dabba
WOMEN:
Oooh the eighties.
MEN:
Yabba dabba
ALL:
What a world we live—

WOMEN:	MEN:
In!	March. March.
	March of the falsettos.
	March of the falsettos.

WOMEN:
What a world we live in!
Oooh
Wa-oooh!

MEN:
Who is
Man enough to march to
March of the falsettos?

ALL: *(Clapping.)*
Yabba dabba dabba
WOMEN:
Screwy families.
DR. CHARLOTTE:
Women internists.
CORDELIA:
Kosher caterers—
ALL:
Who are trying to expand.
Everybody on your mark.
WOMEN:
Congregate in Central Park.
MEN:
Pretty boys are in demand.
ALL:
Welcome to Falsettoland.
Heey!

(Ingenious scissor-kick formations.)

Hooo!

(Great joyous havoc.)

What a world we live in!

*(*MARVIN *looks around, perplexed.)*

Heey!

(They're wheeling around on furniture.)

Hooo!

(Setting the scene.)

What a world we live in!

(Creating the world.)

Heey!

(The last scissor kick.)

MARVIN: *(Looking disdainfully at them all.)*
It's about time, don't you think?
It's about time to grow up,
Don't you think?
It's about time to grow up
And face the music.
It's about time.

(To the audience.)

Since we last spoke
Two years are waning.
I'll try explaining
Just what you've missed.

*(*TRINA *moves to his side.)*

We called a truce
And fitfully we coexist.

*(*MENDEL *moves to his side.)*

I'm still loose.
She's still with the psychiatrist.

(They both walk away.)

So I don't have a psychiatrist
Except on the Jewish holidays.
But I still have my son on the weekends,

*(*MARVIN *embraces* JASON.*)*

Just on the weekends,

*(*JASON *removes* MARVIN*'s arm and walks away.)*

And some very good friends.

(The LESBIANS, *on either side of him, kiss his cheek.)*

But I don't have a lover anymore.
Oh my God.
When am I going to get over this?
When am I going to get over this?
When am I going to get over this?
WHIZZER, CORDELIA, DR. CHARLOTTE:
Homosexuals.
TRINA AND JASON:
Women with children.
MARVIN, TRINA, WHIZZER:
Ex-ex-lovers.
MENDEL:
And a teeny tiny band.
ALL:
Welcome to Falsettoland.
MENDEL:
Psychoanalysts.
JASON:
Child insomniacs.
ALL:
Welcome to Falsettoland.
Liberal democrats.
CORDELIA AND DR. CHARLOTTE:
Spiky lesbians.
ALL:
Welcome to Falsettoland.
CORDELIA:
Kosher caterers.
add MENDEL AND JASON:
Short insomniacs.
add DR. CHARLOTTE:
Hypochondriacs.
add MARVIN:
Yiddish Americans.
add WHIZZER:
Screwy families.
add TRINA:
Radiologists.

ALL:
Intellectuals.
Nervous wrecks.
Ugh. Ah!
Welcome to Falsettoland.

(ALL but MARVIN leave, singing, through the door MARVIN has opened.)

MARVIN:
It's about time, don't you think?
It's about time to grow up,
Don't you think?
It's about time to grow up
And face the music.
It's about time.

One day I'd like to be
As mature as my son,
Who is twelve and a half
And this tall

(His hand indicates JASON-height. JASON slides in, right under his hand.)

That's all I'd like to be, that's all.
It's about growing up,
Getting older,
Living on a lover's shoulder,
Learning love is not a crime.
It's about time.
It's about time.
It's about time.
It's about . . .

The Year of the Child

JASON: *(Listening to a Walkman and singing along.)*
Baruch
Baruch atoh
Baruch atoh adonai
Baruch atoh adonai elohenu
Meluch haolum . . .
TRINA:
Jason, dear, hello.
Are you packed and waiting?
But before we go,
Let me speak with Father alone.

(To MARVIN.*)*

Now as this bar mitzvah nears—
Jason, put your Walkerman on and hum—

(To MARVIN.*)*

Since this is the last loving thing
We'll probably ever do together,
Let's act adult and not go crazy.
MARVIN:
Have you chose yet who'll cater?
TRINA:
What about it?
MARVIN:
I know a person who should cater.
TRINA:
It's a personal opinion who should cater.

MARVIN:
Can we consider who's gonna cater?
TRINA:
Shh.
MARVIN:
Please.
TRINA:
Shh.
MARVIN:
Please.
TRINA:
Shh.
MARVIN:
Please.
MENDEL:
Stop!
This is so much crap.
Throw a simple party.
Religion's just a trap
That ensnares the weak and the dumb.
Stop with the prayers.
TRINA:
How can you stop with the prayers
At a bar mitzvah?
MENDEL:
The whole thing's voodoo,
And I know more than you do.
MARVIN AND TRINA:
This is the year of Jason's bar mitzvah.

MARVIN:
We're more excited
Than we should be.
We're more ex—

TRINA:
We're more excited
Than we should be.

BOTH:
This is the year of the child
When he spreads out his wings.
There's music in his heart,
His life's about to start—
His body's going wild.

(JASON is twitching to the Walkman.)

My child.
MARVIN:
My child.
TRINA:
Our child.
MENDEL:
Children, please,
Throw the kid a celebration and relax.
I'll bring women
From the wrong side of the tracks.
We'll have a ball.
I guess I'll have to raise this Jason myself.

TRINA:	MARVIN:	MENDEL:
	Isn't he an asshole?	My own bar mitzvah was
Yes he is.	Isn't he too much?	A miserable occasion,
Yes, but so are you.	Jesus,	The cause for such abrasion
Really, kiddo,	What an asshole!	In my family.
So are you.	Jason, where's my hug?	It still gives me hives.
Where's my hug?		
	Where's my—	

MARVIN AND TRINA:	MENDEL:
This is the year for Jason's bar mitzvah.	This is the year for Jason's bar mitzvah.
This is the year for Jason's bar mitzvah.	This is the year for Jason's bar mitzvah.

(Doorbell. Enter the LESBIANS.*)*

DR. CHARLOTTE: *(In the doorway.)*
Look look look look look—
It's a lesbian from next door.
CORDELIA: *(Carrying a tray of food.)*
Followed by her lover,
Who's a lesbian from next door too.
And I've got food for you,
Delicious food for you,
Nouvelle bar mitzvah cuisine.

TRINA:
Oh!
CORDELIA:
Here's dietetic knishes,
Gefilte fishes.
Food that's from the heart.
So take a bite and see
If all your friends agree
It's good.
ALL:
Yummy, yummy, yummy, yummy
Yummy, yummy, yummy, yummy
Yummy, yummy, yummy, yummy, yum.
We'll have one perfect time.
We'll spend billions of dollars.
MENDEL:
Conga!
ALL: *(In a joyous, almost psychedelic conga line.)*
We'll have flowers galore. Whoo!
And the band will sound fine. Whoo!
There'll be chandeliers set round the room,
With the men in tuxedoes.

*(*MARVIN *exits with the chair* JASON *is sitting on.)*

There'll be food like food never before.
What a day to remember!
This is the year,
is the year,
is the year of Jason's bar mitzvah.
JASON:
They're more excited than they should be.

*(*MARVIN *returns with a chair on which the word "Jason" is written in Hebrew-like lettering.)*

ALL:
This is the year of the child,
When he spreads out his wings.
There's music in his heart.
His life's about to start
His body's going wild
My—

JASON AND MARVIN:
Chi-ild.
CORDELIA:
Chi-ild.
TRINA:
Chi-ild.
DR. CHARLOTTE AND MENDEL:
Chi-ild.

(A Flying Wallenda finish.)

Miracle of Judaism

Lights come up on JASON, *leaning on a bat, wearing a "Jewish Center" T-shirt.*

JASON:
Dot Nardoni.
Tiffany Axelrod.
Zoe Feinstein.
Angelina Dellibovi.
Bunny Doyne.
Or what's her name?
Mo Christafaro.
Or Heather Levin.
Brittany Rosenthal.
Which?
Flo Giu . . . Giu . . .
What is the name of that bitch?

(He remembers.)

Oh—Flo Giuseppe.
Right, but it borders on kitsch.

*(*JASON *swings a baseball bat.)*

Of these girls,
Which should I invite to my bar mitzvah?
I've a problem to flaunt:
I don't want the girls I should want.
VOICE: *(Of the piano player.)*
Batter up!

(Bleachers are pushed on stage, and our friends, TRINA, MENDEL, MARVIN, CORDELIA, *and* DR. CHARLOTTE, *sit down on them. Crowd noise as they watch the baseball game.)*

JASON:
I want girls for whom I lust.
Girls who wear a lot of makeup.
Girls who smoke and show their bust.
Girls with whom I always wake up.

(He takes a lousy swing.)

VOICE:
Strike one!

(Reaction from bleacher group.)

JASON:
Would they come, though,
If they were invited?
And not
Laugh at my Hebrew?
And not
Laugh at my father and his friends?
VOICE:
Strike two!

*(*JASON *takes another awkward swing.)*

JASON:
Excluding them I find exciting
And I'm left with them I'll be inviting.
Selecting girls for one's bar mitzvah—
God, that's the miracle of Judaism.
VOICE:
Strike three! You're out!
JASON: *(Walking away.)*
That'd be the miracle of Judaism.

(Consolation and cheer from bleacher group.)

The Baseball Game

MARVIN, MENDEL, TRINA, CORDELIA, DR. CHARLOTTE: *(Sitting together on the bleachers.)*

We're sitting
And watching Jason play baseball.
We're watching Jason play baseball.
We're watching Jewish boys
Who cannot play baseball
Play baseball.
We're watching Jewish boys
Who cannot play baseball
Play . . .
MARVIN:
I hate baseball.
I really do.
Unlike the rest of you.
I hate baseball.
CORDELIA AND DR. CHARLOTTE: *(About* MARVIN.*)*
We really wish he'd take this more seriously.
MENDEL:
Ach, I like how he swings the bat.
MARVIN:
It's good how he swings the bat.
But why does he have to throw like that?
ALL THE SPECTATORS:
We're sitting
And watching Jason make errors.
The most pathetical errors.
We're watching Jewish boys
Who almost read Latin
Up battin'

And battin' bad.
MENDEL: *(Getting carried away.)*
Remember Sandy Koufax.
You can do it
If you wanna do it.
Take heart from Hank Greenberg.
It's not genetic.
Anything can be copasetic.
I think
I think
I think it can.
I think it can.
ALL THE SPECTATORS;
We're sitting
And watching Jason play baseball.
We're watching Jason play baseball.
We're watching Jewish boys
We're watching Jewish boys
We're watching—
Slide, Jason—slide Jason, slide!

*(*WHIZZER *has entered.)*

MARVIN:
What is he doing here?
TRINA:
What are you doing here?
WHIZZER:
Jason asked me to come.
Since he asked me to come, I came.
TRINA:
Just what I wanted at a Little League game—
My ex-husband's ex-lover.
Isn't that what every mother
Dreams about having
At a Little League game?
MENDEL:
Looking at Whizzer is like
Eating *trayf.*
CORDELIA: *(Yelling at the umpire.)*
The kid was out!
DR. CHARLOTTE: *(Yelling at the umpire.)*
The kid was safe!

CORDELIA: *(To* DR. CHARLOTTE.*)*
The kid was out.
DR. CHARLOTTE: *(To the umpire.)*
The kid was safe!
WHIZZER: *(Answering* MARVIN*'s question.)*
Hey, I love baseball.
I love baseball.
That's what I'm doing here.
DR. CHARLOTTE: *(Speaking, disgusted.)*
Where the hell did they
Get that umpire?
Oh, hi, Whizzer.
MARVIN:
Look who's here.
Say hello.
WHIZZER: *(Speaking.)*
Hello.
MARVIN:
You're looking sweeter than a donut.
WHIZZER: *(Shaking hands.)*
Marvin.
MARVIN:
Whizzer.
WHIZZER: *(To* TRINA.*)*
He still queer?
MARVIN: *(Overhearing.)*
Am I queer?
TRINA:
I don't know.
MENDEL:
Does it matter?
MARVIN:
It's been so long since I could tell.

(To WHIZZER.*)*

Sit in front of me.
I wanna see the bald spot.
C'mon, c'mon, move in front of me.
It gives me pleasure to see the bald spot.
Since it's the only physical imperfection that you've got,
I wanna see it.

I wanna touch it.
I wanna run my hands through it.
ALL:
We're sitting and watching the kid as he misses.
We're watching Marvin throw kisses.
We're watching sixty-seven pounders,
Watching Jewish boys miss grounders.
Watching boys field, boys bat,
Boys this, boys that.
Watching Jason on deck
Swinging the bat.
WHIZZER: *(Speaking.)* Hey, Jason.
JASON: *(Speaking.)* Oh, hi, Whizzer.
WHIZZER: *(To* JASON.*)*
Keep your head in the box,
Don't think of a thing.
Keep your head in the box,
Your eye on the ball,
Take a breath,
Then let it out and swing.

*(*WHIZZER *swings, beautifully.)*

MENDEL, CORDELIA, DR. CHARLOTTE:
Oooh.
WHIZZER:
Keep your head in the box.
Don't think of a thing.
Keep your head in the box,
Your eye on the ball,
OTHER SPECTATORS:
Keep your head in the box.
Don't think of a thing.
Keep your head in the box,
Your eye on the ball,
ALL THE SPECTATORS:
Take a breath,
Then let it out and swing.
WHIZZER: *(Speaking.)* Go get 'em.

*(*JASON *runs off.)*

MARVIN: *(About* WHIZZER.*)*
Even bald he looks good.
WHIZZER; *(About* MARVIN.*)*
Just remember he's psychotic.

MARVIN: *(About* WHIZZER.*)*
He looks damn good
But he's cheap as dirt.
WHIZZER:
Even maniacs can charm—
Which he does,
So beware.
MARVIN:
And just be careful.
WHIZZER:
When he smiles that smile, avoid him,
Or else sound the alert.
MARVIN: *(Speaking.)* Whizzer.
WHIZZER: *(Speaking.)* Marvin.
MARVIN: *(Speaking.)* So you think there's hope for the kid?
WHIZZER: *(Speaking.)* I love Jason, but this is not his venue.
BOTH:
How could I know
Without him
My life would be
Boring as shit?
MARVIN:
But it is . . .
WHIZZER: *(Yelling.)* Jason, move closer to the plate!
MARVIN:
Yes, it is . . .

(He punches WHIZZER *for suggesting that.)*

He's gonna be hit by the ball!

*(*WHIZZER *punches* MARVIN *back. They rub their arms.)*

BOTH:
Please, God, don't let me make the same mistake.
(A ball rockets in.)
MENDEL: *(Yelling.)* Heads up!

*(*MENDEL *catches it.)*

ALL THE SPECTATORS:
We're sitting and watching Jason the batter.
We know our cheering won't matter.

It is the very final inning
And the other team is winning.
And there's two outs, two strikes,
But the bases are loaded, and—
MARVIN: *(To* WHIZZER *on the other side of the bleachers.)*
Would it be possible to see you
Or to kiss you
Or to give you a call?
ALL THE SPECTATORS: *(On their feet, celebrating.)*
Anything's possible.
Jason hit the ball!

(They sit. JASON, *never having hit a ball before, is still at home plate.)*

Run!

A Day in Falsettoland

WHIZZER: *(Speaking.)* A day in Falsettoland. Dr. Mendel at work.

PATIENT: *(Speaking.)* You go out on the street and there are all these people asking for a handout. Then you go home and open your mail, and it's full of people asking for donations. Then you turn on your TV and they want money for starving children in Ethiopia.

MENDEL: *(Speaking.)* How does that make you feel?

PATIENT: *(Speaking.)* I mean, I just want to be left alone . . .

MENDEL:
I don't get it.
I don't understand.
In the sixties,
Everyone had heart.
In the sixties,
We were all a part
Of the same team.
In the sixties,
We had a new world to start.
Could this—
Oh God, don't say it is—
Could this be the new world we started?
There I sit brokenhearted.
And . . .

PATIENT: *(Speaking.)* Do I wait for the promotion, or do I take the IBM job?

MENDEL: *(Speaking.)* Well, uh, Diane—

PATIENT: *(Speaking.)* Caroline!

MENDEL: *(Frantically looking through his notes.)*
Caroline?

(She cries hysterically.)

PATIENT:
Yes, Caroline!
MENDEL:
I don't get it.
I've been left behind.
Half my patients:
Yuppie pagans.
Modeled on the
Ronald Reagans.
Now the world is too pathetic
And I don't get it at all.
PATIENT: *(Speaking.)* I'm in a deep quandary about my career. What do you think I should do?
MENDEL:
Time's up!
PATIENT:
Oh!

(In another part of the stage, TRINA *is stretching, preparing for a jog.)*

MENDEL:
At least there's Trina at home.
Trina in bed.
Trina obsessing
And sort of caressing
My head with her feet.
I once thought it was sweet
But I don't anymore.
Now I just snore.
'Cause I'm so exhausted
Listening as these yuppie farts complain,
Listening as their shallow hearts explain
Their lives.
DR. CHARLOTTE: *(Speaking.)* Trina works it out.
TRINA: *(Warming up.)*
Marvin's back with Whizzer.
Just like how it was.
If I don't like Whizzer,
It's because my ex
Sure does.

Why should that upset me?
Sometimes I'm a lout.
Mendel serenades and Jason calms me.
Why should I be wilting
When their precious love
Is not in doubt?
Work it out!
JASON: *(Speaking.)* The neighbors relax after work.
CORDELIA: *(Shaking a martini.)*
How was your day at the hospital?
DR. CHARLOTTE:
Unbelievable.
What is that smell?
CORDELIA:
Nouvelle bar mitzvah cuisine.
I've been practicing
Cuisine, bar mitzvah nouvelle.

(She hands the DOCTOR *some food.* MENDEL *approaches* TRINA, *sneakers in hand.)*

MENDEL: *(Speaking.)* Hi, honey.
CORDELIA: *(Asking if she likes it or not.)*
Well?
TRINA: *(As* MENDEL *kisses her.)*
Hi, honey.
MENDEL:
How was your day?
TRINA:
It was terrible.
Did you hear that
Marvin's back with Whizzer?
Marvin's back with Whizzer.
MENDEL:
Drop it, sweetheart.
Give it up.
You know I love you.
What's the matter,
Trina darling?
I don't get it.
Why can't you let go?
TRINA:
Maybe in a mile I'll be okay.

I'll be happy when we finally have this bar mitzvah.
MENDEL:
Isn't it enough
I want you every night?
TRINA:
Ha!
MENDEL:
Every other night.
TRINA:
I wish.
MENDEL:
Every third night.
TRINA:
Hm.
MENDEL:
Drop it!
Everything will be all right.

(MENDEL bumps her ass with his ass.)

TRINA:
Everything will be all right.

(They're panting even before *the run.)*

BOTH:
Everything will be all right.

(They run off. CORDELIA *has just poured* DR. CHARLOTTE *a martini.)*
CORDELIA:
How was your day
At the hospital?
DR. CHARLOTTE:
It was wonderful.
For the first time in months
Nobody died.

(She raises her glass in celebration.)

There were just
Heart attacks and gallstones;

Light bulbs up the ass;
Fake appendicitis which was gas,
Which I diagnosed;
People overdosed and I saved them.
I saved young people, old people,
One priest and one high-school principal.
Saving lives I feel invincible.
Yes I do.
Do you know how great my life is?
Do you know how great my life is?
Saving lives and loving you.
CORDELIA:
You save lives
And I save chicken fat.
I can't fucking deal with that.
DR. CHARLOTTE:
Do you know how great my life is?
CORDELIA:
Yes, I know how great your life is.

DR. CHARLOTTE: Do you know how great my life is?	MENDEL AND TRINA: *(Jogging.)* Everything will be all right.

CORDELIA:
Yes, I know how great your life is.

DR. CHARLOTTE: Do you know how great my life is? CORDELIA: Yes, I know how great— DR. CHARLOTTE: Saving lives	MENDEL AND TRINA: Everything will be all right.
BOTH: And loving you.	MENDEL AND TRINA: Everything will be all right.

Racquetball

WHIZZER, all in white, looking great. MARVIN, in baggy and colorful jams, looking baggy. No ball is used; rather, when they make a shot, the racquet scrapes the floor and sounds like a ball ricocheting off a racquet. In the course of the scene, WHIZZER decimates MARVIN, as you would expect.

WHIZZER:
It bounced twice.
MARVIN:
No it didn't.
WHIZZER:
Once, then twice.
You know it did.
MARVIN:
That's not nice.
WHIZZER:
No it isn't,
But you're a pain in the ass.
MARVIN:
You're a beast,
But at least
When you play me you win.
WHIZZER: *(Serving.)*
You give up.

(MARVIN tries to race the ball down, but can't.)

MARVIN:
I perspire.

WHIZZER: *(Serving.)*
Where's the heat?
Where's the fire?

*(*MARVIN *tries to hit, to no avail.)*

Used to be you'd desire a fight.
So fight.
MARVIN:
So play.

*(*WHIZZER *doesn't move an inch; he's in total control.* MARVIN *is killing himself, trying to get his racquet on the ball.)*

WHIZZER:
One—two—three—four.
MARVIN:
One—two—three—four.
WHIZZER:
One—two—three—four.
MARVIN:
One—two—three—four.
WHIZZER:
One—two—three—four.
MARVIN:
One—two—three—four.
WHIZZER:
One—two—three—four.
MARVIN:
One—two—three—four.

(Finally, by mistake, MARVIN *hits a good shot.)*

WHIZZER:
Lucky dink.
MARVIN:
I'm finessing.
WHIZZER:
Something stinks in how you play.
MARVIN:
Don't you think it's a blessing
I'm so pathetically bad.

WHIZZER:
Just stay back.
Serve with force.
I'll attack
And, of course,
I will win.
Just give in to bliss.
And kiss . . .

MARVIN:
Let's go.
Do you know?
All I want is you.
Anything you do
Is all right.
Yes, it's all right.
Do you know?
All I want is you.

WHIZZER: *(Speaking.)*
Down the alley
High lob
Low drive
Ceiling shot
Into the corner
Four walls
Dink.

WHIZZER:
Hit your shoe.
MARVIN:
No it didn't.
WHIZZER:
Yes it did.
The game is through.
MARVIN:
That's not nice.
WHIZZER:
No it isn't.
MARVIN:
God, you're a pain in the ass.
WHIZZER:
Play it raw.
Don't play pretty.
Sex and games in New York City
Have gotta be played with flair
And passion,
With passion and flair.

MARVIN AND
WHIZZER:
Do you know?
All I want is you.

DR. CHARLOTTE:
Do you know
How great my life
is?

TRINA AND
MENDEL:
Everything will

	CORDELIA: Everything will be all right.	
MARVIN AND WHIZZER: Anything you do. Is all right.	DR. CHARLOTTE: Do you know How great my life is?	TRINA AND MENDEL: Be all right. Everything will
	CORDELIA: Everything will be all right. DR. CHARLOTTE:	
Yes, it's all right.	Saving lives BOTH: and loving you.	Be all right.
Everything will Everything will Everything will Everything will	Everything will Be all right. Everything will Everything will	Everything will Be all right. Everything will Be
Feel all right For the rest of your life. Fell all right For the rest of your life. Feel all right For the rest of your— Rest of your—	Everything will Be all right. Everything will Be all right. Everything will—	We'll Feel feel feel feel We're gonna be Feel feel feel feel We're gonna be Feel feel feel feel We're gonna be—

JASON: *(Speaking.)* You people are so white.
ALL EXCEPT JASON:
Everything will be all right!

(Blackout.)

The Flight

JASON: *(With a knapsack on his back.)*
Just look at me:
I'm a world-class traveler.
Each Friday night
Travel travel travel
From her house to his house.
First take the 104
With my computer.
I'm just a little kid,
Not a commuter.
And each Sunday night
Mother comes to get me
And I hear them fight.
Everybody's yelling about the bar mitzvah.
It's not a wrestling match.
Why are they sweating?
It's not a funeral.
What's so upsetting?
It's a celebration
Where I get presents.
But everybody's yelling
And everybody's ruining it.
It's a celebration
Where I get richer.
But everybody's yelling
And everybody's ruining it.
Everybody's ruining it.
Why oh why,
What have I done that
They'd ruin my bar mitzvah?

JASON:
What have I done that
They'd ruin my bar mitzvah?

THE OTHERS:
What have we done that
We'd ruin his bar mitzvah?

TRINA:
I want the Applebaums.
They're lovely, and they like me.
MARVIN:
They're boring, and they like the way you dress.
MENDEL:
Well, who wouldn't?
TRINA:
Have the Applebaums.
MARVIN:
Screw the Applebaums.
JASON:
Please don't do this.
MARVIN:
He's no jerk.
TRINA:
Have them.
MARVIN:
Nix them.
MENDEL:
Long live the Applebaums!
Arguing takes work!
JASON:
I hate this.
MARVIN:
Blame her.
It is all a waste.
TRINA:
Look at your couch, it is homo-baroque.
Don't talk to me about taste.
JASON:
Stop! I don't want a bar mitzvah!
Okay! I don't want a bar mitzvah!
MARVIN AND TRINA: *(Quietly, sweetly.)*
Whaddya mean you don't want a bar mitzvah?
Whaddya mean you don't want a bar mitzvah?
How do you think we
How do you think we
How do you think we feel about that?

(Their faces are right in JASON*'s.* MENDEL *sticks his face between* TRINA*'s and* MARVIN*'s and scoots them out of the room.)*

Everyone Hates His Parents

MENDEL:
Jason,
I am agitato grande.
Jason, I am muy disgutante
And muy disappointe
Any muy nauseatus
And me mitzraim
Hotzionoo
Dayenu.
Oh—
Day, dayenu.
Day, dayenu.
Day, dayenu . . .

(To JASON.*)*

Everyone hates his parents.
Don't be ashamed.
You'll grow up,
You'll come through,
You'll have kids
And they'll hate you too.
Oh, everyone hates his parents,
But I confess,
You grow up,
You get old,
You hate less.
JASON:
Still I don't want it.
Nothing that gives them pleasure
I'll do.

I don't want a bar mitzvah,
Stupid bar mitzvah,
Any bar mitzvah,
Would you?
MENDEL *(Sliding* JASON *onto his knee.)*
Everyone hates his parents
That's in the Torah.
It's what history shows.
In fact, God said to Moses:
"Moses, everyone hates his parents.
That's how it is."
And God knew
Because God hated his.

*(*MARVIN *re-enters and pulls* JASON *aside.)*

MARVIN: *(Trying desperately to sound reasonable.)*
You are gonna kill your mother.
Don't feel guilty,
Kill your mother.
Rather than humiliate her,
Killing your mother is the merciful thing to do.

*(*TRINA *enters.)*

TRINA: *(Trying to calm herself.)*
Jason, darling, don't get nervous.
I'm right here and at your service.
Look, I'm calm and self-deluded.
Grateful 'cause I hope you'll do
What I pray you'll do.
MARVIN:
Go ahead and kill your mother.
TRINA:
Not with guns, but kill your mother.
MARVIN AND TRINA:
Rather than humiliate her,
Killing your mother is the merciful thing to do.

*(*JASON *is fed up. He tries to hide by pulling his shirt over his head so that only a very squeezed face is visible in the neck hole.)*

MENDEL:
Everyone hates his parents.
Now I see why.
But in time
They'll cool out
And you'll think
They were only fooling.
It's a strange thing about parents:
Push turns to shove—
What was hate
Becomes more or less love.
MARVIN AND TRINA:
Jason, please see a psychiatrist.
MENDEL: *(Speaking.)* I'm a psychiatrist. Get lost.

*(*MENDEL *pulls his shirt over his head and sings.)*

Everyone hates his parents.
This too shall pass.
You'll grow up.
JASON:
I'll come through.
I'll have kids.
MENDEL:
And they'll hate you too.
MENDEL AND JASON: *(Dancing.)*
Oh, everyone hates his parents.
MENDEL:
But, kid, I guess
You'll grow up.
JASON:
I'll grow up.
MENDEL:
You'll get old.
JASON:
I'll get old.
JASON AND MENDEL:
And hate less.

(They dance a great dance.)

And hate less.
Yes!

(They high-five.)

(Blackout.)

What More Can I Say?

The lights rise on Marvin *and* Whizzer *in bed. Slats of morning light cover the designer sheets. Above their heads is a Mapplethorpe of a calla lily.* Marvin *is wearing a white T-shirt;* Whizzer *is wearing nothing. During the whole song,* Marvin *barely moves.* Whizzer, *sleeping, is slowly moving—next to* Marvin *or apart, into* Marvin*'s arms, onto his stomach or his back. Whatever, it's both hot and incredibly innocent.*

Marvin:
It's been hot,
Also very sweet.
And I'm not usually indiscreet.
But when he sparkles,
The earth begins to sway.
What more can I say?
How can I express
How confused am I by our happiness?
I can't eat breakfast,
I cannot tie my shoe.
What more can I do?

If I said I love him,
You might think my words come cheap.
Let's just say
I'm glad he's mine awake,
Asleep.

It's been hot
Also it's been swell.
More than not,

It's been more than words can tell.
I halt.
I stammer.
I sing a rondelay.
What more can I say?

I'll stay calm.
Untie my tongue.
And try to stay
Both kind and young.

I was taught
Never brag or shout.
Still it's hot,
Just like how you read about.

And also funny,
And never too uncouth.
That's the simple truth.

(WHIZZER is sleeping face up. MARVIN looks underneath the sheet and is stunned by his good fortune.)

Can you tell
I have been revised?
It's so swell,
Damn it, even I'm surprised.
We laugh,
We fumble,
We take it day by day.
What more can I say?

(Blackout.)

Something Bad Is Happening

On one side of the stage, DR. CHARLOTTE *is reading a medical journal; on the other,* CORDELIA *is devising recipes from a cookbook,* New Jewish Recipes.

DR. CHARLOTTE:
People might think
I'm very dykish.
I make a big stink
When I must—but god damn;
I'm just professional,
Never too nonchalant.
If I'm a bitch—
Well, I am what I am.
Just call me Doc.
Don't call me Lady.
I don't like to talk
When I'm losing the game.
Bachelors arrive sick and frightened.
They leave weeks later, unenlightened.
We see a trend, but the trend has no name.

(She holds up the journal.)

Something bad is happening.
Something very bad is happening.
Something stinks,
Something immoral,
Something so bad that words
Have lost their meaning.
Rumors fly and tales abound.
Stories echo underground.

Something bad is spreading
Spreading
Spreading round.

(CORDELIA *gives* DR. CHARLOTTE *some food.)*

CORDELIA:
Tell me how it tastes.
Tell me if it's good.
Tell me, dear, if you'd like seconds.
DR. CHARLOTTE:
Stop!
CORDELIA:
Go ahead and wound my pride.
DR. CHARLOTTE:
Just stop!
CORDELIA:
You're feeling very sick inside.
I can tell.
And it's something I cooked.
I just knew how you looked.

(To the audience.)

Look what I've done to my doctor.

*(*DR. CHARLOTTE *cannot believe she is hearing this. She picks up and reads a copy of* Interview *magazine.)*

She's my doctor, and I love her.
She's got passion.
She's intelligent and, Jesus Christ,
A doctor. Very wealthy.
And I love her.
Doctor of Internal Medicine.
I'm sorry that you're queasy.
DR. CHARLOTTE:
I'm uneasy.
CORDELIA:
She's got something on her mind
That makes her nervous.
DR. CHARLOTTE:
This is fucking ridiculous.

CORDELIA:
She's my doctor, and I love her.
She's got—

DR. CHARLOTTE:	CORDELIA:
I scan the mag.	Heart!
Very chic tabloid—	
The men dressed in drag	
Next to their moms.	
Fashion and passion and filler	
But not a word about the killer.	
I like the ball gowns,	
But Jesus Christ!	
Something bad is happening.	Something bad is happening.
Something very bad is happening	
Something stinks.	
	Look, I made her sick.
Something immoral,	
Something so bad that words	
Have lost their meaning.	She ate the food and she got sick.
Rumors fly and tales abound.	Oh, woe is me.
Stories echo underground	Oh, woe is me.
Something bad is—	

BOTH:
Spreading
Spreading
Spreading round.

DR. CHARLOTTE:
Look, a virus has been found.
Stories echo underground.
Something bad is—

BOTH:
Spreading
Spreading
Spreading round.

Second Racquetball

MARVIN *is winning when the game is called.*

WHIZZER: *(Winded.)*
It bounced in.
MARVIN:
No it didn't.
WHIZZER:
Hit the line—
You know it did.
MARVIN:
Just begin.
WHIZZER:
Are you kidding?
Who's telling who how to play?
MARVIN:
Let me live,
Please forgive me for winning one game.
WHIZZER:
Serve it up.
MARVIN:
I attack.
WHIZZER: *(On the defensive.)*
Hold him down,
Keep it back,
Something's gone out of whack.
MARVIN: *(A great shot.)*
I hit—
WHIZZER: *(Sprawling on the floor.)*
Aw, shit.
MARVIN:
My game.

(Serving.)

One—two—three—four.

WHIZZER: *(Missing the ball;* MARVIN *is very pleased.)*

One—two—three
Damn it.
MARVIN: *(Serving.)*
One—two—three—four.
WHIZZER:
One—two—

(He can't get the serve.)

Good serve, Marvin.
MARVIN:
One—two—three—four.

*(*WHIZZER *blows the shot, trips over his own feet.)*

WHIZZER:
One—
Hit my heel.
MARVIN:
Don't be bitter.
WHIZZER: *(Walking off the court.)*
No big deal.
The game is yours.
MARVIN:
It's unreal,
You're a quitter.
WHIZZER:
I can't go on anymore.
MARVIN:
Be a jerk,
My sweet bruiser.
Try to be a decent loser.
At least you could give me that.

(Disgustedly, MARVIN *throws his racquet toward* WHIZZER.*)*

WHIZZER:
Excuse me, I'm ready to go.
I'm ready to . . .

*(*WHIZZER *goes to pick up the racquet and almost collapses.* MARVIN *rushes to hold him up.)*

MARVIN:
Do you know
All I want is you?
Anything you do
Is all right.

*(*WHIZZER *tries to walk away but can't. He stands, bent over, trying to catch his breath.)*

MARVIN: *(Holding* WHIZZER *up.)*
Yes, it's all right.
Yes, it is.

THE OTHERS EXCEPT WHIZZER:
Everything will be all right.
Everything will be all right.
Everything will be all right.

Holding to the Ground

As MARVIN *and* WHIZZER *slowly make their way upstage,* TRINA *draws a white curtain across the stage. We see* TRINA *look at* MARVIN, *who looks scared to death; and then* WHIZZER *sitting on a hospital bed, being examined by* DR. CHARLOTTE. TRINA *fleetingly sees* MENDEL; *she sees* MARVIN; *voices are singing "Everything will be all right."* TRINA *turns to the audience.*

TRINA:
I was sure growing up I would live the life
My mother assumed I'd live.
Very Jewish.
Very middle class.

And very straight.
Where healthy men
Stayed healthy men
And marriages were long and great.

I smile.
I don't complain.
I'm trying to keep sane as the rules keep changing.
Families aren't what they were.
Thank God there's a husband and a child whom I adore.
But then there's more.
So many more.
There's always more.
Life is never what you planned
Life is moments you can't understand.
And that is life.

I'm plain.
I don't astound.
I hold to the ground as the ground keeps shifting,
Keeping my balance square.
Trying not to care about this man who Marvin loves.
But that's my life.
He shared my life.
Yes, that's my life.
Life is never what you planned.
Life is moments you can't understand.
And that is life.

(The curtain is opened on WHIZZER, *white as a ghost, lying in a hospital bed.)*

Holding to the ground as the ground keeps shifting.
Trying to keep sane as the rules keep changing.
Keeping up my head as my heart falls out of sight.
Everything will be all right.
Everything will be all . . .

(She can't finish and walks out.)

Days Like This I Almost Believe in God

MARVIN *enters the hospital room with great, hearty enthusiasm. He is obviously petrified.*

MARVIN:
Whizzer,
Kid, you're looking very good today.
You had to see yourself a few days back.
I had a heart attack.
Jesus.
But today you seem to be
On the way to recovery.
Oh, Whizzer, I want to applaud.
It's days like this I almost believe in God.
Days like this I almost believe in God.

*(*CORDELIA *enters with a tray of Jewish stuff.)*

MARVIN AND WHIZZER: *(Speaking.)*
Hello.
CORDELIA: *(Speaking.)*
Hello.

(Displaying the tray for WHIZZER, *she sings.)*

Rugelach. Gefilte fish.
It's so good you'd think it's Italian.
Also a soup made from chicken
That, though unexotic,
Is antibiotic.
Oh, I'm up to my ass

In a kosher morass.
For aches and croup, try my chicken soup.

(They start the descant.)

MARVIN:
Whizzer,
Kid, you're looking
Very good today.
You had to see yourself a few days back.
I had a heart attack.
Jesus.
But . . .

CORDELIA:
So let's begin. It's medicine.
It could be we're both going to cure you.
Me with my soup,
She with her medication.
Such elation.
But . . .

MARVIN AND CORDELIA:
Today
You seem to be
On the way to recovery.
Oh, Whizzer, I want to applaud.
It's days like this
We almost believe in God.
Days like this we almost believe in—
CORDELIA:
Gefilte fish.
MARVIN:
God.
CORDELIA:
Canadelach.

*(*TRINA *walks in with a plant.* MENDEL *follows.)*

TRINA:
Hi.
He had trouble parking.
Just like on our second date.
MENDEL:
I hyperventilate.
But since I'm parking in the city,
I've improved.
Or else the hydrants moved.

(Only CORDELIA *laughs.)*

Yeah, go ahead,
Be good and pissed.
"How can I help?" says the wiry psychiatrist.
TRINA:
He'll make you well.
WHIZZER: *(Speaking.)* Right.
MENDEL:
I'll make you well.

*(*JASON *enters with a chessboard.* DR. CHARLOTTE *follows.)*

JASON AND DR. CHARLOTTE:
Whizzer, hello.

*(*DR. CHARLOTTE *hugs* CORDELIA.*)*

JASON: *(Going to the bed.)*
Gee, you look awful.
I think you need to play some chess.
WHIZZER:
Jason, sit down and begin.
JASON:
I'll let you win, Whizzer.
I'll let you win.
I'll let you . . .

MARVIN AND CHARLOTTE:	CORDELIA:	MENDEL AND TRINA:	JASON:
Whizzer,	Rugelach.	I'll make you well.	Win.
Kid, you're looking very	Gefilte fish.	He'll make you	Whizzer hello.
Good today.	It's so good you'd	Well. I'll make you	
You had to See yourself a	Think it's Italian.	Well. He'll make you	Gee, you look aw—
Few days back. I had a	Also a soup made	Well. I'll make you	Ful.

MARVIN AND CHARLOTTE:	CORDELIA:	MENDEL AND TRINA:	JASON:
Heart attack	From chicken that though	Well. He'll make you	
Jesus.	Unexotic, is	Well. I'll make you	I think you need to play
	Antibiotic.	Well.	some chess.

ALL EXCEPT WHIZZER:	WHIZZER:
But today you seem to be	Sshhh!
On the way to recovery.	
Oh, Whizzer, I want to applaud.	
It's days like this we almost believe in God.	
Days like this we almost believe in God.	
Days like this we almost believe in God.	
Days like this we almost believe in—	

TRINA: *(Speaking.)* What is this?
CORDELIA:
Gefilte fish.
MENDEL:
I'll make you well.
MARVIN:
Right.
TRINA:
You're looking very good today.
CORDELIA:
Canadelach.

(Everyone tastes CORDELIA*'s food.)*

ALL: *(Speaking.)* Ugh.
(Singing.)
God!

Canceling the Bar Mitzvah

TRINA:
Jason, if you want a bar mitzvah
God knows you can have a bar mitzvah.
But I have to know
And I have to know now
Just what it is you want.
I've addressed the invitations;
Here's your chance to give me hell.
If you think it's bust,
It is probably just
As well.
JASON:
Can't we wait till Whizzer gets better?
Can't we wait till he's out?
That's what bar mitzvahs should be all about.
Good friends close at hand—
Don't you understand?

(Long pause. Music plays.)

MENDEL:
We can't be sure when
He'll get better,
When or if
He'll ever get better.
But the hall is booked
And the band's been retained.
So Jason, please,
What we'll do is your decision.
There's no right and there's no wrong.
Just say yes or no

And we'll promise to go along.
JASON:
Finally now it's all my decision.
Like it's my bar mitzvah.
Just like nothing's happened.
Hell, let's have a party,
Just like nothing's happened.
Why don't you make this dumb decision yourselves,
Okay?
Why don't you make this dumb decision yourselves?

(JASON *moves upstage with his back to the audience.)*

MENDEL:
We'll have the bar mitzvah.
JASON: *(Speaking.)* No.
TRINA:
Then we'll cancel the bar mitzvah.
JASON: *(Speaking.)* No.

(JASON *storms out.)*

MENDEL AND TRINA: *(As* JASON *storms out, still in control.)*
We'll wait until you make a decision.
MENDEL: *(Speaking.)* I think that went well.
TRINA: *(Singing.)* Holding to the ground as the ground keeps shifting.
MENDEL:
Trying to keep sane as the rules keep changing.
BOTH:
Keeping up my head as my heart falls out of sight.
Everything will be all right.

Unlikely Lovers

In the hospital room, MARVIN *is fussing with the bed. In bed,* WHIZZER *plays solitaire and seems content.*

MARVIN:
Who'd believe
That we two
Would end up as lovers?
WHIZZER:
Do you want me to reply?
MARVIN: *(To the audience.)*
Him and me.

(To WHIZZER.*)*

You and I.
Passionately lovers.
WHIZZER:
Please don't get morbid.
MARVIN:
Right.
WHIZZER:
It's just—
MARVIN:
Don't fight.
WHIZZER:
—that I haven't died yet.
MARVIN:
Just stop it.
WHIZZER:
I'm sick but kicking.

MARVIN:
Geez . . .
WHIZZER:
All right.
MARVIN:
Louise!
WHIZZER:
Good night.
MARVIN:
I'm staying here in this spot
Whether you want me to or not
I'm staying.

(Fully dressed, he crawls into bed.)

Here I am
By your side
One old horny lover.
WHIZZER:
Please go home and don't be scared.
MARVIN:
What's the fuss?
I'm not scared.
What good is a lover
Who's scared?
Hit me if you need to.
Slap my face, or
Hold me till winter.
Oh, baby, please do.
I love you too,
My lover.
WHIZZER:
Marvin, just go home and
Turn on TV.
Drink a little something till you're dead.
Think of me around
Sleeping soundly in our bed.
Marvin,
Did you hear what I said?
MARVIN:
Shut your mouth.
Go to sleep.
Time I met a sailor.

Are you sleeping yet, or
What is what?
Whizzer, but
I can't help but feeling
I've failed.
Let's be scared together.
Let's pretend that nothing is awful.
WHIZZER:
There's nothing to fear.
MARVIN:
There's nothing to fear.
WHIZZER:
Just stay right here.
BOTH:
I love you.

*(*DR. CHARLOTTE *and* CORDELIA *poke their heads in the door. They sing to each other a little too loud.)*

DR. CHARLOTTE:
Shhh. Maybe he's tired.
CORDELIA:
Shhh. Maybe he's waiting for us.
DR. CHARLOTTE:
Shhh. Maybe he's waiting for a visit?

(They enter gingerly.)

BOTH:
Is it a bad time?

*(*WHIZZER *starts laughing.)*

We'll come back. If it's a bad time,
We'll come back.

*(*MARVIN *waves them in.)*

We'll come in.

(They join the men around the bed.)

MARVIN:
Look at us.
Four old friends.
Four unlikely lovers.
CORDELIA:
We don't know what time will bring.
WHIZZER:
I've a clue.
MARVIN:
I have too.
WOMEN:
Let's look like we haven't.
ALL FOUR:
And each say nothing.
WHIZZER:
Sky.
DR. CHARLOTTE:
It's blue.
MARVIN:
I love the sky.
CORDELIA:
I love the trees.
MARVIN:
I love bad weather.
DR. CHARLOTTE:
I love the earth beneath my feet.
WHIZZER:
I love friends
That hover.
ALL FOUR:
Gee, we love to eat.
And we need something sweet
To love.
What a group
We four are.
Four unlikely lovers.
And we vow that we will
Buy the farm
Arm in arm.
Four unlikely lovers
With heart.
Let's be scared together.
Let's pretend that nothing

ALL FOUR:
Is awful.
There's nothing
To fear.
Just stay right here.
I love you.

MARVIN:
There's nothing to fear.

I love you.

I love you.

I love you.

ALL FOUR:
Who'd have thought
That we four
Would end up as lovers?

Another Miracle of Judaism

JASON:
Hello, God.
I don't think we've every really spoken.
If you'd kindly allow,
How about a miracle now?
I don't know if you exist.
I can't hear your fingers snappin'.
Are you just a big psychiatrist?
Or can you make things not happen?
Do this for me
And I'll get bar mitzvahed.
In exchange for:
Could you please make my friend stop dying?
I am not naïve.
It won't be easy,
But if you could make my friend stop dying,
God,
That'd be the miracle of Judaism.
That'd be the miracle of Judaism.

Something Bad Is Happening (Reprise)

DR. CHARLOTTE: *(Outside the hospital room, to* MARVIN.*)*
Something bad is happening.
Something very bad is happening.
Something that kills.
Something contagious.
Something that spreads
From one man to another.

You Gotta Die Sometime

WHIZZER:
Okay—
When the doctor started using phrases like
"You'll pass away,"
What could I say?
I said, Doctor,
In plain English,
Tell me why was I chosen,
Why me of all men?
Doctor,
Here's the good part:
At least death means
I'll never be scared about dying again.

Let's get on with living while we can
And not play dumb.
Death's gonna come.
When it does, screw the nerves,
I'll be eating hors d'oeuvres,
It's the roll of the dice and no crime,
You gotta die sometime.

Death is not a friend
But I hope in the end,
He takes me in his arms and lets me hold his face.
He holds me in his arms and whispers something funny.
He lifts me in his arms and tells me to embrace
His attack
Then the scene turns to black.

Life sucks.
People always hate a loser
And they hate lame ducks.
Screw me and shucks.
That's it.
That's the ballgame.
I don't smoke, don't do drugs,
And then comes the bad news.
I quit.
That's the ballgame
It's the chink in the armor,
The shit in the karma,
The blues.
Can I keep my cool despite the urge
To fall apart?
How should I start?
I would cry if I could.
But it does no damn good
To explain I'm a man in my prime.
You gotta die sometime.

Death's a funny pal
With a weird sort of talent.
He puts his arms around my neck and walks me to the bed.
He pins me up against the wall and kisses me like crazy.
The many stupid things I thought about with dread
Now delight.
Then the scene turns to white.

Give me the balls to orchestrate
A graceful leave.
That's my reprieve:
To go out
Without care,
My head high
In the air,
It's the last little mountain I'll climb,
I'll climb.
You gotta die sometime.
You gotta die sometime.
You gotta die sometime.
You gotta die
Sometime, sometime,

Sometime, sometime,
Sometime, sometime,
Sometime, sometime.

(Someone is knocking on the door.)

Jason's Bar Mitzvah

*(*JASON *appears in the doorway.)*

JASON:
Whizzer, hey,
Suddenly it all came clear
I said, let's have my bar mitzvah here!

(The champagne bottle he was holding behind his back is held out triumphantly.)

ALL EXCEPT WHIZZER:
Surprise!

(Behind JASON, *the others stream in, loaded with flowers, food, candles, clothes, and decorations.)*

MARVIN:
This was Jason's first-rate idea.
And I brought the prayer shawl.

(Lovingly he throws the tallis around WHIZZER*'s shoulders.)*

ALL:
It's Jason's bar mitzvah.
MENDEL *(To* WHIZZER.*)*
Don't you move.
Everything will soon be great.
Close your eyes.
While we redecorate.

(TRINA *finds the camera.)*

CORDELIA:
I'll unwrap the billion hors d'oeuvres.
And someone please eat them.
TRINA: *(Gathering everyone and speaking.)* Photo!

(Group ad lib.)

ALL:
It's Jason's bar mitzvah.

(More group photo ad lib.)

TRINA: *(Setting out the candles.)*
Lovely.
Flowers make things lovely.
Champagne makes things lovely too.
Something is amiss.
MENDEL: *(Passing around champagne.)*
Drink up.
Anyone for bubbly?
TRINA:
Probably it's doubly
Useful at a time like this.
Cheers.
MENDEL: *(To* WHIZZER.*)*
Cheers.
TRINA:
And aren't things lovely?
I feel more helpless than I have in years.

(MARVIN *hands* WHIZZER *a robe or a bag.)*

MARVIN:
Try this on.

(Quietly to MENDEL.*)*

Mendel, get this thing in gear.
WHIZZER:
Please excuse me
If I interfere,

But I feel that since I'm the host,
It's me who should toast him.
ALL EXCEPT JASON:
Oooh, oooh.
WHIZZER: *(As everyone raises their glasses.)*
To Jason's bar mitzvah.

(Everyone leaves but the three women.)

DR. CHARLOTTE:
I notified the nurses,
Told them please to not intrude.
CORDELIA:
I passed around the food
And dumped some extra food
'Cause, Lord knows, we've got plenty.
DR. CHARLOTTE:
She's cooked for some two hundred guests.
CORDELIA:
We number not that many.
Actually we're . . .

(She stops to count. Pause.)

Seven.
DR. CHARLOTTE:
Maybe it's not dumb
The way this whole thing ends.
The food tastes really yummy.
CORDELIA: *(Hugging* DR. CHARLOTTE.*)*
Oh, Mummy.

*(*TRINA *can't believe what she's heard.)*

DR. CHARLOTTE AND CORDELIA:	TRINA:
The flowers seem to sparkle	Lovely.
Candelabra sets the tone.	I must make things
The wine is very soothing.	
Soothes the "something something"	Lovely.
	Put everything
Someone needed soothing.	

DR. CHARLOTTE:
I think perhaps I'm overdressed.
CORDELIA:
I think perhaps it doesn't matter
that you are, but
BOTH:
Here we are,
Jason's bar mitzvah looks
Like the books
Say it should.
Cheers.

Everything is lovely.

In its place.

Ready for the

band.

Cheers.
And aren't things
Lovely?

*(*MENDEL *escorts* WHIZZER *in.* WHIZZER, *in his bar mitzvah robe, offers his arm to escort* TRINA.*)*

DR. CHARLOTTE AND CORDELIA:
I feel more rotten than I have in years.

TRINA:
I feel more rotten than I have in years.

MENDEL AND WHIZZER:
Here he comes.
MENDEL: *(To* TRINA.*)*
Fix his tie.

*(*MARVIN *enters with* JASON. JASON *is dressed in a black suit and solemn tie.)*

Trina, try
To make him smile more.
ALL EXCEPT MARVIN AND JASON:
Don't know why
But he looks like Marvin.
MARVIN: *(To* JASON.*)*
How did you turn out so great?
Who do I thank for the man you turned into?
Kid, do you know
How proud I am?
If I don't show
How proud I am . . .

You hold my dreams,
Kid, I burst at the seams
'Cause of you.
MENDEL:
Son of Abraham, Isaac, and Jacob.
Son of Marvin, son of Trina, son of Whizzer, son of Mendel,
ALL EXCEPT MENDEL:
And godchild to the lesbians from next door,
MENDEL:
Sing.
Oh-oh, sing.
Oh-oh, sing.
JASON:
Vie-eme-low yae-o-leh.
Heh-oh-non vi-low.
Ah-yis-is-ooh ay-ysi-ro-ale.
Ha-ooh low toe vo-o-meem aboh.

*(*WHIZZER *can't go on anymore, and taps* JASON *as he leaves, escorted by* DR. CHARLOTTE. *Everyone else but* MARVIN *follows.)*

What Would I Do?

MARVIN: *(Left alone.)*
What would I do
If I had not met you?
Who would I blame my life on?
Once I was told
That all men get what they deserve.
Who the hell then threw this curve?
There are no answers.
But who would I be
If you had not been my friend?

You're the only one,
One out of a thousand others,
Only one my child would allow.
When I'm having fun,
You're the one I wanna talk to.
Where have you been?
Where are you now?

(WHIZZER appears behind MARVIN, dressed as we first saw him. MARVIN turns around, sees WHIZZER and catches his breath.)

What would I do
If I had not loved you?
How would I know what love is?
God only knows, too soon
I'll remember your faults.
Meanwhile, though, it's tears and schmaltz.
There are no answers.
But what would I do

If you had not been my friend?
WHIZZER:
All your life you wanted men,
And when you got it up to have them,
Who knew it could end your life?
MARVIN:
I left my kid and left my wife
To be with you,
To be insulted by such handsome men.

(They face each other.)

WHIZZER:
Do you regret—?
MARVIN: *(Stopping him.)*
I'd do it again.
I'd like to believe that I'd do it again
And again and again . . .
And
What more can I say?
WHIZZER:
What more can I say?
MARVIN:
How am I to face tomorrow?
BOTH:
After being screwed out of today.
Tell me what's in store.
MARVIN:
Yes, I'd beg or steal or borrow
If I could hold you for
One hour more.

WHIZZER:	
One hour more.	MARVIN:
	One hour more.
One hour more.	
One hour, one hour more.	One hour, one hour more.

MARVIN:
What would I do
WHIZZER:
What would I do
MARVIN:
If I had not seen you?

WHIZZER:
If I had not seen you?
BOTH:
Who would I feast my eyes on?
Once I was told
That good men get better with age.
MARVIN:
We're just gonna skip that stage.

There are no answers.
But what would I do
If you hadn't been my friend?
WHIZZER:
There are no answers.
But what would I do . . .

*(*WHIZZER *exits.)*

MARVIN:
No simple answers.
But what would I do
If you had not been
My friend.
My friend.
My friend.

(First JASON, *then everyone else gathers around* MARVIN.*)*

MENDEL:
Homosexuals.
Women with children.
Short insomniacs.
We're a teeny tiny band.
Lovers come and lovers go.
Lovers live and die fortissimo.
This is where we take a stand.
Welcome to Falsettoland.

*(*DR. CHARLOTTE *walks in and joins the circle at the same time as* MENDEL. TRINA *consoles* MARVIN.*)*

(Fade to black.)

THE SUBSTANCE OF FIRE

by

Jon Robin Baitz

Jon Robin Baitz comments:

To be human, I think, is to be essentially an exile, and to be a Jew is to be a traveler within the Diaspora of the present—all those centuries of flight, the endless wandering, the search for safe haven. Instilled within us are the virtually atavistic sensations of impermanence and even, occasionally, of chaos (under the surface, perhaps, but nevertheless present, detectable). I seem continually to write of a displacement which is linked to that. My foreboding as a writer is, in part, that of a Jewish traveler, worried about his papers not being in order. All disenfranchised people feel that to some degree. To be gay, to be a Jew, to be black, any number of things left out in the cold—I insist that we share different versions of the same experience.

The Substance of Fire concerns a man who, as a child, escaped the slaughterhouses of Europe. In journeying to the United States (the New World) to seek salvation in the life of the mind, he finds that the horrors of the twentieth century (the Old World) have, of course, hounded him. No matter how hard he toils at re-inventing himself as a Manhattan bon vivant, his past insists on being heard.

So one hopes that the lesson of all our centuries of travel, of searching for safe haven, is that they are part of the essential human business of being an expatriate. And one often hopes that to be a Jewish writer is to understand that most of the time, it's the same for everyone, no matter what their port of entry or final destination.

The Substance of Fire had its world premiere in 1990 at the Long Wharf Theatre, with M. Edgar Rosenblum, Executive Director, and Arvin Brown, Artistic Director, having workshopped Off-Broadway at Naked Angels.

The Substance of Fire premiered in New York City, Off-Broadway, in 1991 at Playwrights Horizons, Inc. It was directed by Daniel Sullivan and included the following cast:

SARAH GELDHART	*Sarah Jessica Parker*
MARTIN GELDHART	*Patrick Breen*
ISAAC GELDHART	*Ron Rifkin*
AARON GELDHART	*Jon Tenney*
MARGE HACKETT	*Maria Tucci*

The Playwrights Horizons production was remounted in January 1992 at the Mitzi Newhouse Theatre at Lincoln Center with the same cast.

CHARACTERS

SARAH GELDHART
MARTIN GELDHART
ISAAC GELDHART
AARON GELDHART
MARGE HACKETT

SYNOPSIS OF SCENES

ACT I

Spring 1987
A conference room, Kreeger/Geldhart Publishers
New York City

ACT II

Three and one half years later
An apartment on Gramercy Park

ACT I

Spring 1987.

A conference room, Kreeger/Geldhart Publishers, in the Broadway-23rd Street area. There is a conference table, five chairs, some filing cabinets. There are many books. SARAH GELDHART, *a woman in her mid twenties, sits reading. She smiles, and nods to herself.*

MARTIN GELDHART, *her brother, late twenties, enters, smiling. He watches her for a moment, unnoticed.*

MARTIN: Whenever I walk into this room, I tell you, I expect some *guy,* you know, with a manuscript to kick me out. Hey, Sarah.

SARAH: Oh, God, hello, Martin. I know. I've always hated this room. Look at all these books. *(*SARAH *shakes her head, rueful.)*

MARTIN: Miss Barzakian just cornered me in reception and told me that last week Ventrice, that poet? Know him? So he's—he chases Dad down the hall and he says, and I repeat . . . "I'll kill you—you-dirty-Jew-kike-bastard, I'll kill you, you prick." *(Beat.)* It wouldn't be so bad if he were a decent poet.

SARAH: The publishing world, eh? So. What do you think of all this?

MARTIN: *(Thinks for a second, simply.)* It's a bore. You know? What're you reading?

SARAH: Oh, something Dad's thinking of publishing. It was sitting here. God knows what he—what he's thinking. "Hobson-Jobson. A Glossary of Colloquial Anglo-Indian Words & Phrases." I mean, tell me, Martin, am I out of touch here or will, like, two people buy this?

MARTIN: Well, I mean, please. No wonder, is it, we're going bankrupt?

SARAH: No, but still, I do feel funny being dragged into it, don't you?

MARTIN: *(Cheerful.)* Well, you *are* a stockholder.

SARAH: Right. I was kind of hoping that by the time I flew in, they'd have it all sorted out. You know? When you're actually happy they've delayed the flight? Anyway, I read the manuscript they're fighting about on the plane and, I mean—

MARTIN: It was bound to come to a head, wasn't it? Look—just take a look at these shelves. You can't do it. You can't go on publishing accounts of—look at this: a two-volume tome on the destruction of the Sephardim during the Spanish Inquisition? Reprints of Traven and Pirandello. Firbank? *That's* big. How many Kreeger/Geldhart books do you see in the stores?

SARAH: Oh please, we don't have bookstores on the coast, Martin. Let me tell you, I went into a Crown or Dalton or something. You walk in. It's like a Burger King. There're "blips" from the video games . . . it's like, "Buy a Coke, getta Book." I said to the clerk, I'm looking for E. E. Cummings. He said, "Self-help, second aisle on the left." And I said, "Are you people still in the *book* business, or what?"

MARTIN: So what'd you think of the manuscript?

SARAH: The thing is, the plane was, there wasn't an empty, and so you can't really focus on the—

MARTIN: You're saying you skimmed? Is that it?

SARAH: Hey, you know I hate to read, it's not fair. But actually it seemed funny, the dirty part, the thing with the two guys.

MARTIN: I hate being dragged into this. And I swore not even to come down here. I sat there after Dad called, you know, I hung up and said to myself, "This is their trip, I'm not part of it. Let them sort it all out because I just don't care."

SARAH: Cut to: Here we are. And . . .

MARTIN: Of course to say "No, sorry, I can't," is not an option.

SARAH: Yeah. *(Beat.)* Why *do* we come? I mean, because I'm shooting the show, we're doing three shows back-to-back, and I beg them to rearrange the schedule. Because

I've had a summons from Dad. Who said to me, *last* time I was home, "Sarah, how do you actresses remember your lines?" And I go, "What do you mean?" And he said, quite earnestly, "Because none of you are, let's face it now, all that bright, really. Are you?"

MARTIN: *(Smiles.)* Well, he calls me a "gardener's apprentice," whatever *that* is. At Passover he asked me how the tree-pruning business was. I mean, I teach landscape architecture at Vassar, for Christ's sake. Which is silly, but still. *(Beat, peeved.)* They're late.

SARAH: When has Dad ever not kept you waiting? They're in the library with Aaron's novelist. What's his name?

MARTIN: Val Chenard.

SARAH: Val Chenard. It's like the name of a bad restaurant. In Toronto.

MARTIN: Duck, with a pop-tart filling glaze— Val Chenard. *(Beat.)* And how is the show?

SARAH: Better than I thought. It's very hip for children's television. A little too hip, I think, sometimes frankly. And everyone is like, way too thrilled. But still. "Safe-Sex-Tips-for-Tots" *is* a good skit. *(Beat.)* We didn't really do it—a joke.

MARTIN: Yeah well, no. I saw one. We recently got television in Poughkeepsie. You were a caveman's wife. You were singing "When I'm Sixty-four."

SARAH: Martin, can I ask you something? Does anything happen up there? Are you having a life at all?

MARTIN: *(Smiles.)* And do you know of anyone now who has any sort of a life? Today? People sit alone at diner counters eating meatloaf and thinking of Mom. No one has a life.

SARAH: No.

MARTIN: No. I have my orchard, my bonsai. And *they're* fun.

SARAH: Hey, listen. What I have to do is fly right back to L.A. tonight. I have to turn right back around, but let's grab dinner, can we? After all this?

MARTIN: I can't. I'm sorry. I have to get back, I—

SARAH: No, I understand. No, no. Don't say a thing—

MARTIN: But, Sarah, hey, it's only that there just won't be time. Once we get outta here, and then, you know, I'd miss the ten-twenty, and the next train is like, two-o-*seven* or something. And I have to be in Rhinebeck at *dawn* 'cause I'm putting up a windbreak on the Hudson with the sophomores, which is fun. I still seem to get tired, I don't know.

SARAH: Hey, Martin, remember when we were kids, waiting in this room with some awful thing going on down the hall. Mom and Dad screaming at each other.

MARTIN: Are you kidding? Who could forget?

SARAH: And we were royalty. There used to be so many people working here.

MARTIN: There were never very many people working here, sweetie.

SARAH: It seemed like it. Listen, I don't mean to sound like an idiot, but does bankruptcy actually mean there's a day when this whole place folds up?

ISAAC: *(Entering. Wearing a dark suit of impeccable cut. He has the slightest of accents—Belgian/German, barely detectable.)* It's not that bad. Aaron exaggerates. Hullo, sweetheart, I'm glad you're here—to get on a plane!

SARAH: Daddy?

ISAAC: You know your brother has his little Stanford-Wharton-Mafia-Flow charts he waves in my face and screams.

SARAH: Daddy. What do you think you're doing? *(Picks up book from atop the desk.)* I mean, "Hobson-Jobson. A Glossary of Colloquial Anglo-Indian Words and Phrases"?

ISAAC: So what's the big deal? A dictionary? A *dictionary*, do you know how few people bother to publish 'em anymore? (And I'm not talking, please, about the university presses for a tax loss.) I've always done a dictionary now and then if it was interesting enough. Hi, Martin. So. My God, you came, huh. Well. Your brother must've been very pushy with you. You always ignore me when I ask you to come.

MARTIN: Always nice to see you, Dad.

ISAAC: So, tell me, did you get the Edmund Wilson I sent you? I never heard from you. The memoirs.

MARTIN: No, I got it.

SARAH: So what is it? You're not bankrupt, I'm not going to, like, find this place turned into Rug City?

AARON: *(Enters. Younger than* MARTIN *and dressed more like an ad-exec than a publisher.)* You don't think you were rude to Val?

MARTIN: *(To* AARON.*)* Hi.

ISAAC: Was I? I don't think so. I was really rather even-keeled, maybe a little blunt, but he virtually spat on the Krasslow manuscript.

AARON: *(With absolute relish.)* Yes, he did, didn't he? But the Krasslow, Dad, is the last word in boredom. Let me tell you, Val is right. These ossified old academic frauds you trot out every couple of years. You knew Val would be openly contemptuous of your Krasslow, and you deliberately maneuvered him into insulting you.

ISAAC: That's simply paranoid. I'm not that clever.

AARON: Yes, you are. I've seen you do it to me. It's something you do. You navigate a conversation into this place wherein not to insult you would be psychically impossible. Hey, you know something? I don't want to get into a word thing with you, Dad. Do you realize he's about to bugger off to Knopf? And they, Father, let me assure you, this'll hit the stores by Wednesday or something. They'll publish it in a second.

ISAAC: Nevertheless.

AARON: And reap a hell of a lot of cashola so doing, damn it!

ISAAC: So what do you think of your brother's little agenda to take over the company?

MARTIN: Oh come on, Isaac, you're not serious.

ISAAC: I've seen it fermenting in him! What do you think, I'm a village idiot?

AARON: Please.

ISAAC: Please! A blood lust for profitmaking. You knew the kind of work we publish—and you have this arrogant idea that you could—God knows the lingo you people use—

AARON: You people? *You people?* What is that supposed to mean?

ISAAC: You know exactly what I mean. You wanna accuse me of bigotry toward MBA's, fine, go ahead. You're not working at Gulf and Western.

AARON: Just this morning, he actually asked me if I wouldn't be happier as a sales rep.

SARAH: Oh dear.

(There is a silence.)

ISAAC: The reason the stock of this company has been kept in the family is because I wished to avoid precisely the kind of confrontation we are having now. If Aaron cannot make peace with the mandate by which *my* company is to be run, he should not be vice-president. No company would settle for less. It is unfortunate, sure, I wanted at least one of you here, but perhaps—

AARON: *(Quiet.)* That's very clear, yeah. Thanks. But the reason I'm here, you know, is that I actually value the stock I hold in this house. Do you need to be reminded? I own twenty percent of this place, Martin, a quarter, and Sarah fifteen. And if you continue the course you're on, we will be flattened.

ISAAC: Not necessarily. You don't know that I'm not going to come up with—

AARON: No you won't, and we will be taken over by someone who is in the book business by accident—some real-estate developer dying for a salon, and this town is full of 'em! A lonely guy lookin' for a tax loss, they'll sniff this place out, hey. Simon and Schuster is owned by an oil company, Dad. These people come in, hang new wallpaper and dollar bills before the end of the first day. You're going to leave us with nothing—a dead company.

ISAAC: The Chenard book is crapolla, kiddo, there's no denying that.

MARTIN: Actually, I don't think so.

ISAAC: Ahh, you read it. You have a literary opinion, Mr. Johnny-Appleseed-of-the-Hudson here?

AARON: I sent it to both of them.

MARTIN: I finished it on the train coming down here. I think it's powerful. I cried. I don't know why.

ISAAC: You're a gardener, Martin, please.

MARTIN: *(Smiles at Sarah.)* You can't imagine how much we look forward to seeing you, Isaac. I don't know. It's just the way you make everyone feel so welcome, or . . .

SARAH: And hey, please? What's with this "gardener" business, Dad? Your son's a Rhodes Scholar. You're starting to sound like some sort of Fulton fish market thug, calling names. And besides, what little I read of the book, I sort of liked too.

AARON: *(Turns to* MARTIN.*)* You like the book? You really do? I thought you would. I thought you might, both of you. It's something, isn't it?

ISAAC: Excuse me. I've made up my mind. I don't need a little shit-ass democratic committee here to tell me, please, you got it? *(Pause.)* Sorry. To talk like that, to lose my temper. I'm gonna publish Louis Fuchold's six volumes on the Nazi medical experiments.

AARON: What? What are you—?

ISAAC: *(Calm.)* Yes, that's exactly what I'm going to do. That I even let you near a . . . a . . . decision on such a matter is . . . You think that I am going to publish some trashy novel by a slickohipster?

AARON: Dad, this is exactly the problem, this is what I . . . you just decided this? What am I doing here? Just to balance the books?

ISAAC: Abraham Kreeger, your mother's father, started this imprint to publish serious work that was valuable in the larger world. We've played fast and loose with that mandate and made some bucks, and God knows I don't intend to lose any sleep over *that.* I knew how far we had to go in order to grow. Fuck-you money is fine, but now is the time to get back what we lost. And let me tell you—the Chenard book is meretricious bullshit! I wanted my time back after I read it.

MARTIN: Well, I think you're misreading it.

ISAAC: *(A low growl.)* I tend not to misread books. I tend to know exactly the lay of the land.

MARTIN: You have no doubts about your judgment?

ISAAC: Not in regard to this matter.

AARON: Then tell me—why have we been losing so much money?

ISAAC: *(Softens, shakes his head.)* Something has happened. The way in which people read. Perceive. There used to be some silence to life. There is now none. Just static, white noise, fireworks, and boredom all around you. We lose money because we do something that is no longer held to be vital, we're a side-thought to life. And now here you come, Aaron, wanting to save us from destruction, running around here with your manuscript like some kind of Typhoid Mary. *(ISAAC looks at the manuscript.)* You come to me here with bright-lights-little-people, less-than-nothing Tammy Yannovitch—a *hydra*—she's not a writer, she's a monster out of ancient Greece come to swallow cultures, lives, whole cities. These kids with eyes like pinwheels, typing out their little baubles of syntax. *This ain't literature. It's a dress.* You don't read this book. You get a nice little, strung-out, anorexic model who doesn't need a lot of covering, and you put it on her to wear to a gallery opening. *(Beat.)* So listen, Aaron, what I'm saying to you is—it's simple—you've never burdened anyone with your editorial ambitions until now. You're doing fine. You've learned a lot. But these are very tricky waters out there. Forget about this. Go back to your ledgers and you'll be fine. Leave the heavy stuff to me, okay?

AARON: You begged me to come into this business. I mean, these two had sense enough to run a million miles. Now you're trying to kill it off. I can't just sit back and—

SARAH: Listen. Please. It's just books. Really. Please. I see this behavior and I know what's up. You feel usurped.

ISAAC: No, sweetie, please, uh-uh, no.

SARAH: Oh yes, no, you feel "threatened." De-balled by your son.

ISAAC: Sweetheart, please, none of your Neighborhood Playhouse psychologizing. I published Willhelm Fliess while you were at tap class learning shuffle-ball-flap. "Threatened."

AARON: Hey, you know, I'm not gonna argue that this is not a trashy world out there. I mean, come on, but so what?

MARTIN: Aaron tells me if you go ahead and publish the Fuchold Nazi medical experiment book, you won't be able to handle anything else on the spring list except for a couple of the old reprints. Is that right?

ISAAC: The Nazi is six volumes. I can't hold off production. He's been working for thirty-four years. The man practically, he comes to editorial meetings in his casket. Look, we've never been a big house, so now for a while maybe we're a little smaller. It's not a matter of bankruptcy. It's scale. I'll take a reduction in—

AARON: That's really great. You'll take a cut? Have you seen your Visa bills? For a man who has such rigorous standards—

ISAAC: *(Dangerous and insistent.)* Don't! Don't you *dare* to presume to tell *me* how to spend, nobody—nobody has *ever* told me what to do. Nobody. Not your mother, not the banks, and most certainly not my accountant son. *(Beat.)* Listen. Why are you so certain the Fuchold will not be read anyhow? Do you know something I don't?

MARTIN: *(Gentle, reasonable.)* Maybe you're not wrong. But why not let Aaron run with this. What harm can it do?

ISAAC: A lot, a lot, in ways you can't imagine, it can all slip away, everything.

MARTIN: *(Reluctant.)* The thing is, we've all noticed—you're becoming unapproachable. And it's like you're on some sort of end-run to self-destruct. We don't know what to do. Do you like to know—there's a whole hell of a lot of phone-action. The topic? *(He gestures at* ISAAC.*)* And it's not unwarranted, it's a *bore,* but it's *not* unwarranted. You worry us. No end. Look at what you've been publishing. That Englishman's book, Jonally—*The Failure of Art and the Triumph of Technology*? A swipe here at Diaghilev and Stravinsky, a sneer at the Bauhaus, and why not knock off abstract expressionism while you're at it just for a laugh? *(Beat.)* I mean, it's time for another tack, Pop, 'cause you're starting to come off as some sort of neo-con.

ISAAC: *(Picks up manuscript.)* Uh-huhm, sure, a neo-con, well, may I, I'll just read you a little passage here. *(He pauses to make sure they're with him.)* "Alter leaned against the bar, mouth open in recollection of those black hands on his jeans. The feeling of release and submission that comes when someone else unsnaps the buttons—and then, the intrusive rightness of the kid's lips on him, surrounding him in the alley—the cold—the heat—and wetness as his shirt is lifted up towards the spire of the Chrysler building, glowing above them" . . . etc, etc. *(He looks at* MARTIN, *triumphant.)*

SARAH: Well, Dad, I don't understand. What's the big deal here? We all know about blow jobs, don't we?

ISAAC: Yes, we know about blow jobs. That's hardly the . . .

SARAH: Well then maybe you publish all these politico books because there's no sex in them? They're totally flaccid. This whole thing is about hormones. You need to get out more, is all, Dad.

MARTIN: The thing of it is, Dad, you see, I promised Aaron that if I liked the book, I'd support him. Whatever that meant. Understand? I do like the book. Aaron is your partner. You drew him in, made promises. And you are able to be the fairest man I know. Occasionally. So publish the book and what's the big deal? Come on.

ISAAC: What do you think, I'll be cornered? What do you think I am? I'll be dictated to? *(He looks around the room.)* What the hell is going on here? *What?*

AARON: I'm sorry, Dad. I don't understand the Nazi obsession. It has silenced me. I mean, what do you say to it? Look at the spring and fall lists last year. *(Beat.) An Atlas of the Holocaust.* Maps. Blueprints. I.G. Farben's structural reports. All of it on acid-free paper with a handsewn binding, a Japanese printing, wholesaling at one-twenty-nine-ninety-five? *(Beat.)* You take the bread out of our mouths. It's heartbreaking to say how much we lost on that. And please, I won't even discuss the losses on *Water on Fire, an Oral History of the Children of Hiroshima.*

SARAH: Hey. It's just books. You know? I see what's happening here. You'll all use these issues as leverage, whatever the cost. Hey, I know what I'm talking about. Listen, I talk to other actors, and it's so fucking dull. It's just this crushing bore—they're all dying from their dogmas. What they will or will not do, and it's a total snooze. Who cares? It doesn't matter. It just doesn't make a difference.

ISAAC: No, it does matter. It does make a difference. They should care. It matters to them. Otherwise, you end up? What? Heinrich Mann doing little drawings at his desk at Warners. Kazan in a cold sweat, saying yes to anything. All the little failures of spirit—they add up and they add up badly. But, of course, that's the American seduction, isn't it? Not a thing matters here, it's all disposable. Forget your history, forget what you believed in, forget your fire. Forget your fire. *(Pause.)* Leave your fire at the door. You see, Sarah, it matters very much what I choose to fight for. *(Beat.)* So, Aaron. Let me ask you, from a literary standpoint, not a commercial one, why should I publish "Rising Tide"?

AARON: *(Laughs slightly, closes his eyes.)* No. Please. Hey, I'm not that dumb.

SARAH: Well, it's true, honey, you've given, you know, all these terribly mercantile reasons and all, but no literary—

AARON: Yeah, well, don't count on my weakness as a critical thinker, Dad. I'm hip to you. One by one, point by point, I could say, "Oh, the book deals in themes of blah-blah-blah." And you would say, "On, no, it doesn't. If that's what you think the book deals in, you're wrong. A book that *does* deal in blah-blah-blah, I would be very interested in publishing. But this book here doesn't, son. Sorry. Find me a nice German novel about a village in '34 to have translated."

ISAAC: Do me at least the favor of not telling me what I would say to you if you presented an argument to me I haven't heard.

AARON: No. Of course. *(Beat. He smiles.)* No, I'm not much of a reader, we know. I'm more comfortable, you tell me, with the balance sheet and the projections. The numbers don't lie. All that. *(Pause.)* And all done with a smirk, as if you've always held the opinion that making a lot of money was somehow vulgar. For a publisher. *(Beat.)* I just don't get it. Are your literary opinions so profoundly held that they hold to the point where your children have to halt you? Is this ceaseless drive to run us into the ground circling any particular point, Dad, or is it just that in the six years since Mother died, you've become suicidal? Because you're way too smart to stand on ceremony over Anthony-fucking-Trollope. *(Beat.)* I *think*.

ISAAC: This, Aaron, is simply beneath contempt. This line of reasoning, it's gutter reasoning, kiddo, and—

AARON: Maybe, but ever since your wife died, if we had a graph curve it would look like the north face of Everest from '81 on.

ISAAC: I wouldn't confuse high standards with missing your mother.

AARON: Yeah, well, the thing is, I don't think this has anything to do with "standards." What I think is that you are a man who has lost his sense of humor.

ISAAC: My *what*?

AARON: You've lost your sense of humor. What happened to the low joke? The frivolous gesture? Bawdiness? You have no time for a laugh. That's why you should publish this book. That's my best argument.

ISAAC: Excuse me, let me get this straight here. I've lost my sense of humor and if I publish the Val Chenard book, I'll get it back? What're you? Nuts?

MARTIN: It's true, Dad, you've become this Cotton Mather type. You're gonna drop dead from rigor any day now. It's true, Sarah, tell him.

SARAH: Hey, I don't know what to say. I see you smirking, Martin, and I hate this. And besides, what do I know about it? I sing songs to eight-year-olds about trichinosis. I shouldn't even be here. But it's true, Daddy, you get more and more intractable, more isolated in your positions.

AARON: You don't go out. You don't see anyone, you sit around with your illustrated letters, your collection of first editions, signed postcards, sneaking off to auctions—

ISAAC: Please, please, this is—

AARON: He bought a postcard of Adolf Hitler's. A little drawing.

ISAAC: Enough.

AARON: Well, what is that *about*?

MARTIN: A postcard of Hitler's?

ISAAC: He painted, you know that, as a boy. I mean, once he was a boy. He sent a postcard on which he had painted a little watercolor of a church. He painted mostly churches. Landmarks in old Vienna. It had a fascination for me. Done in 1916. It wasn't cheap, but it triggered something. I don't know. A view of a world. I am out of step with myself lately, here in New York. I am out of step with myself.

MARTIN: I understand all that, but I don't understand why that precludes publishing Aaron's book. It's a comic novel. A little book. You just can't give everything equal weight, equal moral weight—

ISAAC: Maybe you can. Maybe you should. Maybe that's exactly the problem.

MARTIN: No. I don't think so. For you, rejecting this book becomes this—affirmation—of how you're supposed to live your life, saying "no" to everything. Let me ask you this: You've become a pretty good publisher of books about horror. It's all death camps and napalm and atrocities with you.

ISAAC: Martin—

MARTIN: The question is—just because you've started to deal in historical hardware, do you imagine that makes you above some sort of reproach? It's "Oh, we can't criticize Isaac Geldhart, we've gotta take him dead serious. After all, he published *Hazlitt on Cannibalism.*" Well, to my mind, all that makes you is a very cautious academic pornographer, a sensationalist with Sulka ties. "See the bodies pile up, watch the dead, see how bad everything is. Why bother engaging?"

ISAAC: This is rich coming from you who has deliberately shut himself away from all interaction up there in Poughkeepsie. You, with your seed-hybrids. Humorless? No, I don't think so. I am just so afraid of this trash piling up around us. I am afraid of the young. *You.* Let me tell you—I am. "Publish this book 'cause you're not funny anymore." My God, I prefer at least your arguments about fiscal doom, but spare me that playing-to-the-balcony crap about missing your mom. I am destroying this company because life is not worth living without your mother? Let me tell you, that wasn't the greatest marriage in the world. I don't think about her a lot these days. So phooey to that approach—stick to the numbers, Aaron.

SARAH: *(Cuts him off—furious.)* Who do you think you're talking about? That's my mother you're talking about. Please! What the hell is the matter with you? Do you hear yourself? Aaron's trying to help. But all I can see is you treating people badly. Treating Aaron with this superior bullying contempt.

AARON: No, hey, it's what I signed on for. You get used to it. It's like you can insult anyone as long as it's done sort of elegantly.

ISAAC: Who? I do this? I really do this? But think about what you're asking me to do. You want me to change the direction of this company. To do so will drive me mad. I don't even know how to. You've gotta bear with me a little. So what if I'm humorless? Surely that's not a valid reason for taking over my life's work? I would say that a sense of humor is nice, but really, in the end, beside the point.

MARTIN: Maybe. I hope not. When was the last time we had dinner together, Pop?

ISAAC: I always ask, but you turn me down cold, so I don't ask anymore. Don't blame me for that. I made an effort to remain close but—

MARTIN: Yes, sure. On terms that are unlivable. *(He lights a smoke.)*

ISAAC: I know. I'm tough in a restaurant, but I—what is this *smoking* business? What are you doing *smoking*? You have no business smoking, Martin.

MARTIN: Your obsession over the martini, for instance. Only a miserable man could require such precision in his drink. The little ice container that has to be three-quarters filled to keep the extra martini perfectly cold. The "problem" with the twist. You actually, I sat there—you said to the waiter, "There's a problem with the twist." You actually—I mean, it used to be funny. But grimly gnawing and hacking away at your salmon—sending it back—you sent it back *three times.*

ISAAC: *(With a contemptuous shrug.)* It wasn't right.

MARTIN: Yeah, well, the maître d' practically stabbed you. I would have applauded. That was the last time we had dinner together.

ISAAC: I thought we had a nice time, Martin.

MARTIN: It was like dinner with Duvalier. Both of them.

AARON: Dad, do you remember when we had a best-seller? It was seven years ago. And it kept us alive. This book can go the same way. Can't you just simply trust me—once. Just now—once.

ISAAC: No. Not on this.

MARTIN: Then I'll sign over my shares of this company to Aaron. He'd be the majority stockholder. I don't want to do that to you, but believe me, I will. Because Mom left us those shares to do what we pleased with. So why push it?

SARAH: Hey, hold on, Martin, what are you doing? Come on, are you kidding here?

ISAAC: Oh, so that's where we are. So how did it go, Aaron? You called up your brother and made him an offer? That is what you learned at Wharton? Bought you a nice degree, didn't I?

SARAH: Listen, Aaron. This is not just some faceless takeover. Martin. People don't recover. Families, they just fold up, you know? Never to speak again. Are we like that? That sort of family? Over money? You've got to find some way to compromise. All of you. Because this is just horseshit.

ISAAC: I sense your little sister would not be in on your takeover. So, Sarah, darling?

AARON: You cannot possibly win this one, Dad. There's just no way.

SARAH: Hold it. Why don't you bother asking me? I'm not going to sit here like some dumb—nobody bothers asking me what I think. "What does she think?" *(Beat.)* What I think is this. I don't want to turn this into some sort of horrible little . . . *thing.* But, Martin, if you hand your stocks to Aaron, then I'll hand mine over to Dad. *(Shrugs, shakes her head.)* Well, sorry. But nobody asks *me.*

AARON: Sarah.

MARTIN: Hey, you know, Sarah, it might not be such a bad idea to let this thing run its course.

SARAH: Why? Because you're enjoying yourself?

ISAAC: So, there you have it. This is, I think, a stalemate.

AARON: Sarah, what are you doing?

ISAAC: Think now, Aaron, didn't Wharton provide you with the next step? *(Silence.)* Why don't you take some time to think it over?

AARON: I have Val in the library. He'll be outta here. He's not just gonna . . .

ISAAC: Well, I will ask him to wait. You talk this over without me. My position is clear. I will *not* compromise. I will not be manipulated. But I am not sure that you should either. *(He exits. Silence in his wake.)*

SARAH: God, he is a tricky bastard.

AARON: Oh, yes.

MARTIN: I need, I think, a drink about now.

AARON: I mean, the idea of you selling your stock to Dad—and, by the way, what's he going to pay you with? Some first editions? Terrific. His collection of illustrated letters? He just went into hock on that Hitler postcard. You want that on your wall?

SARAH: He hung it up?

AARON: Look, there's no cash. We're on empty here.

SARAH: He needs to see a negotiable way out. Bend a little, he'll bend too.

AARON: It's way past that. He got you to offer him your stock. The man'll have fifty-five percent, just what he's after. And if you do that, ultimately, you'll be killing him.

SARAH: But wouldn't taking control from him do him in just as surely—and a hell of a lot more viciously? Have you ever thought that you're acting out of sheer anger towards him? Nothing to do with saving the company? Just rage?

AARON: And if I am? So? What if you're giving in to him out of some need to be loved? That's not just as bad?

SARAH: Hey—

AARON: Get ready for next season—"Lullabies from the Warsaw Ghetto." On every remainder shelf in the country.

MARTIN: I'm going to have a drink. This is exhausting. *(He exits. Silence.)*

SARAH: Why is he smoking and drinking all over the place? What's with him? When did he start? He knows he's supposed to be careful.

AARON: I don't know. I've never been able to read anyone in this family, so don't ask me. *(Beat.)* What do I do now? 'Cause I guess I actually seem to have finally blown it here.

SARAH: I'm sorry, Aaron.

AARON: Well, I just have to find a way to think of this as a positive.

SARAH: Aaron, I'm trying to do the right thing, to do the most right thing.

AARON: No, you're trying to do exactly what I did. You're trying to get his approval. *(Beat.)* I had this idiot notion that he and I'd sit here at this table talking about books. And really he has—not once solicited my opinion, not once asked me what I was reading, over a cup of coffee, which is all I wanted.

SARAH: I know. Listen I'm so dumb I fly across the country because he asks me to. I—look at me—dress like a refugee from *Little Women.* I think of important issues to—I actually sat on the plane tearing through back issues of the *New Republic* and *The Nation,* trying to find witty things to knock him dead with. And last month, he sent a bunch of S. J. Perelman first editions. Why? No note. Nothing. But I sit there for hours thinking, "What's he trying to tell me? Be funnier?" I mean, really.

AARON: Last week, someone asked him what you were up to. He told them you were a clown for hire for children's birthday parties. This, after he saw you on the UNICEF anniversary show. Looked at the TV and mumbled, "Americans," as if you were a foreigner.

SARAH: A birthday clown. That's terrific. I love it.

AARON: Yeah, well, he introduced me at the ABA as his bookkeeper, so you're not alone. *(Beat.)* Look. Seeing as this is pretty much over, we should, at least, be able to have a meal together. Brooklyn. "Garjulos"? The puttanesca is still like blood.

SARAH: Oh, shit, Aaron, I can't. Really. I have to catch the nine o'clock to the coast. We're doing "K" tomorrow.

AARON: "K"?

SARAH: The letter "K," yeah. It's my letter.

AARON: Oh. May I ask you this? Are you still involved with your producer? Is that still on?

SARAH: Why? I mean?

AARON: I'm just curious. It was an issue for you last time I saw you. "This older man." That's still happening?

SARAH: "Happening" implies action, you know? Motion. I just sit around waiting for the guy, repeating lines to myself that would send a sane person running a million miles. Like, "Oh, he's leaving his wife of fifteen years. It was over anyway." So mostly, I wait. *(Beat.)* And yes, fine, he goes days without calling.

AARON: But you settle for that? An older man pushing you, doling out little bits here and there—?

SARAH: No, I admit it, you don't have to press the goddamn point. He's absolutely the cliché of a father fixation.

AARON: Well, just last week, our father accused me of being a person most free within a cliché. He said I was liberated by banality, so. That is that?

SARAH: What're you going to do?

AARON: What can I do? I'm gonna back down, and help steer us through bankruptcy. It's okay— This thing was doomed from the beginning, from the start. I went out with Chenard in college.

SARAH: With? Oh, my God, Aaron, honey. Is that why the book has been so—

AARON: No, I don't think so. I mean, the book is good. This is not a clouded issue.

SARAH: I didn't know, Aaron. I knew that you were . . . but I mean, I just didn't know. You've been so silent.

AARON: No, well, yes. It was a thing. We used to have things. Everybody had a little "thing." Judy doesn't know. Nobody. He liked me because I admitted I knew nothing about literature, only about maybe making a profit in the service of art. He thought I was actually totally naive. Which, of course, I was. *(Beat.)* We have dinner. The people we went to school with are off, you know, doing bad performance art in Hoboken, or in closed sessions with the SEC over insider jobs downtown. Nothing in between. I'm in publishing. We have this link.

SARAH: So this has been with you?

AARON: And I am almost totally domesticated. Judy bought me these slippers from Brooks Brothers. With lamb's wool. I looked at them and thought, "Shackles, goddammit. How do I end up here?"

SARAH: I am sorry, Aaron. That's hard. That's so hard.

AARON: No. It was pathetic to have thought of this as my

big chance. To prove to Dad—I mean, I must think like a seven-year-old.

SARAH: Well, I'm still a toddler, so at least you're ahead of me.

AARON: Too bad we couldn't have a bite.

SARAH: Yeah, well, I've gotta get back. I have the letter "K" to take care of. Such as it is.

AARON: And a father fixation to nurture, right?

MARTIN: *(Enters with a drink in hand.)* Dad is sitting in the library with your writer, Aaron.

AARON: What's he doing?

MARTIN: His Decline of the West, Part Three speech. Chenard is laughing.

AARON: Look, Sarah, if you were to back me, the very worst is that Dad will have been wrong. Well, he should be able to learn to live with that. It's not the end of the world. He'll simply have been mistaken, and I'll have helped him—we'll have helped him. Come on.

SARAH: Look, maybe we should all just pull back. When he comes in, we'll try and start this from scratch. Just reason it out, okay?

MARTIN: I'm not pulling back. Hey, it's Aaron's. I'm out, and I don't give a fuck what you publish really.

SARAH: Hey, come on Martin. Please. What are you talking about?

MARTIN: We go months without speaking to one another. We're all afraid of each other—slightly put off. There's some sort of competitiveness under the surface, and I've never cared for it. We're better off keeping away from each other. And more than that, let me tell you—I am above this struggle.

ISAAC: *(Entering.)* So, it's getting late. We all have places to go, and I'm tired. How do you want to handle this?

MARTIN: Publish *Hustler* or publish Proust. I don't want to have anything to do with it anymore. Your books. God. I am so tired of these books. And your endless posturing, position-taking, ranting, judging. The only thing I miss is Mom. She wouldn't put up with any of this crap for a second. She'd know what to do. Damn it. I just—coming down here is too much. It's done me in. I miss Mom.

ISAAC: The only part I believe is the last. Such poison. Why such poison, Martin? Always?

MARTIN: Poison! You want to talk about poison? Look at

what you've done. You've created a family of literary zombies. You know that people are afraid of you. It's why you've gotten so far. Yes. "Isaac Geldhart knows something, he came from some awful childhood in Europe that nobody knows about." He has a "seer-like standing in the book world." Blah-Blah-Blah—phooey. Let me tell you, we're fucked up by it. I grew up running around this building. When I was eight, you gave me the Iliad in Greek so that someday I could read it. Monster! People's lives are ruined by books and they're all you know how to relate to, Dad. You too, Aaron, for all your talk. You too, Sarah, pretending you hate to read. Sometimes I want to take a pruning shears and do an Oedipus on myself. I counted my books last week. Do you know how many I have? Want to take a guess? *(No one says anything.)* Fourteen thousand, three hundred and eighty-six. The sixty crates of books that Mom left me. Well, I finally had them carted up the Hudson, but I had to have shelves built. The whole house. Every room. And instead of just guessing—I was, I mean—speechless. A wreck of a life. It just flashed before my eyes. No sex, no people, just books till I die. Dickens. In *French.* The bastard didn't write in French. What the fuck am I doing with *Dombey and Son* in French? The twelve-volume *Conquest of Mexico.* Two hundred cookbooks. The *Oxford World Classics,* the little ones with the blue bindings, you know?

ISAAC: You got that?

MARTIN: They're all just words. And this is life, and besides, I hear the book chains are now selling pre-emptive strike video games, so why bother anyway? I'm out.

ISAAC: But really, there are limits, sweetheart.

MARTIN: Yes. That's exactly right. There are limits. I believe I know that. Hey, I spent most of my sixteenth year getting chemotherapy, remember? And it's not that long ago, I can still feel it. I cannot waste my life. I feel you people dragging me into this thing. You want this confrontation, Dad. You want nothing more than your children gathered around you, fighting. Well forget it. You don't know what I feel in my back, in my bones. I wake up some days and I'm crying. I think I'm still at Sloan-Kettering, lying there hairless and white and filling up with glucose from a drip. Hey! I can't get that time back. I feel all the needles, some days, my lymph nodes, and I'm sweating. And part of my life is spent in fear, waiting. I know none of us has forever, know that very well, and I care very much how I spend my time. And involved in an internecine war over a publishing house, is, by my reckoning, Father, a dead waste. *And* if I choose to live with plants as an assistant lecturer at an overrated seven-sisters school, *that* is my goddamn choice. But let's clear up something finally: I am not a goddamn gardener, and you are never going to goad me back into this life by calling me one. And Sarah is not a clown at children's birthday parties, Dad, and Aaron isn't a fucking accountant. You are really charming about your superiority, Dad. But you're really alone, too. This Nazi book jag of yours—it scares me.

ISAAC: I spent a couple of days, a little boy, wandering about after the liberation. I saw a particular kind of man—a wraith-like figure—who could only have been in the camps. But with a brown pinstripe suit, a fleur-de-lis on his tie and manicured nails, trying to pick up where he left off, as if you could. I never say anything about this. Why talk? Why bother? I wasn't in the camps. You know? They're busy throwing the Farbers and the Hirsches into the ovens, and I'm happily eating smoked eels in the basement, with my Stendahl and Dumas. What did I know? I was protected, sheltered by my cousins. And then I got out of the basement and into the wrecked world. I came to this country. You re-invent yourself. Make it as a bon vivant in Manhattan. Meet this woman—this extraordinary woman. Marry. Have these kids. Go to so many cocktail parties, host so many more . . . and they . . . haunt. *(Beat.)* I have kept my eyes closed to the world outside the basement for so long. The wrecked world all around us. But I can no longer close my eyes. *(He turns to* AARON.*)* My son. You are fired. I will give you a week to clear your desk, and I will give you letters of recommendation. But I will not speak to you, I will not communicate with you, I will not . . . *(Pause.)* . . . *give at all.* Kiddo. To the victor go the spoils.

SARAH: Wait a second, wait a second. I see what you're doing. You want to use *me* to screw Aaron. And you think I would go along with that? You think that's the kind of person I am? That I'd just sit still and watch you? Why—because I feel sorry for you because you weren't in a camp?

ISAAC: Sarah—

SARAH: No. I am going to hand my shares to Aaron. Because you just don't understand. You don't know how to love.

AARON: Wait a second. Let's be clear about this. You just handed me control of this company.

SARAH: Yes. I did.

AARON: You did this to yourself. It didn't have to happen.

ISAAC: Do what you must.

AARON: *(Quietly furious.)* I warned you. I explained it to you. But you ignore all the signs. You just proceed self-destructively, asking for help, asking to be usurped, upended, damn it. Do you want to hate me? *(Beat.)* Well, go ahead. Hate me. But we need cash. I have had an offer. Japanese. And you will no longer run the company, you will be kicked onto the board. I have tried to warn you. But with Martin and Sarah's stock—with control in my hands, I have no choice. We will be backed by some men in Tokyo who won't give a fuck whether I publish Val Chenard or Racing Forum so long as it turns a buck in their direction. And you knew this was coming. You knew it could only end up like this. Well, at least you'll be taken care of. You won't starve to death. I'm sorry. I simply have no choice.

ISAAC: You understand, Aaron, sweetheart. You will just be part of the big pile, the big carcinogenic pile of trash, building up all around you, as life itself no longer seems real.

AARON: Yeah, well, you know, that's not my problem. That's *your* problem, Dad. It's not my fault that life does seem real to me, and I can make peace with that. I don't have a holocaust to pin on my chest. I have my family. My city. Some continuity. The way I think. My friends. I don't want to set life back to its beginnings, and I'm not burdened by thinking I'm one of the world's great thinkers, either. All I can do with the "carcinogenic pile of trash" is sift through it. That's all anyone can do. But my life does seem totally real to me. I do not need to suffer in order to feel alive, Pop. I'm sorry. I'm going to have dinner with my author.

ISAAC: *(As* AARON *starts out.)* Aaron. I hope it works out for you.

*(***Aaron** *exits.* **Isaac** *crosses to the window, looks out.)*

Isaac: This city. When I got off the boat, I said, "It's going to be so good now, this life, it's all going to be so full." It was snowing.

Sarah: I'm sorry. I have a plane to catch. Daddy . . . *(She exits.)*

Martin: Dad, why don't we get some dinner? We could take the car. It never gets used. Go across the bridge.

Isaac: That is not possible.

(The lights fade.)

ACT II

Three and a half years later. An old apartment in Gramercy Park. ISAAC *is sitting in a chair, staring out the window. A fierce winter snowstorm swirls around and down over the park. The radio plays, and the radiator hisses steam, gurgles, protests, coughs. The apartment is not so much a home as it is an archive. Floor to ceiling—the room is dominated by books. Though there are also gaping holes, gaps on the shelves where volumes are missing. There are also framed letters—all of which are embellished with drawings.* ISAAC *has a frayed, fogged-in air about him. The door buzzer rings.* ISAAC *sighs, turns off the radio. He puts on his tie and shoes, and is getting on his jacket as* MARTIN *enters—layered in snow, parka, scarf, gloves, and boots. He stands for a moment, catching his breath.*

MARTIN: *(Putting his coat, etc., on a hook in the hall.)* Didn't you hear the buzzer?

ISAAC: *(Eager.)* You want tea? Is it cold? It looks a little cold outside?

MARTIN: I had to stand there, struggling with these keys in the ice and the . . . *(Pause. He sighs.)* How are you?

ISAAC: *(Shrugs.)* Who the hell knows, you know? I didn't think you'd get in. I hear on WNYC the trains are backed up to Lake Placid.

MARTIN: No, I came in last night, I—

ISAAC: I see. I see. I see. Last night. You . . . ?

MARTIN: Stayed at a friend's.

*(*ISAAC *nods, not thrilled.)*

MARTIN: You ate?

ISAAC: *(Not interested.)* Maybe with the snow, the girl won't come.

MARTIN: The cleaning girl?

ISAAC: This place is—who can live this way? *(Yells suddenly.)* Goddamn it! Who? The kitchen is—have you ever tried to steam a squash? I stand there. It's a room full of yellow pulp.

MARTIN: *(Smiles.)* Please.

ISAAC: *(Resigned.)* Martin, I'm telling you, you can't run a place this big with only a woman who comes in once a week from Belize. The dust, it's like a nuclear winter in this place. I'm—*(*ISAAC *runs out of steam.)* You have to take three showers a day.

MARTIN: Dad. The social worker. That's today. You remember?

ISAAC: No, no, no. What do you think, I'm an idiot? Today is the maid and Thursday is the Sotheby lady.

MARTIN: *(Quiet.)* It's the psychiatric social worker. You agreed. I came into town because you asked me—

ISAAC: *(Yelling.)* Do I look to you like a man who hasn't got a calendar? Thursday is the social worker. Today is Tuesday, the cleaning lady! Please!

MARTIN: Today, actually, Isaac, *is*, in point of fact, Thursday.

(There is silence.)

ISAAC: Without Miss Barzakian, how'm I supposed to know my appointments? Idiotic. To have even consented to this.

MARTIN: It would help if you could remember the days of the week.

ISAAC: What for? Just a slab of days, this. What do you do? You go back to Aaron? With reports?

MARTIN: Yes. He asks.

ISAAC: He asks? And you tell him, "He's doddering, he's slobbering, he's mortifying, the kitchen is a horror? He can't tie his shoes." That sort of thing? Because frankly, if that's the case, I'm better off—

MARTIN: *(Suddenly suspicious.)* What do you mean the "Sotheby Lady"—what were you talking about before?

ISAAC: I didn't say anything, I didn't say—

MARTIN: What did you do? Have you been trying to get rid of more stuff?

ISAAC: Musselblat the attorney tells me if I can raise enough, I should be able to make a reasonable offer to get back the company, so—

MARTIN: *(Disgusted and exhausted.)* Oh, Jesus, Dad. Isaac. What's the matter with you?

ISAAC: I've gotta try, don't I?

MARTIN: We're in chapter 11. What do you think you can do? It would take a superhuman effort, and you're not in any shape . . .

ISAAC: What do you know about business? What have you ever known about business? Please. Please. (ISAAC *takes a moment.)* You know, yesterday, I saw the most magnificent pair of shoes on Irving Place on a young guy, and he had to have someone makin' 'em, I tell ya, 'cause there ain't no guy in this hell hole of a town who can do that particular suede—in one *piece*—I tell you. Probably he was English, and I followed him. I'd buy 'em, even if they were the wrong size. You get a guy to copy 'em, there you are. *(He looks bitterly at his son.)* I'll tell you something. I can waste my day in so many goddamn ways, I tell you.

(They both just sit for a moment.)

MARTIN: Dad, have you been for a walk? The park is white. Maybe if it stops snowing.

ISAAC: Do we have to talk? To sit here talking with you—it's like talking to strangers. I really, these little trips in from the country of yours. I don't need 'em, I really don't. I can handle the Sotheby people just fine.

MARTIN: It's the social worker, and it wasn't my idea.

ISAAC: *(Scornful.)* No, of course not. But if Aaron says I'm incompetent, there's gotta be something to it, right? After all, he sure did such a good job with the company, didn't he?

MARTIN: Nobody is saying anything about your being incompetent—

ISAAC. *(Explodes.)* Please! Remember who you're talking to! The impertinence! *(ISAAC crosses away from MARTIN.)*

MARTIN: *(Looks at a pile of bills.)* But why didn't you pay the phone people? It's past due. Can't you see this only serves to substantiate—

ISAAC: It's a maelstrom of papers. Who can keep track of them all? Maybe if they were at least in different colors. *(He sees* MARTIN *looking at some empty bookshelves.)* I have to sell it all. Besides, the disability is up any day now. That's a big check every month to do without. What am I supposed to do?

MARTIN: You sold the old Everyman Encyclopedias?

ISAAC: I got nothing for it. You know what I did? I had to go see those pricks at Gotham. I had to walk in the door like some kind of huckster, like it's a grapefruit. I wish your brother'd seen it. *(He looks at* MARTIN.*)* Tell me something, why do you dress like you're some sort of Paul Bunyan character? It's unbecoming.

MARTIN: I'm sorry. I'll wear a suit next time.

(Silence.)

ISAAC: What do you hear from your sister?

MARTIN: That you still hang up the phone on her.

ISAAC: I'd like to get the hell out of this town. A building blew up just across the park. Apparently there was a cloud of asbestos and now there's cancer for everyone. A janitor was parboiled. The whole street was a freak show.

MARTIN: No, I know. We've talked about this.

ISAAC: Of course, the management company on this property, I think I last saw them in '59, when we signed the papers, and—

(There is a buzz. MARTIN *crosses to the hall for the intercom.)*

MARTIN: *(Into intercom.)* Hello?

ISAAC: They can't hear you. It doesn't work. You can only buzz, not talk, so if, per chance, it happens to be a mugger, well, you're fine.

MARTIN: *(Into intercom.)* Hello?

MARGE HACKETT: *(Over intercom.)* It's Marge Hackett.

ISAAC: Occasionally, it works.

MARTIN: Come up to three. (MARTIN *pushes the button.)* Dad, Can I give you some advice?

*(*ISAAC *says nothing.)*

MARTIN: Just try and answer yes or no. You don't have to—you don't have to do the Isaac Geldhart show. It's not required. They don't let you off on charm. They don't even get it, these people, and if you—

ISAAC: No, I get it. Quit your carping, would you? Making me ill. *(He turns his back to* MARTIN.) Standing here giving instructions like I'm your photosynthesis class or something.

(A knock is heard.)

MARTIN: Dad, she's here.

*(*ISAAC *exits.* MARGE HACKETT *enters. A woman in her fifties—maybe, hard to be sure.)*

MARTIN: Hi. We talked on the phone, we spoke. Martin Geldhart.

MARGE: Oh, yes, right. Sure.

MARTIN: I didn't know if you'd make it here.

MARGE: The snow doesn't bother me. I don't mind it.

MARTIN: *(Shakes his head, looks at her.)* Listen. I know you came all the way here, but I don't think this is the greatest time.

MARGE: On the phone, you said there are bad days.

MARTIN: I would say this appears to be one of them.

MARGE: The depression? It's also, the weather doesn't help much. It can do people in.

MARTIN: Maybe you should come back.

MARGE: Well, I'm here. And your brother . . . ?

MARTIN: Aaron?

MARGE: Was very insistent. Look. The Department is swamped. To get these appointments, and then to get someone to come to the house, it's tough. Why drag it on?

MARTIN: *(Resigned.)* Okay. *(Beat.)* He yells. He was always a bit of a yeller, but now—

MARGE: I am used to it. I don't—it doesn't scare me. But I have to call in. Is there a phone anywhere I can use?

MARTIN: The kitchen *(He points.)* Miss Hackett, I just want you to know—I think this whole business is a big mistake.

*(*ISAAC *enters.)*

MARGE: Noted. *(She exits.)*
MARTIN: She's calling her office. I'll leave you alone.

*(*ISAAC *says nothing.)*

MARTIN: Please don't stand here yelling at her. Would you? Don't do a number on her. *(Pause. No response.)* When she comes in, I'm going to leave you alone.
ISAAC: What? You think I need you to sit here in the room with me?

*(*MARTIN *nods, starts to exit.)*

ISAAC: Martin, how's my tie?

*(*MARGE *enters.)*

MARTIN: *(Adjusting* ISAAC*'s tie.)* It's fine. (Exits.)
MARGE: Your phone, it doesn't seem to be working, it's out.
ISAAC: The weather. But you found it?
MARGE: I did find it.
ISAAC: Because sometimes I misplace it. You see, it doesn't ring. *(Beat.)* Isaac Geldhart.
MARGE: Yes. Marge Hackett.
ISAAC: Listen to that. "It doesn't ring." Already that sounds like special pleading.
MARGE: Not necessarily.
ISAAC: Actually, to tell you the truth, what it is, is a *relief.* I spent so many years waiting for phones to ring, sitting about, so now . . .
MARGE: The silence is welcome. I understand.
ISAAC: Do we know each other? You look . . . no. Tell me, did the woman offer you a coffee?
MARGE: I didn't see anyone.
ISAAC: It's Tuesday.
MARGE: No. It's not Tuesday.
ISAAC: No, it's *Thursday.* She has a tendency not to show. Also, she ain't listed, so I'm fucked. *(Pause.)* Forgive me. I'm trying to be competent. That's the thing you need to know, is it not?
MARGE: Mr. Geldhart, nothing is being determined here.
ISAAC: Oh, forgive me, I was under the impression that something *was* being determined.

MARGE: No. This is a process. No one person can make a dispensation, come to a conclusion.

ISAAC: No one person? There's more of you to come? A tribunal?

MARGE: It's not that bad.

ISAAC: *(Looks at the disarray around.)* There is a mess. You should watch out, because there was asbestos across the park. I'm sure it drifted over. I try not to breathe, which is a hell of a trick. So.

MARGE: So. You understand, then, why I came here, what it is I'm doing here? I repeat—nothing is being determined by just one visit and—

ISAAC: *(Suddenly furious.)* They send a woman into my house to see if I'm a whacko, and nothing is being determined here? The—the—the paperwork that has come flying into this apartment from all the—

MARGE: Please, Mr. Geldhart, you have to, you don't have to—

ISAAC: Why the hell don't you just tell me exactly what I have to do?

MARTIN: *(In the doorway.)* Dad.

ISAAC: Oh, for God's sake, Martin, they sent over here a—look at this woman.

MARGE: *(To* MARTIN.*)* It's okay. Why don't you just leave us for a bit, see how it goes?

ISAAC: Maybe both of you should please just leave me alone. Do you think anyone wants to be seen like this? I mean, it's so fucking vulgar . . .

MARGE: *(To* MARTIN.*)* It's all right.

*(*MARTIN *looks at* ISAAC*, exits.)*

MARGE: We usually do this at the office. It took a bending of the rules to even get the department to think about letting someone come to the house.

ISAAC: I see. Well.

MARGE: Your son, Aaron, he wanted it not to be a nightmare for you.

ISAAC: How thoughtful, such a thoughtful boy, always has been.

MARGE: Our offices aren't so great. He saw that. He was very protective, and he's quite persuasive. So. Here I am.

ISAAC: Yes, you can imagine how grateful I am that I don't have to go to the Cloisters to see a shrink.

MARGE: Actually, we're not in the Cloisters. We're just around the corner, so to speak, across from Bellevue. *(Beat.)* Your son said you might be a little cranky.

ISAAC: A little cranky? Fuck him. That's Aaron's brilliant analysis of my situation, "a little bit cranky"?

MARGE: No, that was Martin. Aaron wasn't so mild.

ISAAC: Aaron. Do you know when last I saw him? Three and a half years ago! Three and a half years. Years!

MARGE: Do you know why I'm here, though? Aside from—

ISAAC: *(Cuts her off, savage.)* I don't give a shit. Three and a half years, I said, and every day I don't see him is a victory. And as for this one, a couple of times a year only, and only because he's weaker then the other two, and I'm not *that* hard. "A little cranky." Fuck them! You got any children, Miss Hackett?

MARGE: Yes, I have children, yeah. I do have children, and—

ISAAC: And do your children think you're crazy?

MARGE: Yes.

ISAAC: Do they really? Well then, Bob's your aunt, as the Brits like to say. So, how are things at Sotheby's?

MARGE: Sotheby?

ISAAC: What do you think of the collection?

MARGE: Pardon me? What are you talking about?

ISAAC: *(Pointing to some framed letters on the wall.)* The illustrated letters, those. Believe me, I've seen you eyeing 'em. You'll see, just like I said on the phone, the collection—I have one piece that's exquisitely ironic.

MARGE: I'm not from Sotheby. I'm from Social Services.

ISAAC: *(Letting that one go.)* I have here something that's not up on the walls . . . There was a filing system when—I used to have Miss Barzakian rummaging around in here doing alphabetical orders and such. The perfect job for a person who was never married. She had an Eastern European's passion for chaos. *(*ISAAC *takes a moment.)* Of course, what she is now is dead, of course. You know? And we had a link, let me tell you.

MARGE: What was that? *(Beat.)* Mr. Geldhart?

ISAAC: We were both refugees. New York, for some of us, for many, who got out of "that kind of Europe"—how do you explain such a link? We didn't come as husks. We came with some decent socks and some hand-made shoes. Our Europe. *(He stops, looks at her.)* But you are not interested in this, forgive me.

MARGE: No, it's interesting.

ISAAC: *(Overriding her with a small, sad smile.)* No, of course you're not. You came to look at the collection. Forgive me. My mind wanders, so they tell me.

MARGE: Are you toying with me, Mr. Geldhart?

ISAAC: I'm not toying with anyone, Miss Hackett, not at all.

MARGE: Do you mind if I smoke?

ISAAC: Nobody smokes anymore.

MARGE: Well, I do.

ISAAC: Yeah, me too. Must be nuts, eh? I'll join you.

MARGE: At the hospital, they don't permit it. Which seems a kind of one-upsmanship to me. Frankly, you know. Bash the smokers. Lord over 'em. Give it to 'em. And there are all these signs on the wall. Well, it's a hospital, so you can't complain. But they give you these looks. That's even if you step outside. They have this little quadrangle, and they won't even put a *bench* there.

ISAAC: *(He lights her cigarette.)* Uh huh? Yes, it that so? That's very interesting, uh . . .

MARGE: And they give you these little breaks. It's all highly regulated. But the very worst of it, the worst is—there are these women. These insufferable women in white nurses outfits—not even real R.N.'s—just volunteers who come in on the Long Island Railroad from *Merrick*. And they create these little *dramas*. My smoking. That constitutes a drama, so I guess life's lost its luster for them, huh? You should see 'em. They have their own refrigerator, and they put labels on cans of Tab. "Do not touch—Molly's Tab." "Debbie's Tuna." And you're forced into the position of acquiescing to them.

ISAAC: Excuse me, I'm sorry, but, do I make you nervous or something?

MARGE: Yes. Why?

ISAAC: I know your type. Divorced. New York State College at New Paltz. Tried to be "with it."

MARGE: If it makes you comfortable to create a little scenario for me, fine. Understand that your son Aaron has suggested competency proceedings be—

ISAAC: Please!

MARGE: Because you have demonstrated a credible inability to manage your own affairs.

ISAAC: And what makes you think you could do such a job? Do you have a formal means of determining levels of responsibility? Rational adult behavior? What? Does the Mayor and Cardinal what's-his-name get together? What? The Skinner people, the Sullivan people? Dewey-Decimal? At least in the *library* world . . . *(*ISAAC *halts.)* No. I can't take this seriously. No.

MARGE: No. Well, neither does your son Martin.

ISAAC: Ah, the Neville Chamberlain of sons.

MARGE: Well, the fact is, we were called upon. It is to be taken seriously.

ISAAC: Did the woman give you a coffee?

MARGE: And you agreed. You said. "Yes." An evaluation was acceptable to you if it would result in your being left alone. Nobody wants to come into somebody's life and—

ISAAC: You are speaking to me as if I were someone to whom logic was a worthwhile approach. If I am ga-ga, logic means nothing, right?

MARGE: Well, I'm new. Maybe with a little experience, I'll begin treating people badly. Look, I really, all I have to do is ask you some questions. *(She stares at* ISAAC.*)* We can get it over with. And—it's not as if what I say can determine your fate. If that's what you're afraid of . . .

ISAAC: What a relief. Okay, shoot.

MARGE: What country, state, city are we in right now?

ISAAC: Are you kidding me? What kind of question is that?

MARGE: It's a perfectly reasonable question.

ISAAC: Next.

MARGE: What month is it?

ISAAC: July, can't you tell?

MARGE: Mr. Geldhart, look.

ISAAC: Okay. There is a book company. It has my name on it. And some forty percent of it still belongs to me. Some Japanese own the rest, along with Aaron, who has helped them grind it down into a kind of bankrupt dust. *(Beat.)* So, you see, I've been trying to put together a package. I still know a little money in this town, and at the same time, my son also wouldn't mind eighty-sixing the Nips, and he thought if he could get me out of the picture, maybe he could use my forty as leverage. This is what we've got here.

MARGE: You're saying your son is doing all this just to get your stock?

ISAAC: Yes, so. You are a dupe, sweetie. Now, I've got coffee cake, linzer torte, and sacher torte. You want some?

(Nobody says anything for a moment.)

MARGE: Aaron tells me you spent $43,000 on hand-cut suits. What made you think you needed them?

ISAAC: I thought it was going to be a busy year.

MARGE: He says you hardly ever leave this apartment. Is that true?

ISAAC: It was *not* a busy year.

MARGE: And that you've cast off all your friends, you've disengaged.

ISAAC: What? I need to have friends?

MARGE: And the credit card bills?

ISAAC: Staggering! Guilty.

MARGE: You're living on—I mean—I don't understand. What did you think would happen to you when it was all gone?

ISAAC: *(With exaggerated good cheer.)* Who cares?

MARGE: You were diagnosed last year as chronically depressed. You've been on Elavil three times a day.

ISAAC: I stopped taking it. I could not read. *That* I will not accept! *(Suddenly bright.)* Let me show you the collection. Enough of this, right? You said on the phone that you are a fan of Herzen? Well, I have the first English edition of *Childhood, Youth & Exile.* London. 1921. *(He hands her the Herzen.)* How many can there be of that? A private printing of *Pilgrim's Progress*, 1898. All this shelf, Private Press stuff—Coleridge was here, sold it to Bertie Rota in London. Wordsworth here. *(He picks up a catalog.)* See? The Geldhart Collection. Look at the prices. That's what you get in London where there's still a market, but here . . . Jack London, and Conrad here. And of course, I still got the *Illustrated Letters*. I only sold a couple, to make the Visa people happy. They were getting shrill. *(He sits next to her on the sofa, with the* Illustrated Letters *file on the coffee table.)*

MARGE: And this is what you love? Books.

ISAAC: Yes. Funny.

MARGE: What? What is it? Did I say something? I—

(She smiles. He is amused.)

ISAAC: No, you had this marvelous tone. This anti-intellectual tone one comes across. So. You hate books.
MARGE: Not at all.
ISAAC: *(Opening the folder.)* There was a time when people used to revel in words. In stories. A kind of perfection, in the air about you, at all times. And people, of course, they used to write. To each other. And how marvelous to accompany the letter with a drawing. A gesture of love— *(Pause.)* Thackeray. Look at it. He bombarded friends with letters. Look at the sketches. He used to illustrate his own novels!
MARGE: It's lovely.
ISAAC: Max Beerbohm. Look at this. George Grosz. Here is, from Max Beckmann, a little note, a sketch. (They chased him out, he ended up dead in the States. A teacher.)
MARGE: Oh!
ISAAC: Osip Mandlestam to his wife. Isaac Babel to his. Orwell from Spain. You begin to see such a bloodthirsty century . . . but aren't they all? Maybe. Maybe, I don't know. *(He looks at her sharply.)* Mind you—it's understood from the get-go, you take the entire collection. I can't bear to think of it's being split up, divvied up all over town—it's to be sold as a piece or nothing, got it?!
MARGE: *(After a moment.)* It's a lovely collection.
ISAAC: You like it?
MARGE: Very much.
ISAAC: *(Clear and quiet and bitter.)* Yeah? Well, me too.
MARGE: I'm sorry.
ISAAC: What?
MARGE: Listen, Mr. Geldhart. I'm going to have someone else do this.
ISAAC: What?
MARGE: I'm sorry. Someone will call from my office. I'm not the one to do this. I hate this. I can't do this.
ISAAC: What? Please, what did I say? Look at the rest of the work, would you?
MARGE: *(Rushing to leave.)* I'm not from Sotheby, and I shouldn't be here. Good-bye, Mr. Geldhart.
ISAAC: I have a letter from Adolf Hilter . . .

(MARGE stops walking.)

ISAAC: A postcard actually on which he painted a little watercolor of a burnt-out church. Bought his art supplies from a Jew. Who thought he had talent. And gave him, just gave him his materials. I mean, I think about that, and what came after . . . It's the most crucial part of my collection.

*(*ISAAC *shows the card to* MARGE.*)*

ISAAC: He was not without a certain basic, rudimentary talent, was he not? You would certainly hope that he had been utterly devoid of talent. I mean, it would at least shed some tiny glimmer of light on the subsequent years, on all that came after. But no—it's no slur of muddy-non-color, this. There is something here, yes?

MARGE: I suppose.

ISAAC: It's never actually been appraised, which is why I called your firm.

MARGE: Do you really think I'm from an auction house, Mr. Geldhart?

ISAAC: *(After a moment.)* I have problems.

MARGE: Yes.

ISAAC: Oh, I know I'm getting it wrong a lot of the time. I used to think it was the fog from the pills they gave me, but when I stopped taking the pills . . . the fog will not lift. But to simply stand about, helpless. That is not acceptable to me. I am not used to it. I find my dream life so much more interesting, given my current waking one. *(Beat.)* It's getting dark. So early. Every year a little earlier. Have you ever been out into this park?

MARGE: A few times. When my husband was alive.

ISAAC: Oh. I see. *(Beat.)* Sorry.

MARGE: We had friends who lived across the park. They used to promenade us there, yeah. Fine, it's a nice park, but, the idea of a key bugs me. It's just a *park,* for God's sake.

ISAAC: Capitalism at its worst?

MARGE: Just small-minded. I wasn't looking at the politics of the thing. *(She moves towards the door, to leave.)*

ISAAC: I've always hated this park. You need a key to get in it. And there's never anyone there.

MARGE: I was there once before.

ISAAC: What? What was that?

MARGE: 1974. During the crisis. The city crisis, when New York was broke, I was here, in this apartment.

ISAAC: You were in my house before? In this apartment?

MARGE: At work, there are these gruesome meetings, at which they assign all the cases. And I recognized your name.

ISAAC: So we *have* met before?

MARGE: You must have had a lot going on in those days. Yes. And I recognized your name from the caseload, and I didn't say anything. This room is the same. It's not as clean, it's not what it was, but the same.

ISAAC: Forgive me, but I'm lost, I knew I recognized you, but I can't place it, and anyhow, most often, when I think I know someone, I'm wrong. You were here before?

MARGE: There was a reading. Some essayist you published, it was a fundraiser for the library. Because the books were literally rotting, and nobody worked there, and there—

ISAAC: They didn't have a single copy of Joyce's *Exiles.* I went in and exploded.

MARGE: So it *was* a fundraiser.

ISAAC: It was horrible.

MARGE: My husband liked those kinds of things. Mainly for the food. I remember one thing in particular. You didn't have rumaki, which was standard fare for those things, and for that little bit, I was grateful.

*(*ISAAC *pours a drink, offers it to* MARGE. *She refuses.)*

ISAAC: It *was* a reading. Clayton Broomer, prick of a guy from the *New Yorker*—wrote about architecture. I couldn't stand him, but my wife made me publish his books. He shrilled at everyone in 'em, about how the city got so ugly. Boy, did I hate those things.

MARGE: Me too.

ISAAC: So. Different time, this, eh? Different time.

MARGE: *(Tentative.)* And we talked.

ISAAC: We talked?

MARGE: We stood in the kitchen. And you were intensely annoyed with your wife.

ISAAC: She had a touch of the flag-waver about her.

MARGE: *(Remembering.)* We stood in your kitchen, you and I, drinking vodka and smoking. I remember hearing my husband laughing and making some sort of deal in this room. We'd just watched him rip off a whole plate of Gravad lox from the waitress, and devour it. You were very insulting. You said he had a voice like something from an animal act on public television. I might have been hurt, but we were enjoying the vodka . . .

ISAAC: Your husband. Tell me, who is this? You sound . . . ?

MARGE: Bitter? Yeah, well . . . *(Pause.)* My husband was Adrian Harrold.

ISAAC: *(Nods, getting it.)* Oh, I see. Jesus Christ. And now you work for social services, shlepping around town with a little briefcase? Adrian Harrold. I remember your husband. The Manhattan Borough President. And in the end, made off with a couple of million, didn't he?

MARGE: The last editorial in the *Times* said, "Drinking from the public trough like a maddened pig . . ."

ISAAC: Please, I really, this is not. I did not . . .

MARGE: Do you know how they found him? My husband? On the road to Montauk. Actually, at the end of the road. God knows what he was doing. In February out there, by the lighthouse. He had a Biedermeier table in the back of his Lincoln. His wrists and ankles slashed and a bottle of pills on the floor. And then, for weeks afterwards, the funny part, these women would show up with outrageous claims. *(Beat.)* Good for a laugh, at least.

ISAAC: I'm sorry. I am.

MARGE: My husband lied from morning till night, and they knew everything. The Mayor. All of them. The only one, really, who knew nothing was, in fact, me.

ISAAC: So, your husband, he left you, what? Nothing?

MARGE: No. He left nothing. I mean, he had his hands in the till. And to me, this is funny—he never shared. It was all for him. *(She looks at him.)* I expected to find a drooler. I thought I'd come over here and find a drooler who had had it easy in the old days.

ISAAC: No, unfortunately, I'm not a drooler. So, you came not for an "evaluation," you came 'cause you were curious.

MARGE: Yes.

ISAAC: You came to gloat. You came to see a "drooler."

MARGE: *(Ashamed, perhaps.)* Maybe.

ISAAC: But this is pathetic. It's like nostalgia for a car wreck. So, terrific, you're just another hustler with an agenda.

MARGE: You could say that.

ISAAC: So, what it is is you get a kick out of seeing someone from the old days? And maybe even taking him down? That's a lot of power for the wife of a prick with sticky fingers.

MARGE: Yes.

ISAAC: Well, that's New York. I mean, that's the ultimate. Wonderful. Let me tell you. I came from the worst place. People turning one another in for a hustle, for a piece of ass, for a piece of black bread, whatever. You get it, sweetie? I mean, if they thought you were a Jew, or not. *Or not.* If they were just pissed off at you 'cause you slighted them. But, this city wins on points. You got me? This city wins on points. Because you had a hard-on to see a crony of your crooked husband? Because you were a little lonely, a little weepy for the old days? You come here, raising the lefty flag—you self-righteous, social-worker-tootsie. Tell me, are you going to put in your report to social services that you came her for a vodka and a flirt fifteen fucking years ago? You're going to tell them that at social services? Hey, let me tell you something, *that* was my wife who did the fundraisers. She dragged every downtrodden threadbare cause into this house, from the Panthers on. And now I should pay 'cause you're bitter? *(Pause.)* Please go home and tell them, go home to your little Smith-Corona and type up, "He's got delusions of persecution, and he's probably gonna end up like Schwartz, dead."

MARGE: Who? End up like . . . ?

ISAAC: Delmore Schwartz. He said, "Even paranoids have enemies." He used to come here for dinner before he died in the hallway of his hotel. So arbeit does indeed macht frei, huh?

MARGE: I made a horrible mistake.

ISAAC: What in the world could you possibly think I had to do with your husband? It seems positively lunatic to me. Revenge! My God! You came for revenge!

MARGE: What about you? You don't know anything about revenge?

ISAAC: What are you talking about? What do you mean?

MARGE: Your children! "Every day I don't see him is a victory!" "The Neville Chamberlain of sons!" "Fuck them." You could tell me a whole hell of a lot about revenge, Mr. Geldhart.

ISAAC: Revenge I know.

MARGE: Seems to me revenge is the only thing keeping you alive. I don't walk around Manhattan with a grudge. I don't walk around this city thinking of revenge. It just wells up.

ISAAC: That I understand.

MARGE: But I get out of bed, as bad as it gets. I'm not saying I don't have days where I don't get out of bed. I think I spent most of '88 staring up at my ceiling. But I try, I put one foot in front of the other and—most of the time I don't even know why. I just do it. I just do it. Well, I've got to go.

ISAAC: Miss Hackett, may I ask you to have dinner with me?

MARGE: What are you talking about? You want to have dinner? You kicked me out a minute ago, or don't you remember?

ISAAC: I am a forgiving man.

MARGE: What, you want to sit somewhere? You want to go somewhere and sit at a table?

ISAAC: I think it would be very nice, very good, were we to have dinner.

MARGE: No. That would be crossing a line.

ISAAC: They wouldn't know.

MARGE: I'd get canned. No, worse. I'd have a "letter" put in my personal file.

ISAAC: Listen, they don't follow you around. They wouldn't know. What's the big deal? I still have my Diner's Club Card that hasn't been shredded. Gramercy Park has become decent, restaurant-wise. Food is better now than when we were young. No more sauerbraten and schnitzel. You see, there was a time, emigration let some Italians in in the '70s—they brought with them significant secrets.

MARGE: I don't think so.

ISAAC: I would say that professionalism has already been blown.

MARGE: Nevertheless. We just can't have dinner. I can't start doing this sort of thing, I just can't.

ISAAC: Late in the game for romance?

MARGE: Romance is not even a consideration.

ISAAC: Out of your vocabulary? Well, too bad. Maybe you've had all the human traffic a person can bear.

MARGE: Maybe I have. I look at you and it doesn't look so great for you either.

ISAAC: Tell me, then, what chance do you think you have in this world? I am curious?

MARGE: What do you mean, "chance"?

ISAAC: Yes. "Chance." Exactly. What're you going to do? Wait for a better deal?

MARGE: I'm not waiting for anything. In the last five years I put myself through school and got this job, which, admittedly is not what I imagined, but still. What have you *done*, lately? I had to drive out to Long Island with a suit for my husband, because he was wearing jogging pants and a Drexel Burnham T-shirt when they found him. *(Pause.)* What chance do I have? Fuck you. Man, I hope I don't look fragile or give the impression that I'm on some sort of widow's walk. I have a son who knows his father ripped off everything in this city that wasn't nailed down! I watched my husband on news at five, *weeping*. Chance? What chance do I have? Because I won't have dinner with you? *(Beat.)* Do you know how much I hate having dinner by myself night after night? Well, I'd rather do that, let me assure you, than have dinner with you and compare bad-break notes.

ISAAC: Why? Afraid you're going to see yourself in me? Is that it?

MARGE: We are nothing alike. Whatever has happened to you, you've done to yourself. You had everything and you threw it away.

ISAAC: I threw nothing away.

MARGE: Then this is how you thought your life would go?

ISAAC: You can't even imagine. You have no idea. This is not how I saw my life turn out. But surprised I am not, Miss Hackett. I did this to myself? You don't see any other survivors in your files, do you? You don't see any brothers and sisters? Betrayal? I never even smelt it coming until the fucking *maid* turned us in. The *maid*. She was like my mother, and let me tell you—I don't have self-pity! You don't see a tattoo on my wrist, do you? But they got my grandparents, they got my mother and father, and they got . . . I came here to make a family and they trashed it, they got it.

MARGE: I am sorry. But really, I am going to leave.

ISAAC: Listen to me. You came here with an agenda, but now at least listen to what was taken away from me. *(Pause.)* I loved my children. I sure don't love them now. You walk into this house . . . *(He points to a table.)* Aaron cut his head on the tip of that table and I carried him to NYU Hospital when he was two. *(Beat.)* Sarah got laid for the first time in this house, and I thought I was quite literally going to die. *(Beat.)* My wife found this sofa in Kingston and we had it carted down and we sat on it, and it was the most perfect . . . my wife . . . my wife . . . my wife. *(Beat.)* My Martin. He comes in here from Lacrosse when he was sixteen, sneezing, and the next thing, he was, just like that—no blood count at all. *(Beat.)* I sleep now in the living room, because the bedrooms are too much to bear. *(Beat.)* I am so stupid, Miss Hackett, I thought that if I published Hazlitt and Svevo. I'd be spared. The silence, Miss Hackett. The silence. Pointless.

MARGE: *(Thinks before speaking.)* I could never bear to play on my husband's connections. There were people who actually liked him, held a degree of sympathy for him. Because, mainly, he kept quiet. He had a thief's honor. I am owed favors. The way these things work. Because there are people in this town who actually think my husband *told* me things. Which is rich. *(Beat.)* But. I can make a call. I can call a judge. And they'll just drop it. Like that. And believe me, there'd be nothing your son can do.

ISAAC: Wouldn't that make you just like your husband?

MARGE: No—that's too damn tough, that's just too hard. We're just flesh and blood here. That's all we are. *(Beat.)* Hey, I'm offering you a good hand. What are you gonna do? Wait for a "better deal"? There are so few breaks.

ISAAC: *(After a moment.)* There are, that's true. *(Beat.)* Perhaps you're right. *(Tired.)* I *would* like a break.

MARGE: Then it'll be over.

ISAAC: Over? That would be lovely, if it were over. *(He picks up the postcard.)* Look at this thing. The man fancied himself a serious artist. Lugging his little brushes about Vienna, God knows. Scraggly hair, greasy. Look at it. Look at the sky. When you pick it up, to think of where it's been . . . what the day was like when he made it. *(Lost for an instant, soft.)* All the things to come. So much to come.

MARGE: It's just a lousy postcard. My husband had Post-it notes all over the place, and I didn't save them.

ISAAC: *(Looking at her with a great, sudden affection.)* Goddamn it, it's a pity I could not persuade you to dine with me. I can be amusing. Especially when I take the antidepressants they prescribe. Then I am at my best. Restaurants are so hard to bear alone.

MARGE: You do not have to eat alone. *(She looks at him for a moment. And turns to exit.)*

ISAAC: Miss Hackett? Thank you. Maybe, when the time is more appropriate . . . maybe when the weather turns kinder, we *could* have dinner.

MARGE: That . . . would be nice, Isaac. Good night. *(She exits.)*

*(*ISAAC *picks up postcard, and then, sets it alight. Placing it in an ashtray, he sits looking at it. Snow streams down. The card burns. After a moment,* MARTIN *enters.)*

MARTIN: She left.

ISAAC: She left. Yes. She's gone, she went.

MARTIN: What is that? What are you doing?

ISAAC: Nothing.

(Beat.)

MARTIN: How was it?

ISAAC: Well, you can relax for a while. You won't have to write my checks and listen to complaints of the cook and make sure that my underwear is changed for a little while yet.

MARTIN: Of course not. I know that.

ISAAC: So you can relax, you're free.

MARTIN: Well I wouldn't mind. I'd do it.

ISAAC: You would. Yes, you would. Why wouldn't you mind, Martin? I don't understand . . . why you wouldn't mind after this . . . ?

MARTIN: Because I am not, unfortunately, as strong as you.

ISAAC: What does that mean? Martin? Please? What?

MARTIN: I don't know. I don't have it in me to do this thing that you do: resolving to write people off, to write it all off. I don't. Believe me, I've tried.

ISAAC: And now what're you—you're going back upstate?

MARTIN: There's a train in forty minutes, yeah. But they're all backed up. So, it's good that it worked out with the . . . Look, you call if you want anything. I'll be up there tonight.

(Silence.)

ISAAC: Maybe I'll walk outside with you a bit. It's so lovely with the snow. Do you want to walk through the park?
MARTIN: Sure.
ISAAC: I need to find the key to the park. Let me find the key.
MARTIN: Wait. I've still got mine.

*(*MARTIN *puts on his coat, hands* ISAAC *his. They walk out to the hall.* MARTIN *turns off the light.)*

SIGHT UNSEEN

by
Donald Margulies

Donald Margulies comments:

Our childhoods are inescapable. No matter how far we travel or what we learn as we venture into the world, we are still our parents' children, the products of instilled values and language and cultural concerns. Most of our journey through life is a series of dramas in which we grapple with the legacy of our upbringing. It is a legacy that lives with us every day, that affects our attitudes toward love and work and politics. Our struggle is to make sense of that legacy, to forgive it, even to honor it—or, to reject it entirely.

In this respect, I am a playwright who unapologetically writes what he knows. I am a lower-middle-class, urban American Jew who grew up in the double shadow of the Depression and the Holocaust. My parents weren't themselves survivors of Hitler (they were scarred differently, by economic deprivation) and yet these two enormous events, which preceded my birth by several years, seemed to move in and take uneasy residence with us. They helped shape in me that which is known as a Jewish sensibility.

However, I don't see myself as a Jewish playwright but rather as a playwright who is Jewish. I bristle when ethnicity is used as an adjective. It diminishes the work and seems to suggest that writing what one knows is tantamount to cheating. If one writes about his people honestly and unflinchingly, he is writing about all people.

I try to tell the truth.

Sight Unseen was commissioned and originally produced in 1991 by South Coast Repertory, Costa Mesa, California. It opened in New York at the Manhattan Theatre Club on January 7, 1992, staged by Michael Bloom, its original director, and with the following cast:

JONATHAN WAXMAN	*Dennis Boutsikaris*
NICK	*Jon De Vries*
PATRICIA	*Deborah Hedwall*
GRETE	*Laura Linney*

Setting by JAMES YOUMANS
Costumes by JESS GOLDSTEIN
Lights by DONALD HOLDER

CHARACTERS

JONATHAN, 35–40
PATRICIA, 35–40
NICK, 40s
GRETE, 25–30

JONATHAN and PATRICIA are American, NICK is English. GRETE is German; her English is excellent, if accented. JONATHAN has maintained his working-class Brooklyn accent; NICK's rural, working-class speech finds its way into his university accent, particularly when he's been drinking; and PATRICIA's dialect suggests that of an expatriate New Yorker living in England.

SYNOPSIS OF SCENES

ACT I

1. A cold farmhouse in Norfolk, England. The present.
2. An art gallery in London. Four days later.
3. The farmhouse. An hour before the start of Scene 1.
4. A bedroom in Brooklyn. Fifteen years earlier.

ACT II

5. The farmhouse. A few hours after the end of Scene 1.
6. The art gallery. Continued from the end of Scene 2.
7. The farmhouse. A few hours after the end of Scene 5.
8. A painting studio in an art college. New York State. Seventeen years earlier.

A turntable should ideally be used to ensure quick transitions between the four discrete settings.

ACT I

Scene 1

Lights up: The kitchen of a cold farmhouse in England. Dusk. JONATHAN, *an overnight bag on his shoulder, stands at the open door.* NICK *is eating a hard roll.*

JONATHAN: You must be Nick.
NICK: Mm.
JONATHAN: Jonathan Waxman.

(He extends his hand. NICK *doesn't shake it but takes a bite of his roll instead.)*

JONATHAN: Is Patricia . . . ?

(NICK *shakes his head.)*

JONATHAN: Oh. You *were* expecting me?
NICK: Mm.
JONATHAN: *(Meaning, "Where is . . . ?")*: Patricia . . . ?
NICK: A lamb roast.
JONATHAN: Ah. Well! Nick! Nice to meet you.

(NICK *says nothing. A beat.)*

JONATHAN: I left the car right outside. That all right?

(NICK *looks out the door, shrugs.)*

JONATHAN: 'Cause I'll move it.
NICK: No no.

(A beat.)

JONATHAN: Uh, I think I'm kind of freezing. You mind if I—

(NICK *gestures for him to come in.*)

JONATHAN: Thanks. *(A beat.)* I made really good time, by the way. Left London 'round one; not bad, huh?

(NICK *shrugs. A beat.*)

JONATHAN: Her directions were really good Patricia. *(A beat.)* Boy, this driving on the wrong side of the road stuff —Ever drive in America?

(NICK *shakes his head again.*)

JONATHAN: Uh huh, well it's *weird* cars coming at you like that. A simple thing like the way you perceive the flow of traffic, the way you're used to seeing, gets challenged here, it all gets inverted. You've got to keep reminding yourself, over and over, remember what side of the road you're on. 'Cause all you need's to zone out for one second on the M4 and that's it, you're fuckin' wrapped in twisted metal.

(NICK *just looks at him. A beat.*)

JONATHAN: Will she be long Patricia?
NICK: God, I hope not.
JONATHAN: Oh, I'm sorry, am I interrupting something?
NICK: *(Gestures to a room.)* Well . . .
JONATHAN: Please. Do what you have to do. I want to hear all about your work, though.
NICK: Hm?
JONATHAN: Your work. I really want to hear about it.
NICK: Oh.
JONATHAN: Archeology's one of those things I've always found fascinating, but I don't know much about it.
NICK: Well, I . . .
JONATHAN: Not now. Whenever. Over dinner. I brought you some good wine; we should drink it. *(Takes out bottles of wine.)* Maybe later I'll get you to show me the dig you're working on.

NICK: Uh . . .

JONATHAN: No, really, I'd like to see it. Hey, I know how obnoxious it is when people say they want to see my studio and then I show them and they're not really into it?, all they're thinking about is *after,* telling their friends they were there? No, I mean it, I'd really love to see it.

NICK: It's . . . It's rather dull.

JONATHAN: I'm sure it isn't. What are you working on right now?

NICK: *(A beat.)* A Roman latrine.

(A beat. PATRICIA *enters wearing a bulky sweater and carrying a bag bursting with groceries.)*

PATRICIA: Well! You're here!

JONATHAN: *(Over "You're here.")* Hi. Yeah.

(She moves around the room, unpacks groceries, prepares dinner.)

PATRICIA: Fancy car.

JONATHAN: Rented. *You* know. What the hell.

PATRICIA: Must be fun whipping round these country roads in a thing like that.

JONATHAN: Yeah, as a matter of fact I was just telling Nick . . .

NICK: Um . . .

PATRICIA: What.

*(*NICK *gestures to his office.)*

PATRICIA: Go.

(He hesitates, goes. A beat.)

PATRICIA: He has work.

*(*JONATHAN *nods. A beat.)*

PATRICIA: So. Arrived in one piece I see.

JONATHAN: Your directions . . .

PATRICIA: What.

JONATHAN: Excellent. Just terrific.

PATRICIA: Oh, good. I'm glad you liked them.
JONATHAN: Great spot.
PATRICIA: Yeah? Looks like a lot of mud most of the time.

(Pause.)

JONATHAN: Good to see you, Patty.
PATRICIA: Is it? Well, good.

(Pause.)

JONATHAN: So you got a lamb roast?
PATRICIA: Ground veal, actually. It was on special. I've become quite a resourceful little cook over here, you know.

*(*NICK *returns, gets a bottle of Scotch, gestures offstage, exits.)*

PATRICIA: Nick is painfully shy. Was he shy with you?
JONATHAN: *(Lying.)* Nick? No. *(A beat.)* So you've become a good cook you said?
PATRICIA: I didn't say good, I said resourceful. No one's a good cook here, so no one notices. Stews are the answer, I've discovered. The meat quality is so awful, you stew the stuff for hours till it all falls apart and it's unrecognizable as meat. Bet you can't wait for dinner, hm?

(She puts on water for tea, etc.)

JONATHAN: Mmm. Can I help with anything?
PATRICIA: *(Over "with anything.")* No. Sit. Pretend you're comfortable. Take off your coat.
JONATHAN: *(Meaning the cold.)* No, I'll keep it if you don't mind . . .
PATRICIA: It's so funny having Americans visit, watching their teeth chatter.
JONATHAN: I think it's warmer out*side.*
PATRICIA: Probably. You get used to the cold and the damp, strangely enough. You get used to anything.
JONATHAN: You've kept your accent.
PATRICIA: For the most part. You'll notice little things here and there.

JONATHAN: It struck me on the phone; I thought by now you'd sound totally . . .

PATRICIA: I don't know, I like sounding American. It works to my advantage, really. You have no idea how hard it is being a woman running an excavation.

JONATHAN: I'll bet.

PATRICIA: The sexism here . . . If you think the *States* are bad . . . Being an *American* woman gives me license to be rude, aggressive, demanding. It comes in handy.

JONATHAN: Don't you ever miss it?

PATRICIA: What?

JONATHAN: Home.

PATRICIA: This is my home.

JONATHAN: What, you don't miss Disneyland, or the Grand Canyon, or Zabar's?

PATRICIA: No.

JONATHAN: You don't miss Zabar's? Now I know you're full of it.

PATRICIA: I don't. I don't get choked up when I see the flag, or Woody Allen movies. I've stopped reading about politics. Reagan, Bush, they're interchangeable. No, I prefer my bones and coins and petrified cherry pits.

JONATHAN: You must miss *something*. Insulated housing, *something*.

PATRICIA: No. I'm an expatriate now.

JONATHAN: An expatriate.

PATRICIA: Yes.

JONATHAN: Gee, I've never known an expatriate before, someone who could just turn their back . . .

PATRICIA: On what. I've turned my back on what? America? VCRs and microwaves? If that's what I've "turned my back on . . ." We work hard here. It's not like the States. Everything is a struggle. It shows on our faces, on our hands. I haven't bought myself new clothes in years. We have to save for everything. The electric fire started smoking?

JONATHAN: Yeah . . . ?

PATRICIA: It'll be weeks before we can buy a new one. Everything's a struggle. The weather is hard. Leisure is hard. Sleep is hard.

JONATHAN: Do you ever think about leaving?

PATRICIA: God! What have I been saying! I like it!

JONATHAN: Oh.

PATRICIA: You're just like my mother! I *like* it here! I *like* the struggle! I *like* surviving obstacles. Hell, I survived *you*, didn't I.

(He reaches for her hand, she pulls away. Pause.)

PATRICIA: Who are you to talk about turning one's back?
JONATHAN: What do you mean?
PATRICIA: You with your shiksa wife in Vermont.
JONATHAN: Upstate.
PATRICIA: Whatever.
JONATHAN: I don't understand. What does my wife have to do . . .
PATRICIA: *(Over "have to do.")* You're an expatriate, too, and you don't even know it.
JONATHAN: How?
PATRICIA: You made a choice. When you married your wife, you married her world. Didn't you? You can't exist in two worlds; you've got to turn your back on one of them.
JONATHAN: I hadn't thought of it like that.
PATRICIA: See? We're more alike than you thought. *(Pause.)* God, when I think of all the angst, all the, what's the word?, "cirrus"?
JONATHAN: *Tsuris.*
PATRICIA: After all the tsuris our young souls went through . . . Your wife should thank me.
JONATHAN: You're right; she should.
PATRICIA: I laid the groundwork. I was the pioneer.
JONATHAN: Yeah.
PATRICIA: The sacrificial shiksa.
JONATHAN: You're looking beautiful, Patty.
PATRICIA: Stop.
JONATHAN: You are.
PATRICIA: I look fat.
JONATHAN: No.
PATRICIA: All the meat and potatoes, and nights at the pub. Don't look at me. I'm afraid this place is perfect for women like me, who've let themselves go.
JONATHAN: You haven't.
PATRICIA: We can blend right in with the mud.
JONATHAN: You look beautiful.
PATRICIA: And *you* look rich.
JONATHAN: I don't even. I'm the same old Jonathan.

PATRICIA: Don't be coy. You're rich and famous. How does it feel to be rich and famous?

JONATHAN: It's meaningless. Really.

PATRICIA: Oh, yeah, right.

JONATHAN: No, the whole scene is meaningless bullshit. You know that. It's all timing and luck.

PATRICIA: Timing and luck.

JONATHAN: Yeah. The party's over for me already; I'm not making now what I made two years ago.

PATRICIA: But you still have your millions to keep you company.

JONATHAN: The numbers don't mean anything. I mean, I'm not crying poverty or anything . . .

PATRICIA: Oh! Well!

JONATHAN: My gallery takes fifty percent. Okay? Remember that. Fifty. And then the government on top of that . . .

PATRICIA: Don't you think you're protesting just a little too much?

JONATHAN: Okay, so maybe I've enjoyed a little recognition—

PATRICIA: "A little recognition"?! Jonathan! You're "it"—

JONATHAN: No, no, not anymore.

PATRICIA: *(Continuous.)* —the cat's pajamas. You can't fool me. I read all about you in the *Times.*

JONATHAN: The *New York Times*? You read the *New York Times*? Hypocrite. You were just telling me how you . . .

PATRICIA: *(Over "telling me how you.")* My mother sent it to me.

JONATHAN: You talking about the Sunday magazine piece? Couple of years ago?

PATRICIA: "Jonathan Waxman: The Art Scene's New Visionary."

JONATHAN: Oh, please . . .

PATRICIA: *(Laughs.)* Is that what it was? "New Visionary"?

JONATHAN: "Bad Boy or Visionary?"

PATRICIA: "Bad Boy or Visionary," excuse me.

JONATHAN: What do you want from me?

PATRICIA: Cover story and everything. Wow, Jonathan, how'd you manage that? I was quite impressed. You on the cover, the very model of messy, Jewish intensity.

JONATHAN: They shot me in my studio. That's how I look when I'm working.

PATRICIA: I know how you look when you're working.

(They look at one another. Pause.)

PATRICIA: My mother's always sending me clippings about you.

JONATHAN: Oh, yeah? Why?

PATRICIA: I don't know, I'd say she's trying to tell me something, wouldn't you? The *Vanity Fair* piece was fun. "Charlatan or Genius?"

JONATHAN: I don't believe this.

PATRICIA: Every time she sends me something, I take it as some sort of indictment, some sort of accusation: *"See what you could've had? See what could've been yours if you weren't so crazy?"*

JONATHAN: Is that what *you* think or is that what *she* thinks?

PATRICIA: Me? No. *(Pause.)* So tell me about your show. How's it going in London? *(That English inflection slips in.)* Is it going well?

JONATHAN: Yeah. Pretty much. Oh, I brought you a catalog. *(Hands her one from his bag.)*

PATRICIA: Hefty.

JONATHAN: There are a couple of gaps I'm not too happy about. Particularly in the early stuff. It's supposed to be a retrospective.

PATRICIA: A retrospective? At your age?

JONATHAN: Are you kidding? I'm almost passé.

PATRICIA: You know, I still have that very first painting you did of me, remember?

JONATHAN: Of course I remember. Where is it?

PATRICIA: Over the mantel. Go and see.

JONATHAN: No shit. You didn't just haul it out of the attic, knowing I was coming?

PATRICIA: There is no attic. And, no, Jonathan, I wouldn't do anything at this point to feed your ego.

(He goes to the doorway leading to the living room and sees his painting; it's like seeing a ghost. She watches him in silence while he looks at the painting.)

JONATHAN: Jesus. Look at this. I can't believe you saved it. How old could I have been: Twenty-two tops?

(She nods; a beat.)

JONATHAN: You know? It's not bad. I threw out most of my student work years ago. I couldn't stand looking at anything. But this, this one's different. It's really not bad.

PATRICIA: When do you open?

JONATHAN: What? Oh. Tuesday. *(Re the painting.)* Look at that: see what I was doing with the picture plane?, how it's sort of tipped? I didn't think I started doing that till like much later.

PATRICIA: Nervous?

JONATHAN: No. I don't know. What can I do? It's my first solo show outside of North America, okay?, my European debut.

PATRICIA: Yeah . . . ?

JONATHAN: So the critics are salivating, I'm sure. Ready to chomp into me like their next Big Mac.

PATRICIA: And what if they do?

JONATHAN: I don't know, I can't worry about it. Press is press. Good or bad. My father, God!, my father *loved* seeing my name in print.

PATRICIA: Oh, yeah?

JONATHAN: *My* last name, after all, was *his* last name. Got such a kick out of it. Eight pages in the Sunday *Times*. He couldn't believe the *New York Times* could possibly have that much to say about *his* kid. "All these words," he said, "are about *you*? What is there to say about *you*?"

(She laughs.)

JONATHAN: He was serious; he wasn't just teasing. Oh, he was teasing, too, but it threatened him. No, it did. It pointed up the fact that he could be my father and still not know a thing about me. Not have a clue. What did the fancy-schmancy art world see that he didn't? What were those big dirty paintings about, anyway? So then when all the hype started . . .

PATRICIA: "New visionary"?

JONATHAN: Yeah, and that's very seductive in the beginning, I got to admit. Vindicating, even: "Ah ha! See? I *am* a genius. *Now* maybe my father will respect me." But it had the opposite effect on him. It didn't make him proud. It bewildered him. It alienated him. How could *he* have produced a "visionary"? It shamed him somehow. I can't explain.

PATRICIA: How's he doing?
JONATHAN: Oh. Didn't I tell you on the phone?
PATRICIA: What.
JONATHAN: He died.
PATRICIA: Oh, no.
JONATHAN: Right before I flew to London.
PATRICIA: You mean last week?
JONATHAN: What's today? Yeah, last Thursday it happened.
PATRICIA: Oh, Jonathan. . . . What happened?
JONATHAN: It was long in coming. Did I not mention this on the phone?
PATRICIA: No.
JONATHAN: Sorry, thought I did. Strange to think, four days ago I was in Flushing, Queens, burying my father under the Unisphere.

(Pause.)

PATRICIA: *He* was sweet to me, your dad.
JONATHAN: Yeah, I know.
PATRICIA: What about shiva? Didn't you have to sit shiva?
JONATHAN: There was no time.
PATRICIA: Oh.
JONATHAN: I mean, they were mounting the show.
PATRICIA: Couldn't they have waited? I mean, your *father* . . .
JONATHAN: No. I had to be here. I mean, there was nothing more I could do; he was dead. What could I do?
PATRICIA: I don't know.
JONATHAN: It was good for me, getting away, I think. Therapeutic. Bobby's doing it, though, shiva. He wanted to. I don't know, I just couldn't. It didn't seem like the thing to do. It's like I'd been sitting shiva for him for fifteen years, since my mother. I'd done it already. *(A beat.)* I wasn't a very good son.
PATRICIA: That's not true; I'm sure you made him very proud.
JONATHAN: No no, that's not what I need to hear. I wasn't. *(A beat.)* I went to pack up his house the other day? My parents' house? All his clothes, my old room, my mother's sewing machine, all those rooms of furniture. Strange being in a place where no one lives anymore.

PATRICIA: I know; I do that for a living.

JONATHAN: Yeah, I guess you do. Anyway, what I found was, he'd taken all the family pictures, everything that was in albums, shoved in drawers—hundreds of them—and covered an entire wall with them, floor to ceiling, side to side.

I first saw it years ago, when he'd started. It was his Sistine Chapel; it took him years. He took my hand (I'll never forget this) he took my hand—he was beaming: "*You're* an artist," he said to me, "*you'll* appreciate this." He was so proud of himself I thought I was gonna cry. Proud and also in a strange way competitive?

PATRICIA: Uh huh.

JONATHAN: So, there was this wall. The Waxman family through the ages. Black and white, sepia, Kodachrome. My great-grandparents in the shtetl, my brother's baby pictures on top of my parents' courtship, me at my bar mitzvah.

Well, it was kind of breathtaking. I mean, the sweep of it, it really was kind of beautiful. I came closer to examine it—I wanted to see how he'd gotten them all up there—and then I saw the staples.

PATRICIA: What?

JONATHAN: Staples! Tearing through the faces and the bodies. "Look what you've done," I wanted to say. "How could you be so thoughtless? You've ruined everything!" But of course I didn't say that. How could I? He was like a little boy. Beaming. Instead I said, "Dad! What a wonderful job!"

So, there I was alone in his house, pulling staples out of our family photos. These documents that showed where I came from. Did they *mean* anything to him at all? I mean as artifacts, as proof of a former civilization, when my mother was vibrant and he was young and strong and we were a family?

That's all gone now, Patty. It's all gone.

(Pause.)

PATRICIA: You have your wife.

(He nods. Pause.)

PATRICIA: She must trust you a lot.

JONATHAN: Why?

PATRICIA: Letting you pop up to see how the old lover made out? Or, ah-ha!, you didn't tell her you were coming!

JONATHAN: No, I told her.

PATRICIA: Too morbid for her taste, huh?, she decided to stay in London?

JONATHAN: No. Actually, she didn't come over.

PATRICIA: Oh?

JONATHAN: She stayed home. Up near New Paltz. We moved out of the city a couple of years ago.

PATRICIA: I know. The article said. I thought it said Vermont.

JONATHAN: No. We bought a farm.

PATRICIA: I know. Some "turn of the century" thing; here we have to ask "turn of *which* century?" So why isn't she here *with* you, your wife? Your big European debut.

JONATHAN: She wanted to. *(A beat.)* She's pregnant.

PATRICIA: *(A beat.)* Ah. Well. A baby. My! Aren't *you* full of news!

JONATHAN: She's pretty far along.

PATRICIA: Congratulations.

JONATHAN: Thanks. I mean, flying was out of the question. Third trimester.

PATRICIA: Of course. So I've heard. Well. Isn't that nice. You'll be a father soon.

JONATHAN: Yeah. Nine weeks or something, yeah.

PATRICIA: Well. This *is* something: Jonathan Waxman a father. Just as you've lost your own.

JONATHAN: Yeah. The irony hasn't escaped me. *(A beat. Going to his wallet.)* Would you like to see a picture?

PATRICIA: Of the child already?

JONATHAN: No, of Laura.

PATRICIA: *(Continuous.)* My God! American technology . . .

JONATHAN: *(Over "technology.")* I *did* have a sonogram I carried around. It's a boy.

PATRICIA: A boy.

JONATHAN: You can tell. You can see his, *you* know, his scrotum.

PATRICIA: Yes.

JONATHAN: I meant a picture of Laura. Would you like to . . .

PATRICIA: I've already seen her.

JONATHAN: How?

PATRICIA: The article.

JONATHAN: Oh, right.

PATRICIA: *(Continuous.)* Remember? Gazing at you like an astronaut's wife?

JONATHAN: *(Returns the picture to his wallet.)* Oh, well, I thought you might've liked to . . .

PATRICIA: No, I will, show me.

JONATHAN: It's okay.

PATRICIA: *Show* me.

(He shows her the photo. A beat.)

JONATHAN: That was our wedding.

PATRICIA: I figured, white dress and everything. How long ago was that?

JONATHAN: A year ago May. We waited a while. How about you?

PATRICIA: Me?

JONATHAN: You and Nick, you've been married *how* long?

PATRICIA: I don't know, eight or nine years?

JONATHAN: Eight or nine?, what do you mean?

PATRICIA: We didn't have much of a wedding. I like her dress. She's so thin. A dancer, right?

(He nods. She returns the photo.)

PATRICIA: She seems nice.

JONATHAN: Yeah, thanks, she is, you'd like her.

PATRICIA: I'm sure.

JONATHAN: And Nick seems . . .

PATRICIA: Don't do that.

JONATHAN: What.

PATRICIA: I tell you I like *your* spouse, you tell me you like *mine.* You don't have to do that.

JONATHAN: I wasn't.

PATRICIA: The fact is . . . Nick may seem . . . odd . . .

JONATHAN: No . . .

PATRICIA: *(A small laugh.)* Yes. But he absolutely adores me.

JONATHAN: That's *good*, I'm glad he does. He should.

(A beat. They look at one another.)

JONATHAN: And you?
PATRICIA: Look, what do you want?
JONATHAN: What do you mean?
PATRICIA: Do you have some sort of agenda or something?
JONATHAN: No.
PATRICIA: You just happened to be in the neighborhood?
JONATHAN: I wanted to see you again.
PATRICIA: Why?
JONATHAN: I don't know, it felt somehow . . . incomplete.
PATRICIA: What did?
JONATHAN: We did. *(A beat.)* I came. . . . I wanted to apologize.
PATRICIA: *(Smiling.)* Not really.
JONATHAN: What did you think when I called?
PATRICIA: I don't know, I was nonplused. I buried you years ago, then all of a sudden a call from London. You caught me off guard.
JONATHAN: So why did you invite me up?
PATRICIA: You caught me off *guard*, I said. I don't know, what *should* I have done?
JONATHAN: You could've said it was a bad time, you were busy, you had other plans . . .
PATRICIA: None of which was true.
JONATHAN: You could've said you had no interest in seeing me again. *(Pause.)* Patty . . .

(He makes a conciliatory gesture; she rebuffs him.)

PATRICIA: I'll give you dinner and a place to spend the night, but, no, Jonathan, I won't forgive you.

(Pause. He goes for his bag.)

JONATHAN: Look, maybe this wasn't such a good idea. I should go to a hotel.
PATRICIA: No! *(A beat.)* Hey, no one here calls me Patty. It's a novelty.

(He drops his bag. She picks up a basket.)

PATRICIA: I'm going foraging in my garden for dinner.
JONATHAN: I'll come with you.

PATRICIA: You aren't invited. *(A beat.)* You're cold. I think it actually is warmer inside.

(She puts on her jacket and goes. JONATHAN *soon gravitates toward the painting and looks at it for a while.* NICK *enters, the depleted bottle of Scotch in his hand.)*

NICK: Oops.

*(*JONATHAN *sees him. A beat.)*

NICK: You've spotted your painting.
JONATHAN: Yes.
NICK: I can't tell you how many nights I've stared at the fire and imagined that painting in the flames.
JONATHAN: Excuse me?
NICK: Oh, I wouldn't dream of damaging it. It's a work of art. And I am a preservationist by nature. *(A beat.)* It makes Patricia happy to have a piece of you on the wall. Did I say *a piece of you*? I meant a piece *from* you. Or perhaps I *meant* a piece *of* you. A piece of *yours,* at any rate. She gazes at it sometimes, when we're sitting by the fire. It doesn't move me in the same way. No, the eye of the beholder and all that. Drink?
JONATHAN: No. I painted it a long time ago. When Patty and I were at school. It's strange seeing something I did like twenty years ago and see all these things I couldn't possibly have seen when I painted it.
NICK: You're rich now, aren't you?
JONATHAN: What?
NICK: Patricia tells me you're rich.
JONATHAN: Oh, God.
NICK: Read it in some magazine.
JONATHAN: Well, we talked about that. Actually, I . . .
NICK: *(Over "Actually, I.")* She said you're rich. You're successful.
JONATHAN: Those are two different things, really.
NICK: Are they?
JONATHAN: Yes, I think—
NICK: How much do you make in a year?
JONATHAN: Well, I don't—
NICK: Am I out of line?
JONATHAN: Well, maybe.

NICK: How much then?

JONATHAN: It's difficult to say. I've had years in which I've made almost nothing. It's only in the last couple of years—

NICK: *(Over "couple of years.")* How much would you get for something like that, for instance? *(Meaning the painting on the wall.)*

JONATHAN: A student painting? I have no idea.

NICK: Guess.

JONATHAN: I really don't know.

NICK: Come on. A pivotal work. You said so yourself. A seminal work. How much would a seminal work, given your current currency, if you will, your current notoriety, how much would an old, young Waxman bring?

JONATHAN: I really have no idea.

NICK: Come on, guess.

JONATHAN: In the thousands, certainly. I don't know.

NICK: *(Over "I don't know.")* Oh, I would think more than that.

JONATHAN: Look, I really don't pay much attention to this stuff.

NICK: Don't pay attention to money? Surely you must.

JONATHAN: No, I let my gallery worry about it.

NICK: Art for art's sake, eh? Well, even I, even I who know, or for that matter, *care* very little about contemporary values in art, or, even, the value *of* contemporary art, even I would guess you're being awfully stingy on yourself. Considerably more than in the thousands, I would say. More like in the *tens* of thousands, wouldn't you agree?

JONATHAN: Maybe. I really don't know.

NICK: Oh, I would think. A pivotal, precocious painting like this? A seminal masterpiece?

JONATHAN: I don't know. What do you want to hear? Whatever you want to hear.

NICK: You.

JONATHAN: What.

NICK: I feel as though I've known you all along.

JONATHAN: Oh, yeah?

NICK: Your picture. She has this snapshot.

JONATHAN: What snapshot?

NICK: A Polaroid. The two of you. Patricia the co-ed. The party girl. Lithe and sunny. Her tongue in your ear. You, squirming like a boy caught in a prank. With gums showing. You don't look at all handsome. She assured me you were. A costume party of some kind.

JONATHAN: A costume party?

NICK: Mm. Patricia in a swimsuit dressed as Miss America. You're dressed like a jester. A clown. A clown or a pimp.

JONATHAN: A what?

NICK: Loud clashing plaids, a camera round your neck. Sunglasses.

JONATHAN: Oh. Halloween. I was a tourist.

NICK: Hm?

JONATHAN: A tourist. I went dressed as a tourist.

NICK: A tourist.

JONATHAN: A visitor, a stranger. An observer. The camera, the Hawaiian shirt.

NICK: It doesn't read.

*(*JONATHAN *shrugs.)*

NICK: You look like a pimp.

JONATHAN: The idea was a tourist.

NICK: Hm?

JONATHAN: Never mind.

NICK: Patricia had forgotten what you'd dressed up *as*. She thought a pimp.

JONATHAN: No.

NICK: Mm. *(A beat.)* What was the idea?

JONATHAN: The idea?

NICK: What did it mean? Was there some symbolic value?, dressing as a tourist?

JONATHAN: I don't know . . .

NICK: Symbolic of your perception of yourself at that time, perhaps? A transient person? Dislocated?

JONATHAN: That's interesting. I wonder if—

NICK: Rubbish. Now, that picture, that photo. Was all I had to go on. For years. Until that *New York Times* article. That one Polaroid she keeps in a box with letters. *(Confidentially.)* I've snooped. There's a postal card from you in that box. One picture postal car. No letters.

JONATHAN: I didn't write much.

NICK: Hm?

JONATHAN: There was no need to write. We were in school together. We saw each other all the time.

NICK: No, I imagine there *were* letters. Painful collegiate prose. Heartsick poems. Declarations of lust.

JONATHAN: Sorry.

NICK: I imagine there *were* letters, but she burned them. Like Hedda Gabler or somebody. Watched with glee while the missives went up in flames.

JONATHAN: No.

NICK: I think there *were.* I prefer to think there *were*. And all that remains is an innocuous postal card. From Miami Beach, Florida, or someplace.

JONATHAN: Yes. A visit to my grandparents. Fort Lauderdale.

NICK: Then there are the stories. Tales of Waxman. The Jonathan Stories. Faraway sounding, exotic. Like from the Old Testament, if you will. Patricia's voice becomes especially animated while telling a Jonathan story. She achieves a new range in a different key. A new tune, a new music entirely. Fascinating. I watch her face. The dimples that sprout! The knowing smiles! Remarkable behavioral findings. *(A beat. He drags his chair closer.)* I've become a Waxmanologist, you see. A Waxmanophile. No, a Waxmanologist. It's my nature. Beneath this reticent exterior lies a probing, tireless investigator. A detective. An historian. And I'm good at my work. I'm compulsive. I'm meticulous. I study the past in order to make sense of the present.

JONATHAN: I understand.

NICK: You're smaller in person than I imagined. I held out for a giant. A giant among men. Instead, what's *this*? You're medium-sized. Compact. Razor burn on your neck. Pimple on your cheek. She said you were handsome; you're all right. Perhaps your appeal lies below the belt, but I doubt I'd be surprised.

JONATHAN: Look, I think I'll—*(Pointing to the door.)*

NICK: Circumcision isn't common practice in the U.K., you know.

(JONATHAN *stops.)*

NICK: Jews still do it the world over, don't they. On religious grounds. Here the risk is too great. Too many accidents. Too many boy sopranos. Here we hold on to our overcoats.

*(*PATRICIA *returns with her basket filled with vegetables and herbs.)*

PATRICIA: Oh. Good. You're getting acquainted.

*(*JONATHAN *and* NICK *look at one another.)*

Scene 2

In the black, we hear the din of people chatting in a large room. Lights up: four days later. An art gallery in London. A polished wood floor and a white wall upon which "Jonathan Waxman" is spelled out in display letters. It is after JONATHAN*'s opening; plastic cups of wine are scattered about. An attractive, European new-wave-looking young woman (*GRETE*) arranges two Mies van der Rohe–style chairs and sets up a mini–tape recorder on a table between them.* JONATHAN *enters.*

JONATHAN: Can we do this quickly?
GRETE: Yes. Please. Sit down.
JONATHAN: It's just I promised Antony—
GRETE: *(While setting up her recorder.)* No, no, sit, let us start immediately.
JONATHAN: *(Over "immediately.")* There's another reception for me in Hampstead, I really—
GRETE: *(Over "Hampstead . . .")* I am ready. Please. We can begin.

(She gestures for him to sit; he does. She takes a deep breath.)

GRETE: Now: first may I congratulate you, Mr. Waxman, on such a provocative exhibition.
JONATHAN: Thank you.
GRETE: It has been eagerly awaited and does not disappoint.
JONATHAN: Thank you very much. Can we get to the questions?
GRETE: Of course.

JONATHAN: *(Overlap.)* I really don't have time to schmooze, I'm sorry.

GRETE: You were kind enough to agree to—

JONATHAN: Well . . .

GRETE: It is a thrill and an honor to finally meet—

JONATHAN: Thank you. Really, could we please—?

GRETE: *(Takes out a stack of index cards.)* Forgive me, I have prepared some questions . . . I will begin with the more important ones first.

JONATHAN: However you want to work it.

GRETE: *(After a deep breath.)* Mr. Waxman.

JONATHAN: Yes.

GRETE: Your depictions of the emptiness and spiritual deadness of middle-class American life in the closing years of the twentieth century have earned you both accolades and admonishment in your own country. Your large, bold canvases of nude men and women who seem as alienated from one another as they do from their environment have been generating controversy in the art community in the United States for the better part of the last decade. They have also been commmanding huge price tags in the art market. How do you reconcile the success of your work with its rather bleak subject matter?, and, (b) do you think your work speaks as effectively to the rest of the world?, or, like a joke that loses something in translation, is its popularity purely an American phenomenon?

JONATHAN: *(A beat.)* Your English is very good.

GRETE: Thank you. I was a year at NYU.

JONATHAN: Ah. Now: Do I think my work is intrinsically American? Yes. Do I think that it's the equivalent of an inside joke that excludes the rest of the world? Definitely not. Whether the rest of the world *likes* it is another question. I'm not gonna worry too much about it. What was the first part of your question? How do I, what?, reconcile . . .

GRETE: . . . the success of your work with its rather bleak subject matter.

JONATHAN: Right. Well, I like to think that people are responding to good art. By good art I mean art that effectively tells the truth, effectively *reflects* the truth, and the truth is often rather bleak, so . . . I mean, you're German, right?

GRETE: Yes . . .

JONATHAN: Germany's been way ahead of us on this. American art is just starting to get politicized again. Before AIDS, it was all about style and cleverness; we didn't know what to make art *about*. Your country, in Germany, you had guys like Beuys, and Kiefer, making art that terrified and revolted you. *Because they knew what they were making art in response to.*

GRETE: To . . . ?

JONATHAN: To the most horrible event of our time. Yeah, *that* old thing. They were dealing with a society that had literally gone to hell. They were looking for clues among the ashes, looking for answers.

GRETE: Yes, but is it not arguable that events such as America in Vietnam, America in Central America, the failure of the American civil rights movement, to name a few, should have been sufficiently powerful premises for making art during the last generation?

JONATHAN: Yeah, but we're talking about the Holocaust. The horror by which all other horrors are judged.

GRETE: Horror is horror, is it not? How can you say that one horror is more terrible than another? All societies are guilty of injustice—

JONATHAN: Whoa. Look, maybe we shouldn't get into this. Let's just talk about the work. Okay? Let's talk about the work.

GRETE: Very well.

JONATHAN: Um . . . What was I gonna say? Oh, yeah. So anyway, I don't really see my work as bleak. I'm responding to situations that exist in American society that are bleak, maybe, but I'm presenting them in allegorical ways that I hope are provocative and entertaining, even. I mean, I don't set out by saying to myself, "I'm gonna make this really *bleak* painting of an interracial couple trying to make love in a vandalized cemetery." Bleak never comes into it. It's just an image. Just a story.

GRETE: I'm glad you brought up that painting. *Walpurgisnacht,* no? 1986. A very shocking painting. Some critics have suggested that the couple isn't making love but that the woman is being raped.

JONATHAN: That's what some critics have said, yes. They've accused me of being racist for showing a black man raping a white woman, but I say it's *their* problem 'cause *they're* the ones who can't fathom a naked black man on top of a naked white woman without calling it rape.

GRETE: Yes, I've read that explanation before. Some people have suggested that you were being disingenuous in your protestations.

JONATHAN: Some people would be wrong.

GRETE: But wouldn't you agree that the title, which means "Witches' Night," could easily mislead?

JONATHAN: No. If those people were to look beyond their own fears and knee-jerk attitudes toward miscegenation and actually look at the painting, they'd see that the lovers are in a Jewish cemetery that's been desecrated. Stones are toppled, spray-painted with swastikas. That's what the title refers to. I thought I was really hitting people over the head, but I guess not. Everyone saw red and failed to see the painting. Just when things quieted down, *feminists* got on my case 'cause the man was on top of the woman!

GRETE: *(A beat.)* While *Walpurgisnacht* is probably your most famous work—certainly it is your most controversial—and, fittingly, the centerpiece of this exhibition, the talk of the show here today seems to be a painting that to my knowledge has never before been shown.

JONATHAN: Yes.

GRETE: A student work. *The Beginning,* it is called.

JONATHAN: Uh huh.

GRETE: Painted while you were in your early twenties.

JONATHAN: Yeah. I only recently came across it again. I'd figured it must've gotten lost or destroyed; student work is *supposed* to get lost or destroyed. But when I found it again, this thing I thought I'd lost, it was like a rush. Every painting I ever did suddenly made sense.

GRETE: Hm. It is the only painting from your personal collection, I see.

JONATHAN: Yes.

GRETE: A very curious painting, Mr. Waxman.

JONATHAN: Curious how?

GRETE: On the surface, it appears to be a fairly commonplace, rather youthful study of a seated figure.

JONATHAN: *(Over "of a seated figure.")* Yeah, but you can't fault the painter for being young. The painting may not be brilliant, but it *is* inspired. I mean, I look at it and I feel the excitement and the, the *danger* of that day all over again.

GRETE: What was it about that day?

JONATHAN: I don't know, it was one of those days artists kill for. The kind we always hope we're waking up to, but which rarely comes to pass. I wish I knew what I'd had for breakfast that day or what shirt I was wearing or what I'd dreamed the night before. Burning leaves; I remember the room smelled of burning leaves. Whatever it was, something clicked that day. I was born. My life began. I started seeing things I'd never seen before.

GRETE: There *is* a kind of . . . *openness,* yes?, present in this painting that is virtually absent in your later work. The way the model *engages* the viewer, for instance. Her penetrating, unwavering eye contact. Nowhere else in your work does one find that kind of . . . connection.

JONATHAN: *(A beat. She's right.)* Hm.

GRETE: *(Rhetorically.)* I wonder about the model. Who *was* this woman? What role did *she* play? I wonder where she is today.

JONATHAN: *(A beat.)* I have no idea.

Scene 3

The farmhouse. An hour before the start of Scene 1. PATRICIA *is sweeping the floor.* NICK *watches while preparing tea for the two of them. A long silence.*

PATRICIA: We'll give him our bed.

(He doesn't respond.)

PATRICIA: Nick?
NICK: Yes?
PATRICIA: We'll give him our bed. *(A beat.)* All right?
NICK: Fine.

(Pause.)

PATRICIA: I'll *offer* it. How's that? I'll *offer* him the bedroom. It'll be up to him. All right?
NICK: All right.
PATRICIA: We can sleep on the futon down here. Don't you think?

*(*NICK *shrugs. A beat.)*

PATRICIA: Don't you think it would be easier?
NICK: Fine.
PATRICIA: *Do* you? Do you think it would be easier?
NICK: *(Over "would be easier.")* Fine. Whatever.
PATRICIA: *Tell* me.
NICK: Yes, I think it would be easier.

(Pause.)

PATRICIA: God, I should change the sheets. Don't you think?
NICK: Patricia . . .
PATRICIA: I really just changed them, should I bother to change them?
NICK: For one night?
PATRICIA: That's what *I* thought; it's only one night. No, I'm not going to change them.
NICK: Don't.
PATRICIA: We can get away with it. He doesn't have to know.
NICK: No.
PATRICIA: They're clean. Tomorrow I'll change them. When he leaves. In the morning.
NICK: Yes. Bright and early. When he leaves. In fifteen hours, eight of which will be spent sleeping. Come have tea.

(Pause. She continues sweeping.)

NICK: Patricia, come have your tea.
PATRICIA: Do you mind about the bed?
NICK: What do you mean?
PATRICIA: Do you mind about us giving him the bed?
NICK: Mind?
PATRICIA: I mean, don't you think it would be more comfortable? It's warmer in the bedroom. He'll be cold. Americans are always cold. *(Pause.)* Nick? Do you mind about the bed?
NICK: Have your tea.
PATRICIA: *Do* you? Tell me.

(Pause.)

NICK: It's only for one night. *(A beat. He reminds her.)* Tea.

(She continues puttering.)

NICK: We'll be fine downstairs. We'll light a fire. Warm it up. We've spent nights downstairs in front of the fire before. Right? Haven't we?
PATRICIA: What am I going to do with him?
NICK: What do you *mean* what are you going to do with him? You should have thought about that before.

PATRICIA: *(Over "You should have . . .")* I mean it's been fifteen years. What am I going to *do* with him? What do I say?

NICK: Patricia. Really.

PATRICIA: This is foolish. Stupid. Let's go and leave a note.

NICK: All right, love. Let's.

PATRICIA: "Called away suddenly."

NICK: Yes. Okay. "Dramatic findings in Cotswolds require our presence."

PATRICIA: *(Laughs.)* What time is it?

NICK: Nearly half past four.

PATRICIA: Damn. I've got to get to the butcher.

NICK: Have your tea. He's not bloody royalty, you know.

(She puts on her coat.)

NICK: Where are you going?

PATRICIA: To get a lamb roast.

NICK: Why don't I come *with* you?

PATRICIA: Someone has to be here.

NICK: You don't expect *me* to . . .

PATRICIA: I'll be right back.

NICK: *I* shouldn't be the one who . . .

PATRICIA: Please, Nick. Please.

NICK: Wait for him to get here.

PATRICIA: Nick . . .

NICK: No, take him with you. Show him the town. He'll be here any time.

PATRICIA: The butcher will be closed.

NICK: *I'll* go to the butcher, you stay.

PATRICIA: You won't know what to get.

NICK: A lamb roast, you said. Let *me* go. You can be here when he arrives. He's *your* friend.

PATRICIA: You're mad about the bed.

NICK: I am not mad about the bloody bed!

PATRICIA: *(Over "the bloody bed.")* If you don't want him to have our bed, *tell* me! *Tell* me you don't want him to!

(Pause.)

NICK: *(Simply.)* He has it already.

(Pause.)

PATRICIA: Why didn't you tell me not to invite him?
NICK: Me? Tell you? What do you mean?
PATRICIA: *(Over "What do you mean?")* Why didn't you forbid me from seeing him again?
NICK: Forbid you? How, Patricia? How could I forbid you? *Why* would I? I wouldn't presume to forbid you to do anything.
PATRICIA: *Why?* Why *wouldn't* you?

(They look at one another. Pause. She starts to exit.)

NICK: *(He calls.)* Patricia.

(She stops and turns. Pause.)

NICK: Come home soon?

Scene 4

Fifteen years earlier. Spring. Late afternoon. Blinds drawn. JONATHAN*'s bedroom in his parents' house in Brooklyn, complete with the artifacts of a lower-middle-class boyhood, the notable exception being a sewing machine. Wearing a vest, suit trousers, and socks,* JONATHAN *is curled up on a bed. His hair is long. There is a tentative knock.* PATRICIA *enters. A beat.*

PATRICIA: *(Whispers.)* Jonathan? *(She waits, whispers again.)* Jonny?

(She looks around the room, gravitates toward the bookshelf and begins scanning the titles. After a while, he sits up and sees her looking at a paperback.)

PATRICIA: I love your little-boy handwriting. So round. The loopy "J" in "Jonathan," the "o," the "a"s. "This book belongs to Jonathan Waxman." *(Laughs, shows him the book.) The Man from U.N.C.L.E.* I wish I knew you then, Jonny.

(She returns the book to the shelf and continues looking.)

JONATHAN: What are you doing?
PATRICIA: I love looking at people's books.
JONATHAN: *(Still awaiting a response.)* Patty . . . ?
PATRICIA: It's like looking into their brain or something. Everything they ever knew. Everything they ever touched. It's like archeology. Lets you into all the secret places.
JONATHAN: Patty, what are you doing here?
PATRICIA: Only took me two years to get in the front door.

Hey, not bad. —Why isn't *Franny and Zooey* at your place?

JONATHAN: It is. I have doubles.

PATRICIA: Oh.

(Pause. They look at one another.)

PATRICIA: You look handsome in your suit.

JONATHAN: *(He begins to put on his shoes.)* Thanks.

PATRICIA: I don't think I've ever seen you in a suit. Have I? I must have. Did you wear a suit at graduation? No, you wore a cap and gown. What did you wear underneath it? Anything?

JONATHAN: What time is it?

PATRICIA: I don't know. *(A beat)* Your dad kissed me. When I came in? He kissed me. On the lips. He's very sweet, your dad. Said he was glad to see me, he was glad I came. See? He wasn't upset to see me. I told you you were overreacting. He's always kind of had a crush on me I think. *You* know the Waxman men and their shiksas. They're legend.

JONATHAN: *(Fixing his shirt.)* I should go back down.

PATRICIA: No. Why? Stay.

(She tries to touch his hair, he moves away.)

PATRICIA: *(On his rebuff.)* So this is where you and Bobby grew up. *(She sits on a bed.)*

JONATHAN: That's right . . .

PATRICIA: Funny, it's just how I pictured it. Like one of those Smithsonian recreations? *You* know, those roped-off rooms? "Jonathan Waxman's Bedroom in Brooklyn, Circa 1970." "The desk upon which he toiled over algebra." "The bed in which he had his first wet dream . . ."

JONATHAN: That one, actually.

PATRICIA: *(She smiles; a beat.)* I loved the oil-painting bar mitzvah portraits of you and Bobby over the sofa by the way.

JONATHAN: What can I tell ya?

PATRICIA: Oh, they're great. *(A beat; she sees the incongruous sewing machine.) Sewing* machine?

JONATHAN: She moved it in when I moved out.

PATRICIA: Ah.

JONATHAN: The only woman on record to die of empty-nest syndrome.

PATRICIA: *(She goes to him and hugs him.)* Oh, Jonny, I'm sorry . . .

JONATHAN: *(Trying to free himself.)* Yeah. You know, I really should go back down. My father . . .

(They kiss, again and again; he's bothered as her kisses become more fervent.)

JONATHAN: *(Protesting.)* Patty . . . Patricia . . .

(She tries to undo his belt.)

JONATHAN: Hey! What's the matter with you?

PATRICIA: Lie down.

JONATHAN: Patricia, my father is sitting shiva in the living room!

PATRICIA: Come on, Jonny . . .

JONATHAN: NO, I SAID! Are you crazy?! What the fuck is the matter with you?!

PATRICIA: You won't let me *do* anything for you.

JONATHAN: Is this supposed to cheer me up?!

PATRICIA: I want to *do* something.

JONATHAN: I don't want sex, Patricia.

PATRICIA: I've never known anyone who *died* before; tell me what I should do.

JONATHAN: This isn't *about* you. Do you understand that? This is *my* problem, *my* . . . loss, *mine.*

PATRICIA: But I'm your friend. Aren't I? I'm your lover, for God's sake. Two years, Jonathan . . .

JONATHAN: *(Over "for God's sake . . .")* I thought we went *through* this . . .

PATRICIA: I want to be with you. I want to help you.

JONATHAN: You can't help me, Patty. I'm beyond help.

PATRICIA: Don't say that.

JONATHAN: It's true. I am beyond help right now. You can't help me. Your *blowjobs* can't help me.

PATRICIA: You don't know how I felt not being at the funeral.

JONATHAN: I'm sorry.

PATRICIA: No you're not. I was in agony. Really. I couldn't concentrate on anything all day. Knowing what you must've been going through? What kind of person do you think I am? I wanted to be with you so much.

JONATHAN: So you came over.

PATRICIA: You didn't say I couldn't. You said the funeral. I came over *after*.

JONATHAN: I meant the whole thing.

PATRICIA: What whole thing?

JONATHAN: The funeral, shiva.

PATRICIA: You mean I was supposed to keep away from you during all *this*?, like for a *week*?— isn't shiva like a week?

JONATHAN: Patty . . .

PATRICIA: Do you know how *ridiculous* this is? Don't you think you're taking this guilt thing a little too far? I mean, your mother is dead—I'm really really sorry, Jonny, really I am—and okay, we know she wasn't exactly crazy about me . . .

JONATHAN: I'm so burnt out, Patty . . . My head is . . .

PATRICIA: *(Continuous.)* Not that I ever did anything to *offend* the woman personally or anything. I just happened to be born a certain persuasion, a certain incompatible persuasion, even though I'm an atheist and I don't give a damn *what* religion somebody happens to believe in. But did she ever bother to get to know me, even a little bit?

JONATHAN: Oh, Patty, this is—

PATRICIA: It's like I was invisible. Do you know how it feels to be invisible?

JONATHAN: What do you think, my mother's dying wish was keep that shiksa away from my funeral?! Come on, Patty! Grow up! Not everything is about *you*. I know that may be hard for you to believe, but not everything in the world—

PATRICIA: *(Over "in the world.")* Oh, great.

JONATHAN: *(A beat.)* Let's face it, Patricia, things haven't exactly been good between us for months.

PATRICIA: What do you mean? Your mother's been *sick* for months. How can you make a statement like that?

JONATHAN: What, this is a surprise to you what I'm saying?

PATRICIA: Hasn't your mother been dying for months?

JONATHAN: I don't really have the strength for this right now.

PATRICIA: Hasn't she? So how can you judge how things have been between us? Her dying has been weighing over us, over both of us, for so long, it's colored so much . . .

JONATHAN: *(Over "it's colored so much.")* Look . . . if you *must* know—

PATRICIA: What?

JONATHAN: If you *must* know . . . *(A beat) I* was the one who didn't want you there. It wasn't out of respect to my mother or my father or my grandmother, it was me. I didn't want to see you. I didn't want you there, Patty. I didn't want to have to hold *your* hand and comfort *you* because of how cruel my mother was to you, I didn't want that . . . I didn't want to have to deal with your display of—

PATRICIA: *Display?*

JONATHAN: Your display of love for me. Your concern. It was all about *you* whenever I thought about how it would be if you were with me! I didn't want you there, Patty. I'm sorry. *(A beat.)* I guess when something catastrophic like this happens . . . you get to thinking.

PATRICIA: Yes? Well?

(Pause.)

JONATHAN: I don't love you, Patty.

(He smiles lamely and reaches for her as if to soothe her as she goes to get her bag. She groans, punches his arm, and goes. He stands alone for a long time before moving slowly over to the sewing machine. He clutches a pillow and gently rocks himself. As he begins to cry, the lights fade to black.)

ACT II

Scene 5

Lights up: The farmhouse. A few hours after the end of Scene 1. PATRICIA *and* JONATHAN *are seated at the table after dinner.* NICK *is standing nearby, looking through the exhibition catalogue. The wine is nearly finished; they are all somewhat disinhibited.*

JONATHAN: Drive down with me tomorrow.

PATRICIA: I don't *go* to London, I try to *avoid* London.

JONATHAN: *(Over "avoid London.")* You can take the train back Tuesday night, after the opening.

PATRICIA: *(Over "after the opening.")* The crowds, tourists, everything so bloody expensive.

JONATHAN: Don't worry about money; everything is on me.

PATRICIA: Why should everything be on you? I don't want everything to be on you.

JONATHAN: *(Over "I don't want everything . . .")* What, you think I'd invite you down and make you pay for it?

PATRICIA: God, Jonathan . . .

JONATHAN: Let me treat you to a couple of days in London!

PATRICIA: You sound like such an American!

JONATHAN: Come on, we'll hang out for a couple of days, it'll be fun.

PATRICIA: What are you talking about?

JONATHAN: We'll do the museums, you'll come to the opening, I'll introduce you to people . . .

PATRICIA: I don't need to meet people, I know enough people.

JONATHAN: *(Over "enough people.")* I mean artists. Writers, actors. You wouldn't believe the people coming.

PATRICIA: Uh huh.

JONATHAN: Hey, I'll take you to Caprice.

PATRICIA: Is that a restaurant?

JONATHAN: *Yes,* it's a restaurant.

PATRICIA: I *told* you, your name-droppings are wasted on me.

JONATHAN: Patty, let me do this. I want you to be my *guests,* both of you.

PATRICIA: Well, I don't know about Nick; he *completely* falls apart in London, don't you, Nick.

NICK: Hm?

PATRICIA: *(Continuing, to* JONATHAN.) That's never any fun, holding his hand as we brave the crush on the pavement. Besides, he couldn't get away.

JONATHAN: Then *you* come.

PATRICIA: No. I couldn't. What are you saying? I don't like big cities anymore either, they get me nervous. I don't even remember the last time I was there.

JONATHAN: Then you're due for a visit. It's really changed, London. Even in the five or six years since I was last over.

PATRICIA: You were here? Five or six years ago?

JONATHAN: Yeah, just a . . . quick thing, *you* know. Passing through.

PATRICIA: Uh huh. *(A beat.) I* know: must have been a year ago Christmas. Whenever my mother comes, she drags me to every bit of crap on the West End; Lloyd Webber's latest ditty. Do you know what they get for that slop?

JONATHAN: Patty.

PATRICIA: I can't just take off and go; some of us have to *work* for a living, you know.

JONATHAN: Oh, well! Excuse *me*!

PATRICIA: *(Over "Excuse me.")* I have data to collect. I have responsibilities, people who count on me; I can't just come and go as I please.

JONATHAN: I'm not asking you to quit your job and run away with me. Two or three days!

PATRICIA: Two or *three*? A minute ago it was a couple.

JONATHAN: Patty . . .

PATRICIA: I can't get away. This is a very exciting time for us. Has Nick told you about the project?

JONATHAN: A Roman latrine?

PATRICIA: Is that all he told you? Nick! *Tell* Jonathan.

NICK: What?

PATRICIA: About the project. *(To* JONATHAN.*)* He loves to minimize.

(JONATHAN *nods.)*

PATRICIA: *(To* NICK.*)* Tell him what you found.
NICK: Patricia . . .
PATRICIA: Oh, you! *(To* JONATHAN.*)* He's impossibly modest. Nick found, not only the latrine, but a late-medieval rubbish pit.
JONATHAN: A garbage dump?
PATRICIA: Yes!
NICK: *I* didn't find it, Patricia, we *all* found it . . .
PATRICIA: Do you have any idea what a valuable find that is, medieval rubbish? Seriously. Shoes, rags, broken plates. It was one of those happy accidents and Nick led us to it.
NICK: I *didn't*. I wish you wouldn't . . .
PATRICIA: Everything you need to know about a culture is in its rubbish, really. What they wore, what they ate. It's a treasure trove. Tons of it. I sift through parcels of ancient rubbish every day, analyze it, catalog it. That's what I do. Every day. Now you know. I shouldn't have told you.
JONATHAN: Why not?
PATRICIA: Sounds fascinating.
JONATHAN: No, it does.

(She gives him a look. He laughs.)

JONATHAN: It does. —Come to my opening.
PATRICIA: Stop it.
NICK: Um . . .

(They look at him. A beat.)

NICK: *(Referring to the catalog.)* I'm looking at your paintings . . .
JONATHAN: Yes . . . ?
NICK: And, honestly . . . I don't get it.
JONATHAN: What don't you get?
NICK: I don't get . . . What's all the fuss about?
JONATHAN: What fuss?
PATRICIA: Oh, Nick. Be nice.

NICK: You're supposed to be something of an iconoclast, aren't you?

JONATHAN: An "iconoclast"?

NICK: I mean, is that all it takes to set the art world ablaze?

PATRICIA: Nick's idea of art is the *Mona Lisa.*

NICK: My idea of art, in point of fact, Patricia, begins and ends with the Renaissance. Everything before it was ceremonial, arts-and-crafts—hardly "art," really; everything since, well, everything since has been utter rubbish.

JONATHAN: Are you kidding? How can you say that? *(To* PATRICIA.*)* All of modern art, he's dismissing just like that?

NICK: *(Over "just like that?")*But it's all been done, hasn't it. The so-called modern age, as far as I can tell, has been one long, elaborate exercise, albeit a futile one, to reinvent what had already been perfected by a handful of Italians centuries ago.

JONATHAN: But the world is constantly reinventing *itself.* How can you say that Leonardo's world view expresses *our* world, or Picasso's even?

NICK: Picasso. Now *there* was an energetic little bloke.

JONATHAN: Am I supposed to shrink in the shadow of the great masters and pack it all in? Say the hell with it, why bother?

NICK: If you had any sense? Yes.

*(*PATRICIA *giggles naughtily.)*

NICK: Absolutely. Why bother, indeed? *(To* PATRICIA.*)* How is it that all the artists I've ever known feel that what they do is so vital to society?

(She laughs some more.)

NICK: Does it ever occur to them that if they were wiped off the face of the earth the planet would survive intact?

JONATHAN: *(To* PATRICIA.*)* Gee, you didn't tell me you'd married such an art lover.

NICK: Art was devised as a celebration of beauty, was it not? I mean, does *this* celebrate beauty? *(Waving the catalog.)* This, this . . . pornography?

PATRICIA: Nick!

JONATHAN: *(Smiling, to* PATRICIA.*)* That's okay.

NICK: *(Over "That's okay.")* Because as far as I can tell that's precisely what this is. And not very *good* pornography at that.

JONATHAN: Really. Well.

PATRICIA: Nick was raised by a puritanical mother.

NICK: *Fuck* that, Patricia. I look at this . . . "art" and I see pornography. Tell me what's there that eludes me.

JONATHAN: I'm not gonna *tell* you what to see. If you see pornography . . .

NICK: I don't *get* it, is what I'm saying. If I don't get it, is it my failure or yours? Enlighten me. Help me see.

JONATHAN: You know, you usually don't have the luxury of painters whispering in your ear when you're looking at their paintings, telling you what to see. That's not the job of the artist. The job of the artist is not to spell everything out. *You* have to participate.

NICK: Participate.

JONATHAN: Yes. You play an active role in all this; it's not just me, it's not just the artist.

NICK: All right . . . what's this, then? *(Flips the catalog to a particular painting.)*

JONATHAN: You can't judge the work like *that*, black-and-white reproductions in a catalog . . .

NICK: *(Over "in a catalog.")* What is this if not pornography?

JONATHAN: Come on, Nick, use your head a little. What do you see?

NICK: You actually want me to tell you?

JONATHAN: Yeah. Describe to me what you see.

NICK: All right. I see what *appears* to be a painting—

JONATHAN: Oh, man . . .

NICK: *(Continuous.)* —executed with minimal skill in terms of knowledge of basic anatomy—

JONATHAN: You really have to see the *painting* . . .

NICK: *(Continuous.)* —of what *appears* to be a couple of mixed race fornicating in what *appears* to be a cemetery, is it?

JONATHAN: Don't be so literal! Yes, that's what it appears to be on the surface, but what's it really saying?

PATRICIA: Let me see.

*(*NICK *shows it to her.)*

JONATHAN: *(Continuous.)* What's going on there? It's an allegory, it's telling a story. Use your imagination!

PATRICIA: The woman is being raped.

JONATHAN: Ah ha. Is she?

PATRICIA: Well, yes, look at her hands. They're fists.

NICK: They aren't necessarily fists; they're just poorly drawn hands.

JONATHAN: Jesus.

NICK: That's what I mean by the apparent disregard for basic traditions in art like knowing the skeletal structure of the human hand.

JONATHAN: But you know what hands look like.

NICK: What?! Is that your response, I *know* what hands . . . ?

JONATHAN: What I'm saying is, it's not my job to photographically recreate the skeletal structure of the human hand.

NICK: What *is* your job? You keep talking about what isn't your job; what *is* your job? Is it your job to paint well, or not?

JONATHAN: What do you mean by "paint well"? You obviously have very limited ideas about painting. I'm telling you, if you guys came down to London, I'll take you around, we'll look at art, I could *show* you . . .

NICK: If one were to *buy* one of these . . . paintings—presuming, of course, one could afford to—where would one put it?

JONATHAN: What?

NICK: I mean, they're quite large, aren't they?

JONATHAN: Fairly.

NICK: One would have to have quite a large wall on which to hang such a painting and, preferably, an even larger room in which to view it properly. (Art *is* meant to be seen, no?) And that room would undoubtedly have to sit in an even more capacious house. Not your standard taxpayer, I take it.

JONATHAN: No.

NICK: Say *I* wanted to buy one of these.

JONATHAN: You? One of those?

NICK: Mm. What would I do?

JONATHAN: Well, for starters, you couldn't; they're already sold.

NICK: *All* of them?

PATRICIA: *(Leafing through the catalog; sotto voce.)*

"Saatchi Collection," "Union Carbide Collection," "Mobil Corporation Collection . . ."

JONATHAN: All of the existing ones, yes.

NICK: The "existing" ones?

JONATHAN: Yes. And there's a waiting list for the paintings I have yet to paint.

PATRICIA: A waiting list? You're joking.

JONATHAN: No.

NICK: You mean there are people on Park Avenue or in Tokyo, who have walls in their living rooms especially reserved for the latest Waxman, Number 238?

JONATHAN: Yeah.

NICK: It doesn't matter which painting, as long as they get their Waxman?

JONATHAN: It's not like this is new, you know; artists have always lived off of commissions.

NICK: So, wait, these art lovers, these poor, unsuspecting—rather, *rich*, unsuspecting—patrons of the arts have bought, sight unseen, a painting you have not yet painted?

JONATHAN: Yes.

PATRICIA: Amazing, Jonny. Pre-sold art.

NICK: What happens if they don't like it?

JONATHAN: What?

NICK: The painting. Say it doesn't please them. The colors clash with the carpet; the image makes madam blush. What then? Are they entitled to a refund? Can they hold out for the next one off the line?

JONATHAN: If they really dislike it, I guess, but it hasn't happened.

NICK: So how many can you expect to do in a year?

JONATHAN: One every five or six weeks? Figure ten a year.

NICK: Ten a year. At roughly a quarter million dollars per painting . . .

JONATHAN: *(Over "per painting.")* Now, wait a minute. What is this fascination with my finances? Ever since I got here you've been hocking me . . .

NICK: *(Over "Ever since I got here . . .")* Patricia, are you aware of how fortunate we are to be the proud owners of our own, actual, *already painted* painting by Jonathan Waxman? And a seminal Waxman at that!

JONATHAN: Look, why should I have to *apologize* for my success?

PATRICIA: Nobody's asking you to.

JONATHAN: *(Continuous.)* What am I supposed to do? Reject the money? Lower my price? What would *that* accomplish? Would it make me a better artist if I were hungry again?

NICK: I don't know. Would it?

PATRICIA: *(A beat; looking at the catalog.)* They *do* look like fists, Jonathan.

JONATHAN: What if they are fists? What difference does it make?

PATRICIA: It makes a very big difference. It changes everything. If they're fists, then that suggests that she's being taken against her will. If they're not . . . Is the painting about a black man raping a white woman, or is it about a couple screwing in a cemetery?

JONATHAN: Oh. You're saying it's ambiguous.

PATRICIA: I'm saying it's confusing. You can't have intended both things.

JONATHAN: Why not? I've got you thinking about it, haven't I?

NICK: But thinking about what? What does it *mean*? If *you* can't say, unequivocally . . .

PATRICIA: *(To* JONATHAN.*)* He has a point. It's all about shock, then. Effect. You can't *mean* "what difference does it make," Jonathan, that just isn't good enough.

JONATHAN: *(Over "isn't good enough.")* You know I don't entirely mean that. I mean, *my* intention is irrelevant; it's all about what you make of it.

NICK: Either way you look at it, it has about as much impact as a smutty photo in a porno mag.

JONATHAN: You can't get past the flesh, can you?

NICK: What?

JONATHAN: This is very interesting. All you see is the flesh. Of course! You surround yourself with bones all day. I mean, here you are, freezing your asses off—

PATRICIA: Jonathan . . .

JONATHAN: *(Continuous.)* —cataloging bones whose flesh rotted away centuries ago. No wonder my paintings scare you!

NICK: Scare me, did you say?

JONATHAN: Yes. They're . . . voluptuous, dangerous. They deal with unspeakable things, fleshy things. *That's* what's going on in my paintings. The lengths people go to, living people go to, in order to feel something. Now. Today.

(Pause.)

PATRICIA: We thought we'd put you in our bedroom.
JONATHAN: What?
PATRICIA: We thought we'd put you . . .
JONATHAN: In *your* room? No, you don't have to do that.
PATRICIA: No bother.
JONATHAN: Where are *you* gonna sleep?
PATRICIA: Down here.
JONATHAN: No, no, I'll sleep down here.
PATRICIA: The bedroom is actually warmer.
JONATHAN: I don't mind.
NICK: Are you sure?
JONATHAN: Yeah.
PATRICIA: No, trust me, the bedroom, it's really no problem.
NICK: *(Over "no problem.")* Patricia, he said he doesn't mind.
JONATHAN: I don't.
NICK: See? *(To* JONATHAN.*)* Yes, why *don't* you stay downstairs?
JONATHAN: Fine.
PATRICIA: But the electric *blanket* is upstairs. He's going to need the electric blanket.
JONATHAN: *(Over "electric blanket.")* Don't worry about me.
NICK: I'll bring it down.
PATRICIA: The mattress-warmer, actually. It's under the sheet. You'll have to strip the bed. It really would be easier . . .
NICK: *(Over "easier.")* So I'll strip the bed. The bed needs stripping anyway.
PATRICIA: *(A beat; to* NICK.*)* Are you sure?
NICK: Yes. I'll take care of it. Leave it to me.
JONATHAN: Thank you.

*(*NICK *goes. Pause.)*

JONATHAN: I hope I'm not . . .
PATRICIA: You hope you're not what?
JONATHAN: I don't know, it seems that my being here . . .
PATRICIA: Yes?
JONATHAN: *You* know . . . Things seem a little, I don't know . . . prickly, maybe? I mean with Nick?

PATRICIA: I haven't seen this much life in him in years.
JONATHAN: Really.

(Pause.)

PATRICIA: I married Nick to stay in England.
JONATHAN: *(A beat.)* Oh.
PATRICIA: They would've deported me. After my degree.
JONATHAN: Ah.
PATRICIA: My visa, *you* know, it was a student visa. It expired. I couldn't go home. How could I go home? Back to my broken-down mother? I couldn't. My skeptical father, who humored me through all my crazy pursuits? I had no one to go home to. No, this made sense. I found that I could survive here. I had to stay.
JONATHAN: *(A beat.)* Does he know?
PATRICIA: I'm sure he does. You mean why . . . ?

(JONATHAN nods.)

PATRICIA: I'm sure he knows. It was certainly no secret. He knew I needed a way to stay.
JONATHAN: I don't understand you. How can you be so cool about this?
PATRICIA: What?
JONATHAN: The man is obviously crazy about you; he's like a blushing *schoolboy* around you . . .
PATRICIA: I know.
JONATHAN: How can you do this? I never thought you'd be *capable* of something like this. You were such a passionate girl, Patty . . .
PATRICIA: Oh, God, spare me . . .
JONATHAN: You were the "student of the world"! Remember? No really, how do you . . . I mean, passion, sex, love . . . You just decided, what, you don't need those things anymore? You just shut that part of you all out?
PATRICIA: Yes. Exactly. My "passion" nearly did me in, now, didn't it.
JONATHAN: Oh, come on, don't lay this on me. That's bullshit. You call yourself an expatriate? You're no expatriate, you're just hiding!
PATRICIA: Who the hell are *you* to judge—?!
JONATHAN: Why do you live with him?

PATRICIA: Why? He's my husband.
JONATHAN: That's not a reason. Why do you live with him if you don't love him?
PATRICIA: Who said I don't love him?
JONATHAN: You just said yourself, you married Nick . . .
PATRICIA: *This is the best I can do!*

(Pause.)

JONATHAN: Don't say that. It isn't even true. I know you too well.
PATRICIA: *Knew* me. You *knew* me. You don't *know* who I am.

(A beat. NICK *appears with a bundle of bedding. They look at him. Pause.)*

NICK: Um . . . Shall I . . . Would you like me to make your bed?

Scene 6

The gallery in London. This scene is the continuation of Scene 2.

GRETE: You just said your definition of good art is "art which effectively reflects the truth." Do you think it is your responsibility as an artist to always tell the truth?

JONATHAN: In my work? Yes.

GRETE: And in your personal life?

JONATHAN: My personal life is my personal life. Look, if my work tells the truth, then I think people are compelled, they *have* to deal with it, they can't not. I like to shake 'em up a little, I admit it. People see my stuff at a gallery, a museum, and the work *competes* for their attention. They're preoccupied, overstimulated. All I can hope is maybe—*maybe*—one night, one of my images'll find its way into their unconscious and color their dreams. Who knows? Maybe it'll change their perception of something forever. I mean, in art, as in life, we tend to affect people in ways we can't always see. You can't possibly know what that other person has taken away with her. *(A beat.)* You can't see it. And just 'cause you can't see it doesn't mean it didn't happen.

GRETE: Hm. Getting back to "good art . . ."

JONATHAN: Okay, let me ask you something: When *we* talk about good art, what are we talking about? Stuff we like? Stuff our friends make? We're talking about value judgments. Most people, do you think most people, most Americans—my *father*—do you think most people have any idea what makes good art?

GRETE: Hm.

JONATHAN: The little old lady who paints flowers and pussycats at the YMCA—and *dazzles* her friends, I'm sure—I mean, does that little old lady make good art? I mean, why not?, her cat looks just *like* that. I'm not putting her down; I think it's great she's got a hobby. But is what she does good art? See, most people . . .

I remember, years ago, the big van Gogh show at the Met? New York? The place was packed. Like Yankee Stadium. Buses emptied out from all over; Jersey, Westchester. All kinds of people. The masses. Average middle-class people. Like they were coming into the city for a matinee and lunch at Mamma Leone's. Only this was Art. Art with a capital A had come to the shopping-mall generation and Vincent was the chosen icon. Now, I have nothing against van Gogh. Better him than people lining up to see the kids with the big eyes. But as I braved that exhibit—and it was rough going, believe me—I couldn't help but think of Kirk Douglas. Kirk Douglas should've gotten a cut of the house.

See, there's this Hollywood packaging of the artist that gets me. The packaging of the mystique. Poor, tragic Vincent; he cut off his ear 'cause he was so misunderstood but still he painted all these pretty pictures. So ten bodies deep they lined up in front of the paintings. More out of solidarity for Vincent (or Kirk) than out of any kind of love or passion for "good art." Hell, some art lovers were in such a hurry to get to the postcards and prints and souvenir place mats, they strode past the paintings and skipped the show entirely! Who can blame them? You couldn't *experience* the paintings anyway, not like that. You couldn't *see anything*. The art was just a backdrop for the *real* show that was happening. In the gift shop!

GRETE: Hm.

JONATHAN: Now, you got to admit there's something really strange about all this, this kind of *frenzy* for art. I mean, what *is* this thing called art? What's it for? Why have people historically drunk themselves to death over the creation of it, or been thrown in jail, or whatever? I mean, how does it serve the masses? *Can* it serve the— I ask myself these questions all the time. Every painting I do is another attempt to come up with some answers. The people who crowded the Met to look at sunflowers, I mean, why *did* they? 'Cause they *thought* they should. 'Cause they thought they were somehow enriching their lives. Why? *'Cause the media told them so!*

GRETE: You seem to have such contempt—

JONATHAN: Not contempt; you're confusing criticism with contempt.

GRETE: *(Continous.)* —for the very same people and the very same system that has made you what you are today.

JONATHAN: What am I today? What *am* I today? I just got here. People like *you* suddenly care what I have to say.

GRETE: I *do* care.

JONATHAN: I know you do. It cracks me up that you do; it amuses me. You know, up till like eight or nine years ago, let's not forget, I was painting *apartments* for a living. Apartments. Walls. Rooms. I was good at it, too. I'd lose myself all day while I painted moldings, then I'd go home and do my *own* painting all night. A good, simple, hard-working life.

Then, like I said, like nine years ago, my world started getting bigger. I couldn't even retrace the steps; I can't remember how it happened. All I know is I met certain people and got a gallery and a show and the public started to discover my work. The night of my first opening, it's like these strangers witnessed a birth, like the work had no life before they laid eyes on it. We know that's ridiculous, of course, but this is what happens when you take your art out of your little room and present it to the public; it's not yours anymore, it's *theirs,* theirs to see with their own eyes. And, for each person who sees your work for the first time, you're discovered all over again. That begins to take its toll. You can't be everybody's discovery. That gets to be very demanding. Who *are* these people who are suddenly throwing money at you and telling you how wonderful and talented you are? What do *they* know? You begin to believe them. They begin to want things from you. They begin to expect things. The work loses its importance; the importance is on "Waxman."

GRETE: Would you prefer to have remained an outsider?

JONATHAN: Preferred? No. It's cold and lonely on the outside.

GRETE: And yet being cozy on the inside—

JONATHAN: "Cozy"?

GRETE: *(Continous.)* —seems to make you uncomfortable as well. Is this not an illustration of that Jewish joke?

JONATHAN: What Jewish joke?

GRETE: Forgive my paraphrase: Not wanting to be a member of a club that would also have you as a member?

JONATHAN: That's not a Jewish joke, that's Groucho Marx.

GRETE: Groucho Marx, then. Is he not Jewish?

JONATHAN: Yeah, so?

GRETE: Well, does not that joke apply to the problem Jews face in the twentieth century?

JONATHAN: What problem is that?

GRETE: The problem of being on the inside while choosing to see themselves as outsiders?—

JONATHAN: Is that a Jewish problem?

GRETE: *(Continuous.)* —even when they are very much on the inside?

JONATHAN: "Very much on the inside"? What is this?

GRETE: *(Over "What is this?")* Perhaps I am not expressing myself well.

JONATHAN: No, I think you're probably expressing yourself *very* well.

GRETE: All I am suggesting, Mr. Waxman, is that the artist, like the Jew, prefers to see himself as alien from the mainstream culture. For the Jewish *artist* to acknowledge that the *contrary* is true, that he is *not* alien, but rather, *assimilated* into that mainstream culture—

JONATHAN: *(Over "mainstream culture.")* Wait a minute, wait a minute. What is this *Jewish* stuff creeping in here?

GRETE: You are a Jew, are you not?

JONATHAN: I don't see what that—

GRETE: *(Over "what that.") Are* you?

JONATHAN: Yeah; so?

GRETE: I am interested in the relationship between the artist and the Jew, as Jonathan Waxman sees it.

JONATHAN: Who *cares* how Jonathan Waxman sees it? I'm an *American* painter. *American* is the adjective, not *Jewish, American.*

GRETE: Yes, but your work calls attention to it.

JONATHAN: How?

GRETE: The Jewish cemetery in *Walpurgisnacht*—

JONATHAN: *One* painting.

GRETE: One *important* painting—the depictions of middle-class life, obviously Jewish—

JONATHAN: How can you say that? "Obviously" Jewish.

GRETE: I have studied your paintings, I have done research on your upbringing—

JONATHAN: Oh, yeah?

GRETE: *(Continuous.)* —I have written many critical studies for art journals in my country. The middle-class life you explore— It is safe to say that your paintings are autobiographical, are they not?

JONATHAN: In what sense? Of course they're autobiographical in the sense that they come from *me*, they spring from *my* imagination, but to say that the subjects of my paintings are *Jewish* subjects, because a Jew happened to paint them, that's totally absurd.

GRETE: Mr. Waxman, I cannot tell to what you have most taken offense: the suggestion that was made, or that it was made by a German.

JONATHAN: *(A beat.)* Look, maybe we should . . .

GRETE: Please, just one more question . . .

JONATHAN: Can we please move on? Let's move on.

GRETE: Of course. *(A beat.)* Mr. Waxman, you speak with charming self-effacement about your much-celebrated career. You say you are amused by your sudden fame—

JONATHAN: Yes.

GRETE: *(Continuous.)* —and seem to view it as an unwanted but not unwelcome bonus, that making good art is all you have ever wanted to do.

JONATHAN: Yes.

GRETE: And yet—forgive me, Mr. Waxman—I am confused. If, as you claim, you had no interest in celebrity, why would you hire a public relations firm?

JONATHAN: This is how you change the subject?

GRETE: There have been whispers, Mr. Waxman. *(She says "vispers.")* Why would you hire a publicist if—

JONATHAN: You think I'm the only painter who has a publicist? This is the reality. You reach a certain point in your career, an *artist* reaches a certain point, where he achieves a certain amount of recognition—

GRETE: Yes, I know, you said. I do not question that.

JONATHAN: Will you let me finish please? If you're gonna make a statement like that—

GRETE: I am sorry.

JONATHAN: *(Continuous.)* —then at least let me make my point.

GRETE: Please.

JONATHAN: An artist who's achieved a certain amount of celebrity, very quickly, there are suddenly all these demands being placed on him. I've talked about that.

GRETE: Yes.

JONATHAN: People want you. Interviews, parties, schools. The problem becomes *time*. Where do you find the time to work?, to do the thing that made you famous? This is where having a publicist comes in. The publicist helps manage your social obligations. and if the painter doesn't have one, the gallery does, so what's the big deal?

GRETE: No, no, I understand. Perhaps I did not phrase my question correctly.

JONATHAN: Cut the crap, miss; your English is impeccable.

GRETE: Mr. Waxman, the whispers I have heard . . .

JONATHAN: Again with the "vispers"!

GRETE: It is true that you hired a public relations firm *two years before* your first success—

JONATHAN: Oh, come on. What is this, the Inquisition? Art is a business, you know that.

GRETE: Two years *before*, to promote your standing in the art community—

JONATHAN: My "standing"—?

GRETE: *(Continuous.)* —more importantly, in the art-buying community.

JONATHAN: What are you saying? I bought my career? I bought my reputation? What?

GRETE: Mr. Waxman . . .

JONATHAN: *(Continuous.)* What about the work? Why aren't we talking about the work? Why must it always come down to business? Huh? *I'm* not doing it, and yet you accuse *me* . . .

GRETE: *(Over "and yet you accuse me.") Is* it true or is it *not* true?

JONATHAN: That's irrelevant. True or not true, who cares?

GRETE: *(Over "who cares?")* It *is* relevant.

JONATHAN: How? How?

GRETE: It is relevant if you espouse to be a visionary of truth.

JONATHAN: *(Over "visionary of truth.")* I espouse nothing! What do I espouse? I paint pictures! You're the one who comes up with these fancy labels, people like *you*!

GRETE: *(Over "people like you.")* How can you talk about

truth? Mr. Waxman, how can you talk about truth when your own sense of morality—

JONATHAN: What do *you* know about morality?

GRETE: *(Continuous.)* —when your own sense of morality is so compromised and so—

JONATHAN: Huh? What do *you* know with your sneaky little Jew-baiting comments.

GRETE: I beg your pardon.

JONATHAN: Don't give me this innocence shit. You know exactly what I'm talking about.

GRETE: *(Over "what I'm talking about.")* No, I am sorry, I have no idea.

JONATHAN: You think I haven't picked up on it? Huh? You think I don't know what this is all about?

GRETE: Mr. Waxman, this is all in your imagination.

JONATHAN: My imagination?! I'm imagining this?! I'm imagining you've been attacking me from the word go?

GRETE: Mr. Waxman!

JONATHAN: You have, miss, don't deny it. You expect me to sit here another minute? What do you take me for? Huh? What the fuck do you take me for? *(He abruptly goes.)*

GRETE: Mr. Waxman . . .

(Pause. She presses a button on the tape recorder. We hear the tape rewind.)

Scene 7

The farmhouse. A few hours after the end of Scene 5. The middle of the night. JONATHAN, *bag packed, his coat on, tears a sheet of paper out of his sketchbook, turns off the tea kettle before its whistle fully sounds, and prepares a cup of tea. The painting, wrapped in newspaper, leans against the kitchen table. He takes six fifty-pound notes out of his wallet and leaves them under the honey pot on the kitchen table.* NICK *has quietly come downstairs and lingers in the darkness. He emerges from the shadows.* JONATHAN *is startled when he sees him and spills his tea.*

JONATHAN: Oh. Shit. Hi.
NICK: Sorry.
JONATHAN: I didn't see you.
NICK: My fault. *(A beat.)* Are you all right?
JONATHAN: A little wet; I'm all right.
NICK: *(A beat.)* Couldn't sleep.
JONATHAN: No.
NICK: I mean *I* couldn't.
JONATHAN: Oh. Me, neither.
NICK: Was the futon . . . ?
JONATHAN: No, it's fine. Did the kettle—? I'm sorry if the whistle . . .
NICK: No. *(A beat.)* Shall I get the fire going again?
JONATHAN: No, you don't have to do that, I could've done that. No, I think I'll just head back early.
NICK: Oh. I see.
JONATHAN: Yeah, I think I'll, *you* know . . .
NICK: Back to London.
JONATHAN: Yeah.
NICK: Hm. *(A beat.)* You won't even wait until breakfast?

JONATHAN: No, I'd better not.
NICK: Patricia will be disappointed.
JONATHAN: Yeah, I'm sorry about that.
NICK: She had planned something, I think. Breakfast.
JONATHAN: Oh, that's too bad.
NICK: *(A beat.)* So you won't get to see the dig.
JONATHAN: I guess not.
NICK: I was going to take you.
JONATHAN: Next time.
NICK: Yes. Next time.
JONATHAN: *(A beat.)* It's just, I've got so much to do when I get back.
NICK: *(Nods; a beat.)* Did *I* . . . ? Was *I* . . . ? I mean I hope I wasn't too . . . *(A beat.)* You weren't . . . sneaking out, were you?
JONATHAN: Sneaking—? No. No, I just thought I'd get an early start.
NICK: It's half past three. You'll be in London before seven. That's quite an early start you're getting.
JONATHAN: I couldn't sleep. I thought I might as well hit the road.
NICK: I see. Well. Patricia will be so disappointed. *(A beat.)* You weren't sneaking out on Patricia.
JONATHAN: No. Of course not. I was gonna leave her a note.
NICK: I'll give it to her.
JONATHAN: I haven't written it yet.
NICK: Oh.
JONATHAN: I was just gonna sit down and write it.
NICK: Please. Carry on.

*(*JONATHAN *sits. Pause.)*

NICK: What were you going to say?
JONATHAN: Hm?
NICK: In this note. What were you going to *say*?
JONATHAN: I'm not sure.
NICK: What were you going to tell her? That would be difficult. Finding the right words. Patricia will be *so* disappointed. She was so looking forward to breakfast. I don't know what she'll do. I might have to comfort her. *(A beat.)* She doesn't sleep with me, you know.
JONATHAN: Oh.
NICK: Not that I was ever her type. There was a certain chal-

lenge to be found in that. I thought she would *never*, not with me. She was so . . . *attractive*, you know, so confident, so American. The first time she slept with me I thought it must have been because I was her supervisor. I'm sure that was why. When it happened a second time, well, I didn't know *what* to think; I chose to think there was hope. Yes, I opted for hope. In a moment of uncharacteristic brazenness, I asked her to marry me. She accepted. I don't know why. I have my suspicions. *(A beat.)* From time to time, I'll fortify myself with stout and kiss her neck, feel her tit, lay with my head there.

JONATHAN: Nick.

NICK: Sometimes she'll let me. She'll even stroke my hair. Once she kissed my head. I wanted to reach up and kiss her mouth, but why get greedy and piss her off?

JONATHAN: Why don't you go back to bed?

NICK: Some nights she'd respond—oh, she'd respond, or initiate even—and I would rush into it foolishly, trying not to feel I was somehow being rewarded.

I take what I can get; I'm English. *(A beat.)* She succumbed to my charms tonight, though. Tonight she acquiesced. Did you hear us?

(JONATHAN shakes his head; he's lying.)

NICK: Oh. What a shame. It was brilliant. *(A beat. He sees the money.)* What's this?

JONATHAN: What?

NICK: Under the honey pot. Money is it? A gratuity? Leaving a gratuity?

JONATHAN: No. Just a little cash.

NICK: A little cash? This is three hundred pounds. Why are you leaving three hundred pounds?

JONATHAN: I thought . . .

NICK: What?

JONATHAN: I thought it could be useful.

NICK: Useful? Of course it could be useful. Money is always useful. Why are you leaving three hundred pounds?

JONATHAN: I thought I could help you out.

NICK: Me?

JONATHAN: You and Patricia.

NICK: With three hundred pounds?

JONATHAN: Yeah. I happened to have a lot of cash on me, I thought I . . .

NICK: *(Over "I thought I.")* You thought you could help us out, unload some cash—

JONATHAN: You know what I mean.

NICK: *(Continuous.)* —lend us a hand, by leaving three hundred pounds.

JONATHAN: I wanted to say thank you.

NICK: *Thank* you?! *Thank* you?!

JONATHAN: *(Over "you.")* Don't be offended.

NICK: Who's offended? Who even *suggested* offense had been taken?

JONATHAN: I thought maybe . . . You sounded . . .

NICK: Do you wish for me to be offended?

JONATHAN: Oh, please. Look, can we—

NICK: Do you *wish* for me—

JONATHAN: No. I'm sorry, you're taking it the wrong way.

NICK: Am I? You leave three hundred pounds under my honey pot . . .

JONATHAN: Nick. Jesus. I can't win with you, can I. Please. Just accept my thanks.

NICK: Your thanks for what?

JONATHAN: For letting me spend the night.

NICK: Three hundred pounds? For "letting" you? Three hundred pounds for letting you spend the night? If I'd known there was a price, I'd have charged you considerably more than three hundred pounds. Considering the damages to my home and happiness. Yes, like German reparations after the war.

I should thank *you*. Your proximity served as a welcome marital aide. Interesting going at it like that. Each for his or her own reasons, yet mutually satisfying just the same. It *is* kind of like war, isn't it.

JONATHAN: I never meant you any harm.

NICK: Never meant me . . . ?

JONATHAN: You act as if I'm to blame for your unhappiness. I'm sorry if you're unhappy. I never meant you any harm. We only met this afternoon . . .

NICK: Have I spoiled the surprise?

JONATHAN: What surprise?

NICK: Were we to awaken to find you gone but three hundred pounds in your stead, under the honey pot? Economic aid, is that it? Jonathan Waxman: Our American Cousin. Our Jewish uncle.

JONATHAN: Enough with the "Jewish," Nick.

NICK: You're right; cheap shot. A Robin Hood for our time, then. Stealing from the rich and giving to the poor. Hey, not entirely off the mark, is it?, stealing from the rich and giving to the— You are quite the charlatan it turns out.

JONATHAN: Am I?

NICK: Oh, yes. You shit on canvas and dazzle the rich. They oo and ah and shower you with coins, lay gifts at your feet. The world has gone insane. It's the emperor's new clothes.

JONATHAN: *(Reaching for it.)* Look, if you don't want my money . . .

NICK: Uh uh uh. Don't get me wrong: I will take your money. Gladly. *And* insult you. I will bite your hand. With relish. Your money is dirty, Wax Man. Hell, I don't care; I could use a few quid.

*(*PATRICIA, *awakened from a deep sleep, enters wearing a robe.)*

PATRICIA: What is happening?

NICK: Our guest is leaving. Getting an early start. He left a gratuity.

PATRICIA: What?

NICK: *(Shows her the money.)* Three hundred quid.

JONATHAN: Look, I thought it would be best for everyone if I was gone in the morning.

PATRICIA: Is that what you thought? Why? Was the evening so unbearable?

JONATHAN: No . . .

PATRICIA: I thought it went pretty well, considering.

JONATHAN: *(Over "considering.")* It did.

PATRICIA: It could have been excruciating.

JONATHAN: I know; it could've been. I was gonna write you a note.

PATRICIA: A note. You know, Jonathan?, you have this incredible knack for dismissing me whenever I've finished serving whatever purpose you've had in mind for me. Just incredible.

JONATHAN: Patty . . . Look: it was really good to see you.

PATRICIA: What kind of shit is that?: "good to see you." I'm not one of your fucking patrons.

(NICK *slips out of the room.)*

JONATHAN: All right, already! What do you want me to say? Did you think it was easy, calling you and coming up here like this?

PATRICIA: Nobody asked you to!

JONATHAN: I had to! Okay? I had to see you again; I had to face you.

PATRICIA: This is how you face me? By sneaking out? *(She sees the painting. A beat.)* What are you doing with *that*? Oh, no you don't. Absolutely not.

JONATHAN: I'm only talking about a loan.

PATRICIA: Why?

JONATHAN: For the show.

PATRICIA: But it's my painting.

JONATHAN: I know.

PATRICIA: You gave it to me.

JONATHAN: I know I did. I'd like you to *loan* it to me. For the show. My gallery'll send you all the legal . . .

PATRICIA: *(Over "all the legal.")* What the hell do you want with this painting? It isn't even that good.

JONATHAN: I don't care how good it is. It's missing something, the show. *I'm* missing something. I've been looking for a link, a touchstone. When I saw this painting . . .

PATRICIA: It's *me* in that painting, Jonathan. You gave it to *me*.

JONATHAN: Don't worry about privacy, the loan can be anonymous—

PATRICIA: I sat for that painting. The day we met. You gave me that painting.

JONATHAN: *(Over "You gave me that painting.")* It'll be anonymous, nobody has to know your name.

PATRICIA: That's not the point. I don't want my painting hanging in a gallery!

JONATHAN: It's only for five weeks. In five weeks, they'll ship it back to you.

PATRICIA: It doesn't mean anything to anyone else; it means something to me. I don't understand—Is *this* why you came?—

JONATHAN: What? No.

PATRICIA: *(Continuous.)* —hoping I'd provide the missing link?

JONATHAN: I wanted to *see* you. I had no idea you'd even have it. As far as I knew you'd hacked it to bits fifteen years ago.

PATRICIA: Why didn't I?

JONATHAN: You tell me.

PATRICIA: So, what was your plan, you were just going to pack it up and go?

JONATHAN: I was going to write you a letter. To explain.

PATRICIA: What, that you were stealing it?

JONATHAN: Borrowing it.

PATRICIA: Taking it. Without my knowledge. That's stealing! You were stealing my painting!

JONATHAN: I didn't think it would matter so much to you. I thought you'd be, I don't know, flattered.

PATRICIA: Flattered?!

JONATHAN: To be in the show.

PATRICIA: God, Jonathan, the arrogance! So you just take what you want now, hm? Is that what fame entitles you to? I don't understand what's happened to you, Jonathan, what's happened to your conscience? You had a conscience, I know you did. Guilt did wonders for you. It made you appealing. Now I don't *know*. You've lost your *goodness* or something. Your spirit.

*(*NICK *has slipped back in.)*

JONATHAN: You're right; I have. I *have* lost something. I've lost my way somehow, I don't know . . . I've been trying to retrace my steps . . . Ever since my father died . . . I'm nobody's son anymore, Patty. They're all gone now, all the disappointable people. There's no one left to shock with my paintings anymore. When I saw this painting, though, it was like all of a sudden I remembered where I came from! There's a kind of purity to it, you know?, before all the bullshit. Patty, I just need to hold on to it.

NICK: How much is it worth to you?

JONATHAN: What?

NICK: *(Gets the painting.)* Start the bidding. What's it worth?

PATRICIA: Nick. For God's sake . . .

JONATHAN: I'm only talking about borrowing it.

NICK: Borrowing is no longer an option. Either you buy it outright . . .

JONATHAN: You're not serious.

PATRICIA: Nick! This is none of your business!

NICK: None of my—? It most certainly *is* my business.

PATRICIA: It isn't yours to sell!

NICK: Oh, let him have the bloody painting and let's be on with it.

PATRICIA: No!

NICK: Please, love. Let him take it out of our home. At long last, please.

PATRICIA: It isn't for sale!

NICK: *Let* him, Patricia. Let him take it to London.

PATRICIA: No, Nick!

NICK: Let him buy it. Doesn't it make sense, love? Think of it: This one painting . . .

PATRICIA: No!

NICK: We'll make some money, love. Tens of thousands.

PATRICIA: This painting doesn't have a price!

NICK: It's our future, love! Our future was sitting on the wall all along. Think of it. We can *save* some money, we can pay our debts. We can get on with it. *(Pause. Softly.)* Let him take the painting, love.

*(*NICK *and* PATRICIA *look at one another for a long time. She lets him take the painting; he gives it to* JONATHAN.*)*

NICK: There you go.

JONATHAN: *(To* PATRICIA, *who is facing away.)* You're sure this is what you want.

NICK: Yes. Absolutely. Send us a check. Pounds or dollars, either is acceptable. As long as it's an obscene amount.

JONATHAN: It will be.

NICK: Good. *(A beat.)* Good-bye, Jonathan.

JONATHAN: Good-bye.

NICK: *(To* PATRICIA.*)* I think I'll . . . go back to bed.

(He starts to go. She takes his hand.)

PATRICIA: Soon.

*(*NICK *leaves. Long pause.)*

PATRICIA: I can't describe the pleasure I had being your muse. The days and nights I sat for you. It thrilled me, watching you paint me. The connection. The connection was electric. I could see the sparks. I never felt so alive as when I sat naked for you, utterly still, obedient. I would have done anything for you, do you know that?

JONATHAN: Patty . . .

PATRICIA: Isn't that shameful? A girl so devoid of self? I would have done anything. *(A beat.)* You know, even after that last time in Brooklyn, I never actually believed that I'd never see you again.

JONATHAN: No?

PATRICIA: No, I always held out the *possibility*. But *this* time . . . *(A beat.)* We won't be seeing each other again. Will we.

(A beat. He shakes his head. A beat.)

PATRICIA: Hm. I wonder what that will be like.

(They continue looking at one another as the lights fade.)

Scene 8

About seventeen years earlier. A painting studio at an art school. Easels in motley array. We can see the model dressing behind a screen. A class has just ended; a youthful, shaggier JONATHAN *continues to paint. Soon, the model, the young* PATRICIA, *enters and finishes dressing in silence.*

PATRICIA: *(Finally.)* How's it going?
JONATHAN: Hm?
PATRICIA: How's it—
JONATHAN: Oh. Fine.

(Pause.)

PATRICIA: You want me to shut up?
JONATHAN: What? No.
PATRICIA: Can I see?
JONATHAN: Uh . . .
PATRICIA: Please? I won't—
JONATHAN: It's . . . It's really not there yet.
PATRICIA: Oh, come on . . .
JONATHAN: You'll get the wrong idea.
PATRICIA: I won't say anything.
JONATHAN: I don't know, I'm still . . .
PATRICIA: Not a peep.
JONATHAN: *(A beat.)* All right.

(She goes to the easel, stands beside him for a long time trying not to show her reaction.)

JONATHAN: I'm playing around with the point of view. See how the—

PATRICIA: Shhh . . .

(She takes a long beat, then walks away, resumes dressing. Pause.)

JONATHAN: Well . . . ?
PATRICIA: What?

(He looks at her expectantly.)

PATRICIA: You told me not to say anything.
JONATHAN: You can say *something* . . .
PATRICIA: I'm going on a diet effective immediately.
JONATHAN: I knew you'd take it the wrong way. It's purposely distorted. I'm trying something. You see how it looks like I'm looking *down* at you and *at* you at the same time? That's why the figure, your figure, looks a little . . .
PATRICIA: Huge. No, I'm kidding, it's good. Really. It's me. I have this mental image of myself . . . I think I'm a Botticelli, but I always come out Rubens. *(A beat.)* You're very good, you know.
JONATHAN: I am?
PATRICIA: Oh, come on, you know it. I looked around during the break. You're the best in the class.
JONATHAN: Nah, I'm just having a good day.
PATRICIA: You want me to shut up so you—?
JONATHAN: That girl Susan's the best I think.
PATRICIA: She is not. Are you kidding?
JONATHAN: She's very slick, I know, but her color . . .
PATRICIA: I'm Patricia, by the way.
JONATHAN: I know.
PATRICIA: I mean, we haven't been formally introduced; you've been staring at my *bush* all *day* but we haven't . . .
JONATHAN: I'm Jonathan.
PATRICIA: I know.

(They shake hands. Pause.)

JONATHAN: You're a good model.
PATRICIA: Yeah? This is my first time ever.
JONATHAN: Is it really? I wouldn't have known.
PATRICIA: You mean it?

JONATHAN: Yeah. I really wouldn't have known. You're good.

PATRICIA: What makes a model good?

JONATHAN: I don't know. You're very steady.

PATRICIA: Steady.

JONATHAN: *You* know, you keep the pose.

PATRICIA: Oh.

JONATHAN: *You* know what I mean.

PATRICIA: So that's all it takes? Steadiness?

JONATHAN: No. I don't know, I mean, when you're working from a model—

PATRICIA: Yeah . . . ?

JONATHAN: *(Continuous.)* —you kinda have to distance yourself.

PATRICIA: Uh huh.

JONATHAN: I mean, just because one of you is naked, it's not necessarily a sexual thing.

PATRICIA: It's not?

JONATHAN: No. It's . . . You have to maintain a certain objectivity, a certain distance. See, it's the whole *gestalt.*

PATRICIA: The *gestalt.*

JONATHAN: Yeah. It's the room and the pose and the canvas. It's the *moment.* The light, the way you look . . .

PATRICIA: You like the way I look?

JONATHAN: *(A beat.)* Yes.

PATRICIA: *(A beat.)* I can't believe I actually signed up to do this (my mother would *die.)* It isn't hard, all I have to do is sit still and let my mind wander. I do that all the time anyway. Why shouldn't I get paid for it? I was watching them burn leaves out the window. The fire was beautiful. —Hey, you want me to get undressed?

JONATHAN: What?

PATRICIA: So you can work.

JONATHAN: No you don't have to do that . . .

PATRICIA: I don't mind . . .

JONATHAN: Your time is up; you don't get paid overtime.

PATRICIA: I don't care.

JONATHAN: No, really, I can paint from memory. Really.

PATRICIA: Why should you paint from memory? I'm *here* . . . I mean, I *do* have my film history class . . .

JONATHAN: Is that your major? Film?

PATRICIA: No, I have no major. I'm a dilettante.

JONATHAN: Oh.

PATRICIA: You want to know what I'm taking this semester? I'm taking American Film Comedy from Chaplin to Capra, Women in Faulkner's South, Poetry Workshop (talk about dilettantes), Introduction to Archeology. And, you know what? It's wonderful, I am having such a wonderful time. I never thought being a dilettante could be so rewarding. I'm interested in a lot of different things so why should I tie myself down with a major, you know?

JONATHAN: *(Humoring her.)* Uh huh.

PATRICIA: You're humoring me.

JONATHAN: *(Lying.)* No.

PATRICIA: My *father* always humors me; you're humoring me.

JONATHAN: I'm not.

PATRICIA: What's wrong with someone admitting she's a dilettante?

JONATHAN: Nothing.

PATRICIA: All it means is that I see myself as a student of the world. A student of the world. I'm young. I have time. I want to try a *lot* of things. Is that something to be ashamed of?

JONATHAN: No. It's just . . . I've never been able to do that. I mean, all I ever wanted to do was paint. I wanted to be an artist, ever since I was a little kid. I was like four and I could copy amazing. I don't know, if I could just paint all the time, maybe once in a while go out for Chinese food . . . that's all I want out of life.

(Pause.)

PATRICIA: You know, you do this *thing* . . .

JONATHAN: What?

PATRICIA: *(A beat.)* I've been watching you. While you work?

JONATHAN: You've been *watching* me?

PATRICIA: Uh huh. There's this *thing* you do I've noticed. With your mouth.

JONATHAN: What do I do with my mouth?

PATRICIA: When you're painting.

JONATHAN: What do I *do*?!

PATRICIA: *(A beat.)* You sort of stick your tongue out.

JONATHAN: Oh. So you're saying I look like an idiot?

PATRICIA: *(Laughing.)* No, it's . . . I'm sorry . . . It's *cute* . . .

JONATHAN: Oh, great . . .

PATRICIA: It *is*. I mean, your concentration . . . *(A beat.)* It's sexy.

JONATHAN: Oh, I'm sure. This dribbling down my . . . a real turn-on.

PATRICIA: *(Laughing.)* It is . . . *(She suddenly kisses his mouth.)*

JONATHAN: *(Surprised, he recoils.)* Hey!

PATRICIA: Sorry. I'm sorry . . . Look, why don't you just paint . . . *(Quickly gathers her things.)*

JONATHAN: No, wait . . . I didn't mean "Hey!" I meant "Oh!" It came *out* "Hey!"

PATRICIA: Are you gay or something?

JONATHAN: No, . . . Surprised. I'm not used to having girls . . .

PATRICIA: What?

JONATHAN: I don't know. Come on so strong.

PATRICIA: Sorry. It won't happen again. *(She goes.)*

JONATHAN: Oh, great . . .

PATRICIA: *(Returning.)* Let me ask you something: If I hadn't kissed you, would you have kissed me?

JONATHAN: No.

PATRICIA: What *is* it with you?! We're staring at each other all day . . . I'm *naked*, totally exposed to you . . . your tongue is driving me insane—the attraction is mutual, wouldn't you say? I mean, wouldn't you say that?

JONATHAN: Yeah . . .

PATRICIA: Then what is it?

(Pause)

JONATHAN: You . . . scare me a little.

PATRICIA: I scare you.

JONATHAN: You do. You scare me . . . A lot, actually . . .

PATRICIA: How could I scare you? I'm the scaredest person in the world.

JONATHAN: Oh, boy . . . *(Takes a deep breath; a beat.)* You scare me . . . 'cause of what you represent. I know that sounds . . .

PATRICIA: *(Over "I know that sounds.")* For what I r— What do I represent? Dilettantism? Nudity? Film studies?

JONATHAN: *(A beat.)* You aren't Jewish.

(He smiles, shrugs. A beat.)

PATRICIA: You're kidding. And all these years I thought I was.

JONATHAN: Look, this is hard for me. It's a major thing, you know, where I come from . . .

PATRICIA: What, your mother?

JONATHAN: Not just my mother. It's the six million! It's, it's the diaspora, it's the history of the Jewish people! You have no idea, the *weight.*

You got to remember I come from Brooklyn. People where I come from, they don't like to travel very far, let alone intermarry. They've still got this ghetto mentality; safety in numbers and stay put, no matter what. It's always, "How'm I gonna get there?"

(She smiles.)

JONATHAN: No, really. "How'm I gonna get there?" and "How'm I gonna get home?" "It'll be late, it'll be dark, it'll be cold, I'll get sick, why bother? I'm staying home." This is the attitude about the world I grew up with. It's a miracle I ever left the house!

(She laughs. They look at one another for a long beat.)

PATRICIA: So now what do we do?

JONATHAN: What do you mean?

PATRICIA: This is it? No discussion? The end?

JONATHAN: I *told* you. I'm sorry. I can't . . . get *involved* with you.

PATRICIA: "Involved"? What does that *mean,* "involved"? You can't *look* at me? you can't *talk* to me? What are you so afraid of?

JONATHAN: I don't even know.

PATRICIA: We're talking about a *kiss,* Jonathan, a kiss, some coffee, and maybe spending the night together.

JONATHAN: Uy.

PATRICIA: We are not talking about the future of the Jewish race.

JONATHAN: See, but I think we are.

PATRICIA: My God, they've got you brainwashed! Is this what they teach you in Hebrew school?

JONATHAN: This is how it starts, though, Patricia: a kiss.

PATRICIA: You make it sound like a disease!

JONATHAN: Well, maybe it is. Maybe it's wrong and destructive and goes against the natural order of things. I don't know. Maybe it just shouldn't be.

PATRICIA: And maybe it's the greatest adventure!

JONATHAN: Assimilation as Adventure. Sounds like one of your courses.

PATRICIA: *Don't humor me!* It's very condescending, Jonathan, it really is.

JONATHAN: *(Over "it really is.")* I'm sorry I'm sorry.

PATRICIA: I come from a tribe, too, you know. Maybe not one with the same history as yours, but still . . . You're as exotic to me as I am to you! You're an artist! An artist has to experience the world! How can you experience the world if you say "no" to things you shouldn't have to say "no" to?!

JONATHAN: *(A beat. He smiles.)* Do me a favor?, get my mother on the phone?

(He gestures to the easel with his brush, meaning: "I should get back to work." A beat. She kicks off her shoes.)

JONATHAN: *(Quietly.)* No, no, don't, really . . . What are you doing?

PATRICIA: Don't paint from memory. *I'm* here, Jonathan. *(A beat.)* Paint *me*.

(They're looking at one another. As she slowly unbuttons her blouse and he approaches, lights fade to black.)

A VOW OF SILENCE

by

Allan Havis

Allan Havis comments:

A Vow of Silence, like my 1988 drama, *Hospitality,* focuses on a profile of Jewish existence which is far from glorious. These two plays are not the heroic *Raid on Entebbe* or the virtuous *Schindler's List. Hospitality,* which was produced in New York, Seattle, Philadelphia, Los Angeles, and London, contains a flamboyant, racist character loosely based on the late Rabbi Meir Kahane, an uncomfortable figure in contemporary Israeli-American politics. Under a cloak of moral relativity, the Kahane character suffers a martyred death at the hands of our government's Immigration and Naturalization Service. *Hospitality*'s central issue of good against evil is distorted and fragmented in the deceptions practiced by its conflicting characters.

Moreover, the very selection of a Kahane character can be misconstrued by some in the Jewish community as fodder for anti-Semitism. A parallel controversy, potentially fueling comparable objections, can be found in *A Vow of Silence,* though this play inhabits a very different political landscape. It is my genuine hope that literal-minded audiences and readers not mistake Jewish self-examination in these scripts for self-hatred.

As a Jewish-American author, I believe that the broad history of Jewish democracy and egalitarianism supports problematic testing of applied ethics and justice. The very nature of Jewish compassion in sacred writings and daily practice transcends race, creed, and religion. It is with this paradoxical point of view that I approached the disquieting Givati Trials, remarkably analogous to our Rodney King affair. The judicial findings in the Givati event take their place in the larger, ongoing search for peaceful coexistence between Palestinians and Israelis. For many, the creation of modern Israel serves as the first miracle to come from the Holocaust. Perhaps a second miracle might lessen the strife between Jew and Arab. The current autonomy plan for Jericho and Gaza offers some cautious optimism among moderates on all sides of the question.

Trust is the most elusive and treasured bond in a world built on selective memory, painful truth, and endless injury. Only time will tell if God's grace will come to the turbulent Holy Land.

A Vow of Silence was presented in a staged reading at the Westwood Playhouse, Los Angeles, January 24, 1994. Directed by Stephen Macht, the cast included:

ELI AVRIEL	*Gabriel Macht*
NISSIM/JACOBS	*Jeff Shore*
DR. MENDELSOHN	*Connor O'Farrell*
BURKE	*Ferrell Barron*
AHMED/JUDGE	*Aharon Ipale*
YOUSSEF	*Glen Beaudin*
LIFFNER/SPOKESMAN	*Scott Craig Jones*
JULIE	*Donna Pescow*
HAROLD	*David Birney*
ISSAM NAJI	*Hector Elizando*
IHAB NAJI	*Joe Maruzzo*
YAAKOV AVRIEL	*Leonard Nimoy*
DEFENSE ATTORNEY	*Michael Durnell*
INTERROGATOR	*Richard Portnow*
NARRATOR/PROSECUTOR	*Bennis Marden*

Another staged reading was held at the Streisand Festival, San Diego, May 9 and 10, 1994. Directed by Shelley Berman, produced by Barcy Stricker, with lights and sound by Christopher L. White, the cast included:

ELI AVRIEL	*Seth Blumberg*
NISSIM/DEFENSE ATTORNEY/PROSECUTOR	*Tavis Ross*
DR. MENDLESOHN/JUDGE	*Richard E. Rottman*
BURKE/INTERROGATOR	*Tim West*
AHMED HAMEN/YAAKOV AVRIEL	*Shelley Berman*
YOUSSEF HAMEN	*Daniel Hernandez*
LIFFNER/JACOBS/ GOVERNMENT SPOKESPERSON	*Mark J. Zufelt*
JULIE MILLER	*Reegan Ray*
HAROLD MILLER	*Kim Bennett*
ISSAM NAJI	*Navarre T. Perry*
IHAB NAJI	*J. D. Meier*
STAGE DIRECTIONS	*Susan Hammons*

This play was commissioned by Mighty Macht Productions and Anasazi Productions. It was developed under a grant from the Center for Jewish Culture and Creativity.

Special thanks to Stephen Macht, Robert Benedetti, John Rausch, Edna Mazya, Smadar Lavie, Ellen Schiff, Shelley Berman, and to the Rockefeller Foundation's Bellagio Center in Italy, where *A Vow of Silence* was written.

To Cheryl Riggins.

A PLAY WITH THIRTY SCENES

CHARACTERS

ELI AVRIEL (Israeli soldier, age 21)
NISSIM (Israeli soldier, age 21)
BURKE (Israeli soldier, age 22)
LIFFNER (Israeli soldier, age 24)
AHMED HAMAN (Palestinian, age 43)
YOUSSEF (AHMED's son, age 15)
JULIE MILLER (American journalist, age 45)
HAROLD MILLER (her husband, American hotelier, age 51)
ISSAM NAJI (Palestinian professor, age 52)
IHAB (NAJI's son, age 20)
YAAKOV AVRIEL (Holocaust survivor, age 52, Israeli director of a Jerusalem Academy and father to soldier AVRIEL)
INTERROGATOR (official from Shin Beth, the Israeli secret police)
DR. MENDELSOHN (American, age 28, who made "Aliyah"—Israeli citizenship)
PRIVATE JACOBS (Israeli soldier, age 21)
GOVERNMENT SPOKESPERSON
DEFENSE ATTORNEY
PROSECUTOR
JUDGE

With Double/Triple Casting—Yaakov Avriel/Ahmed Haman; Nissim/Defense Attorney; Ihab/Eli Avriel; Dr. Mendelsohn/Gov't Spokesperson; Liffner/Jacobs/Judge; Burke/Prosecutor/Interrogator—

A Minimum of Eleven Actors Needed
(One woman, one boy 13–15 years, and nine men)

The play takes place throughout Israel from August 1988 to January 1989. Principal locations are the Jabaliya Army Command in Gaza, the American Colony Hotel in East Jerusalem, the military courtroom near Gaza, the Wailing Wall, a college campus, a detention cell in the West Bank, and a terrorist hovel in the territories. The barest of set design will suffice in this episodic story, based on the Givati Brigade court-martial of 1989, known as Givati One.

Scene 1

The capture at the holding camp. Dr. Mendelsohn cleans off an inspection table, as two Israeli soldiers walk by. August 1988, Gaza.

AVRIEL: What a fucking riot
NISSIM: Little filthy bastards!
AVRIEL: They get younger each day.
NISSIM: On their way to hell.
AVRIEL: On our way to a wedding . . .
MENDELSOHN: Not on my table.
AVRIEL: Shut up, squirrel.
MENDELSOHN: We're low on supplies.
NISSIM: The requisition truck just arrived.
MENDELSOHN: Are there others coming in?
AVRIEL: *(To* NISSIM, *overlapping with* MENDELSOHN*'s line.)* What the hell are you smiling about?
MENDELSOHN: I hate the Reserve.
AVRIEL: Everyone bitches like shit-ass tourists with hemorrhoids.
NISSIM: My brother sold me his Ducati. I'm boring out the engine, so it flies at 180 kilometers.
MENDELSOHN: There's a Palestinian woman down the hall looking for her husband.
AVRIEL: Sexy little thing.
NISSIM: Ducati?
MENDELSOHN: Is she under arrest?
NISSIM: She's with the Albino.
AVRIEL: Ali Hussein. He's whiter than ivory.
NISSIM: Whiter than puss.
AVRIEL: Whiter than a ghost in the Swiss Alps. *(Pause.)* Had a British Triumph. Rattled like a brass skullbasher.

MENDELSOHN: I don't have Hussein on my list.
NISSIM: Albinos bring bad luck.
AVRIEL: His wife's pretty, Ari.

(Suddenly, BURKE *enters, escorting a badly beaten Palestinian in his mid-forties. The Palestinian—*AHMED*—has difficulty walking on his right leg. Although his face is bruised, there is no sign of blood. Plastic handcuffs bind him from behind.)*

MENDELSOHN: He looks awfully bad.
BURKE: Here's the main instigator. And his son.
AVRIEL: Welcome to Hotel Hilton.
NISSIM: We hope you enjoy your stay.

*(*LIFFNER *enters, escorting the Palestinian's son, age fourteen,* YOUSSEF, *his hands bound like his father's.)*

YOUSSEF: *(First in Arabic, then in English.) Awiz eh?* What do you want? *Imshi!* Go away! Leave my father alone!
LIFFNER: Quiet!
YOUSSEF: He's not a well man!
LIFFNER: Who asked you?
AHMED: *(To Youssef) Waif.* ("Stop.") *Bass!* ("Enough!") *Ou'ak* ("Take care!") *(To soldiers:)* I can't breathe. Asthma. Understand?
NISSIM: *(Testing and teasing.)* You want a medic. Tell your son to behave.
MENDELSOHN: He needs a doctor.
YOUSSEF: Let me go back and get his medication!
BURKE: *(To* YOUSSEF.*)* I think you're the one who stoned my brother. *(Slaps* YOUSSEF*'s neck with army cap.)* You should stay in school. Play soccer in kneepants. You don't want to visit this hole. Now you got your father in serious trouble. Sit down on the wood bench. *(Pushes* YOUSSEF *in direction of bench.)*
AVRIEL: What happened to the truck?
LIFFNER: These kids overturned it.
AHMED: *(Now blindfolded by one of the soldiers.)* Be a good boy, Youssef.
NISSIM: He's not related to the Albino.
AVRIEL: How do you know?

NISSIM: I know the village. The boy's father is a merchant. He sells rope.

MENDELSOHN: His mouth's bleeding. Bring him to the table.

*(*LIFFNER *and* BURKE *lift* AHMED *up as though he were a sack of potatoes, and nonchalantly drop him on table.)*

Scene 2

At the American Colony Hotel courtyard café in East Jerusalem. Quiet setting. JULIE, *a Jewish/American journalist, and* ISSAM NAJI, *a Palestinian Professor. A week later in August.*

JULIE: I'm locked out of my room.
NAJI: I'll call the concierge.
JULIE: It's the second time. Yesterday I misplaced my passport. My mind must be on Mars. Didn't we speak at the start of the conference?
NAJI: Yes. We argued about . . . statistics.
JULIE: We both pumped up some numbers.
NAJI: *(Ironic.)* I don't like to pump. I know your husband.
JULIE: Do you?
NAJI: I once beat him at tennis in the Hamptons.
JULIE: Harold hates to lose. In the Hamptons. Are you with the delegation?
NAJI: I'm a panelist without portfolio, a professor at Bir Zeit. An anthropologist, novelist, and glutton. Where is Harold?
JULIE: We had a little birthday fight. Magnified to 70 mm Technicolor.
NAJI: That's Harold's specialty. I like your perfume.
JULIE: It's called Sheer Hostility.
NAJI: I'll buy my wife a bottle. Would you like a drink?
JULIE: Thank you. White wine.
NAJI: *(To* WAITER.*)* Two glasses of white wine. Within this courtyard, there are a dozen intrigues. If you're mutlilingual, bisexual and single-minded.
JULIE: I'm the angel of misguided mercy.

NAJI: Harold and I go back many years. Columbia University.

JULIE/NAJI: Roommates on West End Avenue.

JULIE: Issam Naji.

NAJI: Mind if I smoke?

JULIE: Yes. *(He lights up anyway. Changing subjects abruptly.)* I heard about the Jabaliya riot.

NAJI: A rope merchant died after his arrest. The family is devastated. I had met them during my field work in Jabaliya.

(They drink the wine just served.)

JULIE: Your university closed this month.

NAJI: They found fax machines, short wave radios, and other great weapons of war. I'd love another fax.

JULIE: When's your birthday? Harold loves to give useful gifts.

NAJI: Harold and I loved the opera. He taught me to sneak into the Met without a ticket before the second act. And also Yankee Stadium, but I found baseball too paradoxical. Why should the batter bunt, when TV prefers the long ball? *(Pause.)* I talk in circles. Excuse me. *(Smiling.)* Harold taught me how to cheat at poker. And I taught him to make Turkish coffee, to roll a cigarette with one hand, and to appreciate Islamic logic.

JULIE: How does one appreciate Islamic logic?

NAJI: With perverse wit. You're with . . . ?

JULIE: The *Los Angeles Times.*

NAJI: I was a correspondent for a Cairo paper. Wrote sexy travel propaganda. Of course, my wife had me quit. My wife. Now, after a few drinks I write obscene poetry. My third glass. I can't find the verse. What's noble and anatomical with *s* or *c,* rhymes with intifada?

JULIE: Cerebella?

NAJI: Good. Harold's become very crazy.

JULIE: It's his commitment toward Israel.

NAJI: And you?

JULIE: I don't take sides.

NAJI: We all take sides. Otherwise, we go to hell. Aren't you an apologetic Zionist?

JULIE: I'm not a Zionist. And I never apologize.

NAJI: You've a spiritual air. Are you religious, Mrs. Miller?

JULIE: *(Dryly ironic.)* I was raised an agnostic Jew. The fourth movement of modern Judaism. Harold gave our children a sound Jewish education.

NAJI: Heritage stamps each of us with an indelible destiny.

JULIE: And what is your destiny?

NAJI: Consensus building. Holding the extremes from the improbable center. I just read Le Carré's *The Little Drummer Girl* and was amused by the Semitic games. Yet spy novels never ring true—always a cynic's sentimentality lurking about.

JULIE: Are you as cynical as Harold?

NAJI: I've faith in an ironic, wounded God. Voltaire reinterpreted by a vaudevillian.

JULIE: Voltaire hated Jews.

NAJI: Voltaire hated himself.

JULIE: Do you hate Jews?

NAJI: On the contrary. Tell me that you find me very handsome.

JULIE: Very handsome.

NAJI: I'm not making a pass at you—my wife would kill me before dawn.

JULIE: She's fast.

NAJI: She's Lebanese.

JULIE: Your thoughts about the military beatings?

NAJI: Who would think this intransigence came from the survivors of Auschwitz?

JULIE: I've said the same to Harold. Smoke shoots out his nostrils. He accuses me of being so far left that I'm an honorary shiksa.

NAJI: You?

JULIE: I couldn't watch the circumcision of our two sons.

NAJI: Circumcision has long-term reverberations. I was mistakenly circumcised by a Syrian with a very unsteady hand. Moreover, I'm not Moslem, but the doctor thought otherwise. My son escaped the scalpel. Harold's the godfather of Ihab.

JULIE: I didn't know. Harold's become more Jewish over the years.

NAJI: I gather you don't keep kosher?

JULIE: I can't even cook Jell-O.

NAJI: Another drink? The evening is so young.

Scene 3

(Under routine interrogation, ARMY DOCTOR MENDELSOHN *is smoking a cigarette. Next day, Gaza.)*

INTERROGATOR: Dr. Mendelsohn, do you know my rank with Shin Beth. I'm up there among angels and helicopters in the stratosphere. *(Pause.)* Between 6 p.m. and 11 p.m. a middle-aged Palestinian died during custody.

MENDELSOHN: I gave my account.

INTERROGATOR: What a terrible beating. We have several soldiers' depositions. You wrote a report on this Palestinian?

MENDELSOHN: There was blood from his mouth. He appeared short of breath. I examined him. He was injured, yes, but nothing life-threatening.

INTERROGATOR: Are you certain?

MENDELSOHN: I ran several tests.

INTERROGATOR: The case has caught the unfailing attention of the media and the High Court. The light of God has fallen here.

(Overlapping dialogue, next four lines.)

MENDELSOHN: I'll talk to the press.

INTERROGATOR: That's not necessary.

MENDELSOHN: Insurance against a frame-up.

INTERROGATOR: Not here, Doctor. Your job is to shut up. *(Pause.)* I served in the Reserve. Respect the code. Otherwise . . . We'll have the forensic reports. Someone will be damned by these documents. Maybe you. Let's get our story straight. The victim's son has talked to us. The boy stammers, but says nothing. What did he see? What did he hear? *(Pause.)* You're from the United States?

MENDELSOHN: Yes.

INTERROGATOR: Your career can be ruined. We can accomplish everything today. Speed makes me happy. So boychik, give me some details to make vinegar less sour.

Scene 4

Press conference. A GOVERNMENT SPOKESPERSON *at a podium in front of cameras, a few days later in August. Jerusalem.*

SPOKESPERSON: The Army has suffered minor casualties in Jabaliya. One soldier is in critical condition. Less than twenty Palestinians have been brought in for questioning. A brigade is under investigation for manslaughter. The Israeli Defense Command will prosecute with impunity any serious irregularity of Army policy. I will take your questions now.

JULIE: How do you propose to break the code of silence within the brigade?

SPOKESPERSON: There is no code of silence.

JULIE: Isn't this brutality a consequence of Rabin's "Iron Fist" policy?

SPOKESPERSON: These last eight months we've witnessed tremendous restrain and perspicacity. Now how about a friendlier question from the person in the second row?

Scene 5

PROSECUTOR *and* YOUSSEF *during a brief pre-court exchange. Late August.* PROSECUTOR *may be a voice offstage.)*

PROSECTOR: Youssef, please tell the court how old are you?
YOUSSEF: *(With a stutter.)* I am fifteen.
PROSECUTOR: Do you attend school?
YOUSSEF: Yes.
PROSECUTOR: Have you ever thrown a rock at a soldier before?
YOUSSEF: No.
PROSECUTOR: Did you involve yourself with this riot the other week?
YOUSSEF: *(Pause.)* No.
PROSECUTOR: Please tell the court in your own words how you and your father were arrested. *(Pause.)* Youssef? *(Pause.)* When you were brought into the prison compound, what happened to your father? What did you see? Don't be frightened. *(Pause.)* Youssef? *(Pause.)* Why won't your brother testify? *(Pause.)* It is very important that you answer these questions.

(If PROSECUTOR *was on stage, he exits, leaving* YOUSSEF *alone.)*

Scene 6

HAROLD *and* YAAKOV AVRIEL *are walking the wooded hills just outside Jerusalem—the site of the Academy. The end of August.*

YAAKOV: That's the swimming pool. Makes the Institute less serious. Did you bring your swimsuit?
HAROLD: I can't swim.
YAAKOV: But you like to walk on water?
HAROLD: You scrutinize everything I say.
YAAKOV: It's your diction, Harold. I can't seem to place it anymore.
HAROLD: That comes from two decades of hotel residencies. You did very well for yourself, Yaakov. Who'd ever think it wasn't a resort?
YAAKOV: The goyim. There's no cocktail bar.
HAROLD: Still making meetings Tuesday nights?
YAAKOV: I can't say.
HAROLD: I can guess.
YAAKOV: The command finds my thinking useful. I sit around an octagonal table and lecture on indigenous forms of combat. As I do with West Point and Annapolis. Sometimes I drop a Jackie Mason joke. But I make American lieutenants pick me up in decoration escort.
HAROLD: Vanity?
YAAKOV: Respect. I fit into my uniform. I don't fly coach to New York. They put me on business class, or they can kiss my ass. *(Pause.)* Our leaders are crazy. We're killing ourselves faster than any Arab assault. Choked by these religious arrogant nuts in black hats and coats. My taxes pay for their ultra-Jewish indulgent, no-help existence.

Believe me, when the Haredim* cross the road, I try to run over these Super-Jews.

HAROLD: And what would God say?

YAAKOV: He would pat me on the back, give a tax credit. Population control. You know how fast Hasids breed. Are you making Aliyah?

HAROLD: I wish I were you.

YAAKOV: Don't.

HAROLD: To fight in the Yom Kippur War.

YAAKOV: You can have my medals, and I'll take half your stock options. To pay for my son's defense fund.

HAROLD: I'll give you a blank check.

YAAKOV: A father will kill for his young blood.

HAROLD: Yes.

YAAKOV: I told Eli to cover his ass during those patrols. These boys aren't prepared for Gaza. They get pissed on, shat upon, stoned and humiliated. "Don't shoot back." Christ, sick game?

HAROLD: It's heartbreaking.

YAAKOV: Your wife's enough to drive me crazy.

HAROLD: She has her point of view.

YAAKOV: Which is what, kike self-hatred? I'm sorry.

HAROLD: Don't be. You don't owe her any favors. She'll find what she needs to know about herself here.

YAAKOV: At whose expense?

HAROLD: She can't influence the trial.

YAAKOV: When I get irrational about it, I just want to kill. I don't want my family hurt. I'm just another Holocaust Jew dealing with the Ashkenazic hegemony. And that plays into our politics. Except for my Eli, the defendants are Sephardic. Most of the Givati Brigade are. With their own bitterness toward Arabs. Personally, I hate the territories. We're all fucked up about it here. *(Pause.)* God willing, my son will prevail.

HAROLD: I share that prayer.

YAAKOV: I'll give your wife proper escort. *(Mockingly, pointing.)* Do you want to plant a tree?

HAROLD: Give me a shovel.

YAAKOV: Show me one callus on your hand. *(*HAROLD *taps* YAAKOV*'s stomach with a mock punch.)* All right, show me two calluses. One on each hand.

**Haredim:* Ultra-religious Israeli Jews.

Scene 7

JULIE *and her husband,* HAROLD, *at a bar in West Jerusalem. The next day, early September.*

HAROLD: You're staying at the American Colony? I could have saved you expense at—
JULIE: *(Interrupting.)* It helps to be in East Jerusalem.
HAROLD: So you can be mugged?
JULIE: Can I take you out to dinner?
HAROLD: Yes.
JULIE: Good.
HAROLD: Our little spats are—
JULIE: Cyclical.
HAROLD: Like the weather.
JULIE: Most of the time the weather's predictable.
HAROLD: I worry about your mission.
JULIE: I'm doing everything by the book.
HAROLD: With a heavy slant on the reporting?
JULIE: No.
HAROLD: Why do you want to embarrass me?
JULIE: Harold, we have very separate identities.
HAROLD: That depends who's looking.
JULIE: No one cares.
HAROLD: I do. Why did you leave?
JULIE: Your comments at the conference were extreme.
HAROLD: Should I have censored myself?
JULIE: Yes, for racist language.
HAROLD: You missed my irony.
JULIE: I always miss your irony.
HAROLD: In '47, the UN proposed a fair partition which the Arab League refused. The Palestinians gamble their lives like lemmings off a cliff. *(Pause.)* Jordan is Palestine.

JULIE: Life under Jordan was another form of occupation.

HAROLD: More than half of Jordan's population is Palestinian. You used to think that. We're connected to this land.

JULIE: Can you separate the land from your chauvinism?

HAROLD: Give me an incentive. We haven't kissed in a year. I thought you took up the assignment just to rile me. That was the start of our misunderstanding. Even the kids think we spar too much. *(Pause.)* I'm here to help. Forget politics. I'll do anything for you.

JULIE: I want to believe you.

HAROLD: I love you.

JULIE: I love you too . . . when you're not rabid.

HAROLD: Then stay the night.

JULIE: No.

HAROLD: It's an affliction. I'm a fool without you.

JULIE: True.

HAROLD: And I come on too strong. It's my blood pressure.

JULIE: Or your testosterone. Right now, I'd rather lose myself in work, than in your meshuggeneh Hebraic miasma. You don't look well.

HAROLD: I'm anxious.

JULIE: For the Messiah to eradicate the unions from your hotels?

HAROLD: I'm sick of money.

JULIE: Give it away. You like to play Santa.

HAROLD: Only in December. Red is very sexy.

JULIE: Is it?

HAROLD: Do you remember how hard it was for me to propose to you? How impossible it was to court you? I never wanted to marry anyone. But you gave me a warm heart. You taught me how to love without conditions. You gave me spontaneity, tsuris, and human honesty.

JULIE: Did I?

HAROLD: I've never cheated on you. Even with the separation. Not even phone sex. Can you say the same?

JULIE: I traveled with Gore Vidal to Italy.

HAROLD: *(Laughing.)* I like that.

JULIE: Gore tells the best political jokes outside the toilet. Jealous?

HAROLD: Of a preening, murderous, anti-Semitic gay?

JULIE: Do I chide you about Podhoretz?

HAROLD: He just clubs his victims unconscious.

JULIE: Have dinner with me. Food makes you more sedate.

HAROLD: Not as much as sex. Let's . . .

JULIE: After the trial.

HAROLD: The trial can go on for years.

JULIE: I need your help, Harold.

HAROLD: Is that all you need from me?

JULIE: I don't know.

HAROLD: Rosh Hashanah is on the twelfth. Come to schul. I found a wonderful Sephardic congregation in the old city.

JULIE: Help me, darling, without conditions.

HAROLD: How?

JULIE: You know the Army channels.

HAROLD: Barely.

JULIE: Yaakov Avriel's son is one of the four indicted. Give me a lead. Yaakov won't return my calls.

HAROLD: The intifada gets enough hype.

JULIE: Each day you become more Israeli.

HAROLD: And I see your greater potential.

JULIE: I'm happy as I am. *(Pause.)* Or would a Sabra woman please your pained exotic urges? Something I could never do. I don't have that Israeli mystique. To you, I'm a Tiffany JAP.

HAROLD: I never said that.

JULIE: You think it, which is worse.

HAROLD: Read my heart, not my mind.

JULIE: I met an old friend of yours.

HAROLD: Who?

JULIE: The Palestinian professor from Nabus.

HAROLD: Naji?

JULIE: He's been very helpful.

HAROLD: Like Sidney Greenstreet in *Casablanca.*

JULIE: He's going to introduce me to the two Palestinian boys in the case.

HAROLD: Is Naji at the American Colony?

JULIE: Yes. He's expecting your call.

HAROLD: *(Glancing at his watch.)* I'll ring him at once.

JULIE: He'll like that.

Scene 8

Lecture at Palestinian College Bir Zeit. Second week of September.

NAJI: To conclude, our people have lived here for thousands of years. *(Pause.)* The Jewish people have wandered around the earth for centuries. The terrible events during the middle of this century have exacted an awesome wound among Jews. We Palestinians deplore Nazism and genocide. There is no time for Israel and the U.S. to procrastinate. To the Western media here, I ask that you visit our Arab towns of Palestine. We will tell you only the bare truth. God bless you all. *(Applause. Breaking from his speech, he joins* JULIE.*)* I didn't know you would be here.

JULIE: I want to contact Ahmed's family.

NAJI: Yes, well . . . all right.

JULIE: Today, while we're in Gaza.

NAJI: *(Annoyed.)* I'll arrange something, but you'll have to go without me. Tonight, I've been asked to go on CNN.

Scene 9

JULIE *with* YOUSSEF *at refugee camp, the next day.* YOUSSEF *stutters.*

JULIE: If you like, I can come back later. *(*YOUSSEF *shakes head.)* Then please tell me more. Why won't your brother talk?

YOUSSEF: I . . . I . . .

JULIE: I'm a friend, Youssef.

YOUSSEF: I told you the . . . story.

JULIE: I need details. Try to remember everything.

YOUSSEF: I . . . I . . .

JULIE: I want to know what the soldiers said. Who hit your father? How many times? *(Pause.)* When I come next, I'll be with Professor Naji.

YOUSSEF: I don't want . . . arrest.

JULIE: They won't arrest you. But you have a subpoena to appear in court. You must come to court. Just as the lawyer said.

YOUSSEF: It won't bring my father . . . come back.

JULI: But his spirit is alive. And with you. Youssef, what did your family see when the soldiers came into your house?

YOUSSEF: Guns.

JULIE: Did you fight the soldiers?

YOUSSEF: No.

JULIE: Did you give up?

YOUSSEF: My father . . . didn't let them go . . . into the bedroom. *(Silence.)*

JULIE: Why won't your brother speak to me?

Scene 10

At the military compound stockade. JULIE *and* ARMY RESERVIST AVRIEL. *Mid-September.*

JULIE: I met your wife today, Private Avriel. She was very nice to me. My husband is a good friend of your father, Yaakov.

AVRIEL: What do you want?

JULIE: I can investigate behind the scenes for you, Eli.

AVRIEL: You don't know me.

JULIE: I know you from your fine Army record.

AVRIEL: I shouldn't talk with you.

JULIE: Please let me help.

AVRIEL: I'm a soldier. I follow orders. I support my men and my unit.

JULIE: Let me help. Beatings seem to be—

AVRIEL: *(Interrupting.)* A blow to the knees. A slap to the head. Tear gas. Cars and trucks must travel these roads.

JULIE: And the rule of law?

AVRIEL: American law would be weak here. Every arrest is hell.

JULIE: You and your unit brought in the Palestinian. Was he dying? *(Silence.)* Your father would want you to unburden yourself.

AVRIEL: I didn't kill him.

JULIE: Did your unit?

AVRIEL: No.

JULIE: Then who killed the Palestinian?

AVRIEL: An angel of death.

JULIE: Was there a secret beating? Did anyone at the ward take part?

AVRIEL: Go.

JULIE: This would mitigate your circumstances.

AVRIEL: I am an Israeli soldier.

JULIE: Please give me some details. It'll come out in the forensic reports. *(Pause.)* I spoke with your wife. She knows you didn't kill this man.

AVRIEL: Go.

JULIE: You didn't kill this man. *(Pause.)* Unique to the Israeli Military is the provision which allows a soldier to disobey an illegal command. It comes from the Nuremberg trials.

AVRIEL: I think you're naïve. It's a sad thing to be stoned by hooded children.

JULIE: Yes.

AVRIEL: Flowers don't grow out of a rifle. I doubt what promise you made to my wife and my father.

JULIE: The Star of David signifies many things. Something very moral.

AVRIEL: To me, it is a sharp, barren rock far from your comfortable living room. Out of respect for my father, I spoke with you.

(AVRIEL abruptly exits.)

Scene 11

HAROLD *and* NAJI *at the American Colony Hotel Café. Some days later, mid-September.*

NAJI: You're putting on weight, Harold.
HAROLD: I gave up smoking. And sex.
NAJI: So have I.
HAROLD: And alcohol?
NAJI: It helps me think. She's a beautiful, intelligent woman. I see why you married her.
HAROLD: To this day, I don't know whether I chose her . . .
NAJI: Women choose. That's nature.
HAROLD: And what does that say about nature? Where are you living?
NAJI: Nablus.
HAROLD: Did you renounce your Israeli citizenship?
NAJI: Yes.
HAROLD: You're active now that the university closed?
NAJI: What choice have I?
HAROLD: Return to New York.
NAJI: No, I'm here to resist. Another overeducated misanthrope, in the right place at the right time with the wrong luck.
HAROLD: Your luck's quite spectacular.
NAJI: Are you judging me, Harold?
HAROLD: *(Ironic.)* Yes.
NAJI: I give classes from my home. Publish papers. Make mad speeches.
HAROLD: You're in jeopardy from all sides.
NAJI: God instructs me miserably. How are your parents?
HAROLD: My father died last year.
NAJI: I'm sorry. He was very kind to me. You said Kaddish?

HAROLD: Yes. I'm becoming just like him. The hotels and philanthropies manage themselves. When things blew up with Julie, I got very insecure. Twenty-two years of marriage.

NAJI: And now she's back in your life?

HAROLD: Yes.

NAJI: There's a peasant saying in Arabic: *Nika nika wala tastanika wala ta'alam erak ala kasal.*

HAROLD: Meaning?

NAJI: Screw, screw, don't hesitate—that your cock won't grow lazy. I can be vulgar. Don't worry so. Admire her professional resolve.

HAROLD: It's a selective sense of compassion. There are the Kurds, Ethiopians, Armenians . . .

NAJI: You used to believe in fighting imperialism and fast food franchises. You take your father's mantle.

HAROLD: The real world presented itself with a kick in the ass. You know the kind of Jew I am.

NAJI: You're either married to Julie or to this country.

HAROLD: It's not an either/or proposition.

NAJI: You're entitled to think that.

HAROLD: I think you're the best leader for your people.

NAJI: I'm not a leader.

HAROLD: You can play to any house.

NAJI: I'm a pitiful professor without pension or a pot to piss in.

HAROLD: You've family money, Naji. You've many choices. *(Pause.)* Are you involved in this court-martial?

NAJI: I know the victim's family from my studies in the camps.

HAROLD: How are they?

NAJI: Not well.

HAROLD: The Army won't change. You could rally the moderates.

NAJI: If Americans would stop hating Arabs . . .

HAROLD: It isn't that simple.

NAJI: America finances Israel.

HAROLD: And Egypt. With favored AWAC sales to the Saudis.

NAJI: But nothing to the Palestinians.

HAROLD: Yes. You're looking at me strangely.

NAJI: It's your guilt, boychik.

HAROLD: My love for you doesn't reflect guilt.

NAJI: You love me?
HAROLD: Yes.
NAJI: But not my people?
HAROLD: I don't know your people. When will they be as educated as you?
NAJI: When our universities are reopened and shekles fall from the skies. Who are you, Harold?
HAROLD: You tell me.
NAJI: The wandering Jew with a string of expensive, foreign hotels. *(Laughing.)* We used to smoke hemp.
HAROLD: Yes.
NAJI: Drinking, whoring.
HAROLD: Pissing in the street.
NAJI: Marriage has changed us.
HAROLD: We both got fatter and dumber.
NAJI: Have a drink.
HAROLD: Tell me a joke.
NAJI: Julie has slept with the refugees.
HAROLD: Is that funny?
NAJI: She's an armchair journalist.
HAROLD: We both could give long history lessons.
NAJI: Don't patronize her. You're in alien territory. *(Pause.)* The soldiers will get off. Only one Palestinian died and witnesses aren't forthcoming. In the long run, the case is marginal.
HAROLD: If the case is marginal, why assist Julie?
NAJI: Because I like her.
HAROLD: How do you like her?
NAJI: I like her as I like poetry of another broken language. The poetry of an inquisitive woman. Maybe I can bring you together. Maybe I'll screw everything up brilliantly. *(Pause.)* Teaching has stopped at Bir Zeit. We academics are all farceurs upstaging Arafat's circus. Our brightest students have put aside their reading. Ramadan without sacrifice. An intifada of our minds.
HAROLD: There are rumors about you.
NAJI: Rumors?
HAROLD: Your recent trips to Tripoli.
NAJI: Not true.
HAROLD: I've many friends in the police.
NAJI: Must I lie to make the truth sound convincing. I'm inauthentic to you.
HAROLD: I didn't say that.

NAJI: It's one thing to be an intellectual under the Palestinian flag. Quite another to be that and Christian. Moslems test me twice as hard.

HAROLD: Like a Jew in gentile America.

NAJI: Money makes things worse. The more you have, the more evil in your hand.

HAROLD: I'm worried for you.

NAJI: That I'll be arrested?

HAROLD: Or killed.

NAJI: I won't be. To Likud,* I'm more useful under occupation. And my wife won't let me die prematurely. She's too vengeful. *(Pause.)* Which is better, *Al fadi* or *Al malyan*? Blank bullets or real bullets? Here are the dirty words: *amil, jasus, chain, bishtril.* Agent, spy, traitor, collaborator.

HAROLD: You're hiding things from me.

NAJI: Of course. I wouldn't have it any other way. Julie thinks I rhapsodize your sins.

HAROLD: I need to trust you.

NAJI: And I, you. Help her with her work. Let's score for both teams. We need to get drunk. Waiter! So Harold . . . when did you really last have sex?

HAROLD: On St. Patrick's Day. I wore green jockey shorts. I'm going to win Julie back. Otherwise, I have nothing.

Likud: **Of the two major Israeli political parties, Likud is the more conservative, hawkish rival to the Labor Party.**

Scene 12

The next day, in mid-September, in HAROLD*'s hotel room.*

JULIE: I snuck past the Army brass and got Yaakov's son on tape. I hid the mike. On my way back, my car was attacked.
HAROLD: You went on Saturday? *(She nods.)* Religious Jews can also throw stones.
JULIE: Like Sandy Koufax. I feel for his son.
HAROLD: How far are you taking this?
JULIE: I'm meeting Arafat's top lieutenant in Jordan.
HAROLD: Naji set that up? Let me go with you. I speak some Arabic.
JULIE: Like a Jew from Brooklyn.
HAROLD: Why do you need to reach Arafat's staff?
JULIE: His people contacted me.
HAROLD: Arafat's a joke. *(Pause.)* I spoke to our kids about your trips beyond the Green Line. You're chain-smoking. Hollow-eyed—
JULIE: I covered Belfast, Brixton, and—
HAROLD: Anorexic.
JULIE: Angola.
HAROLD: You were working in large teams with camera crews.
JULIE: I don't scare easily.
HAROLD: Where will you be for Yom Kippur? *(Pause.)* Spend the day with me.
JULIE: Are you helping just to reconcile?
HAROLD: No. *(Pause.)* Stay tonight. Please, Julie. I don't understand the wedge between us. *(Pause.)* I know you're coaching the victim's son.
JULIE: It's necessary.

HAROLD: And ethical?
JULIE: No witnesses are coming forward.
HAROLD: You're crossing a threshold.
JULIE: I can't resist. Something's in my blood. The boy's traumatized.
HAROLD: What do you think the major embassies are saying?
JULIE: Hoping for a major Israeli humiliation.
HAROLD: For want of oil.
JULIE: I know how the UN lines up in the grand scheme. I can see the other side of the coin.
HAROLD: *(He kisses her. She is unresponsive.)* We're thousands of miles away from reality.
JULIE: I'm here on a job. It's as real as that. When I become vulnerable to you, Harold, I lose . . . The other day I wanted you all to myself. You were so gentle and innocent. Old feelings took over.
HAROLD: Give over to them, dammit.
JULIE: I've read the horrendous mail on your desk.
HAROLD: What mail?
JULIE: *(At his desk, tossing several envelopes.)* I know what you're doing behind the scenes. And the sick groups you're supporting.
HAROLD: Julie . . .
JULIE: You're becoming a fascist.
HAROLD: Oh Christ . . .
JULIE: Then show me your sense of balance.
HAROLD: Am I so different than when we first married?
JULIE: Something happened after your father's death.
HAROLD: All I wanted was to share things with you.
JULIE: You can't. Face that fact. That's not my soul. *(Pause.)* I don't want to move here. I'm not religious. I'm not a flag waver for Zion. Life is stunted here. The secular Jew must cater to the religious Jew. And Jewish women are subordinate to their husbands.
HAROLD: Julie . . .
JULIE: A husband can prevent a wife's divorce. It's totally one-sided.
HAROLD: Is that what you want?
JULIE: No.
HAROLD: Thank God.
JULIE: I don't know what I want from you.
HAROLD: And Israel? Something powerful brought you here.

JULIE: It's just work, Harold.
HAROLD: Palestinian autonomy will come.
JULIE: When?
HAROLD: When marriages grow and mature.
JULIE: Only in your dreams.
HAROLD: Tell me one thing. What are you inside?
JULIE: An anorexic Californian journalist.
HAROLD: Who is Jewish. Who once exchanged vows with me.

Scene 13

JULIE *and* YAAKOV *at the square 150 yards away from the Wailing Wall, Yom Kippur, late September.*

JULIE: It's a dirty word?

YAAKOV: Yes. It gives the country an ulcer. Soldiers do their best to control the mobs. TV cameras appear. Cameras fan the violence. And the thugs.

JULIE: Why do you call them thugs?

YAAKOV: Their parents encourage them because they're under age. I mingle with all people. Attended the weddings of many Arab friends. The standard of living is better here and that's why they stay. And they have the vote. *(Pause.)* You blame the Army.

JULIE: Yes.

YAAKOV: Yet when Arabs slaughter their own, nobody knows or cares. Syria, Iraq, Lybia, even Egypt. Pick an open Arab society. Arabs are free to visit their shrines in Jerusalem. They govern such shrines. Before the Six Day War, the Wailing Wall was a urinal for Jordan. See the soldiers at each gate? At any moment, a maniac might try to enter.

JULIE: What if the West Bank were given to the Palestinians?

YAAKOV: Conditions are impossible. Their time was ten years ago.

JULIE: And Sinai?

YAAKOV: We gave back Sinai to Egypt for a piece of paper. The Palestinians could have negotiated under the Camp David accords. Did they cry when Sadat was murdered? Sinai is a desert far from Jerusalem.

JULIE: The French left Algeria, infrastructure intact, after several generations.

YAAKOV: The French had no spiritual ties to North Africa.

JULIE: What's your solution to the territories?

YAAKOV: Offer autonomy. Demilitarized, of course. And if the Palestinians fuck up—they don't deserve a second chance. Strange, you'd think there were oil under our feet the way everyone fights for the right to die on semibarren land. Even you.

JULIE: Me?

YAAKOV: Why the hell are you so screwed up?

JULIE: Am I, Yaakov?

YAAKOV: A liberal heart in the extreme, denies your own people's needs. You compensate like a fool in a masquerade.

JULIE: What do you want for your children?

YAAKOV: Grandchildren. Lasting peace.

JULIE: How about their lives with Arabs in Israel?

YAAKOV: The Arabs who live in Israel, I wish them peace, prosperity, and a genuine education. Most are good people. They deserve good lives. Here it's Eretz Israel. A nation for Jews and their friends. This is the one nation in the world where Jews are allowed to make mistakes. Do you know what that means?

JULIE: I do. Yet you're very critical of your country.

YAAKOV: Because of the religious right and their unholy coalition with Likud. We need to throw all the religious nuts to the madhouse, along with the Chief Rabbinate. There are other Jews holding up the circus tent. *(Pause.)* You drew more information from my son than what was proper.

JULIE: He said what he had to say.

YAAKOV: My son's hanging by a wire. No more tricks.

JULIE: There was a second beating in the compound. Your son's not a murderer. We'll work toward proving that goal. *(Silence.)* I won't argue with you, Yaakov.

YAAKOV: Why should we argue?

JULIE: If Harold said half the things you said, I would walk out of his life. It's enough to see the crap on his desk.

YAAKOV: I'm a bittersweet Jew inside an imperfect society, scarred by a million insecurities. My parents died in Treblinka. *(Pause.)* I hope you can forgive Harold for his new passions.

JULIE: You tolerate my reporting.
YAAKOV: I don't know what to say.
JULIE: I don't blame you.
YAAKOV: I love my son more than anything in this world. *(Pause.)* You've seen the wall many times.
JULIE: Yes.
YAAKOV: What do you feel?
JULIE: Great history. What do you feel?
YAAKOV: I'm drawn to it. I can't pray. Haven't fasted today. I know it's Yom Kippur. But I'll fight for the sanctity. It gives us strength. If my children sense something more . . . I'm glad to be an Israeli. I must be several thousand years old. There are songs I sing, learned in my sleep, kept in my breast, songs which stir my heart. When I get tired of the constant fighting . . . *(Pause.)* As a good friend of your husband, I hope you'll give him your tenderness.
JULIE: He told you to ask.
YAAKOV: No. I appreciate Harold's support. He flew immediately when he heard about my son. That's friendship. Without conditions. See the innocent face of my child, in court and out. Sense our atonement.

Scene 14

HAROLD*'s hotel room. Late evening. Soft light.* JULIE *and* HAROLD, *stripping down while in bed as we hear* JULIE*'s voice-over. They are about to make love. Early October.*

JULIE: *(Voice-over.)* The first-sergeant and the three privates were members of the 432 Battalion of this "elite" brigade. Typically, Sephardic Jews accustomed to Arab culture and their language find themselves in these assignments. *(Pause.)* The first four defendants—Burke, Avriel, Liffner, and Nissim—are charged with manslaughter under Article 298 of the Penal Code. *(Pause.)* Defendant Five, Dr. Mendelsohn, at the time a doctor on Reserve Duty in Division 8117, is accused of causing Ahmed Haman's death out of negligence, according to Article 3204 of the Penal Code. There are unsubstantiated rumors that other soldiers were involved hours after the arrest. *(Pause.)* I'll fax a longer version of this tomorrow with commentary.

Scene 15

Courtroom exchange between PRIVATE JACOBS *and* DEFENSE ATTORNEY. *Later in October.*

DEFENSE ATTORNEY: Private Jacobs, please state your regiment.

JACOBS: 432.

DEFENSE ATTORNEY: On the day of the incident, where were you stationed?

JACOBS: As a punishment, I was on kitchen duty—stationed in the stronghold.

DEFENSE ATTORNEY: What did you see pertaining to the incident? That is, hours after the initial arrest.

JACOBS: The beating happened between 7:00 and 7:30. The Border Patrol was there—

DEFENSE ATTORNEY: *(Interrupting.)* Which is known to be the most brutal, according to military opinion.

JACOBS: And the Regional Forces, some from Regiment 299, soldiers from active reserves.

DEFENSE ATTORNEY: How many exactly?

JACOBS: Fifteen to twenty, each guy would just go by and kick . . . I was away for maybe fifteen minutes. Some devastating blows to the chest, kneecaps . . . not everyone attacked him.

DEFENSE ATTORNEY: This was an unprovoked beating?

JACOBS: Yes.

DEFENSE ATTORNEY: Would you call this a beating of ecstasy?

JACOBS: *(Silence.)* I can't classify it in words.

DEFENSE ATTORNEY: And did you participate in the beating? *(Silence.)* Yes or no? Did you participate in this beating of ecstasy?

Scene 16

Moments before a TV address on CNN, mid-October. NAJI *and* JULIE *near cameras.*

JULIE: I'm not having luck with Ahmed's family. Come with me tomorrow.

NAJI: I can't.

JULIE: You won't.

NAJI: I'm not your genie in a lamp. Harold's talked to me. Julie, we must discuss this later. I'm about to broadcast. *(Lights on for cameras. To TV audience.)* In this trial we're dealing with unusual circumstances which surround the charge of manslaughter. The defense has turned the prosecution into the accused. For now, a successful ploy. Higher officials must be brought to trial.

Scene 17

The next week, late October. HAROLD*'s hotel room.*

JULIE: They've arrested Naji.
HAROLD: When?
JULIE: Last night. His wife phoned.
HAROLD: Was he charged?
JULIE: Administrative detention. Apparently, the Shin Beth has tapped his phone.
HAROLD: Where is he?
JULIE: In the military prison just outside town.
HAROLD: We'll go at once.
JULIE: He's not reachable. I've tried making contact.
HAROLD: I'll make some emergency calls.
JULIE: To whom?
HAROLD: The local authorities.
JULIE: Call the Cabinet Ministers.
HAROLD: Shin Beth is not well-heeled, Julie.
JULIE: Pull a few strings, dammit.
HAROLD: It may be just a routine interrogation.
JULIE: I doubt it. I got him in trouble. We met the PLO command. They'll nail him for inciting a riot.
HAROLD: It'll be stupid to keep him beyond the weekend. The wire services will pick it up.
JULIE: You want him in jail.
HAROLD: How can you say that?
JULIE: His health's not good.
HAROLD: I know. He'll be out by Monday. My word.

Scene 18

Detention cell for NAJI, *days later in November.*

NAJI: It's indecent to close my university.

INTERROGATOR: Bir Zeit was a base of operations. A professor knows the importance of security. *(Pause.)* Who gave you the short wave radio?

NAJI: It is university property.

INTERROGATOR: Without a serial number, or stamped registration?

NAJI: New purchases often slip by.

INTERROGATOR: You know the law.

NAJI: May I see my attorney? *(Pause.)* May I use the phone?

INTERROGATOR: I look at your file and see a brilliant man's career fall to hell.

NAJI: May I use the latrine?

INTERROGATOR: Where is your son?

NAJI: In Cairo.

INTERROGATOR: Are you certain?

NAJI: Yes.

INTERROGATOR: He gave us aid. After his arrest.

NAJI: That was an aberration.

INTERROGATOR: Your articles say attitudes in the West Bank are more dangerous. Are you working with the mayors of Hebron and Nablus? Are you closer to Arafat than George Habash*?

NAJI: Your questions are crude.

INTERROGATOR: You're building a sizeable constituency.

NAJI: How I wish that were true.

*George Habash: Leader of the Popular Front for the Liberation of Palestine (PFL), secular rival to the PLO.

INTERROGATOR: *(Ironic.)* We hope to cultivate moderates. But to be Palestinian in Gaza is to be Hamas.*

NAJI: Leadership reflects only the wants of the population. That's all my articles are saying.

INTERROGATOR: What you're saying is not what you're publishing.

NAJI: Like the German philosopher Leibniz. Both treatises are honorable.

INTERROGATOR: I think you're a candidate.

NAJI: Clearly, I'm not.

INTERROGATOR: You're telegenic, charismatic . . .

NAJI: Stage fright runs in my family.

INTERROGATOR: A regular on CNN. They bought you several silk suits.

NAJI: Rayon. What do you want of me?

INTERROGATOR: We've evidence your son's an operative.

NAJI: Not true.

INTERROGATOR: *(Shows photos.)* We've witnesses. He's in Gaza, not in Cairo.

NAJI: No.

INTERROGATOR: You're lying.

NAJI: I've nothing to gain by lying.

INTERROGATOR: When you lie, I know each minute facial tick. You are an open book. Have it your way. I won't waste time. *(Pause.)* We'll make it known that he was a Shin Beth informer.

NAJI: My son's an archeologist. No one would believe he's worked with you.

INTERROGATOR: We'll see.

NAJI: I need the latrine.

INTERROGATOR: You're a nuisance in captivity.

NAJI: My worth to you is more profound than that.

INTERROGATOR: Is it?

NAJI: Tenfold while I roam my village freely.

INTERROGATOR: You once believed in a federation with Jordan.

NAJI: Jurisdiction under King Hussein would be a farce.

INTERROGATOR: Actually, I like his taste in Western brides.

NAJI: You're closing your file.

INTERROGATOR: You need the latrine. I should ask you one

*Hamas: A militant Islamic fundamentalist group, rival to the PLO.

more thing. Mr. Harold Miller is a personal friend of yours?

NAJI: Yes.

INTERROGATOR: He's a major contributor to Israeli Bond drives. Mr. Miller called on your behalf. Do you know his wife? *(NAJI nods.)* You've been assisting her in her reporting?

NAJI: A little.

INTERROGATOR: Is that wise?

NAJI: Probably not.

INTERROGATOR: Have you slept with her?

NAJI: Go to hell.

INTERROGATOR: Mr. Miller has helped your various projects. His actions are inconsistent.

NAJI: Are they?

INTERROGATOR: He's the one who tipped us off. Here's his letter.

(NAJI refuses to read it.)

NAJI: You'll have to ask him yourself.

INTERROGATOR: I will. Like you, I'm a curious SOB. Tomorrow you'll be formally charged with sedition.

Scene 19

JULIE *visiting* NAJI*'s jail cell. The next day in November.*

JULIE: The two physicians are contesting each other in court, like Abbott and Costello. I'm sure the killing happened in the Army compound subsequent to the arrest.

NAJI: No other Palestinian witnesses have appeared?

JULIE: Just Ahmed's younger son, Youssef. He's tongue-tied. The older son refuses to go near the court. What do you need?

NAJI: Nothing. I've writing paper and a radio.

JULIE: You look awful.

(He holds his finger to his lips, motioning for silence.)

NAJI: You can die from the food. The hummus is like cement. My wife visited today. *(He points to the ceiling light fixture, which is bugged.)* The Army gave her no specific charge. *(He disconnects a wire quickly.)* They're searching for my son.

JULIE: Why?

NAJI: Mistaken identity.

JULIE: Can I help?

NAJI: I don't know how you can.

JULIE: Please. Naji.

NAJI: *(Writing on a slip of paper.)* I'll write out an address. If you find him, tell him not to leave the country. He should stay put and contact a lawyer. Somehow, I'll get money to him. Don't do any more than that. Don't bicker. And don't tell your husband.

JULIE: *(Taking the paper. He reconnects the wire.)* What else?

NAJI: More American cigarettes. Please assist Youssef's testimony. He's not over his fear of court. You can encourage him to go out on the limb, despite his brother's silence.

JULIE: All right.

NAJI: Harold was here today.

JULIE: I didn't know.

NAJI: You don't communicate well.

JULIE: No, we don't.

NAJI: My wife and I communicate nonverbally. She packs my suitcase, and I know I'm on a trip. *(Pause.)* Harold and I made a bet. He thinks I'll leave jail in a week.

JULIE: What did you bet?

NAJI: A case of champagne versus the complete works of de Sade.

JULIE: Are you eating?

NAJI: Involuntary bulimia.

JULIE: I got you into trouble.

NAJI: You didn't.

JULIE: I had no idea things were this bad.

NAJI: How did you get into this building? Harold's attorneys?

JULIE: Never mind.

NAJI: You should not trust anyone.

JULIE: I don't.

NAJI: We're all fools. Jail has taught me that much. And when I'm bored, I sing show tunes from *Jesus Christ Superstar.*

JULIE: Harold can do more for you.

NAJI: Write my obituary for the *New York Times*?

JULIE: Ask him directly to help.

NAJI: Then he wins. *(Mock acerbic.)* He's built luxury hotels around Jerusalem. Give him Sinai, he'd have housed Moses in a packaged five-star. *(Pause.)* Years ago, I owed him a favor. Now he owes me.

(There's a loud knock at the cell door.)

JULIE: I must go now.

NAJI: Perhaps you two will reconcile. Tell Harold I forgive him.

Scene 20

JULIE *and* YAAKOV, *on the Academy's grounds. November, days later.*

JULIE: Why won't you return my phone calls?
YAAKOV: I've been very busy.
JULIE: You think I'm out to hurt your son?
YAAKOV: Yes.
JULIE: I had no intention of doing harm.
YAAKOV: Bullshit.
JULIE: What went wrong?
YAAKOV: The other soldiers heard that you spoke with Eli.
JULIE: So?
YAAKOV: He broke code.
JULIE: This is absurd, Yaakov. There was a second beating within the base. His attorneys know that. You know that.
YAAKOV: I was trained as a navy frogman. Survival is the line to the boat. My son needs us to be that boat. You're looking for an abstract judgment from the clouds. But our sons are too dear. Society won't change because a judge sounds like Solomon. *(Pause.)* If you really want to criticize Israel, move here. Make Aliyah. Prove your Judaism. Don't be ashamed of it. That's something I can't stomach. To me, you're either Jew or gentile.
JULIE: Why did you ever help me?
YAAKOV: For your husband. I love him as my brother.
JULIE: You know my point of view as a journalist.
YAAKOV: I know of your work with the Palestinian boy.
JULIE: You dislike Naji.
YAAKOV: He's a gracious, ever-changing snake. May he rot in jail.
JULIE: I'll go . . .

YAAKOV: Harold put him there. And now he's working to free him.

JULIE: What?

YAAKOV: That's right. Applaud Harold. Neurotic brilliance worthy of a chess grandmaster.

Scene 21

YOUSSEF *on the witness stand, speaking more courageously. Late November.*

YOUSSEF: They ordered my father . . . to stand against the wall. They beat him to the wall . . . several times. And my brother too. My sister ran . . . to the soldier . . . she kicked him . . . he picked her up.

Scene 22

YAAKOV *visits his son* AVRIEL *in the military prison. Late November.*

YAAKOV: I brought a carton of cigarettes.
AVRIEL: Thanks.
YAAKOV: You're not getting much sleep.
AVRIEL: No. It's too noisy here.
YAAKOV: I was wrong to let Julie Miller see you.
AVRIEL: I said nothing to her.
YAAKOV: Then she heard what you didn't say. I put you in jeopardy.
AVRIEL: To hell with her.
YAAKOV: Everything in good time, Eli. Hanna will come next week to see you.

(He reaches for AVRIEL*'s neck affectionately.)*

Scene 23

JULIE *and* ATTORNEY *in courtroom conference room, late November.*

JULIE: Was this the first time a lieutenant general was called to the stand?

DEFENSE ATTORNEY: Rafael Eitan appeared before the commission investigating Sabra and Shatila in 1982. He admitted there was a "gray" area in the use of force.

JULIE: Is the lieutenant general disavowing IDF* policy?

DEFENSE ATTORNEY: It would seem so. Accountability is the finger that points to the sky. Maybe not this trial, but perhaps the next. I'm just one of several attorneys for the defense, but I speak for my colleagues. Be mindful of your contacts with Youssef. Word is getting around.

JULIE: Thanks for the advice.

DEFENSE ATTORNEY: You might find yourself in considerable trouble.

*IDF: Israeli Defense Force.

Scene 24

Defendants BURKE, AVRIEL, LIFFNER, NISSIM, *and* DR. MENDELSOHN—*in detention—speak, informally. December.*

LIFFNER: My wife gave birth yesterday, yet they keep me locked up. Our first child. We've named her Bathsheva. Twenty-seven-hour labor. She has blue eyes. I should be so happy. Here are the Polaroid photos.

BURKE: *(Looking at photos.)* Nothing like you. Who's the father?

*(*LIFFNER *slaps* BURKE*'s head.)*

NISSIM: We're out of legal rebuttals.

AVRIEL: And appeals.

BURKE: That's it.

AVRIEL: Executive order?

LIFFNER: Out of the question.

NISSIM: I hate the Army.

MENDELSOHN: And the Army hates you.

LIFFNER: The new deposition is a lie.

NISSIM: Someone stroked the Arab boy's tongue.

BURKE: Who's telling the truth?

NISSIM/LIFFNER: *(Mocking.)* You and me and brother Moishe.

MENDELSOHN: The forensic reports can help.

BURKE: Bullshit.

AVRIEL: I'm not going to contest it.

NISSIM: You're an idiot and a coward, Avriel.

AVRIEL: I've family waiting for me.

BURKE: So does Nissim and Liffner.

AVRIEL: If you fuck the command, you make it worse for everyone.

LIFFNER: Your father's better connected. Angling for a better deal?

AVRIEL: You cunt.

NISSIM: That's why you spoke to the American reporter.

AVRIEL: I said nothing.

NISSIM: You opened your trap.

AVRIEL: I said nothing!

BURKE: You weaken our stance.

NISSIM: Plea bargaining is for little boys.

LIFFNER: All this crap because of one Arab.

BURKE: Sick justice.

NISSIM: I wish Dayan were alive.

LIFFNER: In charge of IDF.

MENDELSOHN: It wouldn't matter.

AVRIEL: There are insects in my cell.

BURKE: Catch them.

LIFFNER: Train them.

BURKE: A clever bug will be your friend.

AVRIEL: You're a bug, Burke.

MENDELSOHN: Shut up. We're hours from a decision.

NISSIM: You're from the States, Doctor Doctor. *(Pause.)* You don't look religious. Why did you come?

LIFFNER: I'm not going to make fun of him. He's operated on my friend.

MENDELSOHN: You're older than the rest.

LIFFNER: The Army's my profession.

BURKE: Pity, Liffner.

MENDELSOHN: A season in hell.

AVRIEL: What did you imagine?

MENDELSOHN: Purpose.

AVRIEL: Within the Army?

MENDELSOHN: Yeah, and the country.

LIFFNER: Americans dream a child's idealism.

NISSIM: We have our idealism.

BURKE: And it's dead.

LIFFNER: Keep it to yourself, Burke. We're blessed with children.

Scene 25

NAJI*'s cell, early December.*

NAJI: At Columbia, I amassed a tremendous library fine. They withheld my degree, but the dean did something behind the scenes for me. I found the books years later in an old trunk. I donated them to Bir Zeit's library, including the novels of Saul Bellow. *(Pause.)* Books, like friends, are ubiquitous weapons.
HAROLD: I've a visitor with me.
NAJI: Who?
HAROLD: The young son of Ahmed Haman.
NAJI: In your custody?
HAROLD: I've friends at the gate.
NAJI: Harold . . .
HAROLD: He wanted to meet you. A cigarette? You went back to smoking.
NAJI: Out of nerves.
HAROLD: American or Turkish?
NAJI: American. *(*HAROLD *throws him the pack.)* Thank you.
HAROLD: I've tried maneuvers all the way to the Cabinet. You must help me.
NAJI: I'm not Houdini.
HAROLD: There are other choices. *(Pause.)* Be a comfort to this boy. Julie's made headway with him. He's bright, likeable. I want to set up a scholarship fund for Youssef.
NAJI: How generous.
HAROLD: Be his personal mentor, when he's of age to enter your university. I gave money to his family. The boy's not much younger than yours.
NAJI: What's the deal?

HAROLD: If the court exonerates the soldiers, what will happen in the territories?
NAJI: Ecstasy of violence—Arab style.

(NAJI disconnects the microphone wire in the ceiling lamp.)

HAROLD: *(Aware of their momentary privacy.)* You could help contain the violence.
NAJI: From my cell?
HAROLD: There's a gambit. *(Pause.)* Julie's missing. She's with your son. We don't know where they're going. You do. And we both know what he can do. *(Knock at the door.)* First, talk with Youssef. We can't keep him waiting. *(NAJI reconnects wire. HAROLD knocks back on the door.)* You set her up.
NAJI: No.
HAROLD: You filthy liar.
NAJI: Harold . . .
HAROLD: I pray she's not in danger.
NAJI: She's not.
HAROLD: I should rip your tongue from your mouth. *(A soldier escorts YOUSSEF into the cell.)* Thank you. *(Awkwardly.)* Youssef, this is Dr. Naji from Bir Zeit University.
NAJI: *Tsarrafna, Youssef. Su maalak?* ("Nice to meet you, Youssef. What's the matter?")
HAROLD: In English.
NAJI: Hello, Youssef.
YOUSSEF: Hello.
NAJI: I'm very sorry about your father. *Salaamtak.* ("Nothing but your comfort and safety.") The trial's been long and hard on your family. Mr. Miller has given you money?
YOUSSEF: Yes.
NAJI: You know his wife.
YOUSSEF: Why are you in jail?
NAJI: I understand you want to go to college.
YOUSSEF: Yes.
NAJI: Mr. and Mrs. Miller will help you. When the university reopens.
YOUSSEF: Are they beating you?
NAJI: No.
YOUSSEF: They will.
HAROLD: Youssef, we can only stay a few moments.

YOUSSEF: They will beat you before you leave.
NAJI: Let's hope not. God is good. *(Pause.)* Stay home, ignore your friends. Your family has suffered enough.

(The soldier motions to HAROLD.*)*

HAROLD: We have to go.
NAJI: I appreciate this visit. I've a son just a few years older than you. *Alla ysallmak.* ("God be with you.")

(The SOLDIER *escorts* YOUSSEF *away.)*

HAROLD: If you speak out to calm things, a release might be obtained.
NAJI: What words will allay the fears?
HAROLD: Go on television. Plead for restraint.
NAJI: On Israeli television?
HAROLD: You were on CNN and Jordanian TV. I've worked very carefully to get your release.
NAJI: After you initiated my arrest.
HAROLD: What?
NAJI: You heard me.
HAROLD: No.
NAJI: You're lying. Good friend.
HAROLD: Why would I do that to you?
NAJI: I'm the vilified enemy.
HAROLD: You've abducted Julie.
NAJI: From jail?
HAROLD: Drop the act, dammit.
NAJI: She's in love with my people.
HAROLD: You've exploited her.
NAJI: Are you pathological?
HAROLD: Friends don't screw one another.
NAJI: Take off your mask, Harold.
HAROLD: I'd rather be diabolical than pathological.
NAJI: You answered my question.
HAROLD: Then answer mine. Where the hell is she?
NAJI: She's not going to die.
HAROLD: I'd never put your life in jeopardy.
NAJI: I'm in this miserable hole.
HAROLD: The truth is, you're out of harm's way. *(Pause.)* Where is Julie! *(Silence.)* What kind of hellish friendship is this?

Scene 26

JULIE *and* NAJI*'s son,* IHAB, *at a tannery in* GAZA. *They are in hiding. The next day, early December.*

JULIE: I need to use the bathroom.
IHAB: It's not safe to go outside now.
JULIE: How long must I wait? *(Pause.)* I can't stand the odor.
IHAB: For a tannery, it's very sweet.
JULIE: This escapade's not over.
IHAB: We've a few chores to do.
JULIE: Your father doesn't know this side of you.
IHAB: He knows.
JULIE: Then he lied to me.
IHAB: You love Arabs.
JULIE: He said you weren't tied to any group.
IHAB: And the moon is made of shit.
JULIE: Are you PLO? Or Hamas?
IHAB: PLO funds banquets and Concorde flights. This is how my people are to dream? I've become Muslim and I spit on Christ.
JULIE: To spite your father?
IHAB: How much money have you?
JULIE: Three hundred shekels.
IHAB: We can't use your car anymore. I'm giving it to my friend.
JULIE: How do I get back to the city?
IHAB: Let me worry for you. *Ce n'est pas la peine.* ("It's not worth the trouble.") A pretty woman shouldn't worry.
JULIE: I'm going back in my car.
IHAB: *(Blocks her exit.)* They'll catch you on the roads. En-

joy my company. Help me with my English. And I'll help you with my French.

JULIE: You're just a kid.

IHAB: Mrs. Miller, I have a devastating headache.

JULIE: How old are you?

IHAB: Twenty. And you?

JULIE: Forty-one.

IHAB: Then we're a good match. Both mature. Keep your good looks and I'll keep mine. Sit down, please. *(Pause.)* Sit down. *(She does.)* Relax. Take off your shoes and jacket. It's very hot in here.

JULIE: I'm getting my period. I want my car back.

IHAB: Too late. My friend paid money for your Peugeot. Say, bye-bye, Peugeot.

JULIE: I don't like this game.

IHAB: *(Looking out window.)* What game do you like?

JULIE: If you need money, I'll arrange to come back.

IHAB: We need a telephone, drinking water, and a police radio.

JULIE: I made a mistake in helping you.

IHAB: You talk too much.

JULIE: I misjudged Naji.

IHAB: My father knows how to charm and I know how to run.

JULIE: Your father's working for the common good.

IHAB: It's a relative term, which is very insulting.

JULIE: And you?

IHAB: I have many things to do at once.

JULIE: Including terrorism?

IHAB: I've a weak stomach. I'm just a missionary at war with Israel. And, now, Hamas. The bastards. A rival of mine stole drug money. But Hamas blames me. I once talked with the police. I informed, Shin Beth gave me room to breathe, I stopped informing.

JULIE: So who are you?

IHAB: I'm the person who falls between obscene cracks.

JULIE: You've enough ammo for a battalion.

IHAB: I don't live here. My friends do.

JULIE: Where are they?

IHAB: Shopping.

JULIE: I can't wait, Ihab.

IHAB: The verdict will be on TV. We'll find a TV. And we'll have a romantic dinner as we watch TV.

JULIE: Stop bullshitting me.

IHAB: Sit down! You're making me nervous. I said, sit down! *(Grabs her firmly.)* I thought you would be easy. But you're one of those American women who complain about the acid in our tap water. It's our urine. *(She's about to say something.)* Shut up! *(Pause.)* I honor my father. But we're different. So noble. Anthropologist, activist, novelist. Yet he's vain and weak. He was to win the Israel Prize for literature. The first Palestinian Israeli to do so. After discreet inquiries, he gave his official address in Nablus, which disqualified him. None of this was made public. *(Pause.)* I thank you for assisting my escape. You risked something. And it feeds your romance. If wishes came true, I would take you in my arms.

JULIE: Against my will?

IHAB: It's your wish too.

JULIE: No.

IHAB: In a few months I'll get you another car with a radio. I'm not an ingrate.

JULIE: You're a child.

IHAB: You want to live a movie. So do I. My father tricked you. He fabricated witnesses and incidents. He's very good at this. Often he likes to fool me too. The refugees of Jabaliya know how to fight. They are not sheep. They kill soldiers and settlers. Hungry for our land. And a genuine flag. You were successful in getting the stutterer to speak. But the verdict is shit. Laws won't change hatred. *(Approaches her, touches her hair.)* The truth is, you don't belong here. You're a bleached Jew. A crazy Jew. My generation might fail. Our next generation won't. I don't believe in little victories. So let's flush decency down the toilet. *(Pause.)* My father wants me alive. Even as we disagree. I'm not afraid to die.

JULIE: Ihab . . . *(They look strongly at each other from close range.)* I must go.

IHAB: I'll let you kiss me.

JULIE: Stop it.

(He pulls away smoothly.)

IHAB: You want me, but not here. *(Pause.)* Pick a cot in the other room. *(Pause.)* Or do you like the floor? With blood and sawdust and shit. I like the floor. *(Silence. Suddenly he laughs broadly.)* Go back to my father and tell him all's well. He's indebted to you. And you'll feel good. He'll talk to Israel like a desperate merchant in a fire sale. He's tricking himself. That's the way his mind is. Too shrewd, and not shrewd enough. *(Pointing gun at her.)* Now for all this wisdom, let me have the money. A friend of mine will drive you back before the next Army patrol. In the meantime, better stay awake. I'm very lonely to-night.

Scene 27

The next day. Fragment of JUDGE*'s decision, broadcast over monitors or read on a LED computer message board.*

. . . Only after much uncertainty we came to the conclusion that indeed this order was clearly and grossly unlawful. Our basic assumption and starting point was that a violent attack upon any person should immediately bring up in each and every one of us the sensation and the inner feeling that this is morally forbidden and reprehensible to the deepest tenet of Jewish righteousness—since the age of Moses. As a civilized people under one law, in view of the horror witnessed this century against body and soul, this court is shocked and outraged at these military findings.

Scene 28

HAROLD *and* IHAB *in front of the tannery, late that night.* YAAKOV AVRIEL *is out of sight by the offstage car.* JULIE *is inside tannery shack.*

HAROLD: Your mother sent me. Ihab . . . listen to me.
IHAB: Take off your jacket.
HAROLD: The last time I saw you . . . you were this high. *(Hand at his waist. Silence. Removes his jacket.)* I don't have a gun.
IHAB: Now your shoes.
HAROLD: *(Obliges him.)* In my attaché case, you'll find a gift. U.S. cash.
IHAB: Who's with you?
HAROLD: An Israeli friend . . . in the car. Unarmed. There's also heroin.
IHAB: Don't profane my God.
HAROLD: You don't need hostages. You have a choice of two cars. The roads are clear until dawn. Think where you could be in six hours.
IHAB: Hand me your shoes. *(*HAROLD *obliges slowly.)* How can you wear these in the desert? Enough to kill for.
HAROLD: *(Handing him a note.)* Your mother wants you to read this, and to respond. *(*IHAB *pockets it.)* I owe your father a favor.
IHAB: An orphan has no obligations. *(Pause.)* Give me your jacket. *(*HAROLD *obliges.* IHAB *finds* HAROLD*'s wallet inside.)* Yesterday, I would have murdered you. My mind is like roulette.
HAROLD: Please let her come out.
IHAB: She's asleep. I sang a lullaby.

HAROLD: I'm giving you an enormous sum of money. Now get the hell out of here.

IHAB: You can have her for free.

HAROLD: Put down your gun.

IHAB: *(Shoots over* HAROLD*'s head, frightening* HAROLD.*)* Next time we meet, you'll lose at roulette. Tell your friend to get out of the car and lie face-down on the ground. I'm taking the Peugeot.

*(*JULIE *enters.* IHAB *exits.* HAROLD *and* JULIE *look at each other.* HAROLD *removes handkerchief from pocket and wipes his brow.* HAROLD *and* JULIE *stand in silence.* YAAKOV *enters.)*

YAAKOV: I called ahead for an Army convoy.

HAROLD: Do we go?

YAAKOV: It's best to wait for them.

HAROLD: And the boy?

YAAKOV: It's his gamble.

JULIE: How did you find me?

HAROLD: Naji's wife. Are you all right?

YAAKOV: I've aspirin in the car.

HAROLD: I know all about Ihab.

YAAKOV: We could have warned you.

JULIE: All he wanted was money.

YAAKOV: How much did you give him?

HAROLD: Enough to start a small hotel.

YAAKOV: Wasted money.

HAROLD: Talk to me.

JULIE: I just want to be quiet. *(*YAAKOV *exits.)* I'm about to lose my mind.

HAROLD: Julie . . .

JULIE: I could curse all of you. *(Pause.)* Why is Naji a good liar? Why are you?

HAROLD: We've become hideous.

JULIE: Do I lie to myself?

HAROLD: Come with me to the car.

JULIE: Yaakov told me you put him in jail. *(Pause.)* Is there no grace between you and evil?

HAROLD: There is grace . . . between knowing evil and doing evil.

JULIE: And is that you?

Harold: Naji believes what he tells other people. When I lie, I know the lie.

Julie: I rehearsed Youssef, leading him on. Which makes me . . .

Harold: No.

Julie: I want to go home. Without Yaakov in the car. Let him ride with the convoy. I hate the way he looks at me. We don't belong here.

Scene 29

Julie's voice-over, while we see three masked men surprise Ihab *while he's asleep inside a tent. Late January 1989. We might see either video footage or slides of* Julie*'s report somewhere in the midst of the stage action.*

Julie: *(Voice-over.)* An Israeli military court acquitted four soldiers of manslaughter charges in the death of a Palestinian man in Gaza last year. However, it found them guilty of lesser charges of brutality and their actions "manifestly illegal"—implicating the brigade's chief officer and the entire Israeli Defense Force, the IDF. The emotionally charged trial marked the first time since the beginning of the fourteen-month-long Palestinian uprising that soldiers had been tried for beating an unarmed man to death. *(We hear* Ihab *struggle upon awakening.)* Outside the courtroom, the defendants and their parents comforted one another. The IDF Chief Defense Attorney said the defense won't contest the court's moral lesson despite the fact that those who are really guilty aren't being tried. *(*Ihab *is dragged from his tent.)* A round-the-clock curfew has been put into effect in both Gaza and the West Bank.

Scene 30

NAJI*'s cell.* HAROLD *and* JULIE *are with him.* NAJI *looks ill, breathless. Two days later.*

NAJI: I lost my wind. An asthma attack. I'm not getting the right medication.
HAROLD: You're about to be released.
NAJI: Noblesse oblige? And my university?
HAROLD: Will open next month. *(Pause.)* There were twenty deaths in last night's riot.
NAJI: Where?
HAROLD: Ramallah.
NAJI: What prompted it?
HAROLD: The verdict.
NAJI: You know my wife's very ill.
HAROLD: We just found out.
NAJI: Hello, Julie. *(She is silent.)*
HAROLD: Something good happened for your people.
NAJI: What?
HAROLD: A long day in court.
NAJI: A Pyrrhic victory.
HAROLD: It'll influence the elections.
NAJI: If Satan quits Likud. *(Looking at* JULIE.*)* Silence doesn't become you.
JULIE: I have nothing to say to you.
NAJI: We feel sorry for ourselves.

(The following seven lines overlap.)

JULIE: Not quite.
NAJI: Watching our pain magnify.
JULIE: You're a filthy liar.

NAJI: Wanting to see officers punished.
JULIE: Played me for a fool.
NAJI: Balm in Gilead.
JULIE: You hypocrite.
NAJI: Blaming an entire army is facile.
HAROLD: Then all blame is facile.
NAJI: The bowels of Palestine shall explode.
HAROLD: Is that what you want?
NAJI: I don't know anymore. Anger at the Army, at myself, at you . . .
JULIE: And your well-mannered son.
NAJI: My son's a mystery to all of us.
JULIE: I think not.
NAJI: We've a common ancestor, but our blood has gone bad. Back to Abraham. Look at me, Harold.
JULIE: You can't even apologize.
NAJI: Why? We used each other.
JULIE: Ihab took my car, my purse, my tape recorder.
NAJI: You have seventeen tape recorders.
JULIE: He made me piss in the desert.
NAJI: To grow a fruit tree. My son liked the desert.
JULIE: You might have warned me.
NAJI: It was exactly what you wanted. A thrill beyond the Green Line.
JULIE: You feel no responsibility.
NAJI: Apropos your travails, no.
JULIE: Harold proved more honorable.
NAJI: He can afford to be. I inhabit a jail. *(Wheezing.)* He had no qualms about throwing me behind bars. You only half believe it.
JULIE: I heard it before.
HAROLD: Ihab's over his head in trouble.
NAJI: My son's too sacred for this discussion.
JULIE: He could have killed us all.
NAJI: I'm sorry if you think that.
JULIE: I risked my life for him.
NAJI: No. My son risked his life for you.
HAROLD: We can drive you home.
NAJI: Why bother?
HAROLD: Friendship.
NAJI: Lifelong friendship.
HAROLD: It still means something to me.
NAJI: I despise your generosity.

HAROLD: I'm sorry.

NAJI: We've disgraced each other. Greatly. How to atone? *(Pause.)* A man in jail has no power. Only shame. We all inhabit a prison. Jewish life is dedicated to learning and peace, but the Army has shamed every Jew.

HAROLD: What of every armed terrorist?

NAJI: My son's not a terrorist.

HAROLD: Your legacy. My godchild.

NAJI: Enough, Harold.

HAROLD: Thank God, your wife had the decency to help.

NAJI: Duplicity is our sickness. If I press you, you'll say jail was my haven. And I'd give a comparable rationalization. So please, let's forgo this falseness. Shit is shit. *(Shows wrists bandaged, under his sleeves.)* The money you've given me over the years went to causes you loathe. Something you can guess. When your back was turned. I am all things to all people. The Columbia-educated chameleon. "Constructive ambiguity." I worked with PLO, tried to appease Hamas. Now I hate Hamas with all my life. Ihab is dead. *(Pause.)* He was found yesterday. Tagged by his group as a traitor. A heroin sale went bad. His drug habit. Shot with a pistol point-blank to his temple. Friends from Hamas.

HAROLD: Who told you?

NAJI: The lieutenant, last night. With photos. We kill our own even quicker. For no one kills a "collaborator" like a Palestinian. All of us, a firing squad in circle formation. *(Pause.)* Last night I dreamt of Ihab in my arms as we crashed in a plane. We were reconciled. Yes. He wouldn't give me grandchildren but promised a searing nation. *(To* JULIE.*)* He was a confused young man. *(Has trouble breathing.)* I can't speak.

HAROLD: I'm deeply sorry.

JULIE: Naji . . .

HAROLD: Catch your breath.

JULIE: We'll drive you home.

HAROLD: There are several fires along the main road.

NAJI: Fire purifies. In the Bible, the Torah, and in the Korean. *Watan-al-badeel.* The substitute homeland. A lost dream. *(Pause.)* Where will you go?

JULIE: Back home to the States.

HAROLD: For now.

NAJI: You love each other, have the heart to face me . . .

JULIE: Yes . . .

NAJI: . . . while the devil lives in each of us.

HAROLD: We'll exorcise our demons. From nakedness.

NAJI: *(He knocks against the cell door.)* There will come a time—soon—when we will see two nations astride an unhostile border. It's your dream. And mine.

JULIE: Yes.

NAJI: If we bear true witness. Jesus turns the other cheek. Yet Islam says: *Allahu akbar.* God is greater than the enemy.

(The door opens, NAJI *exits out of the cell.* JULIE *and* HAROLD *follow.)*